Gender
Gymnastics

JAPANESE SOCIETY SERIES
General Editor: Yoshio Sugimoto

Japanese Politics: An Introduction
Takashi Inoguchi

A Social History of Science and Technology in
Contempory Japan, Volume 2
Shigeru Nakayama

Gender and Japanese Management
Kimiko Kimoto

Philosophy of Agricultural Science: A Japanese Perspective
Osamu Soda

A Social History of Science and Technology in
Contempory Japan, Volume 3
Shigeru Nakayama and Kunio Goto

Japan's Underclass: Day Laborers and the Homeless
Hideo Aoki

A Social History of Science and Technology
in Contemporary Japan, Volume 4
Shigeru Nakayama and Hitoshi Yoshioka

Scams and Sweeteners: A Sociology of Fraud
Masahiro Ogino

Toyota's Assembly Line: A View from the Factory Floor
Ryoji Ihara

Village Life in Modern Japan: An Environmental Perspective
Akira Furukawa

Social Welfare in Japan: Principles and Applications
Kojun Furukawa

Escape from Work: Freelancing Youth and the Challenge to Corporate Japan
Reiko Kosugi

Gender Gymnastics: Performing and Consuming Japan's Takarazuka Revue
Leonie R. Stickland

Social Stratification and Inequality Series

Inequality amid Affluence: Social Stratification in Japan
Junsuke Hara and Kazuo Seiyama

Intentional Social Change: A Rational Choice Theory
Yoshimichi Sato

Constructing Civil Society in Japan:
Voices of Environmental Movements
Koichi Hasegawa

Deciphering Stratification and Inequality: Japan and beyond
Yoshimichi Sato

Social Justice in Japan: Concepts, Theories and Paradigms
Ken-ichi Ohbuchi

Gender and Career in Japan
Atsuko Suzuki

Status and Stratification: Cultural Forms in East and Southeast Asia
Mutsuhiko Shima

Globalization, Minorities and Civil Society:
Perspectives from Asian and European Cities
Koichi Hasegawa and Naoki Yoshihara

Advanced Social Research Series
A Sociology of Happiness
Kenji Kosaka
Frontiers of Social Research: Japan and beyond
Akira Furukawa

MODERNITY AND IDENTITY IN ASIA SERIES

Globalization, Culture and Inequality in Asia
Timothy S. Scrase, Todd Miles, Joseph Holden and Scott Baum
Looking for Money:
Capitalism and Modernity in an Orang Asli Village
Alberto Gomes
Governance and Democracy in Asia
Takashi Inoguchi and Matthew Carlson

Gender Gymnastics

Performing and Consuming Japan's
Takarazuka Revue

Leonie R. Stickland

Trans Pacific Press

Melbourne

First published in 2008 by
Trans Pacific Press, PO Box 164, Balwyn North, Victoria 3104, Australia
Telephone: +61 (0)3 9859 1112 Fax: +61 (0)3 9589 4110
Email: tpp.mail@gmail.com
Web: http://www.transpacificpress.com

Copyright © Trans Pacific Press 2008

Designed and set by digital environs, Melbourne, Australia. www.digitalenvirons.com

Printed by BPA Print Group, Burwood, Victoria, Australia

Distributors

Australia and New Zealand
UNIREPS
University of New South Wales
Sydney, NSW 2052
Australia
Telephone: +61(0)2-9664-0999
Fax: +61(0)2-9664-5420
Email: info.press@unsw.edu.au
Web: http://www.unireps.com.au

USA and Canada
International Specialized Book
Services (ISBS)
920 NE 58th Avenue, Suite 300
Portland, Oregon 97213-3786
USA
Telephone: (800) 944-6190
Fax: (503) 280-8832
Email: orders@isbs.com
Web: http://www.isbs.com

Asia and the Pacific
Kinokuniya Company Ltd.

Head office:
3-7-10 Shimomeguro
Meguro-ku
Tokyo 153-8504
Japan
Telephone: +81(0)3-6910-0531
Fax: +81(0)3-6420-1362
Email: bkimp@kinokuniya.co.jp
Web: www.kinokuniya.co.jp

Asia-Pacific office:
Kinokuniya Book Stores of Singapore Pte., Ltd.
391B Orchard Road #13-06/07/08
Ngee Ann City Tower B
Singapore 238874
Telephone: +65 6276 5558
Fax: +65 6276 5570
Email: SSO@kinokuniya.co.jp

ISSN   1443–9670 (Japanese Society Series)

ISBN   978–1–876843–51–9 (Paperback)

The National Library of Australia Cataloguing-in-Publication entry

Author: Stickland, Leonie Rae.

Title: Gender gymnastics : performing and consuming Japan's
Takarazuka Revue / Leonie Rae Stickland.

ISBN: 9781876843519

Series: Japanese society series.

Notes: Includes index. Bibliography.

Subjects: Takarazuka Kagekidan. Sex role – Japan. Musicals – Japan.
Social structure – Japan. Popular culture – Japan. Ethnology
– Japan. Gender identity – Japan.

Dewey Number: 305.30952

Cover illustration: The dazzling finale to a typical Takarazuka Revue show. © Takarazuka Revue Company.

Contents

Plates

Acknowledgements

This book owes its existence to the support, generosity and patience of many people over nearly a decade of research. Above all, I thank Associate Professor Sandra Wilson of Murdoch University for her meticulous and untiring guidance. The encouragement of my mentors and colleagues at that same institution and at the University of Western Australia has also been much appreciated. My further gratitude is extended to Professor Yoshio Sugimoto and Ms Machiko Sato of Trans Pacific Press for their kindness and advice in the publishing of this volume.

I heartily thank my informants, whose frank and generous responses to my survey afforded many valuable, unique insights; and numerous past and present members of the Takarazuka Revue Administration, especially Mr Kōhei Kobayashi and Ms Yokiko Haruuma, for their generous cooperation and assistance in arranging interviews. Ms Masako Imanishi, Deputy Principal of the Takarazuka Music School, warmly welcomed me to the School on several occasions, and provided invaluable textual and photographic material. I also thank Ms Satoko Kōsaka and the office of Ms Riyoko Ikeda, original author of *The Rose of Versailles* series, for their permission to reproduce copyrighted photographs. During my fieldwork, I greatly appreciated the hospitality and help of Terry Martin (who also kindly supplied photographs for this volume), Yasuyo Buro, Makiko Hoshide, Mariko Minegishi, Yōko Moriwaki, Kazumi Noda and many others.

Finally, I dedicate this book to the loving memory of my late parents, Harry and Rae Stickland, who gave me licence and encouragement to pursue my dreams.

Notes on names and translations

Japanese surnames precede given names in the body of this work, except in citations of works published in English by Japanese authors; however, the Western order is maintained throughout the Bibliography, to avoid confusion between surnames and family names. Macrons indicating long vowels are omitted in the case of place names, but retained in direct quotations and in citations of Japanese-language sources. Romanisation of Japanese words follows the Hepburn system, with slight modifications. Unless otherwise indicated, all translations are my own.

Introduction

The artifice of gender performance – sometimes playful, mostly conscientious – has enthralled and entertained audiences of Japan's all-female Takarazuka Revue for more than ninety years. On 1 April 1914, the amateurish stage debut of sixteen girls in their teens, hired by the innovative chief executive of a private railway company, signalled the formal beginning of the Revue's history. The young performers presented childish operetta, songs and dances in an improvised auditorium for the entertainment of visitors to a virtually unknown hot-spring resort in a riverside hamlet, tucked into the north-western corner of the Osaka Plain. Now, in the same location, the girls' successors play to thousands of people daily in a 2500-seat theatre boasting state-of-the-art facilities, while similar numbers of spectators patronise the Company's equally large, modern theatre in central Tokyo, or watch its touring performances in other urban and regional centres, or even overseas.

In Takarazuka's lavishly-costumed productions, tall, romantic, masculine heroes with slicked-back hair, tanned faces, wide shoulders and long legs embrace more petite, wide-eyed women in glamorous dresses on the vast, spot-lit stage; dialogue melts into song or dance; audience members applaud enthusiastically at the entrance of a favourite star; and, irrespective of the mood of the drama played out over three hours (including one intermission), the exit doors are not opened until the curtain has fallen on a finale full of dazzling smiles from which all traces of dramatised tragedy or passion have been expunged, and even the dead seem to return to life. Outside the stage door, crowds of mostly female fans wait excitedly to glimpse their favourite performer in her street clothes, minus her heavy greasepaint.

Takarazuka is a performing art combining singing, dancing and acting in live theatres, where carefully-rehearsed performance is directed and augmented by the work of other artists and artisans, including in-house writer/directors, choreographers, composers, musicians, set- and property designers and builders, lighting and sound technicians, costume designers and costume makers. The Takarazuka Revue Company thus comprises not only a group

Plate 1: Takarazuka Grand Theatre and Music School, 2007. A Hankyu Railways train emerges from between the Takarazuka Revue's headquarters and main theatre, at left, and its training school, now housed in upper floors of the building at right. (Photograph courtesy of Terence Martin)

of performers, known collectively as *Takarasiennes*,[1] but also a community of creative staff, as well as supporters, critics and workers in peripheral industries, created and developed over almost a century. Its prestige is considerable, and the name 'Takarazuka,' though now that of a largish municipality in its own right, has become synonymous throughout Japan with the Company itself, even among the millions of Japanese who have never seen a performance. Moreover, the Revue's frequent tours to such centres as New York, London, Paris, Berlin and major cities in China during recent decades, as well as to Japanese-occupied areas in Asia during wartime, have introduced it as a form of 'Japanese culture' to overseas audiences. Arguably, its melding of native and exotic dramatic forms and practices makes it an apt symbol of modern Japan, which has incorporated and adapted so many exotic influences into its culture, especially since the mid-nineteenth century. Its entertainment value aside, Takarazuka has also been popular as an avenue for the training and employment of women. Over 4000 girls have actually joined Takarazuka since its inception, and countless thousands more have aspired to do so, in spite of the notorious difficulty of entrance to its mandatory training course, its demanding schedule, and the harsh treatment meted out to its junior students by their seniors, in addition to the low possibility of promotion to stardom.

My analysis of the place of gender in Takarazuka is informed not only by published material from the public domain but also by my thirty-seven years of engagement with the Takarazuka Revue, during which time I have been by turns a fan, a would-be Takarasienne, a disillusioned observer, a fan once more, a translator and voice actor within the theatrical Administration, and finally a researcher. Drawing upon exclusive interviews, historical accounts, autobiographies, fans' writings, academic and popular analyses, as well as close-hand observation by the author, this book offers insights into the dreams, endeavours and experiences of many who have trod Takarazuka's stage, or who have aspired to do so, or who, as members of its audience, have been captivated by the charisma and talent of its performers. In its use of an eclectic range of source materials, the majority in Japanese, the book also augments and critiques existing scholarship on Takarazuka, especially that of Jennifer Robertson[2] in the United States. At the same time, this volume aims to shed light upon gender issues which have impacted upon the life-stages of women in Japan throughout the past century: through the voices of individuals associated in various ways with the Revue, it places Takarazuka into the context of Japanese women's whole lives; and, by citing accounts of the experiences and views of performers, it examines not only their direct involvement with the Revue but also how childhood and formal schooling led up to their joining, and how Takarazuka influenced such later life-stages as marriage, childbearing and other careers.

Setting the stage

First, however, let me lay the ground for the following chapters by briefly outlining salient structural features of the Takarazuka Revue; defining the terminology used throughout the book; and tracing historical developments from the late nineteenth century onwards which impacted upon the girls and women whose life-stories, observations and opinions comprise the bulk of this volume.

Takarazuka is one example of a distinct genre within twentieth-century Japanese popular culture, the 'all-female revue (*shōjo kageki*),' composed of a number of different performance groups with common features (Mochizuki 1959: 165–74). Though it shares certain similarities with other companies mostly now defunct, Takarazuka has always been larger and better-known, and has proved to be longer-running than its rivals. Certain commonalities with other theatrical genres can also be identified, but Takarazuka is fundamentally distinct from all other entertainment forms developed in twentieth-century Japan. Part of Takarazuka's uniqueness stems from the sheer scale, frequency and extravagance of its productions, whose casts of around eighty members for each major season are chosen from a permanent company of more than 400 attractive unmarried women, who belong either to one of five fixed troupes (*kumi*), or to the 'superior members' (*senka*)' group mostly made up of senior performers. Another distinctive feature of Takarazuka is the invention by the founder and his successors of Takarazuka 'traditions' (*dentō*),'[3] in which certain mottoes and philosophies have been invoked to discipline performers, staff and audiences, culminating in the elevation of the founder to semi-divine status. Now that its 'traditions' have been established, contemporary Takarazuka is a site of struggle between dynamic forces of reinvention and innovation on the one hand, and anachronistic elements of nostalgia and sentimentality, on the other.

In particular, it is Takarazuka's focus upon the portrayal of both genders by an all-female cast that differentiates it from other theatrical genres and provides the main theme of this volume. Takarazuka takes notions of gender from mainstream society, the media, arts and popular culture, both from Japan and from other countries, and adapts, edits, distorts and reinvents them for its own purpose: namely, to project an alluring 'other world' which its fans and performers alike can enjoy. The fans of Takarazuka are also complicit in this manipulation of gender. Countless thousands of fans actively participate in 'grooming' favoured performers into ideal stars, as well as directly or indirectly communicating their opinions and desires to the Takarazuka Administration regarding such matters as casting and choice of productions. Thus, they not only passively consume its entertainments, but also strongly and actively influence the way gender is constructed and performed in Takarazuka, through their support of particular kinds of performers, and by their demands as to how performers should look and behave.

Issues of gender identity and gender performance, and the allure of cross-dressed performers for fans of the same sex, are, of course, not restricted to the all-female revue genre, but also apply to Kabuki, and, to a lesser extent, the masked dramatic genre, Noh (also spelt

Nō).[4] Moreover, other theatre traditions in the world, including the English theatre as epitomised by Shakespeare, have also featured cross-dressing (Ferris 1993; Senelick 2000). In Takarazuka, however, issues of gender identity are particularly acute. Though Kabuki – probably Takarazuka's nearest rival in terms of the regular crossing of gender lines – does cultivate enthusiastic audiences that appreciate the skilled artistry of the cross-dressed *onnagata* or *oyama* (actors who specialise in female roles), the Kabuki repertoire also incorporates categories of performance in which the conscious portrayal of gender is not always important: *aragoto* (lit. 'rough stuff') plays, for instance (see Kawatake 1971: 60–61). In Takarazuka, on the other hand, gender mimicry is the very essence of the performance, on each and every occasion.

Notions of gender are constantly manipulated by Takarazuka performers, and to varying extents by fans as well. During performances, Takarazuka actors may play males or females of almost any age or social status. Moreover, a male-role player may dress off-stage in androgynous clothing to appear before her fans, thus extending her non-feminine portrayal beyond the confines of the theatre, but may don feminine clothing at home. On the other hand, a female-role player who is coquettish in her frilly or figure-hugging stage costume, with red lipstick and fluttering eyelashes, may enjoy wearing trousers and no makeup when out of the public eye. Such manipulation of gender – which occurs both within the context of public performances and in the private, everyday lives of its performers and fans – is critical to Takarazuka's appeal, both for those who perform and those who watch.

It is clear, however, that a large part of the pleasure sought and gained by all parties concerned derives from the performance of a particularly elegant version of masculinity by the *otokoyaku* (male-role players), which is enhanced and supported by fellow performers, and ultimately consumed and interpreted in various ways by the audience. An *otokoyaku*, especially, challenges notions of orthodox gender roles, as she can change her gender according to the requirements of each situation in which she finds herself, at least while she is officially a Takarasienne. By the same token, even a female-role player (*musumeyaku*, who portrays a girl or young woman, or *onnayaku*, who plays a more mature woman, often in a supporting, rather than a leading, role) exposes the constructed nature of gender by her exaggerated performance of femininity, which is not necessarily simply an extension of her everyday persona as a female.

Takarazuka is a complex construct in which performers, fans, writers, observers and critics have their own diverse interpretations of what Takarazuka is and what it means. Takarazuka is part of popular culture, which constitutes not only 'mass culture,' but also 'culture consumed...in various ways, by different people' (Martinez 1998: 6). Moreover, the categories of Takarazuka fan, performer and member of the creative staff are not necessarily mutually exclusive – an avid fan may join Takarazuka; an ex-performer may become a 'second-wave' fan, or groom a daughter or protégé for entry to the Company; and a fan or performer may develop into a writer, director or choreographer, and thus participate in Takarazuka in a different manner.

A fantasy Takarazuka, or even multiple fantasy Takarazukas, evoked in the imagination of each performer and fan, apparently coexists with the Takarazuka of her or his actual, lived experience. The Revue's actors cross and recross the boundaries of these various Takarazukas, also creating for themselves a special persona which itself is part of the fantasy, and which may or may not be androgynous. Other scholars have argued that it is the female masculinity of Takarazuka *otokoyaku* which enables fans of either sex to 'temporarily transcend their everyday gender expectations and roles' (Nakamura and Matsuo 2003: 59). It seems, however, that the performed femininity of the *musumeyaku* and *onnayaku* makes a similarly significant contribution to the construction of the fantasy world of gender gymnastics shared by performers, fans and Revue staff. Many fans also apparently create for themselves a 'fan persona,' which is kept separate from other facets of their lives in some cases, but seems to preoccupy a great part of their waking hours, in others.

One crucial issue in the examination of the significance of gender in Takarazuka is the source of the Revue's appeal for its fans. Recent Anglophone scholarship has addressed this issue at length through one specific focus: that of sexuality. Two opposing opinions emerge: that the main attraction of Takarazuka for its fans is sexual (as 'unaligned erotic play') on the one hand (Robertson 1998b: 145); or that it is 'asexual and a-gendered' (Nakamura and Matsuo 2003: 59), on the other. In this volume, I argue that the true nature of Takarazuka's allure cannot be encapsulated in either of these polar positions. Ultimately, it is impossible to know how important erotic sexuality is to individual fans, or indeed to performers, as Takarazuka's official insistence on 'purity' effectively dissuades most fans and performers from overtly linking fandom or performance with sexuality, especially that perceived as 'deviant.' Sexuality is in fact one area about which the Revue Administration, performers and fans are loath to speak or publish, as to do so would encroach upon the so-called 'Violet Code (*Sumire kōdo*),' a set of largely unwritten but longstanding guidelines said to govern the acceptability of anything connected with Takarazuka, both in performance and off-stage. Fundamentally, however, I believe that the appeal of Takarazuka cannot be expressed in precise terms. It certainly involves erotic sexuality and sexual desire for some who attend its performances and worship its performers, but it represents a different kind of 'love' and enjoyment for others, who appreciate the skill and beauty of cast members in their portrayal of gender, and the entire fantasy world their characters inhabit. The book's whole-of-life perspective shows that an appreciation for Takarazuka begun in some cases in early childhood, and perhaps continuing into old age, is not necessarily a matter of erotic love, though it certainly can be so.

Takarazuka undoubtedly does, however, call forth strong emotional responses from both its performers and its fans. Clearly, engagement with Takarazuka involves a broad range of issues, many of which are gender-based and have implications in terms of the social construction of gender in Japanese society. For girls and women, who now comprise approximately ninety per cent of the Takarazuka audience, the *otokoyaku*, in particular, represents not only the 'ideal man,' as Kobayashi and the Revue Company insist, but also a type of 'ideal woman,' a positive model of female agency, whom they admire and often wish to emulate.

Moreover, it is clear, from the efforts of the publicity machine that surrounds and sustains Takarazuka, that girls and women are given both implicit permission and active encouragement to love other women – specifically, the male-role players – under the pretext that this affection is not (homo-)sexual in nature, because the object of their love is 'male,' and therefore does not compromise the subjects' 'normal' sexuality. On the other hand, the very fact that Takarazuka *otokoyaku* are not biological males means that they are apparently not usually perceived by the husbands of married fans as rivals, nor by the parents of single fans as a threat to the marriageability of their daughters. For many women, Takarazuka is also a place of respite from a boring, unpleasant or unfulfilling everyday existence as a female in Japanese society. The euphoria generated by contact with Takarazuka seems to be the very thing that enables these women to cope with the more mundane aspects of

their lives. In addition, through their choice of clothing or specific
fan-club activities such as amateur theatricals, these female fans
can enjoy performing femininity (or, in some cases, masculinity)
specifically for the sake of other women. It is obvious, therefore,
that the appeal of Takarazuka is much more complex than the above
two extreme positions on eroticism and sexuality suggest.

Getting terminology straight

What do we mean by such concepts as sex, gender and androgyny,
which are so central to any discussion of Takarazuka? Though sex
determination is not always unproblematic, a person's biological
sex is usually determined at birth as male or female according
to the appearance of external genitalia, the existence of sexual
reproductive organs, or through chromosomal structure, with the
criteria for judgement having become more sophisticated throughout history as medical knowledge has increased (International
Foundation for Androgynous Studies 2003). In a different sense,
the word 'sex' generally refers to physical lovemaking in all of
its permutations. By contrast, gender can be seen as a 'social
creation' in which a person is identified as masculine or feminine,
without this decision being based necessarily upon the individual's
anatomy (Poynton 1985: 4). Gender roles can be defined as 'cultural
expectations of behaviour as appropriate for members of each sex,
relative to location, class, occasion, time in history, and numerous
other factors' (International Foundation for Androgynous Studies
2003). Deviation by an individual from stereotyped norms of masculinity or femininity, seen by some people as 'natural' (or even
'god-given') outcomes of biological sex, can lead to such negative
consequences as ostracism or physical punishment. Some scholars
argue, however, that biological sex is as much a construct as gender,
or challenge the idea of the sex/gender dichotomy. Judith Butler,
for one, questions whether there is really a difference between
sex and gender, and demonstrates that 'strategies of exclusion
and hierarchy' are at work in 'the formulation of the sex/gender
distinction and its recourse to "sex" as the prediscursive' (1999:
188), while Michel Foucault even earlier denies the notion of 'sex'
any existence outside a discourse which defines it (1978: 154). In
this volume, I employ the term 'gender' in its learned or socially-
constructed sense.

    Androgyny, or an approximation of it, is an ideal which has been
identified as one of the Revue's central attractions by Robertson

(1998b: 38), Kawasaki (1999: 192) and others. An androgynous person or androgyne is said to be intermediate in gender, exhibiting a 'full range of masculine and feminine qualities' (Tong 1989: 4). Such individuals, according to one recent definition, have assumed (rather than inborn) characteristics that are 'not limited to either of the two traditionally accepted gender classifications, masculine and feminine,' and these can include 'a variety of experiences including androgynous presentation, physique, behaviour, wardrobe and social roles' (International Foundation for Androgynous Studies 2003). According to Jungian psychoanalyst June Singer, androgyny starts 'with our *conscious* recognition of the masculine and feminine potential in every individual, and, is realized as we develop our capacity to establish harmonious relations between the two aspects within the single individual' (2000: 23; emphasis in original). The Takarazuka *otokoyaku*'s portrayal of masculinity is different from that of a typical man, sometimes seeming sexless or gender-neutral, sometimes deliberately seductive and erotic. Kawasaki calls the *otokoyaku*'s 'erasure of the boundary between masculinity and femininity' her main allure (1999: 192).

Butler further argues that a person's gender must be continually reinforced in a patriarchal culture by that person's repetition or 'citation' of gender-appropriate acts, his or her 'doing' or 'performing' of gender (1993: 12–16). Indeed, she sees gender as 'an act which has been rehearsed,' according to a 'script,' which needs successive generations of 'actors' to perform it and bring it into reality (Butler 1990: 272).[5] In other words, gender is not determined by anatomy, but is constructed by countless repetitions of certain actions by innumerable individuals, resulting in a composite picture, shared by society in general, of how persons of a particular gender should look, sound and behave. In the case of Japanese theatre, writes Jennifer Robertson in her discussion of Takarazuka, the gender ideal is 'carefully crafted from a repertoire of markers or forms (*kata*) – gestural, sartorial, bodily, cosmetic, linguistic – that are coded masculine or feminine' (1998b: 38). In both the everyday and the theatrical sense, 'acting like a woman' is undoubtedly a skill that must be 'taught, learned, rehearsed, and repeated' (Kano 2001: 3). The same, surely, can be said of 'acting like a man,' Takarazuka being one place where the techniques of acting as a certain type of man have become well established. My fourth chapter will expand on Robertson's analysis of the various kinds of *kata* employed in Takarazuka, to include examples from actual performances.

Gender and women's history in contemporary Japan

Takarazuka performers, fans and creative staff are all affected by gender issues in general, though the artificial nature of gender in quotidian life may not be obvious to many. On a theoretical level, gender is widely accepted as one of the significant factors influencing the ways in which individuals in Japan, as elsewhere, participate in society and make choices during their lives.[6] However, most analyses of orthodox notions of gender in contemporary Japanese society completely ignore the existence of all-female revues, probably because the revues' artful manipulation of gender represents a radical departure from the very norms discussed in most works. Scholarship in such areas as the social construction of gender, gender socialisation, education and careers for women, and marriage and the family is nevertheless highly relevant to this book. An understanding of major historical developments related to women's place in Japanese society, especially those regarding schooling, employment and social participation, is also essential, especially as some of my informants were born and raised in the pre-war period.

Many scholars have pointed out that being female in Japan has been a considerable disadvantage to girls and women in terms of self-determination. Takarazuka performers, all of whom are female, and most of whom have been born and raised in Japan by Japanese parents, directly experience this disadvantage, which was especially marked under pre-war laws and the Confucian-inspired Meiji Civil Code of 1898, which, Ann Waswo argues, 'enshrined patriarchy and patrilinealism as the norm for all Japanese families' (1996: 149). The Code contributed to the construction in the early twentieth century of what Barbara Sato calls a 'widespread mythology of a monolithic Japanese woman' (2003: 1). It vested authority over family matters in the household head (usually a male); wives were treated as minors and had no property rights; and sons, specifically the first-born, took precedence over daughters. Where family members lived, whom they were permitted to marry, and even whether they were sold to a recruitment broker as labourers or to a brothel as prostitutes, depended legally upon the decision of the head of the household. Moreover, as the Code promoted the samurai model of family life as the one 'proper' model throughout the nation, the warrior-class practice of arranged marriages and strict chastity for women replaced the less formal matches and casual sexual mores hitherto the norm in peasant society, where premarital sexual relations and a free choice of spouse had been commonplace.[7] Then, during the 1890s, a 'significant reformulation of gender ideology' occurred when the government began to encourage married women to shoulder the responsibility for running the household and raising children, under the catchphrase of 'good wives and wise mothers (*ryōsai kenbo*)' (Garon 1997: 102). This ethos formed the basis for the socialisation of girls at home and at school, and was echoed in the moral philosophy of Takarazuka's founder, who, as later chapters will show, regarded Revue performers' membership of Takarazuka as a brief interlude between childhood, on the one hand, and respectable married life and motherhood, on the other.

Early twentieth-century developments in the social participation of women in Japan are especially pertinent to this volume, as that was the time when the Takarazuka Revue was established and became popular. In the 1910s, the expression 'new woman (*atarashii onna*)' was coined to refer to 'an indulgent and irresponsible young Japanese woman, who used her overdeveloped sexuality to undermine the family and to manipulate others for her own selfish ends' (Sievers 1983: 175–76). In the 1920s, Japan saw the emergence of the apparently relatively autonomous but apolitical young woman who began to wear short skirts, cut her hair and seek social and sexual freedom – the so-called 'Modern Girl (*moga*),' who is described as a 'highly modified construct crafted by journalists who debated her identity during the tumultuous decade of cultural and social change following the great earthquake of 1923' (Silverberg 1991: 240).[8] Women's magazines were particularly influential in moulding the image of the Modern Girl, who 'symbolised mass culture' (Sato 2003: 10, 49). Moreover, the interwar Japanese public encoded 'mass' culture as feminine (Sato 2003: 82). Amongst other things, this encoding undoubtedly reflected the burgeoning popularity of all-female revues at the time.

A Japanese female like the 'modern girl' could also be categorised as a 'new woman.' Both defied the 'good wife and wise mother' model of exemplary Japanese womanhood as noted above. It was not only 'modern girls' and 'new women' who worked outside the home, however. As Nagy (1991: 199–216) reveals, paid employment for ordinary, middle-class women dramatically increased in the early decades of the twentieth century. It was still unusual for daughters from well-off, middle-class families to work in the 1920s, however, except in cases of financial hardship (Sievers 1983: 133). The 'proper place' for middle-class women was 'in the home working as unpaid members of the family labour force' (Fukutake 1989: 110).

The patriarchal household was replaced after the Second World War by 'a "democratic" but nevertheless strongly gender-role-determined unit' (White 2002: 64). In other words, in legal terms, women may have gained an equal voice of authority in the family, but marked differences persisted between men's and women's levels of participation in various aspects of family life, and a strong expectation has remained that women will continue to be 'good wives and wise mothers,' irrespective of whether they pursue a career outside the home (see Uno 1993: 293–322). By the 1970s, for example, the typical housewife's role had come to include various forms of social participation, including employment, but the new role models thus produced did not, according to Kumiko Fujimura-Fanselow and Anne Imamura, 'contradict the primacy of the domestic role' even if they 'allow[ed] for a great deal of flexibility within it' (1991: 243). In spite of the current high rate of female participation in paid employment, women have seldom occupied senior administrative positions in the business world, indicating that they still face significant barriers in competing with men for equal status in society – a fact which also impacts upon the post-performing career prospects of Takarazuka retirees.

In spite of the achievement of equally high male and female enrolments in secondary education, post-war formal schooling in Japan still retains certain aspects of the gender discrimination of previous decades, and differences have persisted in such matters as curricular content (Buckley 1993: 360). Though 49.8 per cent of girls continued their education at universities or two-year junior colleges (*tanki daigaku*) in 2005, compared to 51.3 per cent for boys (Gender Equality Bureau 2007), girls still make up the vast majority of enrolments at two-year institutions.[9] Moreover, the aim of some, if not most, women's junior colleges is not only to impart academic knowledge but also to socialise their students to become 'ideal Japanese women,' a process which Brian McVeigh contends is 'as much a bodily experience as it is a mental process,' conducted through direct instruction, school rules and mandatory participation in various rituals (1996: 28–29, 147). These aims parallel the dual purpose of the training given students at the Takarazuka Music School, as I will show in Chapter Three.

The post-schooling life-course of Japanese girls and women over the past century has changed dramatically, arguably much more than that of their male counterparts. Career opportunities for women are widening, due in no small part to legislation and government campaigns for gender equality, though female workers are still more likely to have lower-paid, part-time positions than males, and be greatly underrepresented in positions of authority in most fields. A trend towards delayed marriage and non-marriage has become particularly evident in the past decade, and single Japanese women in their twenties and early thirties who commute from their parental home to their workplace long after they have the financial means to live independently, whose income is largely spent on fashion, travel and other luxuries, and who appear be in no hurry to find a husband, have attracted the unflattering nickname of 'parasite singles.' According to Laura Dales, such 'unreproductive' women, especially those aged 25–29, 'represent the greatest challenge to expectations and ideals of the feminine life cycle,' they having 'the potential to reform the social and family structures which maintain [Japan's] gender-based expectations' (2005: 134). Takarasiennes who choose not to retire within seven years of their debut, but remain single and fully-employed through their late twenties and beyond, also challenge these expectations, though their status as entertainers or celebrities may place them largely outside the norms for gender behaviour, in spite of the claims of Takarazuka's founder to the contrary.

Outline of chapters

Chapter One of this book traces the establishment and growth of the Revue from its beginnings in 1913 to the present day, placing it within its historical context and also emphasising the influence and philosophies of the founder, Kobayashi Ichizō, with special note of his attitudes towards women. It shows that, though the Revue has become a phenomenon in itself, the great diversity among its members has made it anything but monolithic, as it is constantly developing in response to changing internal and external conditions. The historical treatment includes a discussion of the wartime Revue and its links with nationalism, demonstrating that the Company's apparent complicity with a militaristic agenda was sufficiently shallow to allow the Revue's continued operation after Japan's defeat and a fairly smooth transition to the changed circumstances of the post-war period. I further outline significant issues in the Revue's post-war development, showing Takarazuka's response to changes in women's social position, attitudes to sexuality, and other matters.

Chapter Two discusses how prevailing gender norms have impacted upon the lives of girls in twentieth- and early twenty-first-century Japan, especially in relation to matters of education and vocation. It examines the avenues by which prospective Takarasiennes have learned of the Revue, their reasons for applying to join, and how families, schools and others view their thespian aspirations. I also compare Takarazuka with its various rival groups in terms of attractiveness to recruits. Overall, the chapter will show how gender issues in general, and orthodox notions of suitable careers and life-paths for girls, influence the reaction of parents and others to a girl's wish to become a Takarasienne, or other kind of professional entertainer.

In Chapter Three, I explore would-be Takarasiennes' preparation for and experience of the Takarazuka Music School entrance examination, and the subsequent training of the successful examinees, who begin to develop an awareness of how gender is portrayed in Takarazuka during their period as trainees. It shows how determined some girls are to follow their dream of eventually performing on the Takarazuka stage, even if it means diverging from the typical life-path of their female peers. The chapter then reveals the School's dual agenda of preparing students for their stage debut by means of performing arts classes, while simultaneously indoctrinating them with gender-based rules for being demure, virtuous females in Japanese society, as well as with the values of hierarchy, self-discipline, group cohesion and respect for tradition. I show how most girls dislike, but nevertheless accept, the vertical organisational structure imposed upon them and implemented by their seniors to keep order within the school. In addition, I examine the way Music School students begin learning how to manipulate gender in terms of appearance and manner, in preparation for full membership of the Revue Company.

Chapter Four, which discusses performance on and off the stage, challenges the common assumption that playing a female role is 'natural' for a biological female, while playing a male is 'unnatural' for her, and thus must be 'learned' by artificial means. I argue that the gender socialisation to which performers are exposed during childhood gives them a certain understanding of what society expects of them as females, but that the limitations of this early training, coupled with a lack of worldly experience, a tradition of 'mental immaturity' seemingly celebrated in Takarazuka, and the sugar-coated view of the world which Revue productions present, make it necessary for performers to be taught how to portray adult women or men on stage. I discuss the formal and informal processes by which Takarazuka performers learn to be specialists in one stage gender, while simultaneously assuming an off-stage persona as a Takarasienne, bound by the rules of the Administration and the expectations of fans and the general public. Here are defined the aspects of appearance, behaviour and attitude that have been deemed appropriate at various stages of the Revue's development for each gender role, as performed on the Takarazuka stage and at rehearsals, as compared with stereotyped gender-role expectations and representations in Japanese society.

Chapter Five focuses upon the significance of gender in Takarazuka fandom, exploring the importance of the sex and gender of fans, and the stage gender of performers, in determining players' relative popularity. In examining the historical development of Revue fandom, I refute the stereotype of the Takarazuka fan as a particular kind of female, showing that considerable diversity in gender, attitude and practice exists among the larger population of people who make an 'emotional investment' in the Revue. I debate the possibility of a sexual basis for their enthusiasm and the outspoken resistance to this idea. I also discuss the ways in which fans participate in the creation of Takarazuka's fantasy world through their loyalty or fickleness towards performers, their criticism or support of Company policy, and through their contribution to the pool of future Takarasiennes. The chapter also explores the concept of the gaze in relation to Takarazuka, showing how the interplay of gazes among performers and audience members constitutes an important part of the pleasure of Takarazuka fandom, and blurs the boundaries of gender and sexuality of the subjects and objects of those gazes.

Chapter Six discusses the return of Takarasiennes to the non-Takarazuka world, with its concomitant responsibilities and challenges. First, it examines performers' diverse reasons for quitting Takarazuka. Overwhelming support from performers for the enforcement of the Company's 'retirement upon impending marriage' rule reveals the strong identification of the Takarasienne, and especially the *otokoyaku*, as the shared dream lover of fans and fellow performers, a fantasy which would be destroyed by the sexual nuances of a formal relationship with an individual man. Then, continuing the overall theme of the flexible 'construct' of gender and the wide range of attitude and experience among Takarazuka members, the chapter shows how performers who were expected to remain chaste and (hetero-)sexually inexperienced during their membership of the Revue – as 'girls' rather than 'women,' or even as androgynous hybrids of male and female – anticipate or manage post-performing life, which may entail marriage and childbearing, or other manifestations of adult sexuality. The chapter also discusses the relative merits of Takarazuka training in terms of retirees' ability to begin a new career in entertainment or an unrelated field, restart an interrupted education, or forge a cordial relationship in marriage. It shows how an *otokoyaku*, in particular, usually must learn, or re-learn, how to enact a prescribed feminine role in society. Finally, it ties the mentoring and nurturing functions of ex-Takarasiennes to the encouragement of fans, and the cultivation of future generations of Takarazuka performers.

Overall, the central concern of this book is to explore the significance of gender in the Takarazuka Revue, in relation to the broad social context in which it is situated. Arguably, Takarazuka simultaneously reinforces gender norms in contemporary Japanese society, and challenges those same norms, in fact constructing masculinity and femininity according to its own distinct notions of maleness and femaleness, on its stage and off, by and for performers and fans alike. The reader, it is hoped, will gain from the chapters which follow not only a greater appreciation of the Revue itself and the people it touches, but also a deeper understanding of the complex ways in which orthodox notions of gender can be variously interpreted, reproduced, manipulated or subverted, in 'real life' or in the fantasy world beyond the orchestra pit.

1 The Takarazuka Revue, 1913–2007

For more than nine decades, the Takarazuka Revue has grown and reinvented itself in various ways, enduring cyclical fluctuations in popularity, capitalising on periods of prosperity and adapting to adversities such as war and natural disaster. It is unquestionably the most successful of Japanese all-female revue companies, for it still flourishes while its rivals have mostly vanished. Takarazuka is not static, however, and has never been monolithic: it is a heterogeneous organisation, shaped by a combination of diverse interests, personalities, and creative and expressive talents. While its development has been strongly influenced by its founder's artistic, entrepreneurial and moralistic philosophies, various external conditions – social, political, economic and geographical – have also provoked many changes in Takarazuka.

This chapter will sketch the development of the Takarazuka Revue over more than nine decades from its beginnings in 1913, relating its emergence with the earlier history of drama and mass culture in Japan, and women's participation as professional stage performers. Such historical context is essential not only to facilitate an understanding of Takarazuka's development, but also for more specific reasons. Memories of particular moments, melodies and stars from Takarazuka's past are cherished by many performers and fans, including some who no longer frequent performances. Further, the informants who allowed me to interview them include performers who made their debut as far back as around 1930. This historical context, then, is vital in interpreting their testimony, as well as that contained in the numerous published primary sources used in this volume.

Women on the Japanese stage

Although Takarazuka was founded in a climate of burgeoning mass culture after 1910, its distant roots lie in what Marilyn Ivy (1993: 242) describes as the 'extraordinarily vibrant popular culture' of the urban bourgeoisie in Osaka and Edo during the Tokugawa period (1603–1868). Moreover, in artistic terms, it also owes much to the

gradual introduction of Western music, literature and drama during
the Meiji era (1868–1912).

As in the Britain of Shakespeare, women were long barred from
the public stage in Japan. Theatrical entertainments such as Kabuki
and Bunraku (the puppet theatre genre also known as *ningyō jōruri*,
lit. 'dolls and narration') flourished in Tokugawa times (Shively
1978: 7), but though Kabuki itself was originally developed by a
woman, Izumo-no-Okuni, in Kyoto in the early seventeenth century,
Japan's ruling military regime issued repeated bans on female stage
performers from 1629 onwards, though numerous transgressions
have been recorded (Kawasaki 2005: 125). The bans were ostensibly
a counter-prostitution measure, though probably also arose because
of brawls among male spectators over favoured performers. Female
roles in Kabuki were subsequently played by *onnagata* (lit. 'female
form,' also known as *oyama*): male actors who specialised in
impersonating women on stage, to the extent that their private lives
were also lived as women. The *onnagata* developed a technique of
portraying exaggerated femininity that was said to surpass that of
real women. This 'unnatural' representation of gender then took on
aesthetic value because of its very 'unnaturalness.'

From 1890, theatrical performances by mixed casts were
legalised, enabling women to return to the professional stage
(Kawasaki 1999: 166). A few female actors, including Ichikawa
Kumehachi (1846–1913), performed in Kabuki-style plays during
Meiji, though their participation was limited (Gilbert-Falkenburg
1985: 30; Kawasaki 2005: 127). A former geisha, Kawakami
Sadayakko, made her Japanese stage debut as Desdemona in
Othello in 1903, and became the first woman to be called an 'actress
(*joyū*).' This term replaced the old word for 'female player,' *onna
yakusha* (Kano 2001: 32). In 1908, Kawakami founded Japan's
first training centre for actresses, which became the Teikoku joyū
yōseijo (Imperial Actress Training Institution) in 1909 under the
auspices of Tokyo's Imperial Theatre.[1]

While mainstream Kabuki, Nō and Bunraku remained exclusively male genres, women found a vehicle for participation
in theatre through an innovative dramatic form called *Shingeki*
(new drama), which employed dialogue in place of the songs and
dances of Kabuki, and featured women in female roles instead of
Kabuki-trained female impersonators (*onnagata*). Actresses such as
Matsui Sumako, Mori Ritsuko, Hatsuse Namiko, Kawamura Kikue,
Suzuki Tokuko and Murata Kakuko were 'spectacularly promoted'
under the guidance of a committee of Kabuki actors including

onnagata Onoe Baikō VI and Sawamura Sōjūrō VII (Sawamura 1969: 21–22). Ironically, the female actors were taught how to play women's roles by men, underlining the idea that femininity is not a natural outcome of being female, but is an 'art' which must be learned and practised.

Western-style naturalistic acting and the use of actresses were also promoted by the Shakespeare translator Tsubouchi Shōyō, who had formed an amateur company in 1906, while Jiyū gekijō (Freedom Theatre), a professional group directed by Osanai Kaoru, performed Henrik Ibsen's play *John Gabriel Borkman* in 1909 with a mixed cast (Mason and Caiger 1997: 311). Tsubouchi's company, expanded and renamed Bungei kyōkai (Society of Literature and Art), premiered another Ibsen work, *A Doll's House*, with Matsui in the role of Nora, in 1911. The final scene of the play, especially, stirred wide controversy and even some feminists were apparently 'appalled' by its portrayal of a married woman's 'irresponsible' abandonment of home and family in order to live as herself, not as a 'doll wife' in the 'doll's house' of the play's title (see Birnbaum 1999: 28; Rodd 1991: 175, 177; Gilbert-Falkenburg 1985: 37). Matsui also achieved notoriety for her 1914 performance of the title role in Oscar Wilde's *Salome*, in which she revealed considerable amounts of voluptuous, bare flesh during the 'Dance of the Seven Veils.' According to Ayako Kano (1999: 48), Matsui was 'the embodiment of the new Taishō[2] alignment of sex, gender and performance.' The unconventional behaviour of Matsui herself, who left her husband, cohabited with a fellow actor, Shimamura Hōgetsu, and eventually killed herself following Shimamura's death, helped to make professional acting a scandalous career for women in the eyes of many Japanese at the time. The case of Matsui also contributes to an understanding of the rationale behind well-publicised efforts later made by Takarazuka's founder and his successors to differentiate the Revue from its commercial theatre counterparts in terms of morality.

Western operetta, drama and music had been performed in Japan since 1870 by a variety of amateur groups in the Yokohama foreign settlement. Some Japanese (including Osanai and Tsubouchi) attended performances there out of an interest in Western theatre and music (Masumoto 1986: 193–94). Occidental theatrical dance was first taught in Japan by an Italian ballet master, Giovanni Vittorio Rosi, who was engaged by the new Imperial Theatre in 1911 as a director, choreographer and dance instructor in its Opera division for four years (Suzuki 2002).

Kobayashi and Takarazuka Choir's founding

The idea of females acting, dancing and singing on the professional stage was thus still quite novel in 1913 when Kobayashi Ichizō (1873–1957), a senior executive of the Osaka-based Minoo–Arima denki kidō (Minoo–Arima Electric Railway), sought to increase passenger numbers on the company's electric tramline between Osaka and its terminus, a small riverside hamlet later to be formally named Takarazuka. The latter was situated some twenty-five kilometres to the north-west of Osaka, surrounding a mineral spring which had been open for public bathing since 1892 (Kobayashi 1955: 445–46). By 1913, this spa was run-down, recording only about 100,000 visitors per year (Geinōshi Kenkyūkai 1990: 92). In 1911, Kobayashi's Minoo–Arima Railway had established a new spa facility on reclaimed land on the eastern bank of the Muko River, naming one building, which was an exotic structure with a Vienna Secession-style exterior, 'Paradise' (Kawasaki 1999: 22). The building originally housed an unheated, indoor swimming pool, but this proved a failure because mixed swimming was legally proscribed, and the water was reputedly too cold for bathing on all but the hottest summer days. The pool area was converted to a theatre, apparently even before any specific use had been determined for such a facility (Takagi 1983: 49).

During the first two years of the new spa's establishment, men comprised its chief clientele. Indeed, in the Kansai region and probably elsewhere as well, adult men tended to be the ones to have 'the freedom to work, go out to amuse themselves and have money to spend freely' in the early twentieth century (Sakata 1983: 145). By 1913, however, Kobayashi had recognised another, untapped potential market for his company's services: women and children of the burgeoning middle class, who were starting to have sufficient disposable income and leisure time to seek 'wholesome' entertainment, presumably while their husbands or fathers were working to support this lifestyle.

Kobayashi's company had already developed a suburban sub-division of pleasantly-situated housing in Ikeda, on the western fringe of Osaka Prefecture, halfway between Osaka City and Takarazuka, and had extended loans to enable families to purchase a house and land for the equivalent of three to four years' salary for a civil servant, with cheaper monthly repayments than housing rents in Osaka (Kojima 1983b: 184–90). This development exploited the growing trend towards the separation of workplace and domicile which had begun in late Meiji, in which middle-class husbands and fathers spent their working days in inner-urban areas, returning home nightly to the outer suburbs where their stay-at-home wives and children passed most of their time (Sand 1998: 191–207). The suburban railway network radiating away from Osaka, including that developed by Kobayashi's company, provided such men with a rapid and convenient way of commuting to their workplaces.

Kobayashi further predicted that the emerging middle-class family, as a unit, would begin to demand 'wholesome' entertainment and leisure facilities which all of its members could enjoy, in the vicinity of their suburban homes, or at least away from city centres, and he planned to cultivate this hitherto unmet demand by offering musical entertainment at 'Paradise' (Tsuganezawa 1991: 85). As noted above, Takarazuka was conveniently located not far from populous Osaka, a city that had recorded spectacular industrial growth since mid-Meiji, and, by then, according to sociologist Tsuganezawa Toshihiro (1991: 84), had become a smoke-polluted, industrial centre complete with slums, earning it the nickname of 'the Manchester of the East,' or, as Jeffrey Hanes (1998: 276–77) adds, the 'Capital of Smoke (*kemuri no miyako*)' – though the latter perhaps could be interpreted either as a criticism or as a favourable epithet for a prosperous urban centre whose populace could afford to cook meals at their own kitchen hearths.

The negative aspects of inner-city living were highlighted by Kobayashi in his appeal to potential purchasers of his suburban Ikeda real estate, his advertising copy claiming that sanitation in Osaka was so bad that more than eleven deaths occurred for every ten births (Kojima 1983b: 184). Thus, he probably had a shrewd appreciation that his Takarazuka spa facilities would fit the ideal of a verdant, semi-rural paradise, offering residents or workers from the inner city a place of escape for a few hours. Furthermore, Takarazuka was sufficiently removed from the urban dweller's everyday environment to be 'exotic,' a kind of tourist destination. Even as late as 1930, novelist Kawabata Yasunari described Takarazuka as 'exclusively a trysting place (*tsurekomi senmon*)' for lovers from Osaka (cited in Kawasaki 1999: 137).

In 1913, faced with the necessity of reversing the fortunes of his Paradise pool venture in the shortest possible time, Kobayashi decided to form a girls' musical performance group, to be named Takarazuka shōkatai (Takarazuka choir). He took his inspiration from the popularity among women and children of a boys' musical band, established around 1910 by Mitsukoshi gofukuten, a leading department store in Tokyo's Nihonbashi district, and which also performed at Mitsukoshi's Osaka branch (Kobayashi 1955: 447; Kawasaki 1999: 43–44). Kobayashi was not the first to employ the concept of girl entertainers, either: Shirokiya, another Tokyo department store opposite Mitsukoshi, had already established a musical group called Tōkyō shirokiya shōjo ongakudan (Tokyo shirokiya girls' band), whose repertoire included short operetta-like items (Sakata 1983: 159). Nor was Kobayashi the last, as he in turn inspired the foundation in 1921 by Inoue Kochō of the all-female company, Seitai-za, in Hakata, Kyushu (Fukuoka City Foundation for Arts and Cultural Promotion 1999). Similarly, in 1922, Shōchiku gakugekibu (Shochiku musical theatre division), later renamed OSSK (Osaka shōchiku shōjo kagekidan: Osaka shochiku girls' opera company), was set up by Shochiku, a major theatrical organisation; and its Tokyo-based counterpart, SSKD (Shōchiku shōjo kagekidan: Shochiku girls' opera company) was formed in 1928.

Kobayashi and young women

Kobayashi chose girls for his new venture because they would be cheaper to hire than boys, and he believed they would be ready to perform after only minimal training: he held the stereotyped view that though maleness was a prerequisite for specialisation in any field, females did better at an amateur level because of their versatility and quickness to learn (Kojima 1983b: 240; Kobayashi 1955: 447). Using a culinary allusion to argue his point, Kobayashi claimed: 'The only ones to excel in gourmet cuisine are men, but it takes a woman to whip up something adequate in an instant at home' (Tanabe and Sasaki 1987: 146).

Kobayashi may also have had another, covert motive for choosing girls, though, in spite of his stated aim of providing 'family' entertainment: girls would be a magnet for male patrons, who had comprised the bulk of his spa's customers until then, and whose favour he could not afford to lose. All the same, Kobayashi did conscientiously set out to guard the choristers against any moral danger, thus assuaging the fears of the girls and their parents that the choir might be a front for unlicensed prostitution. Such anxiety was not altogether misplaced, given the seedy reputation of the older Takarazuka Spa, on the opposite bank of the Muko River, where even casual clients could purchase the sexual favours of geisha, at least according to one contemporary short story, *Bonchi* (The young master), by Iwano Hōmei, published in 1912 (Sakata 1983: 142). Certainly, Takarazuka recruits had been promised generous pay from the start of their training, Kawasaki (1999: 202) noting that pre-war pay for Takarasiennes surpassed even that of the railway company's mid-ranking managers (*kachō*) and writer/directors in the Revue itself – unusually fine remuneration, indeed, for morally wholesome activities.

Parents' doubts about Kobayashi's venture could also have stemmed from the widespread prejudice among the general populace towards professional performers, due to the legacy of the Tokugawa-period class system which had categorised entertainers of all kinds as *hinin* (lit. 'non-people'), excluding them from the four classes of 'respectable' subjects above them. Kobayashi apparently insisted his performers were 'musicians' rather than 'actresses (*joyū*)' because of the 'comparative prestige' of the former (Ōta 2001: 112). While the new profession of actress was theoretically open to women of any class background, the respectability of actresses was still questioned in early Taishō, and the stage was not deemed the place for daughters from 'good families (*ryōke*),' who were the very girls Kobayashi hoped to recruit. If parents hoped for a socially advantageous marriage for any of their children, for example, then having an actress in the family might have seemed a disadvantage. The term *ryōke* itself, in the opinion of Takarazuka historian Hashimoto Masao (1988: 83), indicated families whose only connection with the performing arts, if any, was 'amateur,' not professional, although the word now tends to be interpreted as 'well-to-do.' A number of early recruits were the daughters of public servants such as police officers or teachers (Hashimoto 1988: 83), though Kobayashi may also have consciously recruited girls whose families were reasonably well-off in order to deflect any suspicion that he might be 'buying' their daughters.

Young women and girls, in fact, had a special place in the heart of Kobayashi Ichizō, due to events in his own life. Born in 1873 in Niresaki, Yamanashi Prefecture, he had lost his mother to illness at the age of eight months. His father, who had been adopted into his mother's wealthy merchant family, was sent back to his birth home upon his wife's death, while the orphaned Ichizō and his three-year-old sister were raised by their great-uncle and aunt, who also had six children of their own (Sakata 1983: 12, 18). It is apparent from Kobayashi's memoirs that he indulged in a life-long, sentimental yearning for maternal affection, though his adoptive family allegedly treated him with fondness and compassion (Sakata 1983:

19). At the age of thirteen or fourteen, he spent one-and-a-half years living in a dormitory while attending school near Mt Fuji, where he became enamoured of his distant cousin, Matsuyoshi: a girl one class below him, she herself was aged no more than about fourteen. This marked the beginning of many years of indulgence in 'love for love's sake (*ren'ai shijō shugi*),' as well as a taste for exceedingly young women. Kobayashi entered Keiō gijuku preparatory school in Tokyo at the age of fifteen, aspiring to 'a career in literature and dramaturgy,' but continued for the rest of his life to yearn for the mother he had never known (Sakata 1983: 16–23).

Kobayashi also continued to pursue young women. After spending large amounts of his family's fortune upon amusement, the twenty-three-year-old Kobayashi, by now a bank employee in Nagoya, began a love affair with Niwa Kō, a fifteen-year-old girl whom he described as 'graceful and elegant, with bright eyes and pearly teeth, a high-bridged nose, fair skin and a slim build.' The pair eventually began to cohabit, according to the frank autobiography Kobayashi penned at the age of seventy-nine, in 1953 (cited in Sakata 1983: 64). However, as his promotion to the bank's Osaka branch depended upon his marrying a 'suitable' woman, he wed a young Christian from Tokyo to whom he had been formally introduced. Undaunted, Kō came looking for him shortly after the newlyweds had arrived at their new home in Osaka in August 1899, and Kobayashi arranged a secret tryst at Arima Spa with his former lover. During her husband's abrupt absence, Kobayashi's new wife found out about his relationship with Kō and abandoned Kobayashi, who then had the temerity to suggest to his family that he should propose to another 'appropriate' candidate in order to retain his job. The scandal was reported in the newspapers, however, and the seventeen-year-old Kō, at the 'peak of her bloom,' subsequently became Kobayashi's legal wife, eventually bearing him five children (Kobayashi 1953, cited in Sakata 1983: 75–82).

Western music and Takarazuka's development

For several months in 1913, the sixteen original recruits to the Takarazuka Choir learnt only singing and instrumental music such as piano and violin, but the curriculum then expanded to train the girls to perform operetta, at the urging of the composer and opera singer Andō Hiroshi, whom Kobayashi had engaged to coach the girls twice a week. Kobayashi himself became convinced that opera had a future in Japan (Kobayashi 1955: 449), and decided that an

all-girl opera troupe, rather than a choir, would be a better advertisement for his railway and the spa. He apparently resisted Andō's
suggestion of forming a mixed opera troupe for fear of the moral
problems that would create, but was enthusiastic at Andō's idea of
dressing girls as boys to play male roles (Kojima 1983b: 240).
Kobayashi changed the group's name in December 1913 to
Takarazuka shōjo kageki yōseikai, or Takarazuka Girls' Opera
Training Association, and recruited four more girls (Kojima 1983b:
240; also Ōzasa 1986: 25). All successful applicants were to be
aged from thirteen to fifteen by *kazoedoshi* reckoning,[3] and were
required to have completed six years of primary education, which
had been legally compulsory for all children since 1907. Andō
wanted a year to train the raw recruits before their stage debut, but
Kobayashi set a limit of nine months, anticipating that the girls
would indeed be able to 'whip up something adequate' in the way
of stage performance by then.

The musical background of the first Takarazuka girls is unclear,
but they certainly would have received some instruction in singing
at primary school, with a few perhaps having taken private lessons
in a Japanese or Western musical instrument, if their families were
sufficiently affluent.[4] Singing had become a compulsory subject at
all primary schools in 1907, and the study of Western music at post-
primary level by girls in the Kansai and Tokyo areas was further
promoted by some private schools (Kubota 2001). The importation
of gramophones and records had begun just before the turn of the
century, providing access to Western orchestral music for those
who could afford it.

By 1914, therefore, Japanese children had become reasonably
familiar with Western-style music, and Kobayashi took advantage
of this to promote an innovative musical theatre style in which the
performers sang Japanese melodies accompanied by a Western
orchestra instead of traditional instruments such as *shamisen*,
flute and drums (Sakata 1983: 70; Ōta 2001: 112). This innovation
served to distance the new entertainment from all-male Kabuki
and other long-established performing arts, and probably also
to differentiate Takarazuka performers from geisha, whose
repertoire included dancing and singing to the accompaniment of
traditional instruments. Kobayashi criticised Japanese music as
being 'unfamiliar, having little to do with [young people's lives],
impossible to understand ... and even detrimental to taste,' though
his opinion was radical, given that the study of traditional musical
instruments such as the stringed *koto* had begun to join the tea

ceremony and flower arrangement as disciplines considered 'suited to the interests of women and girls' within the context of female education in the Meiji era (Sakata 1983: 70; Kumakura 1990: 221). Such 'traditional' artistic accomplishments were to be exercised to enhance the cultural mood of the home, rather than to groom girls and women for the public life of a professional performer. Nor did Kobayashi seek to distance himself from this latter orthodoxy. Current Revue writer/director Ōta Tetsunori links the aim of Kobayashi's training organisation directly to the ideology of 'good wives, wise mothers' promoted by the state from at least the 1890s onward, observing that Takarazuka training was founded 'on a basis of amateurism,' with the aim 'not to nurture professional performing artists, but to heighten the level of general education of the women and girls who would mother the sons who would carry responsibility for Japan in the future' (Ōta 2001: 112).

The first public performance of the Takarazuka Girls' Opera was held in April 1914 in the converted Paradise swimming-pool building, in conjunction with an exhibition on a wedding theme. Patrons could enjoy a hot bath in a vast marble bathtub 'ten times bigger than any in Osaka,' a stroll around the exhibition, a tasty meal in the dining hall and a free seat on the tatami-matted floor of the boarded-over pool for a programme of 'fairy-tale opera (*otogi kageki*),' dances and musical items performed by Girls' Opera members, some of whom played male roles (Kamura 1984: 14–15). In keeping with Japanese theatrical practice, the performers wore 'whiteface (*oshiroi*)' makeup, which masked their own features. From then on, the Opera Training Association continued to recruit new girls and mount seasonal performances, also participating in charity concerts sponsored by the *Osaka mainichi* (Osaka daily) newspaper, which favourably reported the group's activities. The girls were schooled to become orchestral performers as well as singers and dancers, learning instruments such as the violin, piano, cello and mandolin, and when not performing on stage, they could often be found in the orchestra pit helping with the accompaniment.[5]

Kobayashi's choice of the Osaka hinterland as a venue for an all-girl opera troupe was shrewd, in that Osaka's distance from Tokyo enabled the development and refinement of such a novel idea in entertainment before exposure to a presumably more sophisticated Tokyo audience – a process which continues today, as new Takarazuka productions usually première on the Revue's 'home stage' in Takarazuka, then open in Tokyo after a further period of rehearsal: with a greater range of theatrical offerings from which to choose, Tokyo audiences are therefore presumed likely to demand higher quality than the 'tryout' audience from the Kansai area surrounding Takarazuka. In 1918, performances were held for the first time outside the Kansai region, in Tokyo and Nagoya, resulting in the first application for admittance from a Tokyo girl, Torii Eiko, who had seen the Girls' Opera at the Imperial Theatre and was encouraged by her father to join (Sugahara 1996: 36; *Kageki* 1969: 32). Torii's prowess at dancing was soon recognised, and she took the stage name of Amatsu Otome, becoming Takarazuka's most celebrated performer and remaining a Takarasienne for sixty-two years until her death in 1980.

January 1919 saw the opening of the Takarazuka ongaku kageki gakkō, or Takarazuka Music and Opera School, a formally-registered, private school for the training of recruits, with Kobayashi as its founding principal (Sakata 1983: 254). Students received free training, as well as a generous wage of seventeen *sen* per day – an amount similar to that earned by a middle-ranking, male white-collar worker ('Kiyoku' 1980: 147). The Takarazuka Girls' Opera Training Association was disbanded and simultaneously re-launched as the all-encompassing organisation named Takarazuka shōjo kagekidan (Takarazuka Girls' Opera Company), to be made up of remaining Training Association members, current students at the School and its subsequent graduates. Under his own name, Kobayashi had already actively participated in the Opera Training Association's creative output, having patched together twenty libretti from anthologies of well-loved songs taught in primary schools, and he continued to write scripts after becoming principal of the School, using the pseudonym Ikeda Hatao (Kamura 1984: 24).[6]

In accordance with the new legal status of the Music and Opera School, the curriculum was expanded to include academic and practical subjects deemed suitable for girls, such as sewing, Japanese language and English, as well as the morals and ethics class (*shūshin*) common to all schools, in addition to training in dancing, singing, acting and music ('Takarazuka ongaku gakkō' 1985: 4). The School accepted female primary school graduates up to the *kazoedoshi* age of eighteen. After a year in the 'preparatory course (*yoka*),' the girls were promoted to the 'main course (*honka*),' during which they made their stage debut. They were obliged to continue attending classes at the School and performing for at least two further years, as members of the 'research course (*kenkyūka*).' Kobayashi's insistence upon representing both trainees and performers as 'students' did not stop him paying them well, however: one early recruit, Okitsu Namiko, recalls Kobayashi handing out bonuses of one thousand yen in 1923 (a sum described by the recipient as 'enough to build a fine, two-storeyed house'), and advising the girls to use the money to buy property (cited in *Kageki* 1973a: 124).

This generosity was outwardly paternalistic – and Kobayashi did instruct the girls to call him 'Father (*Otōsan*)' (Kasuga Hanako, cited in *Kageki* 1973a: 123) – although it was probably also an extension of his continued taste for the company of beautiful young women, however chaste their association may have been. In the early decades of Takarazuka's development, he was indeed an affectionate surrogate father to his young charges, inviting them en masse to his home to enjoy his garden, and organising 'sports days' like those held in regular schools (Otowa Takiko, cited in *Kageki* 1973a: 125; Sugahara 1996: 206). In an interview commemorating the hundredth year of the founder's birth, one 1913 entrant, Takamine Taeko, stated that since his death she had missed him more than she missed her own parents (cited in *Kageki* 1973a: 125). As Kobayashi grew older, the girls referred to him as 'Grandpa' behind his back, but 'Mr Principal (*Kōchō-sensei*)' to his face (Kasugano 1987: 87).

In keeping with the 'school' metaphor, from that era until the present day, Takarazuka performers have continued to be known as '*seito* (students),' company rehearsal rooms have been referred to as '*kyōshitsu* (classrooms),' and writer/directors have been addressed as '*sensei* (teachers).' When the performers were divided into two groups in 1921 to enable simultaneous performances at different venues, each group was named as if it were a school class (*kumi* or -*gumi*), becoming the *Hana-gumi* ('Flower Class,' now usually translated as 'Flower Troupe') and *Tsuki-gumi* ('Moon Class/Troupe').[7] There was clearly an economic rationale behind the 'student' label, for a licence was mandatory for professional actors from Meiji until the end of World War II; and a company run for profit which employed such actors would have had to pay tax, whereas a not-for-profit organisation whose amateur members happened to perform on stage would not (Tsuganezawa 1991: 185). Kobayashi the entrepreneur, it may be surmised, was loath to pay such licence-fees or extra taxes. Veteran performer Kasugano Yachiyo writes that Kobayashi's solution was to insist that his performers were 'students' and to have them arrange their own hair. Performers who used full wigs apparently qualified as professionals needing licences, so Takarasiennes used a so-called 'half-wig,' an invention which allowed their own hair to appear at the front, disguising the fact that artificial hair was being used (Kasugano 1987: 75). Sakata, on the other hand, claims that Kobayashi so disliked the term '*joyū* (actress)' that he banned the use of wigs, which he associated with actresses (1983: 258–59).

Sociologist Tsuganezawa Toshihiro notes that Takarazuka's non-taxable status continued unquestioned until around 1935, when Hyogo Prefecture authorities apparently investigated the Takarazuka Girls' Opera on suspicion of tax evasion, claiming that it was paying the girls 'splendidly' under the pretext of living expenses, while charging admission to their performances: on 25 February 1935, a local tabloid newspaper, *Osaka yorozu chōhō* (Osaka morning bulletin about everything), reported that Takarazuka had strongly refuted the accusation that its 'students' were nothing but '*yūgei kasegibito* (itinerant players earning money from performing),' by claiming that the girls were charged tuition fees, and were certainly not paid 'wages' (cited in Tsuganezawa 1991: 185). Possibly as a result of this investigation, payment to trainees at the Takarazuka Music and Opera School was abolished in 1936, though performing graduates were still listed on the payroll. Even since the post-war abolition of the actors' licensing system, however, Takarazuka performers have continued to be known as 'students,' with their quasi-amateur status held up as something to be celebrated. Pay is now reputed to be low, about the same as that of a female office clerk, at least according to one ex-performer (Suwa 1980: 23), though popular stars may be offered high salaries after their seventh year in the Company, on an individual contract basis.

Kobayashi evidently did not intend to keep Takarazuka as an exclusively single-sex performing group, for ten boys were admitted to the school in January 1920 as '*senka-sei* (special course students),' to begin a projected four-year course under the tutelage of Tsubouchi Shikō (Sakata 1983: 262–63). Six months later, twenty more boys enrolled, including future writer/directors Shirai Tetsuzō and Hori Seiki, but the special course was abruptly cancelled in November that year because of fierce opposition from the female pupils, their parents and a multitude of fans, who were revolted at the idea of what they termed 'wolf-like, tiger-like, disgusting, filthy males' sharing the stage with the girls (Tsubouchi 1977, cited in Hashimoto 1988: 15).[8] Tsubouchi claimed that 'not a single member of the Girls' Opera Company wished to make a lifelong career as a performing artist if it meant collaborating with boys' (Sakata 1983: 263).

As Takarazuka's popularity rose, the Paradise theatre became inadequate. A 1500-seat public hall in Minoo Park, in north-western

Osaka Prefecture, was bought by Kobayashi, dismantled and moved to Takarazuka in 1920, thus enabling much larger audiences to enjoy Girls' Opera performances. Three years later, however, the entire Paradise complex, including both of the theatres and the training school, was destroyed by fire. A medium-sized wooden auditorium was hastily erected, enabling performances to resume after only two months, while students at the School moved temporarily to Kawanishi, on the rail line to Osaka, until their new classrooms were completed in September 1923. At this time, the school's regulations were amended to admit new trainees up to the age of nineteen by *kazoedoshi* calculation, a change perhaps attributable to the Company's interest in training more mature young women, to impart a more adult mood to its productions (Sugahara 1996: 37).

The 'revue age' and beyond

The 1923 fire ironically provided Kobayashi with the opportunity to fulfil his dream of a theatre with mass appeal, employing the economy of scale to keep admission prices low, for he opened the Takarazuka Grand Theatre (Takarazuka daigekijō) the following year. With an advertised audience capacity of 4000, it was heralded as the largest theatre in the Orient. Admission to the theatre cost 30 *sen*, only a fraction of the price of Kabuki tickets, and the same price as a bowl of *raisu karē* (curry and rice) at the theatre's dining hall.[9] The suitability of the vast auditorium for large-scale spectacles was first demonstrated with the premiere on 1 September 1927 of Japan's first European-style revue, Kishida Tatsuya's *Mon Paris (Mon Pari: waga Pari yo)*, choreographed by Shirai Tetsuzō, one of the original male students of the Music and Opera School, who later earned the title 'King of Revues.' Takarazuka's popularity soared to phenomenal heights as a result, and a recording of the *Mon Paris* theme song sold an astonishing 100,000 copies, igniting a boom in so-called *shanson*, Japanese-language versions of French popular songs (*chansons*), which Kishida and successors had discovered during overseas sojourns (Tsuganezawa 1991: 57).

Whilst Takarazuka was not unaffected by the broader social trends that characterised the 1920s and early 1930s in Japan, the Opera Company did not, for example, hasten to promote the mores and fashions of the so-called 'modern girl.' In *Mon Paris* in 1927, however, there was a dramatic change in the physical appearance of its performers on stage, from childish 'school play' participants to sexually alluring young women. Although doll-like 'whiteface' makeup was still used in *Mon Paris*, the new costumes revealed more bare flesh than ever before, and the administrative office apparently emptied each day during a scene set in Egypt, when the staff rushed to the theatre to watch dancers in brief tunics which bared their legs, shoulders and arms (Hashimoto 1999: 55; Kōbo Opus 2001: 111). Nipple-shaped beading on the breast area and V-shaped panels simulating a deep cleavage further added to the sexual allure of the costumes, even though photographs in Hashimoto (1994: 36), for example, show the wearers themselves to be quite physically immature. While Takarazuka costumes were demure in comparison to the near-nudity seen on the Paris stage at that time, public comment in Japan was stirred by the appearance of performers splashing about in bathing suits in a swimming pool sequence in Kishida's 1928 production, *Haremu no kyūden* (Harem palace) (Hashimoto 1999: 56). Here again, while Kobayashi trumpeted the 'wholesomeness' of his venture, the sexual subtext of a revue on a harem theme would surely have attracted a significant number of men to the theatre to ogle.

In spite of their daring onstage costumes, Kobayashi's 'students' continued to appear conventionally feminine off stage, wearing a demure uniform resembling that of higher girls' schools: an economy-grade silk kimono beneath dark olive green, culotte-like *hakama*. While the usual footwear for actual *jogakkō* students was leather ankle-boots, however, Takarazuka trainees wore plain wooden *geta* (sandals) on their feet. The uniform marked them as belonging to Takarazuka, probably thus enabling better supervision of their behaviour, while its similarity to a regular girls' school uniform also forged a link between the young performers and their *jogakkō* contemporaries in the general population, whom Kobayashi hoped would form a growing proportion of his target audience.

Irrespective of stage gender, all Takarazuka players had long hair until the early 1930s, the *otokoyaku* resorting to tucking it into a hat on stage even during indoor scenes. Mizunoe Takiko, star of the rival revue group Tōkyō Shōchiku gakugekibu (established in 1928), which also employed women to play male roles, had sported a short bob for two years before one Takarazuka *otokoyaku*, Kadota Ashiko, followed suit.[10] Many other Takarazuka performers soon followed Kadota's example, and short hair became the norm for male-role players. Short hair had been fashionable in Japan since the early 1920s among so-called 'modern girls,' but the combination of short hair and masculine costumes must have seemed daring at the time. In addition, traditional 'whiteface' makeup was now abandoned for naturalistic greasepaint, which transformed performers' hitherto 'doll-like' white faces into those of 'fresh young women of flesh and blood' (Hashimoto 1999: 59). It was also in the early 1930s that Kobayashi formalised a motto for the Revue, *'Kiyoku, tadashiku, utsukushiku* (Purely, righteously, beautifully),' perhaps partly to counter any criticism that his mannish, short-haired stars might be morally suspect (Sakata 1983: 317–18). The motto may also have protected Kobayashi and the Company's male creative staff from outsiders' speculation about their exclusive contact privileges with the cloistered girls of Takarazuka, from whose personal company other men were barred (see Nozoe 1997: 99).

While the world economy plunged into depression after the Wall Street crash of 1929, the Takarazuka shōjo kageki flourished, largely due to the popularity of Shirai Tetsuzō's Western-influenced revues, beginning with *Parisette* in 1930 and reaching a pinnacle the following year with *Hana shishū* (Flower anthology) (Takagi 1983: 60; Sakata 1983: 306–07). Although Japanese forces invaded north-east China in the Manchurian Incident of 1931, triggering some weeks or months of 'war fever' in Japan, the lives of most of the populace, as Sandra Wilson (2001: 160) observes, apparently changed little, and popular culture continued to focus on its usual concerns. The *Hana shishū* signature tune of 1931, *Sumire no hana saku koro* (When the violets bloom), became an unprecedented hit, and still remains Takarazuka's best-known song.[11] The period later categorised as the first 'golden age of the revue' reached full momentum in 1934, when *Hana shishū* was restaged for the formal opening of the Tokyo Takarazuka Theatre, which boasted the most modern facilities available in Japan at the time.

Even though payment of a salary to trainees was discontinued in September 1936, as noted above, competition for admission to the Music and Opera School was fierce in the late 1930s, with 12.5 applicants competing for every one place on offer in 1938. At the same time, new school regulations were introduced: applicants who scored highly in the entrance examination (presumably those with some prior training in singing and/or dancing) were immediately promoted to the second year of training, and girls were bonded to perform for a further three years after graduation instead of the two years formerly mandatory (Hashimoto 1999: 67, 1994: 164).

Technological developments in mass entertainment also affected Takarazuka. The rising popularity of cinema during the late 1930s, for example, spurred the Revue Administration to set up its own film unit, Takarazuka eiga (Takarazuka Films). The immediate stimulus was the sudden departure of a vivacious female-role player, Todoroki Yukiko, to join the Nikkatsu film company in 1937. According to Takarazuka's version of events, the young woman herself was reluctant to quit the Revue. She nevertheless farewelled her beloved stage 'in floods of tears,' as her father had apparently already accepted a sum of money from the film studio in question, thereby sealing Todoroki's contract (Takagi 1976: 114). Her case seemingly demonstrates how the authority of the (usually male) household head, which was sanctioned by the Meiji Civil Code and held sway until post-war constitutional reforms, could be used to override a daughter's wishes.

Takarazuka in the war years, 1937–1945

From the 1930s onwards, as Japan moved towards war, multiple facets of life for the populace, including public entertainment, took on a nationalistic aspect. As David Leheny asserts, the Japanese government in the pre-war and wartime periods 'accepted that leisure could be another area for state intervention in citizens' lives, in order to promote the national interest, broadly understood' (Leheny 2003: 177–78). This being the case, it is not surprising that the performing arts in general, including all-female revues such as Takarazuka and Shochiku's two companies in Osaka and Tokyo, as well as the popular media, should have been used to further the state's agenda, their performances increasingly being 'informed by a belief in the imperial prerogatives of the Japanese people' (Robertson 1998b: 106).

Films were part of Takarazuka's contribution to the war effort. The first to be made by Takarazuka eiga was the experimental 1938 release, *Gunkoku jogakusei* (Girl students of a martial nation), an example of the genre known as kinodrama or *rensa-geki*, in which live acting on stage was interspersed with cinematic sequences (*TOYRO Library* 2002). New film studios were purpose-built in 1938 on sports fields near the Grand Theatre, casting current Revue performers in all-female dramas. Most of the latter had nationalistic themes, in accordance with guidelines for producing patriotic propaganda films imposed by the Motion Picture Law of April 1939, and subject to the advance censorship of scripts which began in 1940 (Havens 1986: 24–25). One notable production was *Mabuta no senjō* (The battlefield of memory, 1940), starring popular *musumeyaku* Tsukioka Yumeji. Between 1938 and 1941, when the studios suspended operation, Takarazuka made more than ten films of various lengths. Takarasiennes played both female and male parts in the earliest productions, but were cast only in female roles after 1940. While *otokoyaku* were accepted, even celebrated, in live theatre, their playing of male roles on the screen apparently was criticised in the media and elsewhere as 'unnatural' (Ishii 2002). Takarazuka films of this era were probably unique in the importance they placed upon female characters, or at least upon characters played by female actors (even if they were supposed to be portraying men), because, as William B. Hauser (1991: 297) observes, wartime films in general seldom cast women in anything but supporting roles, if at all.[12]

Takarazuka began to build an additional identity for itself as a representative of Japanese performing arts in 1938, when it undertook its first overseas tour: thirty Takarasiennes performed in twenty-six cities in Germany, Poland and Italy (Kamura 1984: 100, 1981: 54; Sakata 1983: 338). A contingent of forty performers and sixty staff toured Hawai'i and the mainland United States the following year, drawing good audiences on the west coast, but apparently flopping in New York due to lack of publicity and growing anti-Japanese sentiment. In San Francisco, Takarasiennes' impersonation of males was apparently so convincing that a female usher at the theatre was adamant that there were two men in the cast (Kasugano 1987: 112).

Further overseas tours were undertaken during the next several years to give 'solace performances (*imon kōen*)' to Japanese civilians and military personnel in areas under Japanese military control: Northern China in 1939, Manchuria and Keijō (now Seoul) in 1942 and 1943, and Manchuria again in 1944 (Fujino 1990: 114–20; Sugahara 1996: 42; also Robertson 1998b: 89–138).[13] A 1944 tour to the Japanese colony in southern Sakhalin (Karafuto) and to Hokkaido is recorded in Revue archives as a 'domestic' tour. Such tours often caused considerable hardship to the participants. One star recalls riding in open trucks and trudging for miles in snow in China, carrying a heavy rucksack (Kasugano 1987: 129). Accommodation facilities were primitive, often entailing the billeting of individual performers in the isolated farmhouses of Japanese settlers. One informant recalled her terror at having to wait by a railway track in rural Manchuria in pitch darkness until the arrival on foot of her host family for the night (Informant TH 2001, Q. 5.1). It may be imagined that the Takarasiennes' chastity was tightly guarded during these tours, lest their kind of 'solace (*imon*)' be confused with the 'comfort (*ian*)' provided by other women, who worked as sexual slaves to the military.

Following the escalation of conflict with China into full-scale war in 1937, Takarazuka was affected in numerous ways. Various aspects of the Revue attracted criticism, for example, for running counter to the National Spiritual Mobilisation Plan (Kokumin seishin sōdōin keikaku) announced in September 1937 (Kamura 1984: 96). The dresses, luxurious kimonos, permanent waves and cosmetics that the spiritual mobilisation campaign decried (see Havens 1986: 18) all were in common use on the Takarazuka stage, and its productions were better known for their cloying romance than for their staunch patriotism. Girls who expressed a wish to join, and fans who enthusiastically attended performances, were therefore likely to meet with censure from spiritual mobilisation campaign sympathisers, and many schools forbade their students to attend performances. Negative attitudes directed at Takarazuka during wartime are reported by ex-performers Tamai (1999: 16–17) and Kamo (1996: 241). In the early 1940s, Takarasiennes themselves became prone to accusations that they were 'delinquents' or 'un-Japanese (*hikokumin*),' because their singing and dancing seemed frivolous when the rest of the population was being mobilised for the war effort, often having to undertake unpleasant or dangerous work (Tamai 1999: 16). Residents in the Osaka-Kobe area, though, apparently continued to demonstrate their support for Takarazuka by 'packing the theatre to overflowing' on Sundays, and the performers further avoided being 'jeered at' in public by agreeing amongst themselves to stop perming their hair (Kasugano 1987: 118).

Nor did Takarazuka's creative staff evade criticism. After police and prefectural government officials came to Takarazuka with accusations that the Revue was 'a hotbed of Western thought and liberalism,' staff writer/directors like Takagi Shirō apparently set to work to appease the authorities. Inspired by poet Hagiwara Sakutarō's essay arguing for a cultural 'return to Japan (*Nihon e no kaiki*),' Takagi decided that the answer lay in writing and staging *Nihon-mono* (theatrical pieces set in Japan) (Kōbe Shinbun Hanshin Sōkyoku 1984: 120). Some wartime productions, however, including *Manshū kara Shina e* (From Manchuria to China, 1938), *Kōkū Nippon* (Japan flies the skies, 1940) and *Tatakai wa koko ni mo* (The battle is here, too, 1943) were either commissioned or even supposedly entirely written by military bodies including the

Imperial Rule Assistance Association (Yokusan seiji taisei kyōgikai) and the Army Air Administration (Rikugun kōkū honbu) (Kamura 1981: 52–53). In the early 1940s, at least one out of the three or four separate segments comprising each performance programme bore the label of Army, Navy or other governmental sponsorship (Kamura 1984: 97–98; Sugahara 1996: 41–42). Ambivalence on the part of these official commissioning bodies is suggested by their apparent readiness to harness the publicity value of Takarazuka to advertise their aims, even while expressing disapproval of the whole revue genre on the grounds of its Westernised or frivolous facets.

It must be remembered, however, that Takarazuka was certainly not singled out to be a tool of imperialism, in spite of Robertson's account (1998b: 89–138) which seems to suggest the contrary. Titles of wartime revues staged by Osaka shōchiku shōjo kagekidan (OSSK), for example, had a similar ring to those of Takarazuka, and one self-proclaimed 'dyed-in-the-wool son of the military nation (*sujigane-iri no gunkoku shōnen*)' records having excitedly watched such 'stirring' OSSK productions as *Tekikoku kōfuku* (The surrender of the enemy nations) and *Shichishō hōkoku* (Serving our country for seven lives) as a boy (Nakagawa 2003: 46). Robertson's insistence on Takarazuka's complicity in the state's military agenda thus over-emphasises the distinctiveness of Takarazuka in the 1930s and 1940s. Moreover, the theme of complicity in state projects decreases dramatically when the focus turns to the post-war period.

The very 'frivolity' and gaudiness of Takarazuka productions, and their frequent association with Western culture, meant that the Revue was always likely to attract official disapproval during wartime, and some adjustment thus had to be made if performances were to continue. Moreover, there is little or no evidence to suggest that Takarazuka staff or performers were opposed to Japan's war with China and later with the Western powers, and it may be presumed that the conditions of wartime provided a great deal of new material for Takarazuka scriptwriters. Cooperation with the military was probably hard to avoid in any case, not only because the Revue was such a highly visible enterprise, but also because of the political involvement of its 'father,' who entered national parliament in July 1940. Kobayashi did not run for elective office, however, he having been directly appointed by the Prime Minister as Minister of Commerce and Industry in the second Konoe Cabinet; he subsequently lost his ministerial post in disgrace over the supposed leaking of confidential state documents in early 1941

(Sakata 1983: 353–74; Kojima 1983b: 203–12). Although the sixty-five-year-old Kobayashi was by then no longer involved in the actual running of the Revue, his name was indelibly linked with it, and this fact may also have influenced the Company to make efforts to reflect the aims of the ruling regime.

Western-influenced costuming such as spangles, ostrich feathers and swallowtail coats, the latter having epitomised *otokoyaku* elegance, vanished from the Takarazuka stage in 1940, and in the same year, a prohibition was imposed upon the use of show titles featuring such foreign loanwords as 'revue' and 'operetta' (Hashimoto 1993: 50). Though on-stage wear for performers in Japanese-style productions set in a bygone age remained the same, costumes for realistic dramas set in wartime Japan often simulated ordinary citizens' clothing or uniforms worn by students, nurses, members of patriotic associations and military personnel.[14] The official off-stage uniform for Takarasiennes changed from *hakama* over a silk kimono to a skirt suit made from flimsy synthetic fabric known as *suteipuru faibā* (staple fibre, often abbreviated to *sufu*) (Tamai 1999: 18).

In 1940, the then 456 Takarazuka performers were formally organised into a self-contained branch of the Greater Japan Women's National Defence Association (Dai Nippon kokubō fujinkai). In 1942, the latter Association merged with two other women's organisations to become the Greater Japan Women's Association (Dai Nippon fujinkai), a nation-wide body which mobilised women into volunteer activities to support the war effort (Fujii 1985), promoting the ideas that 'good citizens are soldiers' and 'all citizens are soldiers' (Smethurst 1978: 162). Takarazuka performers' identity as 'women' rather than 'girls' had already been suggested in 1940, when the word '*shōjo* (girl)' had been excised from Takarazuka's name, in accordance with performers' wishes, by one account (Kasugano 1987: 80), or by Kobayashi's determination, according to another (Robertson 1998b: 63).[15] As members of the Greater Japan Women's Association, Takarasiennes thus would have had little choice but to demonstrate their dedication to its ethos, both on- and off-stage. Apart from performing or rehearsing regular productions, small groups further showed their patriotism by performing cheerful songs and dances at farming villages, factories and hospitals in their 'spare time,' even paying their own fares to travel to isolated rural areas (Kamura 1984: 104).

The increasing prominence of military values in performances, the drab costumes and simple sets did not go unnoticed by Takarazuka audiences. Suzuki Haruhiko, a middle-school student in the early 1940s, for example, recalls being so dismayed at Takarazuka's increasing use of militaristic themes and the reproduction upon its stage of the drab clothing of the general populace that he stopped attending performances, even though he had adored Takarazuka since the age of five. During a family trip to see a Takarazuka show in January 1944, he explains, he became 'utterly miserable' at the sight of *otokoyaku* clad in military uniforms or 'service caps and gaiters' and the female-role players in *monpe* trousers and *kappōgi* pinafores, with miniature national flags in their hands (Suzuki 1979: 110, 112). Similarly, famed *manga* artist Tezuka Osamu, a Takarazuka resident in his boyhood, is cited in Ikeda (1980: 142) as having remembered seeing an increasing number of 'close-cropped heads and suicide pilots' on stage, and thinking unpatriotically that it was a 'horrid age (*iya-na jidai*).' Many other fans, on the other hand, did continue to attend, although Hashimoto (1999: 67) insists that the wartime audience would not have accepted the militaristic presentations if at least one of the three or four parts of the typical Takarazuka programme had not consisted of pure entertainment, such as was provided by productions like *Pinocchio* (1942). Takarazuka audiences were apparently not the only theatregoers in Japan at that time to dislike militaristic presentations, as wartime Kabuki audiences similarly shunned so-called 'plays of living history (*katsureki-geki*),' which were promoted by the government's Board of Information, with the aim of raising morale on the home front (see Bowers 1974: 206).

Although some girls continued to seek entry to the School, perhaps longing to evade dreary or dangerous war work by joining the Revue, the Company's trainee intake by the early 1940s had steadily declined from a peak in 1938 of seventy-five chosen from among 835 aspirants.[16] One 1943 entrant was inspired to join by a nationalistic Revue production entitled *Tsuyoi machi, akarui machi* (A strong community, a cheerful community, 1942), the authorship of which was attributed to the Imperial Rule Assistance Association (Tamai 1999: 28). The performing arts training she received was poor, however, for first-year students at the school spent their final term doing manual work at an electrical goods factory, leaving them only scant time to practise ballet and vocal technique by themselves. At the end of the school year in March 1944, students from distant areas were sent home to their families, as their safety could no longer be guaranteed. Those residing locally were formally organised into the Takarazuka Music and Dance School [Women's] Volunteer Corps (Takarazuka ongaku buyō gakkō [joshi] teishintai) in 1944, and sent to a nearby factory making aircraft parts (Tamai 1999: 29–30, 32).[17]

Amidst the danger, devastation and privation of the last stages of the war, Takarazuka still carried on, although the content, style and scale of performances had by then been significantly modified, and it is suggested that the Company's survival itself was at risk (Kamura 1981: 53). Many Takarasiennes quit the Company for reasons such as the death or injury of family members, or the loss of their family home and possessions through bombing.[18] Others were dissatisfied with what they were expected to perform, or the 'disrespectful (*hirei*)' attitude of military commanders they encountered while on tour (Shiraishi 1980: 122). Audience numbers fell due to the departure of several well-loved stars whose successors proved less popular, and attendance further shrank 'like the tide going out' after the resignation of the popular writer/director Shirai Tetsuzō – at least according to his disciple Takagi Shirō, who blames Shirai's departure on a movement 'in the name of patriotism' within the ranks of Takarazuka's creative personnel in the early 1940s, which sought to oust Shirai for being 'a free thinker who was enamoured of the West' (Takagi 1983: 239–40).[19]

In spite of the impact of circumstances such as those outlined above, Takarazuka continued to be loved and frequented by many, irrespective of what was actually performed and what costumes were worn. In her series of short stories based on various Takarasiennes' lives, one ex-star describes the scene at a Takarazuka theatre as the war escalated, vividly revealing the nostalgic place held by the Revue even in soldiers' hearts:

Every day, before the curtain went up, a military march was sung in chorus from the stage. And among the young men who were called up into battle, there were many who made Takarazuka their final memory [of civilian life] by attending a performance up to the last moment before they reported for duty. Those were times when there were almost always some young men wearing red sashes [symbolising their imminent departure for the front] in the audience. They were given a round of applause as they set off courageously to fight for their country, in response to a summons made through the [theatre's] microphone in mid-performance (Ashihara 1985: 34).

Attendance at Takarazuka performances thus simultaneously provided respite from and continuity with the wartime situation, for both soldiers and the families who farewelled them, as the Revue somehow managed to entertain as well as spiritually mobilise its spectators, while reflecting what Morris Low (2003: 88) describes as 'a fascination with the sacrifice of young men [in war].'

Finally, on 1 March 1944, all large theatres in Japan's major cities, including Takarazuka's two main venues, were closed by the First Emergency Measures Ordinance (Dai-ichiji kessen hijō sochihō). A uniformed member of the Imperial Rule Assistance Association, wearing a sabre, reportedly stopped a dress rehearsal in Tokyo on the day the theatres' closure was announced, by shouting: 'In these times of war, when we have no alternative but to attack [the enemy], the Takarazuka Revue is unnecessary and non-essential!' (Utsumi 1980: 166). Three days later, huge crowds converged on the Takarazuka Grand Theatre to see the final full-scale performance, at which both performers and audience were reportedly 'moved to tears' (Tamai 1999: 30–32).

The Grand Theatre was taken over by the Navy Flying Corps for training its cadets, and the building was painted black as camouflage (Hashimoto 1988: 146). Robbed of its main performance venues, the Revue Company reportedly chose the only way to survive, by joining the Japanese Federation of Mobile Theatres (Nippon idō engeki renmei) (Utsumi 1980: 166). Mobile troupes of Takarasiennes continued entertaining and 'encouraging' both military and civilian audiences around the country, while a cinema was refurbished and used for small-scale productions in Takarazuka itself, under the name of Takarazuka chūgekijō (Takarazuka Middle Theatre).

While nearby cities were bombed, Takarazuka was left unscathed. According to one account, US planes showered Takarazuka with leaflets saying: 'Be reassured, for we will not drop bombs on Takarazuka' (Shiraishi 1980: 123). A different writer, however, tells of leaflets warning of the Allies' intention to 'make flowers bloom on the Revue town on 15 August [1945],' though 'flowers' meant incendiary bombs in this case. In the latter version, the war's end saved Takarazuka (Nakao 1991: 60), and one memoir tells of the situation on that very date, 15 August, when a group of Takarasiennes scheduled to entertain flying corps personnel (probably *kamikaze* pilots) in northern Kyoto Prefecture heard the emperor's radio announcement that Japan was defeated. The group nevertheless went ahead with their afternoon performance in a 'dream-like' state, before an audience of young men robbed of their chance of a supposedly glorious suicide mission (Fujino 1990: 131). The following day, the same Takarasiennes, dusty and dirty after a train journey from the air base, found a long queue of people encircling the cinema in central Kyoto where they were to perform. Among the crowd were some 'exquisitely made-up young ladies in airy one-piece dresses' (Fujino 1990: 132) who were obviously pleased that wartime austerity measures no longer applied, and that they might again enjoy the Takarazuka Revue of old.

Post-war developments in Takarazuka

With the war's end, Takarazuka began to reintroduce Western themes and performance practices to its stage from September 1945, promptly adapting to the demands of Occupation censorship regarding theatrical activities by jettisoning nationalistic plays and war-glorifying revues from its programmes. Its seeming eagerness to do so even raises doubt about the sincerity of its former dedication to militaristic aims.

Whereas post-war activities in traditional theatrical genres such as Kabuki were hampered by an Allied ban on plays reflecting 'feudal' thought, especially those dealing with martial themes, revenge, suicide and similar matters, which had featured prominently in their repertoire,[20] Takarazuka's in-house writers and choreographers, accustomed to creating new productions at short notice, were able to revive their Western-inspired revue scripts and techniques immediately. The Company did not completely cease operations even in the earliest days of the Allied Occupation, in spite of the near-impossibility of securing a venue in which to perform. Though the Allies confiscated large auditoriums such as the Revue's theatres in Takarazuka and Tokyo for their own use, and the Takarazuka chūgekijō, which had been used for small-scale productions, burned down in December 1945, small groups of Takarasiennes still continued to take classes and rehearse in a former dance hall, or toured to regional areas (Hashimoto 1999: 72). Fortunately for the Revue, however, special guest performances by stars Kasugano Yachiyo and Otowa Nobuko to entertain Allied troops stationed in and near Takarazuka apparently so impressed the Occupation forces that arrangements were made to return the Grand Theatre to Takarazuka's control long before other similar facilities in Tokyo and elsewhere were returned to civilian use, according to a television interview with Utsumi Shigenori, a writer/director from that era (NHK Osaka 1992a).

The immediate post-war period saw a second (and final) attempt by Takarazuka to integrate males into its performing company. In December 1945, it accepted five male recruits, including a twenty-two-year-old who had trained to be a human torpedo, but had evaded an explosive death thanks to Japan's defeat. By the start of the new school year in April 1946, two more groups of boys had enrolled, and while there were separate homerooms for male and female students, ballet and singing classes were mixed. Kamura Kikuo, a staff writer/director at the time, recalls that the training course for boys was one year longer than that for girls (Kamura 1984: 257–58). This was perhaps due to Kobayashi's opinion, noted earlier, that males took longer to teach than females. No further recruitment of boys occurred after 1946, and even after their eventual stage debut at a minor theatre, male graduates were not given the opportunity to perform in full-scale productions with regular Takarasiennes.[21] At the Takarazuka Grand Theatre, for instance, the young men could only be heard, not seen, as their participation was limited to singing in the concealed 'chorus box' (Tsuji 2004: 259). *Otokoyaku* star Sumi Hanayo (1948–63) remarks that the presence of male voices in the pit chorus added 'enormous *hakuryoku* (oomph)' to polyphonous songs (Sumi 1999: 51).

The Japanese populace, full of 'feelings of disappointment and hunger for entertainment' after their country's defeat, greeted with joy the reopening of the Takarazuka Grand Theatre (Utsumi 2000: 67). When the first post-war Grand Theatre season opened on 22 April 1946, the programme consisted of an operetta, *Karumen* (Carmen), and a revue, *Haru no odori: ai no yume* (Spring dance: reveries of love). The passion and dreamy romance of the subject matter, the exquisite costumes made from fabric secreted away during the war years, and above all, the return of the glamorous *otokoyaku*, attracted large audiences. As there had been no significant air-raid damage in Takarazuka, the barely-altered theatre and its verdant environs indeed must have seemed like a paradise to the residents of nearby Osaka and Kobe, both of which had been extensively bombed. As one veteran performer comments, 'people's yearning for beauty and gentleness must have emerged all the more strongly because those days were gloomy, having been long without colour for the war-weary' (Fujino 1990: 137). Similarly, writer/director Utsumi recalls being amazed at the 'beauty of whiteness' on the Takarazuka stage, everything in his hometown of Osaka having being charred and filthy (NHK Osaka 1992a).

As Company numbers had dwindled considerably during the last years of the war – archival records showing a total of only 204 performers as of January 1946, under half the pre-war maximum – it was imperative for the Revue to build up its numbers as soon as possible after the war ended (see Hashimoto 1993: 149–50). Students already in training were promptly promoted to performing, and the newly-renamed Takarazuka ongaku gakkō (Takarazuka Music School) welcomed its first post-war intake of girls in April 1946 for a single year of classes before their stage debut. Whereas would-be Takarasiennes had previously been accepted if they showed potential to become good performers after a number of years' training and stage experience, successful applicants in 1946 were apparently admitted for their potential 'usability' after only a year at the School. Thus they needed to show either exceptional talent, such as that of promising singer Yodo Kaoru, or a 'doll-like' cuteness, as in the case of Yachigusa Kaoru (Tamai 1999: 137). Revue performances began again in Tokyo in March 1947 at the Nichigeki Theatre (Nippon gekijō) in Yurakucho, and thereafter were held more or less regularly at various venues around the capital, for Takarazuka lacked a permanent base in Tokyo for almost nine years after the war. Troupes from Takarazuka were occasionally invited to perform as 'guests' at the Tokyo Takarazuka Theatre (Tōhō gekijō), which the Occupation Forces had renamed Ernie Pyle Theatre. The theatre was not returned to Takarazuka control until early 1954, although the Occupation ended in 1952 (Hashimoto 1994: 167).

After an initial surge in the immediate aftermath of the war, audience numbers dwindled once more. Although stars such as *otokoyaku* Koshiji Fubuki (1937–51) and *musumeyaku* Otowa Nobuko (1937–50) had attracted many fans to Takarazuka, film studios once again vied to entice pretty female-role players (including Otowa herself) away from the Revue.[22] The resulting exodus of popular stars threatened the Revue's survival, but a timely fillip to Takarazuka's fortunes was provided by the staging in 1951 of Takarazuka's first full-length, dramatic spectacular, *Gu bijin* (Miss Yu, the beautiful) – a lavish contrast to the two or more separate items which had hitherto comprised a Takarazuka programme. Written by Shirai Tetsuzō, a post-war returnee to the Revue's staff, *Gu bijin* was a tragic love story set in ancient China. It featured live horses and colourful Chinese costumes, and ran for three months to large audiences. Nevertheless, it was not until the mid-1950s that the Revue returned to the prosperity of pre-war years, according to writer/director Takagi (1983: 240).

Takarazuka reached a milestone in its history upon the death in January 1957 of Kobayashi Ichizō, who had recently retired from a brief third term as Principal of the Takarazuka Music School, after many years of activity in the business world and a short post-war return to national politics. His passing was commemorated by a 'school funeral' befitting his status as founding Principal and respected patriarch. Regardless of Kobayashi's death, however, the Company's connection with the Kobayashi family was continued by his third son Yonezō, who had for some time been a senior executive of the Hankyu railway company (then officially known as Keihanshin kyūkō, or Kyoto-Osaka-Kobe Express), which still operated the Takarazuka Revue.[23]

In 1959, the previous obligation on members to remain with the Company for several years after graduation was abolished. This meant that graduates from then on could, if they wished, use the Music School's comprehensive training and good reputation as an immediate stepping-stone to a different career in show business.[24]

In post-war decades, Takarazuka productions continued to reflect current social trends, including, to some extent, freer sexual mores. 'Gender gymnastics' were an important feature of a 1960 hit entitled *Karei naru sen byōshi* (1000 colourful musical beats), in which leading *otokoyaku* performers switched from one gender to the other on stage. The erotic charm of this transformation from handsome men to alluring women was probably a significant factor in the show's success. Performed at three theatres, in Takarazuka, Tokyo and Osaka, the production drew 730,000 people in a total of seven months (Hashimoto 1999: 77, 82). Archival photographs show its star, *otokoyaku* Sumi Hanayo, whose presumably womanly original body-shape was usually hidden under thick masculine costumes, now clad in an hourglass-shaped leotard and fishnet tights, smiling coquettishly and flirting with audience members by stepping down off the apron stage into the stalls. As regular Revue patrons would have known that Sumi was an *otokoyaku*, some may even have viewed her performance as a type of female impersonation, her costume and heavy makeup being the epitome of 'drag.'

In 1965, the Revue finally resumed its overseas tours, sending a fifty-two-member troupe to Paris, where it set a precedent in its presentation of an Occidental-style revue as well as the Japanese dances that had previously monopolised Takarazuka's touring programmes tailored for Western audiences (see Sugahara 1996: 57). The excellent reception given the presentation was due largely to a combination of the dancing talent of *otokoyaku* star Maho Shibuki and the choreography of Paddy Stone, a Briton whose subsequent work with Takarazuka in such shows as Kamogawa Seisaku's *Shango* (1968) earned him both accolades from audiences, and the nickname 'Demon Stone (*Oni no Sutōn*)' from his dancers because of his unrelenting quest for perfection (Kishi 2000: 116). Stone was a pioneer in a series of British and American choreographers and directors whose work has greatly augmented the Takarazuka repertoire throughout the past forty-two years. Other significant contributors to the raising of Takarazuka to international standards have been the renowned Gemze de Lapp (*Oklahoma*, 1967), Sammy Bayes (*West Side Story*, 1968), Tommy Tune (*Grand Hotel*, 1993), Linda Habermann (the Off-Broadway season of *Takarazuka * Yume*, 1992, and others), and Darren Lee (*Fancy Dance*, 2007).

From the late 1960s onwards, the influx of well-known foreign musicals posed various challenges to Takarazuka performers accustomed to certain ways of performing gender, as well as to staff used to staging in-house scripts tailored to individual performers' talents. Gender portrayals had to be modified, and bodies pushed to the limit to meet the demands of choreography originally created for mixed companies. De Lapp, a champion of the Stanislavski Method of acting, was a stickler for realistic acting in her direction of *Oklahoma* for Takarazuka (Honchi 1974: 30–32). Tight restrictions imposed by the copyright-holders on variation of the character portrayal, dialogue and mood of the original production meant that *otokoyaku* were forbidden to wear coloured eye-shadow or false eyelashes, and had to use brownish makeup which made them appear more like real men than the *otokoyaku* ideal, apparently to the dismay of some performers and fans (Sugahara 1996: 60–61). Again, in *West Side Story*, no allowance was made for the fact that the cast was all female: US choreographer-director Bayes insisted that dancers scale a three-metre-high wire fence at every performance (Haruna 1993: 101).

From the 1970s into the new millennium

The 1970s began amid high economic growth and escalating standards of living in the general population, which affected Takarazuka in both positive and negative ways. In spite of the optimism of the Revue Administration in accepting a large number of recruits, audience numbers slumped during this time of economic buoyancy, perhaps because Japanese people's lives were so full of optimism that they did not need to seek an escape from reality through stage entertainment, or else because material goods were becoming so affordable that family income was directed at these purchases rather than towards a couple of hours at the theatre. Fewer girls applied to the Music School, though similar numbers to previous years were admitted, fifty-four to sixty girls graduating annually in the mid- to late 1960s.

In the year when Japan proudly showcased its technological advancements to the world at Expo '70 in Osaka, however, an unusually large group of seventy girls made their Revue stage debut. Around this time, probably as a response to the sudden increase in student numbers, the School introduced new rules for student self-government, entrusting the discipline (*shitsuke*) of junior students to their immediate seniors. The campus had previously been cleaned by hired staff or on a voluntary basis by students, according to two ex-performers (Informant MH 2001, Q. 2.2; Informant PP 2001, Q. 2.2), but now the buildings and grounds were scrupulously cleaned by first-years, under the critical eye of the second-years, and this activity was well-reported by the local media. The well-publicised stricter discipline at the Music School may have discouraged some girls from applying, but the drop in aspirant numbers probably also reflected the general decline in Takarazuka's popularity noted above, a decline which is usually attributed to overwhelming competition from television, cinema and the 'underground (*angura*)' theatres of the time (Kawasaki 1999: 207).

The mid-1970s saw a spectacular rebound in Takarazuka's popularity. In August 1974, the representative 'face' of Takarazuka was irrevocably changed when it staged *Berusaiyu no bara* (The Rose of Versailles), a flowery musical romance set in the court of Marie Antoinette, based on a best-selling comic book series by Ikeda Riyoko, featuring as its protagonist, Oscar – a girl raised as a boy. With the success of this production, Takarazuka's fortunes suddenly improved dramatically, and the names and faces of its stars rapidly became famous throughout Japan. The total audience for *The Rose of Versailles* in the mid-1970s totalled approximately one and a half million ('Berusaiyu' 1994: 87). The script by Ueda Shinji, multiple versions of which told the same basic story but focused upon different aspects of the relationships among the main characters, proved to be a flexible vehicle in subsequent years to highlight the talents of various performers, and each of several reprises has been both a nostalgic return to an old favourite and an opportunity for reinvention and rejuvenation for Takarazuka.

After three years of *Rose of Versailles* success, Ueda triumphed once more with his script based on Margaret Mitchell's novel, *Gone with the Wind* (*Kaze to tomo ni sarinu*, 1977), in which Haruna Yuri made Takarazuka history by wearing a moustache as the lead hero, Rhett Butler. Audiences were obviously primed for the more adult mood of this production, for some 1.34 million people attended performances of Takarazuka's alternative 'Butler' and 'Scarlett' versions in the first two years, the two being differentiated by a stronger focus on the named character (Hashimoto 1994: 267; Wetmore 2006).

By the end of the 1980s, performers whose inspiration for joining the Revue had been their exposure to the mid-1970s productions of *The Rose of Versailles* had begun to reach prominent positions in the Company. Mori Keaki, for one, was promoted to top *otokoyaku* star in 1989 in the first of a series of reprises of the very play which had prompted her decision to apply to the Music School some fourteen years previously (Mori 1993: 155–57). The restaging of versions of *The Rose of Versailles* from 1989 to 1991 boosted Takarazuka audiences yet again, and the Company now embarked on the replacement of its out-of-date main 'home stage,' the Takarazuka Grand Theatre. Rehearsal rooms and administrative offices were moved to temporary accommodation in a former bathhouse as new premises were built, though productions continued at the old Grand Theatre until November 1992 while the new auditorium took shape immediately adjacent to it. The state-of-the-art new theatre was opened on 1 January 1993, the changeover having been accomplished with a speed reminiscent of the two-month refurbishment in 1935 of the structure it replaced, which had been gutted by fire in that year (Sugahara 1996: 212). It attracted large audiences with its sumptuous facilities, although the actual number of seats had been reduced from 2,750 to 2,500, due to the abolition of the steep, cramped third tier of seating and the widening of first- and second-level seats to accommodate the larger bodies of 1990s Japanese.

Takarazuka's popularity reached unprecedented levels in the early 1990s, but natural disaster interrupted this idyllic period. A record number of applicants had vied for admittance to the Music School in 1994, with only about one in forty-six examinees succeeding, but on 17 January the next year, the devastating Hanshin-Awaji Earthquake hit the Takarazuka area before dawn. The Grand Theatre, built on alluvial soil beside the Muko River, was extensively damaged, necessitating closure for repairs. As one senior member recalls (Kishi 2000: 203–22), performers and Music School students who had a home outside the devastated area were encouraged to leave Takarazuka until summoned back, and some performances were staged in other cities, in a repeat of the situation during the height of the war. With characteristic speed and enthusiasm, repairs to the

Grand Theatre were completed to enable regular performances to resume with a new season's cast from late March 1995, just over two months after the earthquake. The first post-earthquake offering was unusually topical: *Kokkyō no nai chizu* (The borderless map), in which the Berlin Wall was seen to topple and a newly-promoted star played Beethoven's *Ode to Joy* on a grand piano, in her role as a concert pianist.

Audience levels were affected by the earthquake for some time. Serious damage to transport infrastructure made getting to the theatre difficult, as some train lines were cut and vehicular routes were jammed. Many residents in the audience catchment area whose homes had been partially or completely destroyed were preoccupied with daily existence, and the financial burden of rebuilding homes probably left little money for entertainment such as Takarazuka. Within a year or two, however, Takarazuka audiences slowly returned, and the environs of the Grand Theatre soon sported gleaming new apartment blocks, shops and restaurants. In spite of the decade of economic doldrums that dogged Japan from the 1990s into the twenty-first century, Takarazuka recorded an overall average attendance rate of ninety-three percent of capacity during the 1990s, a ten percent rise over the previous decade (Takahara 2001). In the opinion of former Chief Executive Ueda Shinji, Takarazuka benefited from the recession because people look to its colourful, fantasy world for comfort in times of gloom (Takahara 2001). Another Takarazuka producer, a Mr Iwasaki, speculated that Takarazuka tickets might be seen as an affordable alternative to an overseas trip, beyond the means of many Japanese once the economic 'bubble' had burst (Singer 1996: 181).

Certainly, the Revue Administration seemed optimistic at the end of the twentieth century. The Revue nostalgically 're-viewed' its performing history in 1999, when each troupe reprised the Company's best-known or most significant works from the past, with the notable exception of *The Rose of Versailles*, which was reserved until after the turn of the new century. Audiences and cast members alike were thus reminded of the traditions built up over Takarazuka's eighty-seven years, and latter-day stars – such as Makoto Tsubasa (retired 2001), who was mentioned by one of my interviewees (Informant PZ 2001, Q. 3.17) – often paid public homage to the 'legacy' they had inherited from their seniors of past decades (*senpai*). The final year of the millennium saw the relocation of the Music School to a new, multi-storey building adjacent to the theatre complex.

As the first decade of the new millennium draws to its close, it is difficult to predict whether Takarazuka's popularity will endure. The Revue seems already to be anticipating a triumphant centennial in 2014, but both external and internal factors may affect its course before then. Certainly, its own official website and countless fan-based websites on the Internet, a dedicated satellite television channel and other technological advances bring it to a far wider audience than ever before, and the advertising opportunities offered by cyberspace are extensive. On the other hand, electronic forms of virtual reality may prove less attractive to fans than the live performances of fantasy romance offered by Takarazuka, resulting in the maintenance or growth of its theatre audiences. Also, Takarazuka will surely continue to benefit from the nationwide surge in popularity since the early 2000s of stories of 'pure love (*jun'ai*),' rather than of overtly sexual relationships, in television programmes and films. This trend is epitomised by the mass adoration by Japanese women of the Korean actor Bae Yong Joon (nicknamed Yong-sama, i.e. 'Prince Yong'), who portrayed a sensitive and romantic protagonist in the 2004 drama series, *Winter Sonata* (Kamiya 2004). One recent publication even rates various Takarazuka *otokoyaku* in terms of their 'Yong-sama'-ness (Kawasaki et al, 2005).

Some Company policies have been tried and discarded: a new personnel-management system instituted in mid-2001, for example, initially had considerable impact. Rising stars were uprooted from their regular troupes and kept in reserve in a special section of the 'superior members' (*senka*)' group (hitherto comprised of very senior Takarasiennes who were no longer regular performers), ostensibly in readiness for reassignment when a top star's position became vacant (Yabushita 2003: 77). This system apparently caused concern to fans, for the new generation of *otokoyaku* stars who had been assigned to *shin-senka* (new superior members' group) while awaiting promotion to top position were only afforded leading roles for brief terms of between a few months and one or two years before retirement, though a majority of their predecessors had played leading roles for several years, enabling them to hone their stage skills to a high quality and build a large following among fans. Some of the 'stars-in-waiting' eventually quit the company before achieving top-star status. The apparent unpopularity of that human-resources practice seems to have led to its demise less than six years since its institution, however, as only one youngish performer, *musumeyaku* Tōno Asuka (debut 1998), was still awaiting reappointment to a troupe in 2006

(*Takarazuka otome* 2006: 16), but had been assigned to the Star Troupe by early 2007 (*Takarazuka otome* 2007: 107). Moreover, the trend for early retirement seems to have been reversed, or at least slowed, as the Flower Troupe's leading player, Haruno Sumire, due to quit Takarazuka at the end of December 2007, had reigned in top position for five years (*Takarazuka Revue Official Web Site* 2007). It remains to be seen whether other present and future stars will have sufficient charisma and talent to attract and maintain a loyal audience for so long.

In national terms, the problematic shrinking of Japan's birth-rate (Suzuki 2007: 5–6) may mean that there will be fewer and fewer children to become fans, or to aspire to join Takarazuka from now on. The opening of Universal Studios Japan in Osaka in March 2001 was also blamed for an exodus of entertainment-seekers from long-established recreation facilities, including Takarazuka Familyland (by which name the amusement park adjacent to Takarazuka's theatres had operated since 1960). Though the Grand Theatre and its adjacent Bow Hall theatre remain viable, Takarazuka Familyland finally closed in April 2002 after almost three decades of declining visitor numbers, thus enabling redevelopment of the site for residential or commercial purposes and parkland (Johnston 2002). Now, the area sports a green zone with landscaped gardens, a lake, restaurants and a pet-exercise facility, all run by Hankyu Amusement Service Co. (*Takarazuka Garden Fields* 2007).

Now with five troupes of seventy or more members each, Takarazuka is indeed a different organisation from the little band of immature teenagers of 1914, yet the spirit of Kobayashi Ichizō, whose framed calligraphy of the Revue's motto hangs prominently upon the wall in Company headquarters, still urges all comers to conduct themselves 'with purity, righteousness and beauty,' an ideal still actively promoted in the twenty-first-century Revue. Future prosperity, however, depends upon a continuing stream of young girls who yearn to perform on the Revue stage, and seek entry to its notoriously strict training school. The experiences of such girls constitute the topic of the next chapter, which traces their first contact with Takarazuka and their motivation for aspiring to join Japan's most famous revue company.

2 Joining Takarazuka: Motivation and Others' Reactions

Notions held by girls and their parents regarding suitable education, training and careers for females in contemporary Japanese society have played an important role in the steps girls have taken during their teen years to direct their future lives. Even in the twenty-first century, gender is a significant issue, though girls' access to educational opportunities, in particular, is more open now than at any time in Japan's history, as most girls between the ages of fifteen and twenty complete upper secondary schooling, after which nearly half proceed to some kind of tertiary education. Most of the remainder seek employment, stay at home to help their families or engage in other unpaid occupations.[1]

For around a thousand girls each year, however, a very different course beckons – joining the Takarazuka Revue, even if this means curtailing their regular secondary education, and, with rare exceptions, abandoning hope of attending university. For some, joining Takarazuka will lead to a long theatrical career, quite dissimilar to the occupations of most of their female counterparts in the general workforce. If they do not marry or bear children, performers' life history will further diverge from that of the majority of women. Before they decide to join Takarazuka, however, Takarasiennes-to-be represent a broad cross-section of middle- to upper- class Japanese girlhood. What ultimately unites the majority of these girls is a determination to choose the course of their own lives, rather than to allow someone else to do it for them.

Prospective Takarazuka performers become acquainted with the Revue in many ways, and gender issues are involved at every stage of the process of their decision to join it, with or without the encouragement of others. Not all applicants are particularly eager to become Takarasiennes, some being indifferent, others even reluctant candidates. Their families and teachers, too, are far from uniform in their attitudes to daughters or pupils taking the Music School entrance examination. Gender norms established by Japanese society can affect parents' expectations as to their daughters' prospects for higher education, employment and eventual marriage. Once the decision to join Takarazuka is made, however, most applicants show that they do not lack self-determination.

This chapter focuses on why girls seek entry to the Takarazuka Music School, and what results in the short term from this decision. As background to the following discussion, however, I first outline the significant features of gender-related socialisation and education for female children in Japan. Secondly, the chapter examines how girls initially became acquainted with Takarazuka, showing the connection between the development of various media in the twentieth century and the spread of Takarazuka's name and reputation. Thirdly, it discusses the range of factors motivating would-be Takarasiennes to apply for entrance, especially in relation to the girls' own perception of gender issues, and briefly examines other avenues of training and employment for girls who desired a stage career, as well as possible alternative occupations for girls who did actually join Takarazuka, suggesting why these alternatives were not pursued. This is followed by an exploration of the differing reactions of family members and schoolteachers to girls' thespian aspirations, which range from hearty encouragement to strong opposition, and the ways in which girls win parental consent, where necessary. Overall, the chapter shows the wide diversity in attitudes and experiences among the girls who have been admitted for Takarazuka training, suggesting the multiplicity of models of young womanhood in Japan during the past century.

Gender socialisation of girls in Japan

In Japan, as elsewhere, the family is the primary setting for gender socialisation, which constitutes one part of training for selfhood. Mothers are seen as particularly instrumental in this socialisation process, as they are considered destined to be a child's '"first teacher," passing on knowledge in an instinctive and spontaneous manner quite different from the more formal education of the classroom' (Kōsaka 1966: 135–36). Girls typically are socialised to fit female gender norms by others' evaluation of their conduct, attitude, physical appearance or language as '*onnarashii* (befitting a girl/woman; ladylike; feminine)' or the opposite, '*onnarashikunai* (not befitting a lady/woman/girl; unfeminine)' (Smith 1987: 3). A girl's failure to behave in a manner deemed appropriately feminine by the community at large may bring shame upon her entire family.

Within the socialisation process, children also learn from their elders about the hierarchical basis of interpersonal relationships, which, it is usually argued, reflect the structure of Japanese society. That society, according to Chie Nakane, operates on the basis of a 'vertical principle' (Nakane 1970). In the home, children are usually taught to be respectful and obedient to their parents and older siblings, and grow up to expect respect and obedience from younger siblings. The showing of politeness to elders by such means as bowing and the correct use of gender-appropriate language, including honorific and humble expressions, is one important aspect of this early training, and it is essential learning for girls who later join Takarazuka.

Formal education has also played a significant role in the social construction of gender. The philosophy underpinning educational policy for girls during the Meiji and Taishō eras, as well as the first two decades of Shōwa, was, again, to produce 'good wives and wise mothers.' Public girls' higher schools rapidly increased in number from the beginning of the twentieth century, though they were attended only by a privileged few. A stereotyped image developed of the *jogakusei* (girls' school student), with her *hakama* (a long, culotte-like garment) uniform, her penchant for literature and poetry, and her romantic or worshipful relationships with fellow students. The homosocial world of pre-war *jogakkō* (girls' schools) was partly created, partly idealised by illustrators such as Nakahara Jun'ichirō (the husband of Takarazuka star Ashihara Kuniko) and Takehisa Yumeji, whose distinctive style of depicting beautiful women somewhat echoed the Westernised beauty of certain Takarazuka performers (see Ashihara 1985), and writers such as Yoshiya Nobuko, whose novels and short stories featured love and friendship between girls and women. The late nineteenth and early twentieth centuries also saw the establishment of a number of private girls' schools, variously informed by Confucian, Christian or secular philosophies. Nevertheless, most girls were excluded by poverty and other factors from access to post-primary formal education until after World War II, when compulsory education for all children was extended to nine years.

Now, irrespective of gender, most children in Japan remain at school even after the end of compulsory education, girls having gradually caught up to, or even surpassed boys over the past century, at least in terms of years of secondary schooling. Since the Second World War, the proportion of girls continuing on to higher secondary education has risen steadily, both against the total of female junior high school graduates and in comparison with boys. While forty-eight per cent of boys, as opposed to just over thirty-six per cent of girls, proceeded to senior high school in 1950, almost eighty per cent of both girls and boys began senior high school in 1969. From the mid-1980s onward, more than ninety-five per cent of girls have entered upper secondary schools, peaking at 98.0 per cent in 2006, though 97.4 per cent is the highest figure for boys (again in 2006), male students having consistently lagged several points behind their female counterparts (*Monbukagakushō* 2007b). It is thus somewhat unusual for girls in Japan not to undertake upper-secondary education, and so those who enter the Takarazuka Music School immediately following graduation from junior high school, irrespective of their scholastic ability, are deviating from the norm. So strong is the allure of the Takarazuka stage, however, that many girls obviously yearn to enter its world at as young an age as possible, as the discussion below will reveal.

After leaving school, also, Japanese girls and women have been afforded different, and often inferior, opportunities in vocational training and employment compared to boys and men (Waswo 1996: 159–63). The performing arts constitute an interesting exception, however, for though women and girls were barred from the professional stage until only about a century ago, as we have seen, they now seem more likely than men and boys to consider becoming professional actors, dancers or singers, or at least to acquire artistic skills as part of their general preparation for adulthood. While Japanese males have not faced the same historical impediments as females to a career on the professional stage, the theatre seems to have been an uncommon occupational choice for boys in general. Theatrical and musical interests undoubtedly have been deemed by the general populace as less 'masculine' than sports, military training or academic pursuits, and opportunities for boys' participation have accordingly been restricted. Such a stance reflects the common expectation that a man should earn enough to support a wife and children, whereas a woman's 'career,' at least in the case of the middle class and above, has been often regarded as marriage and motherhood (Vogel 1978: 216), and outside employment for such married women has commonly been deemed 'part-time.' Moreover, there has been no theatrical organisation that has offered boys the kind of full-time, formal training as is conducted by schools attached to all-female revue companies such as Takarazuka, or their guarantee of a job for a number of years after graduation.

Initial contact with Takarazuka

The existence of Takarazuka is now well known throughout Japan and even in some other parts of the world, and information about it is obtainable through all kinds of media, especially those targeting a female audience. The inaugural members of Kobayashi's Takarazuka Choir and Girls' Opera Training Association, however, were recruited through newspaper advertisements, personal introduction or word-of-mouth. We have seen that there was no precedent for such an artistic organisation in the Osaka area, except for the Mitsukoshi Boys' Band, which Kobayashi credits as having inspired him. The first trainees, therefore, had little or no idea what to expect. In fact, word-of-mouth publicised the original group as a '*fujin shōkatai* (women's choir),' according to one of the recruits, Takamine Taeko (cited in Sakata 1983: 175; also *Kageki* 1974a: 110). This resulted in a wide range of applicants – from children barely out of primary school (the youngest, Kumoi Namiko, aged about eleven) to a graduate of a women's normal school, who had already qualified as a teacher (Tsukuba Mineko, about eighteen).[2]

As the preceding chapter has shown, the Girls' Opera was established not as an end in itself, but as an 'attraction' to increase patronage of Minoo-Arima Electric Railway trains and the 'Paradise' leisure complex the railway company had built in Takarazuka.[3] Accordingly, posters advertising performances were probably displayed at stations and other facilities connected with the railway, as they are today.[4] Local residents were thus informed of the group's existence and activities, but little other effort apparently was made to advertise the première season. At the beginning of 1914, the railway company's public relations magazine, *Sanyō suitai* (Mountain shapes and river forms), carried a brief description of the forthcoming initial season and the training of the performers, and a single advertisement appeared in the *Osaka mainichi* newspaper on 19 March, prior to the opening on 1 April that year (Hashimoto 1999: 49). The two-month debut performance, presented daily until 30 May 1914, was reported in the *Osaka mainichi* newspaper on 16 April that year as having been 'very well received by women and children' (Geinōshi Kenkyūkai 1990: 94; Takagi 1983: 57), though audiences for the next few quarterly performance seasons were apparently so small that the venture was in danger of closing (Takagi 1983: 52; Kobayashi 1955: 454; *Kageki* 1992a: 54; also, Domenig 1998: 268).

At this point, however, the print media began to play a vital role in the survival of the Takarazuka Girls' Opera. Popularity increased as a result of performers' participation in charity performances in Osaka and Kobe in December 1914 under the auspices of the *Osaka mainichi*, which, with a circulation of about 300,000, was the leading newspaper in the Osaka area at that time (Gluck 1985: 233). These performances, which featured Takarazuka girls reprising their Paradise Theatre fairytale operas and dance items, were then held each winter until 1919. The existence of the group and the nature of its activities thus became known much more widely in the Kansai area than would have been the case through Minoo-Arima Railway efforts alone, thanks to a combination of the newspaper's advance publicity and favourable reports published after the charity shows. Huge crowds flocked to see the *Osaka mainichi*-sponsored performances in Osaka, especially, and a striking upturn in patronage of the Paradise facility, from an annual total of 259,000 visitors in 1915 to 424,000 in 1918, can be attributed to fervent interest in the Girls' Opera (*Kageki* 1992a: 54). At that time, in the decade leading up to the advent of radio, the print media was the main source of news and current affairs information, and the major national daily newspapers 'combined serious reporting with popular features, [and thus] were able to attract a widely diverse readership' (Gluck 1985: 232–33). Without doubt, print media enabled Kobayashi's enterprise to become known to a broad cross-section of the local population, garnering not only potential audience members but also new recruits.

Other printed sources of inspiration for would-be recruits have included anthologies of Takarazuka scripts, the first of which was published in 1916, enabling enthusiasts to rehearse or even to stage their own versions.[5] In addition, prospective trainees have been able to obtain information from the fan-oriented magazines *Kageki* (Opera) and *Takarazuka gurafu* (Takarazuka graphic), which have been published almost continuously from their launch in 1918 and 1936, respectively, to the present day. The magazines' essays, interviews and illustrations furnish readers with myriad details of the upbringing and early family life of Takarasiennes as well as their experiences as trainees and stage performers, thus providing diverse models for would-be entrants. Several Takarazuka preparatory schools have also numbered among the magazines' small list of regular advertisers, offering aspirants a way to ready themselves for the entrance examination.

From the time of its very founding, therefore, newspapers, magazines and other printed matter have been important in the popularisation of Takarazuka, and simultaneously instrumental in attracting new recruits. From the mid-1920s, however, various forms of electronic media also played an increasingly large role. As Christine Yano observes, the electronic transmission of popular songs brought performers into the homes of audiences who had previously needed to go to theatres and other places to listen to them, and also aided in the legitimisation of entertainers' work, as they were now 'situated on at least one cutting edge of modernity – that of technology and the new mass media industries' (Yano 1998: 250). In 1928, the first electronically-recorded gramophone records went on sale, and one such recording, of the theme song from Takarazuka's *Mon Pari* (Mon Paris, 1927), sold exceptionally well throughout Japan (Kawasaki 1999: 103), as was noted in Chapter One. Later, as long-playing (LP) records were developed, fans could enjoy musical numbers from entire productions, recorded live with a full audience, replete with fans' shouting of performers' nicknames to coincide with their favourites' entrances, exits or moments of particular significance. In the mid-1960s, LP records were superseded by audio cassettes, which in turn began losing their market share in the late 1980s to compact discs (CDs), some with *karaoke* tracks for practising Takarazuka tunes.[6] The long-playing recordings contain edited versions of revues and dramatic performances, including songs, dialogue and sound effects (but omitting dance scenes with purely orchestral accompaniment), enabling would-be Takarasiennes to rehearse singing and acting along with their favourite performers.[7]

Takarasiennes' voices were pre-recorded ready for transmission even before the start of public radio broadcasts by the government-owned Nippon hōsō kyōkai (Japan Broadcasting Corporation, known as NHK) in 1925, and Revue performers made their first live radio appearance on 11 March 1927 (Kawasaki 1999: 103). This and other broadcasts over subsequent years certainly reminded many potential recruits and their families of the existence of the Girls' Opera, and the medium probably inspired many girls with promising voices to consider Takarazuka entry (Hashimoto 1994: 163). Kobayashi's specific targeting of well-off consumers as both patrons and performers was aided by radio, as the high cost of receivers, the obligatory licence fees imposed by the Ministry of Communications, and a restricted supply of electricity in the countryside meant that few Japanese apart from wealthy city-dwellers acquired their own wireless sets at first. Affluent urban girls were thus far more likely to be listening to Takarasiennes on the radio, and perhaps to be inspired to join the Girls' Opera, than their working-class urban or rural counterparts, though the government and radio manufacturers took various measures to increase radio-listening in the countryside in the late 1930s (see Partner 1999: 27, 30).

During the 1930s, in particular, Takarazuka was renowned for the quality of its singing, making it more suitable for radio than its main rival company, the Tōkyō shōchiku gakugekibu, whose star, Mizunoe Takiko, was apparently more accomplished as a dancer than as a singer, meaning that her performances probably appealed more to the eye than to the ear.[8] In the early 1940s, however, domestic and overseas radio broadcasts of Takarazuka's more nationalistic performances were utilised by the government for their propaganda value rather than simply for entertainment, and wartime songs infused with patriotic sentiment apparently replaced Western-inspired romantic songs from Takarazuka's earlier years (see Robertson 1998b: 129). By the end of the war, sixty-two per cent of Japanese urban households and thirty-nine per cent of rural households owned a radio, but, for various reasons, most of the sets apparently did not work (Partner 1999: 41, 48). In the early post-war period, too, many people were unable to afford to buy a radio set or to have a malfunctioning set repaired (Partner 1999: 72). Even if girls from impoverished families had heard about the Revue, joining it would probably not have been an option in the early post-war period, as Takarazuka no longer paid its trainees until after their stage debut.

During the Occupation, the fortunes of the radio industry fluctuated, although commercial radio stations were granted licences for the first time in 1951, paving the way for commercial broadcasting, in which Takarazuka actively participated. Kobayashi lamented in 1952 that the Revue Company did not make sufficient attempts to exploit the nationwide publicity value of radio by ensuring that its radio programmes were 'trend-setting and interesting' (Kobayashi 1955: 530). A few years later, however, just such a programme, *Takarazuka fan kontesuto* (Takarazuka fan contest), did begin on commercial radio, its run lasting from 1955 to 1974. It gave Takarazuka fans and aspiring Takarasiennes the opportunity to sing Takarazuka songs and perform excerpts from stage scripts opposite the stars they idolised, for the appraisal of a Revue writer and a musical director. The adjudicators apparently encouraged promising contestants to attempt entry to the Music School, although their praise may have been a little exaggerated, according to one Takarasienne who won accolades as a contestant on the radio programme but received no preferential treatment when she joined the Company in 1973 (Suwa 1980: 29).

While the advent of radio seems to have been advantageous to Takarazuka, the nationwide popularity of cinema in the 1930s was a mixed blessing for the Revue, as Chapter One has shown. It will be remembered that in an attempt to stem an exodus of its most attractive performers to other studios, Takarazuka established its own motion picture studio in 1938, and this enabled a number of its stars to become well known far beyond the audience catchment area for its stage performances, at least in urban centres with cinemas equipped to show its talkies.[9] Some films probably directly aimed to attract recruits, such as *Takarazuka fujin* (Takarazuka wives, 1951), which incorporated scenes of Revue rehearsals and performances, as well as affording glimpses of fictitious Takarasiennes' off-stage lives (Yabushita 2002b).[10]

Takarazuka's dual film and stage system also provided girls from all over Japan who aspired to become screen actresses with a way to receive comprehensive, paid training in stagecraft as well as on-camera experience, while having their morals guarded more tightly, one assumes, than in the environment of an ordinary commercial film studio.[11] Stage-acting, especially in such genres as the mainstream Kabuki theatre, had largely sloughed off the ignoble status it had endured during Tokugawa times, but some stigma apparently still clung to film-acting. The fact that Takarazuka was primarily a stage performance company with large, well-equipped theatres thus probably lent a measure of prestige to those of its members who acted in its films, allowing the Revue Company to attract more aspirants.[12]

We have now seen the important contribution of newspapers, magazines, recordings, radio and film to the popularisation of Takarazuka, especially in the first few decades after its establishment. For the past half-century, however, television has been undeniably the main medium for bringing the Revue into Japanese households, and it has doubtless inspired countless girls to make a pilgrimage to its theatres, and to attempt entry. Takarazuka was quick to appear after regular public television broadcasts started in Japan on 1 February 1953, for a special Takarazuka programme, *Opera ikka* (Opera family), was telecast only a fortnight later by the national broadcaster, NHK ('Rajio, terebi' 2004: 204). For the next several years, however, as had been the case with radio, the daughters of affluent families were far more likely to learn about Takarazuka through that medium than less well-off girls, because the expense of sets initially hindered sales. As the Japanese economy gained vigour, an increasing number of households purchased a television, in some cases even before investing in a washing machine or a home of their own – despite the fact that a television set apparently cost as much as seven-tenths the asking price for a 'modest' house with land in 1955 (Partner 1999: 162–64).[13]

Takarazuka's television appearances became even more frequent upon the opening in November 1958 of Kansai Television (KTV), a Hankyu-affiliated, Osaka-based private television station, which inaugurated a regular programme entitled *Takarazuka terebi gekijō* (Takarazuka television theatre) that same month ('Rajio, terebi' 2004: 204). Since then, NHK and KTV, joined in recent years by satellite broadcast channels such as WOWOW and the Takarazuka Sky Stage, have regularly shown live or pre-recorded telecasts of Takarazuka stage performances, in addition to producing special documentaries or light entertainment programmes featuring Takarasiennes (Kishi 2000: 39–41; Nimiya 1994: 41–50). Over many years until the mid-1990s, KTV produced a series of Takarazuka programmes, which were broadcast on Saturday afternoons in the Kansai area, interspersed with advertising for Hankyu's railway network and department store chain, the Takarazuka Revue and Takarazuka Familyland amusement park. In other parts of the country, however, where other advertisers sponsored the programmes, these were not shown in prime time: in Tokyo, for example, fans had to tune in at six on a Sunday morning.

Such Takarazuka programmes, usually filmed in front of a studio audience, afford fans a close-up view of their idols. While the sheer scale and impact of a live Revue performance (including the palpable energy of audience members) does not usually translate well to the television screen, there are instances in which the charisma of the starring performers, especially in close-up shots of intimate dramatic or romantic moments, can be conveyed quite effectively. The telecast most often cited by Takarasiennes as having captivated them to the point of wanting to join the Revue is that of *The Rose of Versailles*, staged in 1974–76. Sendai resident Mori Keaki, for one, was inspired solely by viewing an NHK telecast of the latter production, and did not see her first live Takarazuka performance until after she entered the Music School (Mori 1993: 155). Mori eventually starred in the 1989 re-staging of *The Rose of Versailles*, and was featured in a television programme entitled *Chikyū hatsu 19-ji* (Seven p.m. ex Earth), which in turn reportedly triggered the Takarazuka aspirations of two 1990 Music School entrants, Chihiro Reika and Kei Natsuki – one of whom had set out to see her very first live performance as a result (*Kageki* 1992: 131–32).

Takarazuka telecasts of various kinds, both in Japan and overseas,[14] perhaps have been especially inspiring to fans who find attendance at performances difficult or impossible, and there are several examples of such girls having applied successfully for Music School entry. In the early 1970s, for instance, television appearances by Takarasiennes on NHK and KTV apparently caused a 'dramatic increase' in Takarazuka fan numbers, as evidenced by a deluge of letters to NHK (Tanimura 1971: 38). The 'shining' world of Takarazuka revealed on one such weekly NHK show featuring Revue stars stimulated one Toyama Prefecture teenager, who was tired of studying technical drawing at a vocational high school, to 'try something new.' With only a few months' ballet lessons by way of preparation, she applied to enter the Takarazuka Music School, eventually becoming an 1980s *otokoyaku* star (Tsurugi 1992: 51–52). Similarly, Okinawa resident Hanamiya Airi was inspired to join Takarazuka by a satellite telecast of the Revue's tour to New York in 1992 (cited in Ishii 2000: 134).

The development of home appliances such as tape-recorders and video-recorders further enabled Takarazuka fans and would-be Revue performers to capture sounds and images of the Revue from radio and television for replaying in their own time. In a magazine interview, 1990s leading *otokoyaku* Asaji Saki recalls being able to watch live performances only once or twice per year while still an aspiring Takarasienne, and, prior to seeking Music School admission in 1981, looking forward eagerly to a weekly television programme entitled *OH! Takarazuka* – the soundtrack of which she would tape-record (*Kageki* 1995: 123). After the devastating 1995 Hanshin-Awaji earthquake brought a halt to regular telecasts of Takarazuka performances on the Kansai Television network, the Revue Company began to release its own range of video cassettes (duly engineered to prevent copying) of regular stage performances and special events. Digital Versatile Disks (DVDs) followed from around the turn of the millennium. Such videos and DVDs enable aspirants and other fans to scrutinise Takarasiennes' makeup, hairstyles and costumes, and, if they wish, to imitate their singing, dancing and acting styles, both for their own pleasure and as preparation for a hoped-for stage career. This parallels the extensive use by actual Revue performers and creative staff of audio and video recordings when preparing to reprise a particular scene, musical number or even an entire work, based on a previous production.

Subsequent innovations in electronic media, such as satellite broadcasting and interactive television, promise to play an ever-increasing role in attracting new audience members and promising candidates for Takarazuka training in the future. Towards the end of the twentieth century, the burgeoning Internet began to provide aspirants not only with an official Revue web site, but also with a link to the Music School. There are also several unofficial sites for the exchange of information about how to prepare for the entrance examination and what to expect. In addition, numerous preparatory schools utilise the Internet to advertise their courses to would-be Takarasiennes.

Various forms of media, therefore, have played a large role in informing potential Takarazuka entrants, their families and their friends about the existence and allure of the Revue. Nevertheless, large numbers of accounts in published sources, as well as my own interviews and personal experiences, show that the most significant event that has impressed the attractiveness of Takarazuka upon the majority of its future performers is attendance at a Takarazuka performance itself. Often, only a single experience as an audience member, even a few moments' viewing of the action on stage, is sufficient to provoke in these girls the tantalising thought that they, too, might some day tread the boards of the Takarazuka stage.

As Chapter One revealed, during the first four years of its existence, Takarazuka was a 'local' phenomenon drawing both its performers and its audience from the populous city of Osaka and its environs, but its performance tours to Tokyo and various provincial centres from 1918 onwards brought its live stage presence to an audience far beyond the Kansai area. The combined effect of print media publicity and these live appearances, especially the first extensive tour in 1924, which included Beppu in Kyushu, as well as Nagoya, Wakayama and nearby Kyoto, Kobe and Osaka, produced applications to enter the Music and Opera School from more distant regions as well as from the vicinity of Osaka (Takagi 1983: 58). Regional tours have continued to attract applicants, such as Kyushu-born Anju Mira, who saw her first performance in Nagasaki as a first-year student at junior high school in the mid-1970s, and nurtured her dream of entering the Revue for the following five and a half years, while looking forward to Takarazuka's annual visits to her home town (Anju 1993: 39–40).

Takarazuka evidently did not anticipate attracting applicants from elsewhere when it began tours to other regions, however. The Revue was initially unprepared for an influx of non-local trainees, for when the first four Tokyo recruits, including Amatsu Otome, arrived to begin training in 1918, they had to be billeted with the family of Takigawa Sueko, a more senior member of the Girls' Opera who lived in Takarazuka, as no dormitory yet existed for girls who could not commute from their own homes. Takigawa's family became the 'home away from home' for a number of girls in subsequent years (Takigawa 1974: 35; *Kageki* 1974b: 63). Amatsu's parents and five younger siblings eventually moved to Takarazuka, and two of her three younger sisters also became Takarasiennes (Torii 1997: 10–11). After accommodation facilities were established, the School could guarantee the care of numerous recruits from distant areas, although archival photographs and descriptions suggest that the original wooden dormitory was far from luxurious. Nowadays, except for those who stay with close relatives living within commuting distance of the Music School, all students must reside in the Revue's 'Sumire ryō (Violet dormitory),' a ferro-concrete building with separate wings for Music School students and Company members, situated across the Muko River from the School. Once they join the Company proper, Takarasiennes are free to live where they choose, although the dormitory is cheap and convenient, and some performers remain there throughout their tenure with the Revue.

Overseas performances began in 1938, bringing Takarazuka to an international audience, and also attracting occasional applications from would-be entrants living outside Japan. One 1985 entrant to the Music School, Natsushiro Rei, who was born in Japan, saw a Takarazuka performance in Paris in 1975, during temporary residence in France during childhood. At that time, Natsushiro recalls, Takarazuka symbolised for her 'the culture of a foreign land (*ikoku no bunka*),' which, for her, was Japan. Just one more viewing when she later returned to her home country, though, made her decide that she wanted to perform on its colourful stage (Natsushiro 2001: 42).[15]

Non-Japanese girls have occasionally been admitted, though they have mostly been of Japanese ethnic background, or at least of East Asian descent, though strong prejudice against ethnic Koreans has probably prompted most entrants of Korean family background to hide their ethnicity, with the notable exception of current star Aran Kei (see *Mindan Shinbun* 2007). Ethnic Chinese girls brought up in Japan, on the other hand, seem mostly to have advertised their Chinese ancestry through their choice of stage name, as in the case of Yō Akira, cited below. Non-Japanese enrolees from overseas possibly were accepted in a spirit of international cultural exchange, without the expectation that such girls would remain long with the Company after Music School graduation. Indeed, each of two Thai graduands from 1961–62 left in the same year as her debut, as did one Taiwanese who graduated and retired in 1970, while a Spanish-Argentinean who also joined the Company in 1962 quit the following year. Another Taiwanese, Li Li, a 1967 entrant to the Music School, retired after three years on the stage. The likelihood of foreign students being admitted seems to rise when Takarazuka's popularity at home wanes. There was a decline in audience numbers from the late 1960s until 1974, for example, but instead of limiting student intake during this period, the Music School did quite the opposite, accepting two Taiwanese and one Japanese-American along with a large number of girls from within Japan. This suggests an eagerness on the part of the Administration to win publicity for Takarazuka, with the aim of boosting its popularity (see Hashimoto 1994: 189; also, *Takarazuka otome* 1970: 37, 108).

Diverse motivations

There are many different motivations for girls to enter the world of Takarazuka. Without doubt, however, exposure to a Takarazuka performance has been the greatest single impetus for would-be Takarasiennes, as has already been suggested, though other factors are also influential. The sights and sounds of the Takarazuka stage or the charisma of a certain performer seem to have an instantaneous, captivating effect upon many female (and some male) members of the audience, impelling them to want to join the Revue. One performer, Misato Kei, recalls: 'The curtain went up. The prologue music began. At that moment, my life was decided!' She thought: 'Here is where my job will be, the job that matches my ideals!!' (Hibino 1986: 18).

A similar reaction is reported by many other girls, and a significant number describe being struck by an 'electric' sensation upon seeing their first performance or gazing at a particular star (usually an *otokoyaku*). This sensation often gave rise to a sudden yearning to join Takarazuka, even though the girls concerned may have had no training in the performing arts whatsoever, and may not have considered such a career until that moment. Various

Takarasiennes' memoirs record remarkably similar experiences. At the sight of *otokoyaku* star Daichi Mao playing James Dean on television, one girl felt 'an electric charge go *zzzzt* all over [her] body.'[16] Another wrote, somewhat exaggeratedly: 'I was immersed in a world of giddy intoxication. My heart floated in mid-air, and electricity ran though my whole body' (Takashio 1989: 20). Yet another reminisced: 'The instant I saw it, I became transfixed by the stage performance. I was hit with a piercing sensation (*bīn to kita*), as if to say, "I'm going to be in this!" Frankly speaking, it was a tremendous shock.' (Anju 1993: 40). This electric sensation may have some physiological basis, as will be suggested in Chapter Five, where the role of the gaze and its manipulation by the various parties involved in order to enhance the pleasure of the Takarazuka experience will be further discussed.

Not only girls, it must be remembered, are thrilled and inspired by the Takarazuka stage – after all, several groups of boys and young men were admitted to Takarazuka training at different times, although little is known of their motivation, and they did not perform with the Revue proper. However, one male entrant who later achieved fame as a creator of revues, Shirai Tetsuzō, joined the short-lived Danshi yōseikai (Male [opera] training association) in 1919. He felt strongly moved and impressed at seeing his first Takarazuka performance, claiming later that this initial reaction became the 'heart and soul (*kokoro*)' of his subsequent career as a Takarazuka choreographer, writer and director (Shirai 1967, cited in Takagi 1983: 39). Another young man had apparently been a 'huge fan' of the Revue since childhood, and wrote to Kobayashi immediately after the war, expressing his view that Takarazuka should develop into a mixed company. He subsequently entered the Takarazuka Music School in December 1945 with four other boys, making his eventual debut in a mixed cast at a minor theatre (Kōbe Shinbun Hanshin Sōkyoku 1984: 179–81; Kamura 1984: 253–60). In another instance, an American adult male choreographer of my acquaintance declared after watching his first Takarazuka performance around 1980 that he would 'give anything to be dancing in that company, even in the very back row of the chorus.' Hearing that only females were admitted, he half-seriously suggested to me that he might gain entry if he 'bound himself' to hide his male anatomy.

In contrast to those who were captivated by Takarazuka as a whole, some aspirants admired a particular star and wished either to emulate her or to perform on the same stage as their idol, as did Kanna Miho, who worshipped Daichi Mao (Minakaze and Natori

1997: 29). The perfume wafting from the stage as the star passed by seemed to cast a spell on one of my post-war informants, who first experienced Takarazuka from the orchestra pit, where she sat as her brother sang in the male chorus which accompanied the Revue for some years from the late 1940s into the 1950s. The *otokoyaku* star, Kasugano Yachiyo, seemed so unworldly that this informant wondered if the performer 'really breathed air,' suspecting that she 'ate nothing but mist (*kasumi*)' (Informant DP 2001: Q. 1.7). Kasugano had a similar effect upon another informant of mine, who, though she did not cite her admiration as the main impetus for her application, nonetheless described the star as 'a man from a dream-world, with a breathtaking radiance and beauty that Japanese men lack' (Informant PZ 2001: Q. 1.8). The word *akogare* appears in countless descriptions of Takarasiennes' and fans' feelings towards Takarazuka performers and the Revue stage. It encompasses such concepts as 'admiration,' 'yearning for a person or thing,' 'a desire to emulate' and 'wanting to become someone or something.' As one informant who joined in the 1960s says, 'I purely and simply felt *akogare*. I wanted to *be* one of those people on that stage' (Informant EF 2001: Q. 1.8, Q. 1.9; emphasis added). Another 1970s entrant who had watched Takarazuka since early childhood spoke of her own longing (*akogare*) to be on its stage, which she defined as a place that was 'out of the ordinary (*futsū de wa nai*),' 'constructed (*tsukurareta*)' and 'pretended (*itsuwatta*)' (Informant NK 2001: Q. 1.8).

For other girls, however, the decision to join Takarazuka was not a sudden one. A number of recruits had grown up watching Takarazuka regularly, and had 'naturally' come to assume that they would join it, such as one informant whose mother and both grandmothers had associated regularly with Takarasiennes (Informant CL 2001: Q. 1.7). Yet other girls enjoyed the performing arts in general, and saw Takarazuka as a place where this interest could be developed (Informant AB 2001: Q. 1.7). Two of my informants who had learnt classical ballet from childhood were attracted by the fact that if they entered Takarazuka, they could perform 'all year round on a glamorous stage, to the accompaniment of a live orchestra' (Informant AA 2001: Q. 1.8), and 'wear gorgeous costumes' (Informant KT 2001: Q. 1.8, 1.9). Another fledgling *otokoyaku*, Kiriya Hiromu, in an interview following her stage debut, explained that she had taken ballet lessons from a young age, but had become interested in singing and other forms of dance when she attended musicals as a junior high school student. Upon seeing a Takarazuka performance, however, she was 'fascinated' by the male-role players, and as her ballet teacher had often said she was 'like a man (*otoko mitai*),' she decided that becoming a Takarasienne might be more appropriate for her than becoming a ballerina (cited in *Kageki* 1994: 132). Some girls, while not overly enthusiastic about the Revue, nevertheless take the Takarazuka entrance examination as a 'safety net' in case an alternative path is closed to them. One informant, who had a dramatic speaking voice, would have preferred to become a voice actor (*seiyū*), but passed the Music School test and decided that it would be just as well to take up her place (Informant PZ 2001: Q. 1.7).

Some girls joined Takarazuka to please a more eager friend or relative who wanted to experience life as a Takarasienne vicariously, as in the case of one of my informants who made her debut in the early 1930s: her elder sister, a devoted Takarazuka fan who apparently could not join the Revue herself, hoped to draw close to the performers she adored through her younger sister's involvement (Informant HO 2001: Q. 1.7). Such excessive enthusiasm on the part of a parent, relative or friend sometimes can be unwelcome, however, leading to a refusal by the girl concerned even to apply to the Music School. Some girls who counted current or past Revue performers among their relatives did not wish to emulate them, in spite of the latters' encouragement. 1990s *musumeyaku* star Morina Miharu, for example, showed no interest in the Revue as child, to the disappointment of her mother, ex-Takarasienne Musashino Hiromi. Her mother later rejoiced when her daughter suddenly announced her intention to try the entrance examination at eighteen (cited in Natori and Takeichi 1996a: 28–29). The two daughters of 1970s *otokoyaku* star Ōtori Ran were sent to ballet lessons during childhood, but both defied their mother's constant urging to follow in her footsteps and flatly refused to consider entering Takarazuka, declaring that they did not want to 'make the same mistakes (*ni no mai*)' as their famous parent, who married comparatively late and divorced several years afterwards, having spent her twenties and early thirties performing male roles (cited in Kaji 2001; also see Chiba 1996: 129–31).

In other instances, the reputation of Takarazuka as a strict training institution wins the approval of a parent who wishes an indulged daughter to be exposed to character-building discipline. One mid-1950s entrant from Tokyo, Nagao Noriko (stage name Matsunami Shibuki), who had never seen the Revue, was 'ordered' by her mother to attempt the entrance test upon graduation from junior high school. The mother explained that as an only child, her daughter must not be allowed to become selfish, and that she should undertake some strict 'training as a human being (*ningen shugyō*).' Takarazuka apparently seemed the best place for such discipline (cited in Natori and Takeichi 1996b: 196).

A small number of applicants had never seen Takarazuka, but disliked academic study, and heard that the Takarazuka Music School offered practical rather than academic training. Kōzuki Noboru, for one, a skilled gymnast from Yamaga in rural Kyushu who went on to become a popular *otokoyaku* star, read about Takarazuka in a magazine, and thought that perhaps dancing or singing would 'suit' her, although she had not taken formal lessons. She was so hesitant to gamble upon her untried aptitude for stage performing, though, that she took a correspondence course in hairdressing once she had entered the Music School, in order to make herself employable should she fail (Kōbe Shinbun Hanshin Sōkyoku 1984: 64). Another gymnast, 1990s star Takane Fubuki, who had apparently dozed through the Takarazuka performance she attended at fourteen, found sitting at a desk to study 'unbearable' while still in junior high school. In spite of her lack of enthusiasm for the Revue, she was delighted to find out about the Music School, which appeared to have few desk-bound theoretical subjects, and decided to enrol (cited in One's Co. Ltd 1996: 121). Another informant of mine, a veteran *otokoyaku*, confessed that she, too, had been 'not very good at schoolwork,' and thus had seen Takarazuka's practical aspects as an attractive alternative (Informant HO 2001: Q. 1.7).

For some other girls, Takarazuka seemed a respectable alternative to an undesired marriage. One informant, born about 1920, was influenced by the unhappy experience of her eldest sister, a qualified teacher. The sister had suffered greatly from her husband's mental cruelty, writing to her family that marriage was 'life's graveyard' (Informant TH 2001: Q. 1.8). A 1970s entrant, Yamashiro Haruka, who had watched Takarazuka from her kindergarten days, attended a private school with an attached junior college, which would have relieved her of the necessity to experience the so-called 'examination hell' of studying for entrance to university. However, Yamashiro joined Takarazuka in a spirit of revolt against what she saw as a pre-determined life in which the 'rails were already laid out': graduation from junior college, followed by 'bride training (*hanayome shugyō*)' in preparation for marriage (cited in Kōbe Shinbun Hanshin Sōkyoku 1984: 23).

Economic and social factors in Japan clearly affect Takarazuka audience and applicant numbers. A vibrant economic climate and wide availability of alternative opportunities for amusement, education and employment seem to have a negative effect upon the popularity of Takarazuka. It was suggested in Chapter One that the high economic growth that enabled much of the Japanese populace to achieve a degree of material affluence from the 1960s onwards may have blunted to some extent the urge to forget everyday life through escapist entertainment such as Takarazuka. Not surprisingly, any downturn in the popularity of the Revue is reflected by a corresponding lack of zeal on the part of girls in general to compete for admission to a highly selective institution like the Takarazuka Music School. Such circumstances seem to prompt the Company to take remedial measures to boost both patronage and recruitment: the decline in audience numbers from the late 1960s until 1974, for example, was accompanied by the offer of large numbers of places at the Music School, as the Administration probably hoped to discover a few charismatic individuals who would revive the Company's fortunes. However, the fact that fewer stars than usual emerged from graduating classes with especially large enrolments suggests that the quality of applicants was comparatively low, in spite of the large numbers recruited. Smaller classes in other years produced several stars each, such as the three leading *otokoyaku* who emerged from the smaller group of fifty-nine who graduated in 1960, and the three other stars from the class of sixty-one in 1963 (Hashimoto 1994: 187–89).[17]

On the other hand, general economic doldrums can sometimes prove fortuitous to the Revue Administration. A spectacular rise in the Revue's popularity due to the staging of *The Rose of Versailles* occurred about a year after the oil crisis of 1973, which had adversely affected the Japanese economy and presumably made people less optimistic, and thus perhaps more likely again to seek escape in a fantasy world. The Music School subsequently received a flood of applications. It will be remembered that the demise of the 'bubble economy' is also credited by Ueda Shinji, formerly Takarazuka's Chief Executive, as having boosted Takarazuka's audience numbers during the 1990s, presumably again because the Japanese populace was in need of a pleasant distraction from its financial woes (cited in Takahara 2001). The middle of this period also coincided with the highest recorded number of applications to the Music School, in 1994. During the late 1990s and into the new century, many girls have faced increasingly 'glacial' career prospects should they pursue tertiary education, especially those contemplating a four-year course (see Morley 1999: 171). Such girls might consider joining an organisation like Takarazuka because it hires only women, offers comprehensive training, and guarantees them employment for up to seven years after the training period, should they want it, even if the salary is apparently low.

Alternatives to Takarazuka

Girls of the middle class and upwards in Japan who are interested in finding employment after leaving school, but are unenthusiastic about traditional careers for women in such areas as nursing or teaching, or employment in factories, shops or offices, may be attracted to some aspect of the performing arts in general. For almost forty years after the founding of the Takarazuka Girls' Opera, live musical theatre was certainly one of the most popular of such entertainment genres, perhaps because it was the only form to combine colour, movement, orchestral music and the sound of the performers' speaking and singing voices. Other alternatives did exist, but Takarazuka offered certain advantages that could not be matched.

Films, which had been imported into Japan from 1896 and made locally from 1899, were very popular, but the Japanese film industry did not offer girls the same comprehensive career preparation as Takarazuka. Moreover, unlike live theatre, films were in black and white, and silent screen characters could neither speak for themselves nor sing, thus limiting the range of expression film actors could employ. Although the first Western talking picture was shown in 1929, it was not until two years later that Japan made its first 'technically successful' talkie.[18] The first domestic colour feature film was not made until 1951.[19] The live stage, therefore, continued for many years after the advent of films to provide the only full-colour, full-sound, moving, visual entertainment in which girls in Japan could aspire to gain training and employment.

Other performing arts genres such as popular singing, which probably entertained many girls through recordings, radio, television and perhaps the screen, may also have stimulated a desire to become a performer, but apart from winning talent contests such as those which spawned such 'idol' singers as Yamaguchi Momoe in the early 1970s, the way to achieving this desire was not as clear-cut as joining a revue company such as Takarazuka, with its attached Music School. A significant proportion of aspiring Takarasiennes, it must be stressed, had had no background in dancing or singing when they decided to try for entry, and probably could not have aspired to a career as a ballerina or opera singer, for example, as they had not begun formal lessons until their teen years. Takarazuka may be the preferred choice for such girls because the intensive nature of Music School training readies its graduates to begin stage work after only two years (or one year, for a decade or so after the war), after which they are expected to continue developing their skills through Company classes in a range of performing arts, including the traditional Kyōgen (comical plays), Japanese dance, ballet, jazz and modern dance, classical and jazz vocal and many other subjects. The 'school' atmosphere of Takarazuka is reinforced by these classes, which are offered free to Company members, utilising various rehearsal rooms and studios within Revue headquarters. Around twenty instructors are now employed to teach these classes (Fujino 1990: 210–12).

As Chapter One has illustrated, in the early decades after its founding, Takarazuka had to compete for audiences and applicants against rival all-female revue troupes such as those set up by Shōchiku in Osaka and Tokyo in 1922 and 1928, respectively, as well as a number of smaller groups scattered around the country (Domenig 1998: 273; Kurata 1990: 94–96). These companies did offer performing arts training, as well as regular opportunities to exercise the skills thus acquired. However, although the two Shōchiku companies did for many decades offer a reasonably popular alternative to joining Takarazuka to girls who hoped for a career in musical theatre, [20] there were also some drawbacks, for the girls and their concerned parents. The companies' prestige did not match that of Takarazuka, and their home theatres were situated in so-called 'meccas of popular entertainment,' in Tokyo's lively Asakusa (near the Yoshiwara red-light district), and in Osaka's bustling Dotonbori and Sennichimae (of even more dubious reputation) (see Hanes 1998: 278). It will be remembered that families of the original recruits to Kobayashi's Takarazuka Choir had also apparently feared for the safety and chastity of their daughters, probably because of the seedy reputation of the original Takarazuka spa, situated on the opposite bank of the Muko River from the Revue theatre. Kobayashi reassured the parents, however, and the girls evidently came to no harm. Over the ensuing years, also, the Takarazuka Administration has so thoroughly downplayed any unsavoury aspects of its location that it is probably seen as nothing but wholesome by prospective entrants and their parents, who might have objected on moral grounds to the locations of other urban groups.

Neither of the two Shōchiku companies, which no longer exist in their original form, had the same prestige or corporate support as Takarazuka. Both apparently suffered more than Takarazuka when the retirement of idolised stars at various times provoked severe drops in audience numbers, and applications to their training institutions fell as a result. Though Kinki Nippon Railway (Kintetsu) had become a major financer of Osaka-based OSK from 1971, and used its rail network's publicity avenues, such as posters in trains and public relations publications, to advertise performances, OSK was on the brink of closure in the late 1970s when performer numbers seemed about to fall below a crucial minimum of forty, according to one of its stars, Shinonome Akira (1977–96) (cited in Sugahara 1996: 104). OSK later enjoyed a sudden revival in popularity, however, beginning with its 1982 season of *Yōkihi* (Yang Gui-fei), written by erstwhile Takarazuka director Kamura Kikuo. After 1999, however, its attached training school, OSK Nippon kageki gakkō, accepted no new recruits, reportedly in an attempt by its then owner, the Kintetsu Group, to reduce expenditure on human resources. To devotees' dismay, the company itself was formally disbanded in May 2003, though more than forty performers re-grouped under the name 'OSK sonzoku no kai (Association for the continued existence of OSK),' with the support of numerous fans (OSK sonzoku no kai 2004; Nasu 2003: 15). It began training new recruits aged up to twenty-two in April 2004, and is now operating as 'New OSK,' with purpose-built headquarters in inner Osaka which incorporate its own performance and rehearsal space (New OSK 2007). The Tokyo-based SKD ceased regular operations in 1990, long after its home theatre, the huge Kokusai gekijō (International theatre) in Asakusa, had been demolished in 1982 to make way for the Asakusa View Hotel, forcing the company to perform in various other theatres (Sugahara 1996: 254).[21]

OSK and SKD had long been regarded as a 'safety net' for girls who had failed to gain entry to the Takarazuka Music School,[22] and during the years since their disbanding, most aspiring Revue performers have had to abandon their dream of a stage career if rejected by Takarazuka. The 2004 resumption of training by the reorganised OSK, however, with a higher entrance age limit than Takarazuka, but with entry still restricted to unmarried applicants, will surely be welcomed by many such girls and young women. Except for Takarazuka and OSK, would-be *otokoyaku*, especially, now have next to no other avenues for performing masculinity in a mainstream professional theatrical context. Television and films, for instance, employ women only to play women, with rare exceptions. Likewise, though mixed companies such as Gekidan Shiki (see *Shiki Theatre Company* 2007), established in 1953 in the Tokyo area, provide interested girls with alternative training to Takarazuka in singing, dancing and acting, these companies seldom cast females in male roles (Moore 1994: 18).

In spite of the arguments for choosing Takarazuka over other alternatives, the Revue is a second-best choice for some girls considering a stage career, because their first choice is denied them due to various factors. One of my informants, for example, a 1950s Music School entrant who lived with her widowed mother in Osaka, had wanted to be an actress in straight drama (*shibai*), but at that time, all large professional theatre companies, such as Bungakuza, Mingei and Haiyūza, were located in Tokyo.[23] The only groups in Kansai were small-scale, and such local companies 'did not seem interesting enough' for my informant, yet she did not want to move to the capital without her mother's permission, which she suspected would not be forthcoming. She realised that Takarazuka would be an acceptable alternative, and attempted the examination after having graduated from high school and begun work as an office clerk (Informant SS 2001: Q. 1.9).

Another aspiring actress (later to become the Takarasienne Kazami Kei) auditioned for entrance to the theatre company Haiyūza in the mid-1960s without telling her parents. She was in her first year of senior high school, and was advised by the examiners to 'try again after having studied play scripts more thoroughly.' The following year, having been elected student council president of her single-sex school, Kazami experienced euphoria at addressing the student body from the stage in the school auditorium, and credits this as motivating her to apply to Takarazuka, where she presumably enjoyed playing an *otokoyaku* before an even larger audience of rapt females (see Fujita 1977a: 119). In yet another instance, a daughter (Minoru Kō) who stated her desire to study overseas in order to make a career of ballet was steered towards Takarazuka by her parents, who obviously did not want her to leave Japan (*Kageki* 1991b: 123). Similarly, the mother of Nishina Yuri surreptitiously read her daughter's diary, becoming alarmed to learn that the girl dreamed of becoming an actress. She then took her daughter to see a Takarazuka performance, in a successful ploy to direct her daughter's interest towards joining the Revue, about which the mother had no reservations because it was 'only girls' (cited in Takarajennu kyatto fan kurabu 1996: 75). Sometimes, Takarazuka is a compromise for girls who dreamed of an occupation unconnected with the performing arts, but were dissuaded by parents with fixed ideas about the suitability or desirability of certain career paths for their daughters. Hyūga Kaoru, for one, loved animals and aspired to become a veterinary surgeon, but her parents vetoed this plan, saying it would be 'too demanding' for a woman (Hyūga 1992: 80). She later decided to join Takarazuka because she was very tall, and realised that her height would be an advantage there. Her parents agreed to let her enter the Music School only upon hearing from acquaintances that Takarazuka was 'a place where [girls] became good brides (*ii yome-san*)' (Hyūga 1992: 101–02).

Family and school reactions

Family reactions to a daughter's aspiration to become a Takarasienne are varied. Some families rejoice, and give their full support, while in other cases opposition is voiced by one or both parents, or by other family members. Nagy (1991: 199–216) observes that early in the twentieth century, especially, it was widely debated whether it was 'proper' for a middle- or upper-class daughter to work at all. It was thus even less likely for such a daughter to be encouraged to make a spectacle of herself by appearing on a public stage as a professional performer, as noted in Chapter One. Even now, some middle-class parents, as well as the wealthy elite, may prefer their daughters not to take any kind of paid employment between leaving school and marrying, though most girls themselves probably now expect to work for at least a few years after finishing their formal education.[24] A daughter's aspirations towards a career in the entertainment industry seem still to be regarded by many parents as particularly unacceptable.

Old prejudices towards acting as an occupation sometimes still underlie familial objection to a girl's joining Takarazuka. The choice of the stage as a profession by children from families with no thespian ancestry may be seen as financially risky and perhaps morally suspect, though, as we have seen, Kobayashi always assured parents that Takarazuka was safe and honourable, unlike other similar companies located in less salubrious surroundings with perhaps less well-behaved audiences. Certainly, many parents seemed to prefer Takarazuka over its closest rivals, OSK and SKD, not only because of the perception that Takarazuka was more morally 'wholesome' than the two groups situated in the inner city, but also because of the perception that Takarazuka's originally semi-rural setting with its natural beauty and fresh air provided a healthier physical environment (e.g. Tamai 1999: 16; also, *Kageki* 1974b: 63). From the 1970s onward, as the city of Takarazuka became more and more densely populated and crowded with buildings and roads, and OSK relocated permanently to suburban Nara, these reasons for preference may have become less valid. Nevertheless, OSK members were still regularly expected to play in such venues as theatre restaurants during regional tours, where spectators were occasionally drunken and disrespectful towards the performers, according to an OSK acquaintance who recounted such episodes to me in the mid-1980s, expressing her particular dislike for the skimpy, bikini-like costumes which OSK performers were sometimes required to wear.

Parental reactions to a child's choice of occupation are frequently based upon common societal expectations which differ according to the sex of the child. In an essay first published in 1942, Kobayashi expressed an opinion that was probably shared by many people, showing why acting on the professional stage was considered to have differing implications for sons and daughters:

> For a woman, becoming a stage performer at the age of nineteen or twenty by no means determines her future. One might say it is merely a means for earning part of her wedding expenses.[25] And far from being a drawback, to be on stage can sometimes provide the opportunity for a good marriage, so the decision to tread the boards can be made more lightly and positively than one might expect.
>
> In the case of a man, on the other hand, conditions are very different. A man in his twenties is at the vital point when he must determine the path he will follow in the future. It is not easy for him to make the bold decision to become a stage performer, because upon earnest reflection about his future and his talents, he cannot indulge in frivolous behaviour (Kobayashi 1942: 436–37).

Kobayashi obviously shared the stereotypical view that boys should enter a 'solid' profession that would support them and their families, whereas girls had more freedom to choose the stage because they were just 'filling in time' until marriage, not starting a life-long career.[26] The instability of acting as a profession has usually not been made an issue in the case of Takarasiennes, because the Company's policy of training and employing recruits for a number of years guarantees them a livelihood until they reach their mid-twenties, considered until recently to be a suitable age for marriage, after which almost all are expected shortly to leave the Revue stage, whether they actually marry or not.

Within the family of a girl aspiring to join the Revue, there is often a marked difference in the reaction of various members, with support for and objection to her wish to seek admission to Takarazuka frequently dividing along gender lines. According to examples from published materials and my interview informants, mothers (or grandmothers, in some cases) seem the most supportive, as many have been Revue fans and/or aspirants in their own youth. The so-called *'kyōiku mama'* ('education mother'), who pushes her children to achieve academic success, became a social phenomenon in the second half of the twentieth century in Japan (see Condon 1985: 120–40), but there also exists a kind of 'Takarazuka stage mother' who dreams of putting her daughter(s) into Takarazuka, perhaps because her own thespian aspirations were thwarted. The mother of *musumeyaku* Itsumine Aki, for one, urged her unwilling daughter to apply in the 1980s, and 'rejoiced even more than the daughter' when the girl was granted admission (cited in *Kageki* 1991c: 123).

Since the 1937 debut of the first second-generation Takarasienne, Hitomi Urara, who was the daughter of Hisano Mitsuko (1921–23), about seventy pairs of mothers and daughters have trodden the Takarazuka stage, with there being two cases of three generations: grandmother (Kurenai Chizuru, 1921–32), mother (Chiharu Kyōko, 1956–59) and granddaughter (Marisa Hitomi, 1989–98); and Takigawa Sueko I (1913–33), Takigawa Sueko II (1954–69) and Takigawa Sueko III (1995–2007) (*Takarazuka otome* 2007: 124; Yabushita 2007a).[27] Similarly, one *musumeyaku*'s mother who had belonged to an all-girl revue troupe in Kyushu, the Kokusai shōjo kagekidan (International girls' revue company), liked Takarazuka and sent both of her daughters to ballet lessons as grounding for a stage career: indeed, one became a professional ballerina, while her sister, Minakaze Mai, entered Takarazuka (cited in Minakaze and Natori 1997: 200). The sisters of many performers also have been inspired to join, with or without their sibling's blessing. Two younger sisters of Amatsu Otome, as noted above, followed her example, though Amatsu initially opposed her sister Kayoko's joining in 1921 (Kumono 1980: 170). A history of the Revue published to commemorate its eightieth anniversary in 1994 records twelve sets of three sisters becoming Takarasiennes, and seventy-nine sets of two, including four pairs of twins (Hashimoto 1994: 19–97).

Some fathers also have been conscientious backers of their daughters' dreams, aiding their preparation for the Music School examination in various ways. Occasionally, fathers' enthusiasm surpasses even that of their daughters or wives. The father of 1977 entrant Kodai Mizuki, for one, always drove his daughter home from ballet classes, travelling an hour each way late at night to collect her (cited in Minakaze and Natori 1997: 81–82). In another case, a father who was a Takarazuka fan himself apparently 'banded together (*kessoku shita*)' with his daughter to help her take the entrance examination in 1969. His wife's full cooperation only came later, when she bowed to the determination of her daughter, Natsuki Teru, who had moved from the family home in Wakayama Prefecture, a four-hour journey away from Takarazuka, to her grandmother's house in Toyonaka, about one-eighth of the previous distance. Subsequently, the entire family relocated to Toyonaka (*Kageki* 1973b: 107). Takarazuka's strictness, too, may win the approval of some fathers who value discipline: Usami (1981: 8) cites the case of one ex-military man who encouraged his daughter to 'go and have a strictly regular lifestyle (*kiritsu tadashii seikatsu*) drummed into [her]' at Takarazuka.

On the other hand, a once pro-Takarazuka father may come to deem a daughter's lack of self-discipline as disqualifying her from aiming to join the Revue. The writer and lyricist Sakata Hiroo, a Revue fan since his childhood, sent his reluctant younger daughter Natsume (who became *otokoyaku* Ōura Mizuki) to ballet lessons from a young age in the hope that she would become enthusiastic about dancing and subsequently aspire to join Takarazuka; later, however, Sakata briefly opposed his daughter's developing desire to become a Takarasienne when he discovered she had played truant from ballet rehearsals in order to watch Revue performances (Sakata 1992: 62–67).

Sometimes, one or both parents are so eager to have a daughter join Takarazuka that they groom the girl for that goal by such means as providing lessons in ballet, singing or Japanese dancing from an early age. One extreme example is that of 1970s *otokoyaku* Haruna Yuri, raised in a family of zealous Revue fans, who took her to see performances each Sunday from infancy. Haruna's parents took positive steps to influence their daughter's physical development from babyhood by eschewing the traditional Japanese practice of *onbu* (carrying her piggyback), and forbidding her to kneel on the *tatami*-matted floor, insisting instead that she sit on a chair.[28] They believed these measures would prevent the child from becoming bow-legged, which they thought would disqualify her from Takarazuka entry. Ballet lessons were postponed until Haruna was about nine, as her mother thought Haruna's leg-muscles might 'harden into a funny shape' if she were to don toe shoes any earlier. Later, when Haruna was at junior high school, her mother had to do her daughter's homework for her so the girl could concentrate upon extra-curricular lessons in preparation for the Music School examination (Haruna 1976: 30–32).

While many parents support their daughters' stage aspirations, a large number of others do object, for various reasons. Examples show that the father has often been more reluctant to give consent, not only to his daughter's dream of joining Takarazuka, but to any idea of her becoming involved in the entertainment world. Sometimes, his permission is granted only after the daughter gains admittance to Takarazuka training, as in the case of veteran Takarasienne Kishi Kaori, a member of her high school's drama club in the mid-1950s who had her heart set upon becoming a voice actor, but whose father had demanded she study pharmacology at a university instead (Kishi 2000: 20). Though it was apparently considered an honour in her native Osaka to have a daughter accepted by Takarazuka, with the names of successful candidates being published in the local newspaper, one of my informants had a father who regarded Takarazuka as 'out of the question (*motte no hoka*).' Having taken the Music School entrance exam in secret, my informant telephoned her family to say she had passed, and was taken aback to hear hearty words of congratulation from her father instead of further objections. Forty years later, she discovered that he had secretly sent her brother to buy multiple copies of the edition of the newspaper carrying his daughter's name, to distribute proudly among relatives (Informant PZ 2001: Q. 2.10).

Similarly, when a female relative of an aspirant has been a Takarasienne, the latter's insider knowledge of the Revue's realities sometimes means that the girl in question will be actively discouraged from applying to the Music School. One of my informants, who had strongly opposed her niece's desire to join, opined that Takarazuka was 'something to watch, not to enter into' (Informant PZ 2001: Q. 4.10).

Some parents of would-be Takarasiennes fear the reaction of relatives who have more authority within the extended family, as in the experience of one of my informants who grew up in a provincial area. Her parents were threatened with ostracism from the family circle by senior relatives if their daughter joined Takarazuka, although ultimately no such action was carried out, largely thanks to favourable publicity given by local newspapers to another girl from the same area who had already joined the Revue (Informant TH 2001: Q. 1.7). Since the Music School has charged fees for the past forty years, and post-graduation wages are now low, other parents may try to dissuade their daughters on financial grounds, believing that the family could not afford to keep a daughter in Takarazuka. The reminiscences of a number of entrants whose parents were not particularly affluent show that such girls could not pay for the extra-curricular classes taken by their Music School classmates, and had to miss out (e.g. Mori 1993: 189–90).

No fathers of my informants seemed to resist the idea of their daughter becoming a 'son' in the form of an *otokoyaku*, and thus not as 'adorable' and 'feminine' as they might want her to be, and perhaps not marriageable. On the other hand, mothers and sisters of many Takarasiennes have idolised certain *otokoyaku*, and are possibly pleased that their daughters and sisters would like to become one. Not all girls are socialised to be ladylike, in spite of a strong tendency on the part of many Japanese parents and schools to prescribe certain gender-specific behaviours and proscribe others. When, for example, the birth of a daughter has thwarted the hopes of parents for a son, the girl herself is sometimes brought up in boyish fashion, as in the case of Haruna Yuri, cited above. Haruna's ex-soldier father was apparently bitterly disappointed that the baby his wife bore was not the boy he had anticipated, and whom he had intended to name Masatoshi, meaning 'Victor.' Haruna claims to have been raised in 'thoroughly Spartan fashion,' without any feminine socialisation whatsoever. '"Masatoshi" lived on, deep in my breast,' she writes, 'and when "he" sometimes showed his face, it made my father rejoice, though it saddened my mother.' Having no interest in 'playing house,' and being taller and better at boys' pursuits than the neighbourhood boys themselves, Haruna became their leader, and she believes this 'laid the groundwork for becoming an *otokoyaku*' (Haruna 1976: 20–21). Her own life experience was later echoed in her portrayal in *The Rose of Versailles* of Oscar, a girl raised as a boy by her father, an army general. Created by Haruna on the Takarazuka stage in 1974, the role won her nationwide renown.[29]

Parents who hope their daughters will pursue higher education are likely to disapprove of Takarazuka, as joining it precludes university studies, and girls often yearn to enter the Music School after only receiving the legal minimum of schooling, as noted above. At least until relatively recently, however, daughters in Japan commonly have been subject to lower parental and social expectations regarding the length and academic quality of their education, as compared to sons. Indeed, for much of the twentieth century, in Japan as elsewhere, a protracted education was considered neither necessary nor desirable for most girls, though it is now taken for granted that most Japanese girls complete senior high school. While a tertiary education of four or more years is considered vital for boys, at least for those of the middle class or higher, and particularly in urban areas, this is not the case for girls – even in the last decade, young women with more than two years of post-secondary education have often found this greatly disadvantageous in job-hunting, if not also in their quest for a husband.

In its early years, Takarazuka offered additional educational opportunities to its girl students compared to the norm, but in recent decades the reverse has been the case. Takarazuka's training institution, whatever its name, has always insisted that its applicants have completed the minimum number of years of schooling mandated by Japanese law, and in pre-war years offered a comprehensive curriculum including not only performing arts classes but also regular school subjects. For many girls in pre-war Japan whose formal schooling had been limited to just six years at primary level, these extra classes probably represented a significant addition to their basic education. This doubtless made the Music and Opera School an attractive alternative to girls' higher schools, especially as no fees were charged at the former until 1936.

Now, however, girls who join Takarazuka before completing their upper secondary education put themselves at an educational disadvantage compared to the majority of their peers, as general subjects of no direct relevance to stagecraft have been excised from the post-war Takarazuka Music School curriculum. Girls from commercial or industrial high schools, however, are likely to gain considerable prestige by entering the Takarazuka Music School, as well as augmenting their education, as the former two types of institution generally have a lower status than academic high schools. Recently, though, the Takarazuka Music School has taken a step to somewhat assuage parental concerns about their daughters' truncated secondary education. In 2003, it arranged a high school equivalency correspondence course in affiliation with a private high school in Osaka Prefecture, for interested Takarazuka trainees who had not completed upper secondary schooling, and the first twenty-four students to complete this programme attained high school graduation in spring 2004 (Kobayashi 2003: 59). The School's web site reports that a total of 101 students gained their equivalency qualifications in the first four years of the scheme, and a dozen or so were studying for them in the 2007–08 academic year (*Takarazuka ongaku gakkō* 2007). This implies that while making their debut on the Takarazuka stage may be the students' immediate goal, high-school graduation is also valued as preparation for their life after performing.

In contrast to those parents who are reluctant to have their daughter's formal education curtailed because of her Takarazuka aspirations, some others may object to the current Takarazuka curriculum which does not prepare girls directly for homemaking. Only in the earliest years of the Revue's existence was sewing taught, and for the greater part of its history, the tea ceremony alone has been retained in the curriculum as a 'polite accomplishment' deemed desirable for a wife-to-be. As the next chapter will elaborate, cleaning has been the only other skill typically expected of homemakers that is actually taught to Music School students, though their prowess lies in specialist cleaning (such as scouring piano keys with cotton buds), rather than general housework using modern appliances and cleaning products. Cooking has never been taught to Takarasiennes, perhaps in anticipation of the fact that students and performers could live in the Company's dormitories, commute from home, or be pampered by fans, so they would not even have to shop for, let alone prepare their own food. The ability to bow to authority (or at least to appear to do so) now seems to be the principal benefit of Music School training in regard to married life, as suggested by a number of my informants cited in Chapter Six.

Suspicions about 'deviant' sexuality, too, might give some parents cause for opposing a daughter's Takarazuka aspirations. Although only one of my informants made direct reference to the issue of homosexuality, archival evidence from 1930 cited by Robertson (1998b: 69–70), for example, shows that male impersonation by Takarazuka performers was blamed in the print media for changing (supposedly) platonic, same-sex crushes between feminine girls into overtly sexual 'butch-femme (*ome*)'-type relationships. Parents who read such articles might have been concerned about Takarazuka in a moral sense because of the apparent possibility of their daughters being subject to lesbian influences in that all-female environment, which might have jeopardised their marriageability. On the other hand, even same-sex love might still have been seen as preferable to premarital heterosexual experience, as long as it was regarded as a 'phase' that would pass with maturity. Repeated efforts by the Revue Administration to quash any rumours of same-sex relationships, as well as reiteration by Kobayashi and the Company that Takarasiennes would make excellent wives, have aimed to assuage any such parental anxiety. Even the most explicit book written by an ex-performer about the less laudable aspects of Takarazuka refutes the existence of lesbian couples among performers, explaining that although many pairs of Takarasiennes do live together, this is because they are far from their families – by not living alone, they are more secure and less lonely, because they have someone to counsel them in times of suffering (Suwa 1980: 52).

Irrespective of the attitudes of a stage-struck girl's parents, though, it is sometimes the school which the daughter attends that hinders her pursuit of the dream of joining Takarazuka. A variety of reasons may exist for a school's ban on students' association with the Revue: vestiges of discrimination against actors in general; a belief that actresses, in particular, represent an immoral type of woman; an idea that idolatry towards cross-dressed females is perverted; a pride in academic achievement to the exclusion of other paths, and so on. Some high schools have strongly discouraged any aspirations towards a theatrical career among their students, though such an attitude has not always had the intended effect. In one case, a girl who attended a strict Catholic high school in Yokohama liked the Revue, but had not thought about applying to the Music School until the idea was put into her head as the unexpected result of her being summoned to the office of the principal, who demanded to know whether (unfounded) rumours about the girl's intention to enter Takarazuka were true. The student concerned (*otokoyaku* star Matsu Akira, 1966–82) passed the Takarazuka entrance examination a year later, but would probably not have been able to return to her high school, had she failed (cited in Suzuki 1979: 186).

Moreover, as middle- and high-school teachers in Japan are vested with the responsibility of guiding their pupils towards achievable goals in further education, training or employment (see Singleton 1967: 37–40), would-be Takarasiennes usually must inform their homeroom teacher of their plans, and win the cooperation of at least one of their teachers in order to submit an application to the Takarazuka Music School. Some teachers are reluctant to aid their pupils in their theatrical ambitions, as in the case of Tamai Hamako, whose mother was subjected to unpleasant comments (*iyami*) from her daughter's homeroom teacher when she requested a copy of the girl's school record for Tamai's Music School application (Tamai

1999: 16). In another instance, the high school attended by Ō Natsuki (1977–85) expected all of its students to proceed to tertiary education, and apparently not a single student had sought to apply to the Takarazuka Music School before Ō in 1975. Ō was summoned to the staff room, where her homeroom teacher angrily demanded to know 'what on earth' the girl was thinking (cited in Natori and Takeichi 1996b: 90).

Similarly, Yō Akira, a student at the Overseas Chinese School (Chūka dōbun gakkō) in Kobe, apparently had a good chance of gaining admittance to a Japanese public senior high school, but she also intended to take the Music School entrance examination. Her school warned that if Yō passed both entrance examinations, but were to decline the offer of a place at a highly-competitive public school, this would prejudice the public education system against later examinees from the Overseas Chinese School. Consequently, Yō was directed by her teachers to change her choice of senior high school to a presumably less-demanding private institution (Minakaze and Natori 1997: 122–23). Other aspirants' teachers, however, have been extremely supportive, and in some cases, a teacher who is a Takarazuka fan has singled out a promising pupil who is unusually tall, attractive or talented, suggesting she apply to the Music School, without the girl herself ever having seen or been particularly interested in the Revue. Ōtori Ran, who did not see her first performance until after her enrolment, but went on to become a star in the 1970s, is one example (NHK Osaka 1992b).

The means by which aspiring Takarasiennes conquer parental or school objections to their determination to try for the Music School are varied, and some girls apparently employ considerable wiles to gain permission. The Music School application requires a parent's name seal, to indicate consent, and this is probably impressed without parental knowledge in some rare cases. One 1980s *musumeyaku* mentioned above, Kanna Miho, who came from what she terms an 'exceedingly unyielding (*chō katai*)' family, vowed to attempt the examination just once, at the end of her first year of senior high school in 1981, promising her parents that she would study hard for university entrance if she should fail. She also extracted permission to attend ballet and singing lessons by pointing out that she would always regret not having made the effort if she were to take the examination without any formal preparation. Kanna's father continued his opposition even after she passed, and her mother ensured that her daughter's place at senior high school was retained by continuing to pay the school fees for a year, in case she found the Music School too strict – a waste of money, ultimately, as Kanna attended only the first day of first term at the high school, though her form teacher apparently included her name in roll-call until the end of the first term (Minakaze and Natori 1997: 23–25). In spite of her parents' initial reservations, Kanna went on to become a leading *musumeyaku*, retiring for marriage at the peak of her stardom in 1988.

This chapter has shown that the desire to enter Takarazuka stems from a variety of motivations, and aspirants are variously aided or hindered in their quest to gain entry to the Music School by the people around them, who in turn are affected by personal or societal attitudes. It must be remembered, however, that unlike most other educational institutions, the Takarazuka Music School assesses not so much its applicants' intelligence or scholastic ability, but their beauty and suitability for training as performers on the Revue stage, as well as their potential to contribute to the Company's future popularity through their mastery of gendered performance. In light of this, the next chapter will explore the process of preparation for Takarazuka entry, the taking of the examination itself, and the unique experience of studying at the Takarazuka Music School: a rite of passage shared by every Takarasienne in history as she anticipates playing out Takarazuka's version of femininity or masculinity on its stage.

3 Negotiating the 'Narrow Gate' to the Music School

Countless girls have dreamed of joining Takarazuka, and many tens of thousands have taken the further step of applying for admission to the Takarazuka Music School, graduation from which is mandatory for membership of the Revue Company. Once enrolled, the students are kept busy, not only training to become professional performers in musical theatre in general, but also beginning to acquire the techniques necessary to specialise in the portrayal of a particular gender on the Takarazuka stage, as well as learning how to take their place in the Takarazuka hierarchy. It is especially important to examine the School, as it is at this institution that the issue of the *conscious performance* of gender affects students, perhaps for the first time in their lives. Here, each trainee is subjected simultaneously to two types of gender-based training: for the portrayal on stage of a gender not necessarily concomitant with her biological sex, and which exaggerates or challenges gender stereotypes in Japanese society; and for the expression of obedient, demure and virtuous femininity which each Takarasienne is expected to sustain throughout her off-stage life. This latter femininity echoes certain societal ideals, but is distinct again from her stage gender performance.

This chapter focuses on how girls gain entry to the School, discussing the attitude of female students to preparing for non-academic training instead of the upper secondary or tertiary education which most of their peers will undergo; what and how Takarazuka expects them to learn while they attend the Music School; and how students respond to these expectations. The chapter illustrates again how much variety in attitude and experience exists among this select group of girls, and how they adopt or resist selected values established by society and its structures.

Preparing for the examination

The process of preparation for entrance to Takarazuka differs widely among individuals, with some girls having no special training except that which they received at school in singing and physical education. Others, though, at the opposite extreme, spend months or years attending preparatory classes in the hope of becoming Takarasiennes.

The upbringing of many Japanese girls, especially those from middle- or upper-class families, includes private lessons in one or more of the performing arts, presumably for their value as polite accomplishments deemed desirable for women generally. Many girls who aspire to join Takarazuka have attended lessons in a musical instrument, ballet or Japanese dancing during childhood, often without any thought of becoming professional performers, as extra-curricular classes in a variety of subjects, known collectively as *(o)keiko-goto* ('practice-things'), are considered an extension of children's education. According to a Japanese belief, children will make rapid progress in a performing art if they start to learn it from the sixth day of the sixth month in their sixth year, and numerous Takarasiennes recall having begun Japanese dancing lessons, for example, on that date (e.g. One's Co. Ltd 1996: 187).

On the other hand, dancing classes appear also to have been chosen by the parents of many a weak or sickly daughter, in the hope that she would gain strength or health through exercise. School clubs, membership of which is often compulsory at junior and senior high schools, also offer students a wide choice of cultural or sporting activities, as noted by Hendry (1987: 93), and many Takarasiennes reportedly believe that participation in dance, chorus, orchestral band or drama clubs nurtured in them a love of the performing arts. Some, though, undertook quite different club activities, such as tennis or volleyball (Fujita 1971b: 109). Practice of a martial art like *kendō*, for instance, though probably not undertaken specifically with Takarazuka in mind, nevertheless could also give a potential *otokoyaku* a useful grounding in sword-fighting, which is quite often required on the Revue stage.

The amount of attention each Takarazuka aspirant can give to regular schooling while she prepares for the Music School examination varies among individuals. Some are never able to study or do homework, thus earning low grades, but others manage to achieve higher grades than previously, probably as a result of efforts to appease concerned parents, and possibly also because such would-be Takarasiennes are more focussed than their contemporaries, whose scholastic efforts may be aimed at the next step in a long ladder of schools and universities, and might not be directly connected with a vocation. As graduation from the

Takarazuka Music School has always guaranteed girls a place on the Takarazuka stage, aspiring entrants know that if they are successful, they will be making their debut as professionals in just two years. Thus, realisation of their dreams must seem more immediate than in the case of most of their classmates at regular school.

In 1980, Music School admission regulations were changed so that applications were barred from girls of senior high school age not currently enrolled in formal schooling, ostensibly out of consideration for examinees who failed to gain entry irrespective of the number of attempts they made. Moral considerations might also have prompted this ruling, for girls might lead an 'irregular' life if not attending day-school, learn too much about the adult world, and thus lose the disciplined, sheltered innocence that Takarazuka seems to value in its recruits. Prospective applicants must now continue their education until the end of the academic year immediately preceding their attempt to enter the Music School. Prior to the amendment of the rules, a considerable number of girls each year apparently left regular school to concentrate entirely upon preparing for the entrance examination for a year or more, which usually entailed taking private dance and/or singing lessons (Usami 1981: 8). In one case under the pre-1980 system, a girl who failed at her first attempt at Music School entrance spent such a year in academic limbo after having been expelled from her senior high school. She had broken a rule forbidding students to apply to any other school during their enrolment, her misdemeanour having come to light when she played truant in order to submit her initial Music School application in person. Her perseverance paid off, however, as she later passed and became the star *musumeyaku*, Minakaze Mai (Minakaze and Natori 1997: 204).

For several decades up till the mid-1990s, many aspiring Takarasiennes who lived within commuting distance of Takarazuka enrolled in a special preparatory programme called Bekka (Separate Department), which was run after hours by the Music School and offered a comprehensive curriculum of ballet, singing and Japanese dancing for girls aged between fourteen and eighteen. Classes were held from six till nine in the evening from Mondays to Saturdays, but attendance did not by any means guarantee a pupil's entry to the School proper. There was some advantage, however, in that Bekka pupils had the chance to become familiar with the School's buildings and acquainted with some of its teachers before attempting the entrance examination. Writer/director Takagi Shirō (1976: 41) noted in the mid-1970s that many girls from Tokyo

went to the extent of taking up lodgings in Takarazuka in order
to attend Bekka classes, which cost considerably less than regular
private lessons. Jun Mitsuki, for example, would rush from daily
after-school volleyball practice to Takarazuka Bekka classes in her
final year of high school, when preparing to enter the Music School:
her evening meal would not be eaten until ten at night (Takagi
1976: 41). For those attending regular school as well, the physically
challenging classes and late arrival home, as well as a long period
of commuting for some, would have left the girls so exhausted that
they had little energy, let alone time, to do academic homework
or study. In one example, a 1963 entrant, Katsuki Miyo, would
rush off to Bekka classes after a full day at a public high school
on six evenings per week, take three hours of lessons in singing
and dancing, then return to her home in Izumiotsu, a city south
of Osaka, at about eleven o'clock at night, still wearing her school
uniform. In spite of her exhausting schedule, she, like many other
aspirants, claims that she never once suffered or felt sad, saying:
'My goal of entering Takarazuka, my dream, must have been my
heart's support' (Katsuki 1971: 78).

Although Bekka ceased operation, a somewhat similar school
was established in 1993 at the Hankyu-run Theatre Drama City in
Osaka, which for some years offered two-hour classes in musical
theatre subjects after regular school hours, three times per week
(Kobayashi 1996: 53). The Takarazuka Music School is still the
venue for the Takarazuka kodomo atene (Takarazuka children's
athenaeum), which has long offered Sunday classes in ballet,
Japanese dance and singing to girls from mid-primary school to
the third year of junior high school. The final class conveniently
ends in time for watching the three o'clock Grand Theatre
performance. Not surprisingly, the pupils are predominantly would-
be Takarasiennes, although a few, apparently including 1990s
otokoyaku Maya Miki, attend without harbouring any aspirations
towards joining the Revue, merely wanting to learn dancing and
singing (Maya 1994: 106).

In Tokyo, Osaka and adjacent areas, there is now a growing
industry in preparing 'wannabe' Takarasiennes for the entrance
examination, with many of the instructors in such subjects as ballet,
singing and deportment being retired performers themselves.[1]
While the majority of such teachers might not have achieved top
stardom, their intimate knowledge of the Takarazuka system, as
well as their contacts within the organisation, enable them to tailor
their teaching programmes to their pupils, and perhaps to enjoy

vicariously the later stardom of the successful ones. As noted in
the previous chapter, advertisements for such preparatory classes
have regularly appeared in the Revue's fan magazines and theatre
programmes for some decades, but would-be Takarasiennes can
now also search the Internet for details of various schools. On the
other hand, some mainstream ballet or vocal instructors whose
pupils are not necessarily aiming for Takarazuka recognise
potential in particular girls, and encourage them to apply, as in the
case of one Kanazawa resident, Sawa Kaori, who had begun ballet
classes in the 1960s at about the age of nine at an academy run by
ballerina and choreographer Ōtaki Aiko, who also taught classical
ballet at the Music School, and served as Company class teacher and
choreographer for Revue performances for decades (see Kishi 2000:
30; *Kageki* 1991b: 136). Sawa was urged by her teacher to consider
Takarazuka, and after becoming a junior high school student, spent
what amounted to 'a week out of every month' in Tokyo, hours away
by express train from her home city, attending ballet and singing
classes (Fujita 1971b: 108). Here, gender is significant because such
an investment of time and energy on non-school-based artistic
activities would be arguably rare among junior (and senior) high
school boys, due to a heavier emphasis on academic and sporting
achievement for male students.

Unlike school sporting or cultural club activities where the
emphasis is upon team-work, independent dancing and singing
classes often foster a spirit of fierce competition among individuals,
for entrance to the Music School is via a 'narrow gate (*semaki mon*)'
through which only a select few may pass. At a ballet class for Music
School aspirants that I observed in Tokyo in January 2001, pupils
were constantly watching their classmates and comparing their
rivals with themselves, looking smug when accomplishing a step or
routine better than others, and appearing vexed when chastised. The
teacher, a retired *musumeyaku*, frequently couched her criticisms in
terms of whether a particular student's pose, movement, attitude or
level of effort would be acceptable at the Takarazuka Music School.
The preparatory establishment in question prominently displayed
large photographs of successful applicants from recent years,
using these to advertise the efficacy of its instruction. Takarazuka
claims it is in the business of 'selling dreams,' so it might be said
that the preparatory industry for intending applicants to the Music
School depends upon 'selling the dream of the Takarazuka dream.'
Aspirants often pay large sums of money to be groomed into ideal
candidates; after all, this investment will turn these stage-struck

purchasers of the Takarazuka dream into its eventual purveyors, if they are admitted to the Music School.

The entrance test

For all but the first few years of its existence, Takarazuka has accepted only a small proportion of the hundreds of girls who have applied annually to enter its training school. As noted above, in early years of the Revue's history, recruits merely had to be of reasonably attractive appearance, have completed primary schooling and be judged by the recruiters as having potential to be trained in music, singing and dance, without necessarily having any background in the performing arts. In 1913, the first applicants to the Takarazuka Choir were apparently examined in a ten-mat room containing a piano, next to the Paradise spa's boiler-room, where the vocal instructor, Andō Hiroshi, requested the girls simply to 'sing any song they liked' (*Kageki* 1974: 110). One 1928 entrant describes her entrance test as consisting of an interview, writing answers to simple questions in arithmetic and literacy, reproducing short texts from memory, walking up and down in front of the examiners in lieu of dancing, and singing scales (Fujino 1990: 13–15). Even after the Second World War, according to the reminiscences of star Sumi Hanayo, applicants in her cohort simply had to walk around in front of the selection panel and sing one song, although the competition was 'as fierce as [that to enter] Tokyo University,' as only about one in thirteen candidates was admitted to the Music School that year (Sumi 1976: 117). However, unlike at Tokyo University, where academic merit would be the main criterion, the beauty of Takarazuka examinees was clearly more important than their talent – women's worth being measured largely by their appearance.

From around the 1960s, the examination system developed into the one in practice today, necessitating more and more specific training by aspirants. The 'Takarazuka boom' attributed to the 1974 premiere of *The Rose of Versailles* apparently led to a sharp improvement in the artistic preparedness of applicants (Kawasaki 1999: 209). Examinees must now perform a previously unknown ballet routine which is demonstrated by a senior pupil for solo reproduction, after a few minutes of practice; sing a pre-rehearsed song; sight-read an unknown melody; and face a panel of examiners at an interview, where the applicants may be invited to demonstrate any special talent that they have declared. Less-promising candidates are culled at this point, while 'short-listed' examinees undergo the testing process once more, at a more demanding level. Given that the Music School trains girls for only two years, aspirants who, for example, demonstrate suppleness and potential to respond rapidly to instruction after having taken only six, or even three, months of ballet classes prior to the examination, will probably gain higher marks than those of similar ability, gained over years of training. A significant number of stars recall that they failed the examination at their first attempt, practised diligently during the ensuing year, and passed with excellent marks upon their second try, having demonstrated an ability to learn quickly when working towards a definite goal. Some examiners (all or mostly males) are notorious for choosing girls whom they find charming over less attractive candidates with some performing skills. Examiners apparently also value a quality described as 'plus alpha (*purasu arufā*)' – that is, something 'extra special.' A very pretty and coquettish acquaintance of mine, who had had little performing arts training, attempted the Takarazuka Music School entrance examination in the late 1970s at the exhortation of a friend who was eager to apply, but was reluctant to do so alone. When asked by the interview panel why she wanted to enter Takarazuka, my acquaintance reportedly declared, 'Because I want to be a star!' She was offered a place at the School, but declined, realising that she was ill-prepared for the rigours of the Music School. Her friend failed to gain admission. Writer/directors such as Shirai Tetsuzō and Utsumi Shigenori are known to have spotted a supposed star quality in otherwise low-scoring examinees. *Otokoyaku* stars Uchinoe Noboru and Ōtori Ran, for example, apparently would have failed the entrance examination had their interview mark not been boosted by such examiners, who later boasted of their 'eye for potential' (see Suzuki 1976: 133–34; Utsumi 1992).

The mystique of the Music School is so strong that quite a number of girls who know they have scant chance of passing apparently take the entrance examination, simply for the memory of having gone through the same process as all Takarasiennes. Even successful entrants often report having been convinced that they would fail the test, but wanting to try anyway, in order not to live with the regret that they had not made at least one effort to become a Takarasienne. The examination is now conducted in two rounds, the first being held at the Takarazuka Music School and a suitable facility in Tokyo, before 'short-listed' candidates are re-examined at the School itself. One examinee from Sendai, north of Tokyo, travelled all the way to Takarazuka to take the initial test. She reasoned that even if she

were eliminated in the first round, she would at least have set foot in
the Music School of which she had dreamed (Mori 1993: 161–62).

While some girls feel isolated and shy among a crowd of seemingly more talented and beautiful rivals at the test venue, others
apparently endeavour to befriend fellow candidates who appear
likely to pass, gathering names and addresses so that they can keep
in contact with the successful ones even if they themselves are not
admitted. The examinations are held in late March or early April,
when spring temperatures are often low, and one candidate, Kanna
Miho, recounts removing her warm cardigan and lending it to a
promising fellow examinee who was suffering from the cold, not
out of kindness, but out of 'a feeling of self-satisfaction' that she
was helping a deserving candidate to pass (Minakaze and Natori
1997: 31–32).

The formal curriculum

The mixture of goals to which Takarazuka Music School students
are expected to aspire is expressed succinctly in two different
mottoes, executed in distinctive calligraphy by the founder,
Kobayashi Ichizō, which are framed and displayed with equal
prominence upon the School walls. Mottoes, according to Chie
Nakane (1970: 20), function to 'bolster the sense of unity and
group solidarity' in Japanese society, and Takarazuka's mottoes are
presumably designed to have the same effect within the Company.
One motto specific to the Takarazuka Music School is '*Gei mata
gei* (Arts and more arts),' also translated in an English-language
official pamphlet as 'One highly developed artistic accomplishment
after another' (*Takarazuka Music School* 1999). Well-known
lyricist and translator, Iwatani Tokiko, a former member of the
Takarazuka staff, paraphrases this motto, saying: 'One can never
achieve perfection in the arts, even to one's dying day. Each art
must be constantly practised, each skill…untiringly honed' (cited
in Suzuki 1976: 106). The other motto, shared with the Revue
as a whole, is the more familiar '*Kiyoku, tadashiku, utsukushiku*
([With] purity, righteousness and beauty),' which expresses an ideal
femininity. Together, they encapsulate the ethos of the Takarazuka
Music School.

The first chapter of this volume traced the evolution of Takarazuka's training institution into the modern school it is today. It will
be remembered that instruction was once given in a number of
musical instruments, in addition to dancing and singing, and that

after 1919, regular girls' higher school subjects were also taught, according to a pamphlet issued in 1985 by the School. One of my informants, a pre-war entrant, recalls the difficulty of theoretical subjects such as the history of music, film and drama, as well as Japanese, English and *shūshin* (moral training). Her practical classes included classical ballet, modern dance, eurhythmic exercises, tap-dancing, acrobatics, Japanese dancing and piano. Examinations were held and report cards issued each term, and unlike today, those who failed were summarily expelled. Student numbers therefore fell steadily, and the initial four classes had shrunk to two in the second year of my informant's enrolment (Informant MH 2001: Q. 2.2). Now, the Music School evidently cannot afford to admit large numbers of students who are unlikely to complete the course, for expulsion seems rare.

The current curriculum offers some forty hours per week of classes in dance (classical ballet; modern, tap and Japanese classical dance), singing (solo, ensemble and choral), acting, a musical instrument and other theoretical and practical aspects of music and stagecraft (Takarazuka Music School 2000). The tea ceremony is also taught as a polite accomplishment, not only for its discipline and elegance, but also as a symbol of Japanese culture, whose etiquette Takarasiennes should know 'in case they are later invited to a real tea ceremony,' according to the Deputy Principal in 1999. Formal instruction concentrates, however, upon skills directly applicable to performing on the Takarazuka stage, even though the school's name might suggest a broader musical curriculum. April 1988 saw the abolition of the largely self-taught marching band (*kotekitai*), once a feature of the first-year curriculum, and students now study only one musical instrument, for a paltry one hour and twenty minutes per week. Those without grounding in a keyboard instrument learn piano, while experienced pianists or organists can choose *shamisen* or *koto*. This contrasts sharply with the comprehensive instrumental music training provided by the School in its earliest years, when members of the Girls' Opera were taught to be instrumentalists in their own right as well as accompanists for others. Perhaps now that Takarazuka can boast of ninety years of theatrical achievements, it no longer needs to pretend that its performers are really musicians rather than actresses, although it still seems loath to discontinue its tradition of calling them 'students (*seito*).'

Students from past decades often reminisce about their eagerness to practise the piano. Many arrived at the School before it opened in the early morning, with some even scaling the hedge in order to

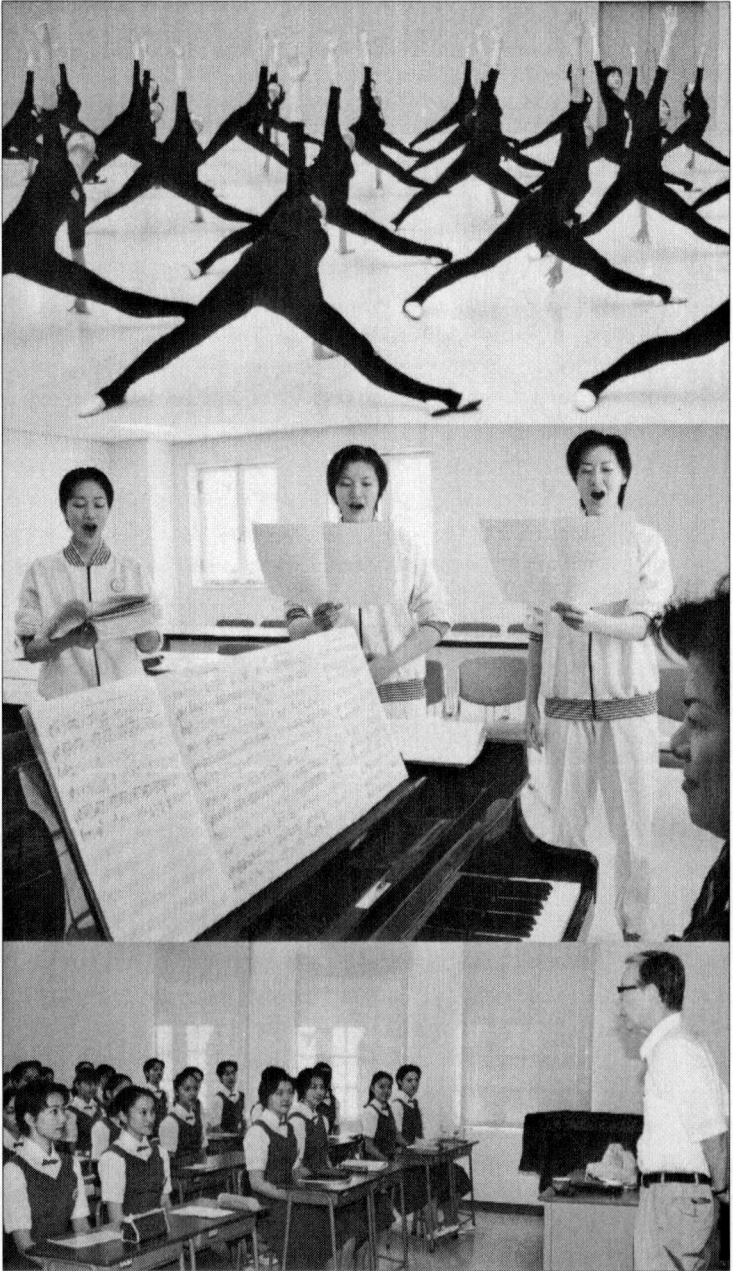

Plate 2: Takarasiennes in training at the Takarazuka Music School.
(Photographs courtesy of Deputy Principal Imanishi)

secure first turn at one of the few pianos available (Kishi 2000: 34). After school, too, the pianos were in demand. One 1930s entrant recalls her junior year, when her extra-curricular keyboard practice would be interrupted whenever a senior arrived. 'I would do the polite thing by saying '*dōzo* (after you),' then leave the classroom with a bow and wait outside,' she recounts. 'I would stay quietly out there, listening to her singing her scales at the piano, until she went home and I could go in again and practise' (Informant HO 2001: Q. 2.1). The School now apparently has forty pianos and almost twenty electronic keyboards, so there should be more than enough to go around (Kishi 2000: 34).

While many schools in Japan have suffered from the problem of *gakkyū hōkai* (classroom breakdown, caused by students' disruptive behaviour: see Yoneyama 1999), classes at the Takarazuka Music School are usually conducted in an atmosphere of eagerness to learn and excel, and of respect (and often affection) for teachers, who include many former Takarasiennes. The first woman to hold the post of Deputy Principal, Imanishi Masako, for one, was once the veteran character player, Hayama Michiko. Such alumnae are also *jōkyūsei* (school seniors) to their students, and are afforded extra respect for this reason. Not all students are serious all of the time, however. One *otokoyaku* renowned for her sense of fun, Takashio Tomoe (debut 1972), writes that she 'loved' piano lessons so much that she 'zealously cut the class' almost weekly (Takashio 1977: 92). Another, Maya Miki, similarly avoided piano classes by bandaging a different finger every week and pretending to be injured (Maya 1994: 182). Reminiscences of other graduates show that the amusement park once adjacent to the school – now defunct – tempted some to skip boring classes and enjoy rides on the roller coaster, monorail and rowboats, which were free for Music School students. Sometimes the truants were discovered by seniors and severely scolded (see Fujita 1977a: 127).

School organisation: hierarchy and discipline

Both the Takarazuka Music School and the Takarazuka Revue are characterised by a hierarchical organisation that maintains discipline among its numerous members by requiring each junior to obey and defer to all her seniors. The ritualistic 'right way' of behaving is narrowly prescribed and taught in a range of Japanese institutions, and justified as being 'important in countless spheres of Japanese social life,' as Brian McVeigh asserts in his discussion of female junior college students (McVeigh 1996: 317). Takarazuka insiders believe that the sex of performers and trainees – female, not male – is crucial to the maintenance of good discipline. Indeed, Kobayashi Ichizō once wrote that it would have been impossible to develop an all-male company of four or five hundred performers, suggesting that men would be 'always fighting (*nenjū kenka darō*)' (cited in Tanabe and Sasaki 1987: 146). Author and self-proclaimed Takarazuka fan Tanabe Seiko further proposes that the Takarazuka Revue has survived because of the unique ability of *Japanese* women to work in harmony within such a system. Tanabe echoes orthodox Japanese notions both of gender and of Japanese-ness in her argument that 'Japanese women's meekness and rich ability to adapt, their obedience, earnestness, cleverness and spirit of cooperation are simply astonishing,' and suggests that a commercial theatre company composed of several hundred 'strongly self-assertive, individualistic Western women' would not survive as long as Takarazuka has done (Tanabe and Sasaki 1987: 147).

Although most executive decisions in Takarazuka regarding productions, personnel placement and casting are made by men in administrative and creative positions, Takarasiennes largely govern themselves in everyday matters, utilising a chain of command based upon seniority, not stage gender. The initial year of Takarazuka training is known as *yoka* (preparatory course), and the second as *honka* (main course), each year being further divided into two (formerly more) classes according to the level of education each student had completed before entry.[2] Real age is considered irrelevant. Instead, one iron rule applies (with exceptions such as that noted below): absolute obedience (*zettai fukujū*) to seniors. Such obedience is first instilled both by direct instruction from second-year students, and by drills conducted by Japan Self Defence Force personnel, who teach new entrants precision bowing, marching and obedience to commands with perfect timing, as vividly shown in the documentary film by Britons Longinotto and Williams (1993).

The latter classes apparently began in the late 1960s, when an instructor from the Ground Self Defence Force base in nearby Itami was invited to the School, possibly by its Dean of Students (*seitokan*), Kagawa Tadashi. Kagawa, himself a retired military officer, was already teaching students conduct (*kikyo*) and deportment (*yōgi*), probably with similar content to that which figured in the pre-war moral education (*shūshin*) curriculum, according to the then principal, Kumano Norikazu (Kōbe Shinbun Hanshin Sōkyoku 1984: 186, 190). One of my informants, who conducted her own informal investigation into the history of the harsh treatment of Takarazuka juniors by seniors, found that the bullying of first-years became endemic from 1970 or just before, probably in connection with the introduction of Defence Force instruction (Informant PZ 2001: Q. 2.3). There were also unusually large intakes of new students in those years, perhaps in anticipation of the need to provide scores of dancers for special attractions commemorating Expo '70 in Osaka, and the stricter discipline might have been imposed to ensure control over such big numbers of inexperienced Takarasiennes.

First-years display the result of their indoctrination as they scurry about the school, pressed closely to the right-hand side of corridors and stairways, supposedly to allow second-years and teachers easy thoroughfare. They bow stiffly and chorus a set greeting whenever they catch sight of a senior, hurrying to open a door for her even if they must interrupt their own activity to do so. The juniors resemble robots in their rigid posture, with arms held stiffly to the sides and fingers outstretched, and in the way they turn corners at right angles – a useless rule, in the opinion of one veteran informant, who says: 'I think it is more important to be able to pull swiftly out of the way the instant you pass someone going in the opposite direction, to avoid spoiling her costume' (Informant MH 2001: Q. 2.3). The School insists, though, that the drilling is not militaristic, and is necessary for training the students to be '*kibin* (able to move with promptness and agility),' as Deputy Principal Imanishi Masako explained to me in 2000. Another ex-Takarasienne offers a different justification:

> Show-business people have to conduct themselves with the utmost politeness, and it is the true intention of the Music School to build a richly artistic character [in its students]. It isn't extraordinarily strict; it is [just] a well-disciplined school. It only teaches what is proper for a human being – the rules of society at large, common sense, courtesy and good manners...Someone from the Meiji era, for example, would say that the school was teaching what was natural,...cultivating a sense of social duty within the performing arts, teaching students to keep in step with each other in such a way that they acquire it naturally (Informant DP 2001: Q. 2.3).

Each individual situates herself in three levels of hierarchy during her training at the Music School: she is subservient and answerable to her immediate seniors; equal to her *dōki* peers; and superior to and responsible for her immediate juniors. This order will remain constant throughout her training, her tenure with the Revue, and even into her retirement. In the Company hierarchy – a broad-based pyramid with octogenarian Kasugano Yachiyo currently at its needle-like peak – rank is determined by two things: the year a particular performer and her peers (*dōki-sei*) enter the Music School;[3] and how she scores among her year-group at examinations held at graduation, then in the December of her first, third and fifth year with the Company.

From the time of entry to the Music School, each student is constantly reminded that her classmates are both her staunchest allies and her fiercest rivals. At the School, her rank initially reflects her entrance examination score, but fluctuates according to subsequent tests. However, while students may strive individually to attain the best grades possible, all are also urged to cooperate to achieve a uniformly high standard during group activity, whether it be cleaning, or learning an ensemble item for a performance. This experience, coupled with the hierarchical discipline to which they are exposed, evidently aids performers later in their careers. One 1980s entrant says, 'When we're up on stage dancing, we have that sense of solidarity, an awareness of those beside us... which we were taught as first-years' (Informant RX 2001: Q. 2.3). The peer relationships forged at the School generally remain strong for a lifetime, and for this reason, one pre-war entrant especially recommends the Music School as a good place to send an only child, as these 'strong horizontal ties' will support her in place of siblings when the death of her parents severs her vertical ties (Informant TH 2001: Q. 4.10).

One more factor unites classmates: fear. We have already seen that beginning students are drilled in bowing, quick response to commands, and obedience to seniors. Punishment for misdemeanours is rarely physical (unlike the 'hazing' apparently inflicted upon male military cadets or members of sporting and martial arts clubs at schools or universities) – Music School punishments apparently include standing or kneeling for long periods of time, or redoing cleaning tasks. The importance of formal lessons in stagecraft almost pales in comparison with the constant scrutiny and chastisement Music School first-years receive from second-years, who watch eagerly for transgression of rules governing posture, grooming, etiquette, movement, attitude, and speech, as is evident in Longinotto and Williams' 1993 filmed exposé. Understandably, juniors spend much of their first year avoiding seniors whenever possible.

In seniors' presence, first-years adopt a rigidly polite, subordinate stance, and even when out of uniform, away from the School, they are constantly on guard lest they encounter a senior and perhaps break some rule. Nearsighted girls apparently suffer the most, for they often cannot detect the presence of seniors, and thus may fail to make the required bow and greeting. Edwin O. Reischauer (1988: 144–45) and others observe that in Japan an acceptance of authority goes together with an expectation of indulgence – at least in theory, Takarazuka seniors are supposed to be acting severely for juniors' benefit, establishing a relationship of *amae* (dependence) and indulgence,[4] in which juniors look to them for example, guidance and approval, though many rules may seem unreasonable to juniors at the time. One *musumeyaku* claims that when she was a first-year, classes were welcome opportunities to 'take a break (*kyūkei*),' free from the fear of being scolded by a second-year for some real or imagined misdemeanour (cited in Takarajennu kyatto fan kurabu 1996: 75). During recess times, tension among first-years is high, but this quickly eases once seniors are out of sight, as I perceived at the Music School in February 2001.

A wartime recruit, recalling that juniors could be chastised or summoned at the whim of seniors, commented: '[A]t times like those, we didn't feel as if we were alive' (Tamai 1999: 21). In a conversation with me in 1972, one 1970 Japanese-American entrant, Yuki Reina, described the Music School as 'the strictest boarding school in the world.' 'There was not a single day when I didn't cry,' she later told director Miki Akio – comic books had taught her Japanese, but not the ultra-polite register demanded of Takarazuka first-years when addressing a senior (Miki 1977: 76). Similarly, *otokoyaku* star Mori Keaki, enrolled in 1977, claims she was so sick with fear and 'culture-shocked' in her first three days at the School and its dormitory, which 'felt like gaol,' that she lost five kilogrammes in weight in that time. 'It wasn't that the second-years did frightening things; their [very] existence was frightening,' she recalls (Mori 1993: 179–80). One young informant of mine (Informant AA: Q. 2.1, 2.4) had thought she knew what to expect, but was still so shocked at the extreme discipline after entering the School in April that, to her, 'by May, it felt as if a whole year had passed.' As first-years, she also commented, she and her classmates 'didn't live like human beings.' 'We were cockroaches,' she declared. The same metaphor is employed by *musumeyaku* Asanagi Rin, who called the nervous scurry of juniors in the corridors '*gokiburi-aruki* (cockroach-walk)' (Asanagi 1997: 105). The student-imposed discipline seems especially harrowing for trainees who had enjoyed freedom as children.

Between classes, the *yoka rūmu* (juniors' common-room) provides something of a haven for first-year students, but the 1970 principal, Kumano Norikazu, describes second-years 'thumping on the dividing wall' to summon particular first-years, who had to hurry next door and kneel on the floor, awaiting instruction or chastisement (Kōbe Shinbun Hanshin Sōkyoku 1984: 186). To address the problem of an indisposed junior possibly having to share a sickroom with a senior, thus compounding her discomfort, the infirmary at the new Music School building opened in January 1999 has beds in separate rooms for each year.

Students can also be scolded for breaches of etiquette towards their instructors, though apparently not for poor mastery of the subjects being taught. In a first-year singing class I observed in 1999, for example, one student who repeatedly hit wrong notes during her rendition of the song 'Bali Hi' from *South Pacific* laughingly apologised each time to the male teacher, but was not chastised.

What Brian McVeigh terms as 'sociolinguistic choreography' is heavily emphasised at the School, where the performance of formalised greetings (*aisatsu*) and set expressions in particular situations is mandatory (McVeigh 1997: 44–45, 56–57). The four top-scoring students in each year carry responsibility for the behaviour and discipline of their entire peer group, and the dux has the heaviest burden, being expected to pass on all messages from above and to accompany any classmate who commits a perceived misdemeanour when she goes to apologise to seniors according to a strictly prescribed formula. 'Language symbolised everything,' writes Amami Yūki of her mid-1980s experience: 'All of Takarazuka's customs, regulations and lifestyle models were encapsulated within the words [we used]' (Amami 1995: 40–46). In the presence of seniors, for example, all informal conversation is forbidden, and the phrase: '*Shitsurei shimasu*,' used to beg pardon for some kind of real or imagined rudeness, rings out at the beginning and end of every interaction. Denied spontaneity, the real voices of first-years are thus silenced. Their situation is analogous to that of Japanese women in general, who can be seen as 'muted' in relation to men, in the same way that the voices of women elsewhere are typically also silenced or 'muted,' as Edwin Ardener (1972: 135–58; 1975: 19–27) and Shirley Ardener (1978: 9–48) have each argued.

Such discipline is justified by the belief that seniors must prepare their juniors to fit harmoniously into the Revue hierarchy and make a positive contribution to its activities. Forcing them to take collective responsibility for each other's shortcomings encourages each member to forestall behaviour on the part of a peer which might jeopardise the quality of stage performances or stain Takarazuka's reputation for impeccable manners and morality. In his analysis of *senpai–kōhai* (junior versus senior) relationships in school sporting clubs, Yoshio Sugimoto (1997: 122–23, 247) writes of a 'rationale that one can become a good player only after one has formed a submissive personality, willing to follow orders.' The same is arguably true not only of Sugimoto's 'player' but also of an 'actor' in the Takarazuka context. As future stage performers, Takarasiennes-in-training must learn to hide their true feelings: to smile when they are suffering, to appear calm even if seething with anger, and to indicate agreement with a senior even if she says something as irrational as 'crows are white,' to use the clichéd Takarazuka example of a senior's pronouncement that defies common sense. In short, novices must learn to pay lip-service to the notion that seniors are infallible, by using a front (*tatemae*) that conceals their real feelings and beliefs (*honne*).[5]

Though they hated the experience of being subjugated at the Music School, most of my informants agreed that the policy of absolute obedience to seniors was indeed useful in a stage career, and in later life. 'As the school is a gathering-place for people with different personalities, each of whom has led a different life,' says one informant whose career spanned the 1970s and 1980s, the discipline functions as 'a kind of spiritual "levelling of the ground (*ji-narashi*)"' which brings them all back to the same starting-point, so they can develop from there into performing arts professionals' (Informant CL 2001: Q. 2.3). The only dissenter I encountered, who thought the system was 'idiotic (*bakabakashii*),' nevertheless conceded that the habit of paying lip-service to superiors' pronouncements, even when these seemed ludicrous, could be a handy skill to employ in marriage, 'especially in dealing with a mother-in-law' (Informant SS 2001: Q. 2.3).

The above examples notwithstanding, it must be understood that some juniors do love and respect their seniors. One informant recalls thoroughly enjoying her time at the School in the late 1920s, when discipline was apparently not as strict as later, saying: 'Every day was like marshmallow, all fluffy. The seniors all treated us with affection, and we in turn thought of them as our big sisters.' She emphasises the importance of sincere respect, rather than the superficial politeness she believes is engendered by today's rules, explaining:

I think [the School] should be exacting about the performing arts aspect, rather than about unnecessary things. ... [I]t is a good thing to be polite, and as for cleaning, it's also good to keep things clean, but it wasn't forced upon us; we did it of our own volition. It's good to bow, but now, everyone thinks that bowing is a kind of gesture, as if they merely needed to go through the motions of bowing – the bow doesn't come from truly heartfelt respect. In that sense, there isn't the same strictness now [as that which we experienced] (Informant PP 2001: Q. 2.3).

The second year

Though competitive striving for personal reward is usually associated more with orthodox masculinity than with orthodox femininity (Devor 1989: 50, 164, n. 19), the second year in the Music School is undoubtedly characterised by a race to graduate with high marks. Ex-performers have told me of pins being hidden in ballet shoes and leotards being stolen by classmates to inconvenience their rivals during the second year. Todoroki Yū (debut 1985) speaks of the facial expressions of all of her classmates, 'even the gentle-looking ones,' growing *kitsui* (severe) in their senior year at the School, but becoming 'a little more childlike again' when they entered the Company (cited in One's Co. Ltd 1996: 8). Good grades win starring roles in the two-day graduation performance, the *bunkasai* (cultural festival), at which students vie to impress their faces and talent upon both the Revue Administration and prospective fans.

The School ethos ensures, however, that second-years do not focus entirely upon themselves. Having endured one year of subjugation, they must now enforce discipline upon their juniors. For one informant enrolled in the 1960s, this duty was simply a 'nuisance,' as she wanted to concentrate upon her studies (Informant CL 2001: Q. 2.2). Failure correctly to supervise the class below invites criticism from those more senior in the hierarchy, since the instruction of each group of juniors is the responsibility of those immediately above them. Many rules are perpetuated simply because they are considered as 'tradition,' and peer pressure can prevent a would-be reformer from speaking out against rules she herself had found unreasonable (Informant KT 2001: Q. 2.2). Some seniors, however, do lobby their classmates and School staff to change rules they consider irrational or out-of-date, or decide among themselves not to repeat hated practices that they had endured. In the late 1930s, for example, one informant and her classmates made a conscious decision to stop bullying juniors, because it was 'contrary to the "pure, righteous and beautiful" spirit of Takarazuka' (Informant TH 2001: Q. 2.1, 2.2). Again, in 1988, seniors voted to abolish the dozens of ugly, metal hairclips that short-haired students had formerly been required to use, to prevent hair covering any part of the face (Amami 1995: 56). At the Music School early in the new millennium, I observed that all budding *otokoyaku*, even first-years, now sculpted their short hair with gel, making them look much more mature, masculine (or at least androgynous) and attractive than when the hairclips were compulsory. Would-be *musumeyaku*, on the other hand, continued to braid their long hair, making them appear more childish than their *otokoyaku* classmates.

Notwithstanding a few seniors' good intentions, other examples show that some second-years are determined to be as strict and fearsome as possible towards hapless new entrants, as a kind of 'payback' for the treatment they received the previous year (e.g. Tamai 1999: 21; Asanagi 1997: 105). In one sense, however, the second-years are also 'indulged' in their tyranny by their juniors. The authority of seniors can be destroyed by group resistance, as evidenced by the actions of the 1973 intake of students to the Music School, who made history by refusing to be cowed by the intimidation of their immediate seniors. According to retired *musumeyaku* Wakaba Hiromi, then a first-year, the class planned and executed a mass escape from school, to avoid a scheduled *hansei-kai* (a meeting called regularly by second-years to 'grill' juniors for their transgressions). One first-year was hurt when she fell downstairs in the rush to flee (Wakaba 1996: 143–44). Teachers and senior students were astounded, and the second-years apparently burst into tears when they realised that all forty-five first-years had defied them. According to Tsurugi Miyuki, a senior at the time, the shame of having their authority thus challenged clung to her class for five or six years into the future (cited in Wakaba 1996: 144).

The cleaning regimen

The stereotypical role of women as cleaners of the household is echoed in the strict cleaning regimen imposed upon students at the Takarazuka Music School, where the unwritten curriculum assumes similar, if not greater, importance compared with the timetable of classes. Cleaning forms a significant part of this non-artistic curriculum. After the entrance ceremony welcoming them to the

School, even before a single dance step is executed or a note sung, new trainee Takarasiennes have their janitorial duties demonstrated to them in great detail by the second-years, as first-years are expected meticulously to clean the interior and immediate exterior of the Music School before class every morning from Monday to Saturday.[6] Such duties are not unique to Takarazuka, but they are enforced in an unusually rigid manner. For example, throughout primary and secondary education in Japan, most schools also expect students to undertake daily cleaning, but in a far less scrupulous manner than at the Music School. Nor is Takarazuka's cleaning regimen unique among performing arts academies in the world. The rival all-female revue company OSK, for example, also expected first-year students at its training institution, OSK Nippon kageki gakkō, to clean the school each day under seniors' supervision.[7] Now that the latter school has closed, however, the Takarazuka Music School is probably unparalleled in the strictness of this aspect of its unwritten curriculum.

In her first semester, each junior is given hands-on instruction by her seniors in the labour-intensive methods used to clean the particular area she is assigned for the entire year, then is left to herself to perfect the prescribed 'choreography' of each task, with an economy of movement and exactness similar to the actions of the traditional tea ceremony. Floors must be swept and mopped, then gummed tape is used to remove every last particle of dust. Windows are polished inside and out, their invisibility apparently luring many a bird to its death, and grime is swept from window-frames with paintbrushes. Cotton buds clean every surface and cranny of piano keys and the consoles of sound-mixing equipment; and toilets are rendered spotless, to the extent that 'one could rub one's cheek against them' (Robertson 1998b: 55). The results are inspected by second-years, who may order the cleaning to be done all over again if they are dissatisfied or churlish. Vacuum cleaners and other potentially labour-saving devices are not used, ostensibly because they are not sufficiently 'character-building.' This attitude echoes the pronouncement of a company president's wife on the merits of a toilet-cleaning roster for young female factory workers: 'Cleaning up after someone is good practice in preparing to be a wife' (Matsumoto 1976: 65). According to Japanese folk wisdom, pregnant women should energetically scrub toilets, supposedly to ensure the birth of a beautiful baby, although the connection seems spurious. Trainee Takarasiennes are likewise exhorted to be diligent at cleaning for the sake of the beauty of their spirits.

The Takarazuka cleaning regimen can also be interpreted as an initiation rite necessary for gaining admittance into the exclusive 'family' or *uchi* (in-group) made up of more experienced Music School students and Revue performers. It takes a year for these newcomers to achieve true membership of this family, to become, as Dorinne Kondo (1990: 141–42) puts it in another context, 'the "us" facing outward to the world.' The *uchi* that is the Music School is akin to a domestic domain, with the first-years resembling new brides, under the thumb of second-years who behave like mothers-in-law. Here, as in the traditional Japanese household (see Smith 1987: 17–18), the physical environment and mood are largely controlled by senior women, even though their authority might extend only as far as the front gate. The thoroughness of the cleaning also serves to differentiate Takarazuka from the outside world in general (*soto*), both physically and spiritually. In her discussion of the concepts of *uchi* and *soto* in relation to the home in contemporary Japan, Emiko Ohnuki-Tierney (1984: 21–22) points out that dirt, germs and disease are associated with the outside world, and cleanliness with the interior of the home, or *uchi*. In the Music School case, however, the cleaning regimen undertaken by beginning students seems not only to remove visible grime, but also symbolically to banish the unseen 'impurity' of the world outside Takarazuka, ridding the School of undesirable influences so that all students can study in an unsullied atmosphere, while simultaneously instilling the socially-prescribed, feminine virtues of meekness, diligence and perseverance in its participants. The first-years can be seen as the ideal group to undertake such a mission, as they occupy a marginal position because of their newness to the 'in-group,' and thus constitute a buffer between the 'sullied' quotidian world and their more refined seniors, who are almost ready in body, heart and mind to join the Revue Company proper.

Music School discipline, including the cleaning, is often the focus of magazine articles and television documentaries produced for both domestic and overseas audiences, and the practices featured in these somewhat sensationalised articles and documentaries are usually assumed by the general public to have a long history, echoing the strict atmosphere known to have existed in many ordinary schools before the end of World War II. However, as writer Kawasaki Kenko and others have pointed out (e.g. Kawasaki 1999: 59), the so-called 'tradition' of scrupulous cleaning by junior students is a quite recent phenomenon, dating only from around 1970. This date coincides with the introduction of military-style drilling, as noted above.

Hired cleaners maintained the school during the pre-war experience of one informant, who was astounded to see present-day first-years on television removing dust from piano keys with cotton swabs (Informant MH 2001: Q. 2.3). No cleaning was done in another informant's initial year, around 1960. 'There weren't any strict rules at all. It was simply fun,' she says (Informant EF 2001: Q. 2.1).

(New) gender roles and new names

Once accepted into the Music School, a present-day student will have to reappraise the gender socialisation she has undergone as a child and adolescent, and begin learning to exaggerate certain aspects of femininity if she aims to play female roles, or, if she is to specialise in male roles, even to unlearn some of the behaviours that she has been taught are appropriate for a girl. Robertson (1998: 9) suggests that graduation from the Music School marks a Takarasienne's 'public debut as a specialist in one gender.' In Takarazuka's early decades, though, according to my oldest informants' reminiscences, training did not prepare students specifically to play male or female parts. Even in the late 1950s, one informant explained, the whole course was devoted to nothing but 'the real basics (*kiso*)' of singing, ballet and so on, and this same informant expressed gratitude for the solid grounding that she received in dancing and singing during her training (Informant SS 2001: Q. 2.8). At that time, the School did not make aspiring *otokoyaku* around the age of seventeen or eighteen sing in a low *jigoe* (chest voice)[8] to simulate masculinity, as it apparently does now, but expected all students to sing using a higher 'head voice (*uragoe*),' irrespective of their future stage gender.

As males typically are taller than females, height is the main criterion for deciding which stage gender a girl will adopt: aspiring *otokoyaku* generally need to measure a minimum of one hundred and sixty-five centimetres tall, but other factors, including personality, looks, body type, voice pitch and individual preference, are also taken into account. Now, according to the yearbook *Takarazuka otome 2007*, performers such as Asanagi Mana (178 cm) and some half-dozen others boast heights of 175 cm or more, so the bottom-line for *otokoyaku* is likely to rise accordingly.

Some students, moreover, grow so much during their enrolment that they have to switch from *musumeyaku* to *otokoyaku* at some point, as did Asaji Saki, who started off at the maximum height for a female-role player, the role to which she originally aspired

(Tsuganezawa and Natori 1997: 69). One informant of mine who was enrolled in the mid-1980s admired *otokoyaku* from afar, but would have preferred to become one of 'the pretty ones' who played opposite them, as she had learnt ballet for many years and yearned to wear the beautiful costumes of the female-role players. She 'cried and cried' when her classmates pointed out that she was too tall, and had an *otokoyaku*'s figure. When she subsequently had her long hair cut short after years of growing it, she brought the severed tresses home to keep for a few days, doubtless being reluctant to leave them on the hairdresser's floor (Informant KT 2001: Q. 2.5).

Most formal gender-role training takes place in drama classes, when female-role players now wear the skirt of their regular uniform, while male-role players don track-suit trousers – though this has not always been the case, as illustrated by a 1970s magazine photograph (*Pacific Friend* 1975: 21) showing two students in skirts rehearsing a love scene, one trying to embrace the other. Both look self-conscious and awkward. Each student probably learns as much, if not more, however, by observing how fully-fledged Takarasiennes play their various gendered roles on stage; and by practising makeup and costuming for her own and her classmates' amusement. Students attend Revue performances in class groups as part of the curriculum, but many also attend in their spare time. Finally, at the annual February graduation performance, second-year students perform in some items in their stage gender, though they are still inexperienced and cannot yet be called 'specialists.' By graduation, the length of their hair signals their intention to become a *musumeyaku* or *otokoyaku*, but it is still a marker of potential for specialisation rather than a *fait accompli* (Informant PZ 2001: Q. 3.4). In the first year at the school, at least, hair length seems to be more related to convenience than future stage gender. It is usually not until months after graduates have finished their debut season and begun their 'apprenticeship' with one of the five troupes that their stage gender and their hairstyle is truly settled, as the next chapter will show.

As well as deciding on the gender she will play on the Takarazuka stage, each Music School student must also choose the professional or stage name (*geimei*) by which she will be formally addressed after her debut. Three suggestions must be submitted to the Administration, six months before graduation. A name will be rejected if too similar to that of a current or past member (except when a daughter assumes her mother's stage name), too difficult to read, or too close to the student's real name, which will henceforth

be used only for strictly private or legal purposes. Nowadays, a girl
might devise a *geimei* herself, consult with family members, ask a
mentor, or even pay a fortune-teller to choose a lucky combination of
symbols. She will also decide upon a nickname, often in consultation
with her classmates and family, for use by her peers, fellow troupe
members and fans alike, to signify familiarity and affection. Many
fans seem to pride themselves on their comprehensive knowledge
of performers' nicknames, which are published along with other
biographical details of each performer in the annual *Takarazuka
otome*.[9]

In the early years of the Takarazuka Girls' Opera, Kobayashi
Ichizō assigned a *geimei* to each young performer from *Ogura
hyakunin isshu*, a thirteenth-century poetry anthology familiar to
children and adults because of its use in a traditional New Year card
game. Certain poems were exhaustively mined for possible name
combinations, reflecting Kobayashi's 'literary tastes' (Takagi 1976:
56).[10] Later, names took their inspiration from various sources, such
as nature, literature, geography, history or a list of admired persons.
A few Takarasienne 'surnames' such as Azuma, Asō, Shirakawa
and Nakahara are not unusual in the general population, but most
names are immediately recognizable as invented, including those of
Mahoroba Yū (debut 1991) and Ayura Kao (1994), both with *hiragana*
surname and *kanji* given name. The Western name 'Michelle' was
the inspiration for the name Mishi Eru (1971), which means literally
'to obtain a beautiful poem.' Koshiro Miyako, a 1970s *otokoyaku*
star, apparently chose her stage name to reflect her birth in China
to Japanese parents, the characters for Koshiro (ancient walled city/
castle) evoking the image of the Great Wall of China (*Takarazuka
otome* 1970: 43).[11] In 2000, the nickname for the US flag, 'Stars and
Stripes' (*seijō* in Japanese), inspired the stage name of Seijō Kaito,
who attended American School (*Takarazuka otome* 2006: 59). There
are limitations on the choice of names, however, for the spirit of the
'*kiyoku, tadashiku, utsukushiku*' motto always rules the choice of
sound and meaning combinations. One extreme example is that of
1979 graduate Kiyo Masami, whose name echoes the motto itself:
kiyo is written with a Chinese character meaning 'pure,' while *masa*
and *mi*, though rendered here in *kana* script, are common readings for
the Chinese characters used to write *tadashi(ku)* and *utsukushi(ku)*,
respectively. Some mischief does occasionally slip past the censors,
however, as in the name of 1980s *otokoyaku* idol Daichi Mao (see
Kihara 1980: 107), which, an ex-Takarasienne friend of mine once
gleefully pointed out, becomes a risqué pun after subtle alteration

to '*daitchimaō*,' a colloquial contraction of '*daite shimaō* (I'm going to "have" you/him/her).'

Takarazuka stage names usually indicate the female sex, regardless of the stage gender of their owners. There are scattered examples of masculine-sounding 'given names' written in *kanji*, but these are balanced by non-traditional 'surnames,' as in the cases of Katsumi Hiroshi (debut 1971), Mio Hajime (1974) and Nachi Masaru (1975). Some *otokoyaku* nicknames, too, including the mannish 'Tom' for current male-role star Todoroki Yū, certainly suggest masculinity, as did 'Big Brother (*Aniki*)' for the pre-war star, Ashihara Kuniko (Robertson 1998b: 73). Of the twenty performers making their stage debut in 1914, all but three (Ogura Miyuki, Matsuura Moshiho and Shinohara Asaji) assumed professional 'given' names ending in the feminine -*ko*, as in the cases of Kumoi Namiko and Takamine Taeko (the first *otokoyaku*, who starred as Momotarō in the 'fairy-tale opera,' *Donburako*). The percentage of -*ko* names in the general population at that time was nearly thirty per cent less than in Takarazuka, which was seen as a trend-setter in girls' names.[12] In 1920, two performers adopted 'given' names that consisted of masculine-sounding infinitive verbs for the first time: Ashirogi Wataru (to cross) and Makino Noboru (to ascend). In the latter case, however, the use of *hiragana* instead of *kanji* to spell Noboru feminised the name's written appearance, if not its pronunciation.

The popularity of -*ko* endings for Takarasiennes' assumed first names then gradually waned, again ahead of the trend in Japanese society, dwindling to a single example in the 1972 graduating class, none among 1975 and 1976 graduates, then fluctuating between five and zero per year since then, with only seven examples in 2006.[13] The fanciful names chosen by most Takarasiennes apparently continue to mark them as artists with poetic imaginations, who inhabit a different world from that of the general population. The deliberate choice of a masculine-sounding name by an *otokoyaku*, too, marks Takarazuka's divergence from the societal norm for female names.

The years a girl spends preparing to enter the Takarazuka Music School and training there are doubtless crucial in defining her life-course thereafter, even if she chooses not to spend many years as a professional performer. By passing the highly competitive examination to enter the School, she proves to herself and others that she has 'something special,' and, by completing the training and successfully graduating, she also demonstrates a mental and physical strength seldom demanded of a girl her age in Japan.

Although each Music School student is different, each undergoes a normalising experience at the School, which bonds her to every other Takarazuka performer from the past nine-and-a-half decades. The exacting discipline of the first year enables members of each graduating class to execute a perfectly-synchronised display of dancing at their professional debut, in identical costumes, makeup and headdresses which obliterate individual differences. The following chapter will show that such beginners then follow divergent paths as they gain experience in the performance of gender on the Takarazuka stage, in its all-female community that constitutes a distorted mirror of the gender norms of wider society.

4 Performing Gender on and off Stage

The carefully-calculated portrayal of the different genders by all-female casts in Takarazuka has probably brought the Company as much renown, and sometimes notoriety, as any intrinsic merit of the singing, dancing or dramatic productions. The Revue, through its performances and in other ways, exposes and exploits the artificiality of assigning gender on the basis of biological sex, while insisting that its performers are orthodox, feminine women in private life. In the absence of real males, Takarasiennes need either to exaggerate their femininity to compensate for the physical limitations of their male-role opposites, or to hide their femaleness and assume the guise of an 'ideal man.' All the while, however, even if they are playing an eighty-year-old 'grandfather,' says one 1990s star, their performance must at all costs be 'beautiful,' 'colourful' and imbued with 'dreams' (Mori 1993: 67). Thus every performer helps to construct a unique Takarazuka version of masculinity and femininity.

Takarazuka itself is like an alternative reality, existing beside, but not really being part of, Japanese society in general, and the genders it portrays are correspondingly somewhat different from the norm. The totality of the fantasy extends beyond the walls of Takarazuka's theatres into the immediately surrounding areas, which take on an unmistakeable air of theatricality. Signed posters showing ambiguously-gendered performers in stage makeup adorn shops and restaurants, and Takarasiennes in distinctive clothing and hairstyles can often be sighted in the streets. Although Kobayashi and other staff insisted that Takarasiennes revert to 'regular young ladies' as soon as they stepped off stage, there is some inevitable carry-over of stage persona (and 'artificial' gender) into private life, both conscious and unconscious, to back up their stage roles and to feed the fantasies of their fans. All Takarasiennes learn, however, to 'exercise discretion (*kejime o tsukeru*)' as to where, when and how they should reveal their various selves.[1]

Kobayashi himself realised that to the female eye, *otokoyaku* were 'superior to actual men (*otoko ijō*),' precisely because the players were women, whom he called 'supreme connoisseurs of masculine

beauty' (Kobayashi 1955: 467). Over the years, Takarazuka has built
up a body of rules and models for gender performance, reproduced,
revised and augmented by successive generations of performers and
creative staff, and taking into account the changing composition and
tastes of its audience. Its fans, in turn, help promote this 'artificial'
portrayal of gender, by their attempts to influence the performers'
efforts through their support or criticism, as will be further
examined in Chapter Five. This chapter, on the other hand, analyses
the performance of gender by members of the Revue itself.

The task of cultivating the ability specifically and consciously
to manipulate her performance of gender begins on the day a
Takarasienne formally joins the Company. Following her graduation
ceremony at the Takarazuka Music School in the morning, she
attends the Company induction ceremony (*nyūdan shiki*) in the
afternoon, in the process turning from a feared and revered second-
year student, administering discipline and favours according to her
whim in the closed world of the training school, to a member of
the lowest-ranking group in the Revue's huge hierarchical pyramid,
required to obey and show deference to every current and past
performer in the history of Takarazuka, irrespective of individual
ability or popularity. Once out of her school uniform, the inductee,
known as a 'first-year postgraduate (*kenkyūka ichinen*, or *ken-ichi*)'
in keeping with the school metaphor still in use in Takarazuka,
can begin to advertise by way of her appearance and demeanour
how well suited she is not only to playing a male or female role on
the Takarazuka stage, but also to acting the part of the off-stage
Takarasienne, itself an identity often incorporating mixed gender
signals.

Every Revue performer, therefore, creates and selectively uses
at least two, if not three 'faces,' each distinguished mainly by its
emphasis upon masculinity, femininity or, especially in the case of
an off-stage *otokoyaku*, a kind of androgyny. The most consciously
assumed gendered 'face' is that of the character a Takarasienne
enacts within the confines of the proscenium arch, but the typical
performer seems obliged to control another, 'public' face, which
she shows to fans and the Takarazuka-savvy general populace when
she identifies herself as a Takarasienne. An *otokoyaku*, for example,
will almost always present herself in trousers rather than a skirt or
dress, and a *musumeyaku* will usually choose frilly, lacy off-stage
wear that is 'cute' rather than chic or sexually provocative. As many
of my informants have commented, a Takarazuka performer must
be aware of 'being seen' wherever she may be recognised, and

modify her behaviour to reflect well upon the Revue's reputation as well as her own. In addition, she may also keep yet another 'private' face for herself, her intimate friends and family, or, on the other hand, for total strangers who are not aware of her occupation. This 'third face' may be more 'normally' feminine, androgynous or even masculine than that she reveals as a Takarasienne. One informant who plays only female roles on stage, for example, states that her private wardrobe includes trousers (Informant WF 2001: Q. 3.6), while an ex-Takarasienne friend commented in January 2001 that one of her Music School classmates was reputed to be 'a real *ossan* (seedy, middle-aged man)' in private life.

In this chapter, I first explore the stylised theatrical techniques (*kata*) employed for portraying specific gender roles on the Takarazuka stage, tracing the changing aspects of appearance, behaviour, attitude and language deemed appropriate at various stages of the Revue's history for each gender role, as performed on its stage and within the Company's confines. I will show that stage genders constitute edited or exaggerated versions of common societal conceptions of womanhood and manhood. I will then argue that Takarasiennes need to resort to *kata* for producing gendered performance, not only because they need to use readily-identifiable gender markers to signal to the audience which gender they are portraying, but also because their scant worldly experience means they must learn gender portrayal in an 'artificial' manner. Although Takarasiennes are all exposed to varying degrees of socialisation as girls during their childhood and early adolescence, their lack of life experience in the adult world outside the Revue means that they are almost as ill-prepared to play a stereotypical woman on the Takarazuka stage as to play a man.

Forms and techniques of gender mimicry

To create appropriate representations of male and female characters on the Takarazuka stage, performers largely rely upon one or more of three methods – the copying of traditional *kata* that signify masculinity or femininity in a theatrical context, the observation of real people in society, and the exercise of imagination. Like many 'traditions,' *kata* have been invented, adapted and discarded at various times, and are mainly learned by mimicking the clothing, makeup, voice, gaze, posture, gait, singing/dancing style and mood of seniors in the Revue. Many Takarazuka *kata*, however, have become stylised to the extent that they no longer relate to 'real' gender in mainstream society, and have meaning only within the theatre's fantasy world. There is a similarity here with Kabuki, in which the portrayal of most stock characters is even more dependent upon *kata*, which are usually based upon the manner of acting established by famous players of the past.

The *kata* method of teaching and learning gender portrayal in Takarazuka is in fact similar to that by which artistic skills in such genres as Japanese classical dance, the tea ceremony, flower arrangement and so on are transmitted from one generation to the next, in a hierarchical structure headed by a supreme teacher known as the *iemoto* (see Hendry 1987: 153–54). Several of the characteristics of the *iemoto* system identified by P.G. O'Neill are reflected in the way Takarazuka seniors commonly pass on their skills to their juniors: 'instruction always consist[s] essentially of demonstration by the teacher without explanation, and then of minute imitation by the pupil'; communication up (and down) the hierarchical pyramid takes place in a series of steps, through representatives of each year-group who are responsible for the dissemination of information, instructions and reprimands from above to their peers and juniors, and who also speak on behalf of their year-group to higher ranks; and junior performers are expected to cultivate 'a strong sense of duty and obligation,' as well as 'gratitude' to their teachers and superiors (O'Neill 1984: 637–38). In the Takarazuka case, the latter are usually the more experienced members of each troupe, especially the stars and older by-players whose stage skills, beauty, charisma and personal warmth inspire fledgling Takarasiennes. Loyalty to one's troupe is foremost, but is inseparable from loyalty and obligation to Takarazuka itself,[2] as well as from reverence for the memory of its founder, Kobayashi Ichizō, the spiritual patriarch of the organisation.

It takes time for Takarasiennes to learn how to portray exaggerated gender roles on stage – many more years for an *otokoyaku* than a *musumeyaku*, given the latter's head-start in femininity afforded by the socialisation most undergo during childhood. In the case of male-role players, a decade or more of practising their art is deemed necessary for internalising the necessary techniques to the extent that these can be applied automatically. Less-experienced Takarasiennes are probably only able to execute their highly gender-marked roles with sufficient skill and panache precisely because of the limited time during which they need sustain character on stage. In the opinion of one former *otokoyaku*, the male-role players are different from biological males who have to 'do' masculinity permanently, twenty-four hours a day, and who therefore have 'lots of problems.' The *otokoyaku* version of masculinity, she claims, is the more beautiful for being concentrated into just three hours at a time (Informant NK 2001: Q. 3.8). Most women who know Takarazuka, whether they be performers or fans, seem to express a preference for *otokoyaku* over 'real' men, precisely because of this beauty. I doubt, however, whether many women would agree with the corollary that the exaggerated femininity of Takarazuka female-role players makes the latter preferable to 'real' women, as they are often portrayed as merely decorative foils for the *otokoyaku*.

Through the use of *kata*, novice performers compare themselves to the models furnished by their more-experienced seniors, in what is actually a process of mirroring. The image of the ideal Takarasienne is one to which all performers aspire, impossible though it may be to achieve. One *onnayaku* informant claims that the example of the stars who 'handed down the Takarazuka dream' to her as their successor has been too dazzling for her to emulate, even after more than a decade as a Company member. 'I still feel as if I'm a long way from becoming a Takarazuka person like them,' she confessed (Informant RX 2001: Q. 3.5). Even a 'model' female-role player, though, is herself forced into the position of a mirror, rather than existing for herself, because a *musumeyaku* is not supposed to shine more gloriously than her male counterpart. The *raison d'être* of a female-role player in Takarazuka is to do everything she can to ensure that the male-role players always look good in reflection. This parallels the more general situation of women in society in Japan and elsewhere, who have long been expected to present an image of being less capable, less intelligent, and less creative than men. As Sally Cline and Dale Spender convincingly argue, '[i]f men seek to look bright then women can assist them by feigning foolishness...[W]omen learn to hide their lights under a bushel, to step back so that men appear more prominent and positive' (Cline and Spender 1988: 41). Robert Smith observes that women in Japan are 'conceived to serve an auxiliary function, albeit a crucially important one' (Smith 1987: 3). To the majority of female fans and performers, therefore, the pretty, cloyingly sweet and dependent *musumeyaku* may be too painful a reminder of their own powerlessness to win much sympathy or affection. Usually considerably younger than her male partner, the Takarazuka female-role player appears even more childish because of her stage gender. As Erica Burman notes (1995: 54), in a general context, 'maturity is equated with masculinity...[T]he competent male model needs the incompetent female for its demonstration, just as the master needs the slave to constitute and maintain his lordly status.'

If the *musumeyaku* can be likened to a mirror, a surface against which the *otokoyaku* bounces 'his' image of ideal masculinity, then it can also be presumed that the typical *otokoyaku* is a narcissist. If an *otokoyaku* is successful in the quest to create the beautiful image of an ideal, other-gendered lover, then 'she' herself, as a woman, might very well become besotted with the imaginary male 'she' sees reflected in the metaphorical mirror of her on-stage partner, or indeed in the real mirror into which she gazes before stepping out on stage.

Looking the part: physical *kata*

The illusion of masculinity or femininity is primarily achieved by clothing the bodies of the actors to hide, reveal or exaggerate their female flesh, but the act begins with the body beneath. Slimness now seems to be a prerequisite for retaining a position in Takarazuka, whichever the gender role. Most performers look underweight for their height, and some are extremely thin. Several of my acquaintances in the Revue claim that stage lighting and costumes make bodies look fatter on stage than off. In past decades there have been a few conspicuously plump performers, such as Mizuho Yōko (who played Mammy in the 1974 season of *Gone with the Wind*). One of my informants (SS 2001), an *onnayaku* who specialised in singing until her retirement in the early 1970s, confided in an aside that she had been warned by the Administration that she was 'getting too fat.' Another female-role singer, Takamiya Sachi, also active in the early 1970s, reportedly started to watch her diet after being advised by the *otokoyaku* star Maho Shibuki that 'a *musumeyaku* must have a beautiful body-line' (cited in Ueda 1974: 72).

Even during rehearsal, gender differences are emphasised by players' choice of clothing and hairstyle. Cast members practise using their own clothes, in one of two rehearsal rooms whose floors are marked to show the dimensions of the theatre stage, and in which floor-to-ceiling mirrors cover one wall corresponding to the position of the audience. Many dance studios around the world probably share this feature, but the mirrors have an additional function in Takarazuka – to show each Takarasienne how successfully she is portraying her stage gender without the aid of greasepaint, body-enhancing costumes, wigs and microphones. Each troupe (*kumi*) claims it has its own distinctive '*kumi* fashion,' but it is common to see *otokoyaku* wearing a towel around the neck, tucked into a loose top to disguise the breasts, a sweater tied around the waist and hanging down to hide the buttocks, thick, dark-coloured tights, leggings or 'sweat pants,' lots of dark, solid colours, and short, loose hair. *Musumeyaku*, on the other hand, usually don long or knee-length skirts over a coloured leotard (often pinned or stitched into a V-shape at the cleavage to emphasise the bust) and flesh-coloured tights, and wear their long hair in a bun or ponytail. At the final full run-through (*hon-dōshi*) of each production in the rehearsal hall before dress rehearsals in the theatre proper, however, when I was preparing to translate the script for the Grand Theatre's 'English Earphone' service, I frequently observed performers clad in rehearsal clothes probably chosen purposefully to resemble significant aspects of their characters' actual stage costumes and accessories. Senior members of the Revue Administration attend these occasions, and doubtless performers are aware that their appearance may win them a better role in future, if they make efforts in the rehearsal hall to 'look the part.'

Ever since *otokoyaku* Kadota Ashiko shed her long tresses in 1932, hair length has been the most immediate symbol of chosen secondary gender. One of my informants, a retired performer, called the growing of hair 'an expression of will (*ishi hyōji*)' to be recognised as a woman, and an invitation to directorial assistants (who are in charge of choosing players of minor characters) to cast the individual concerned in female roles (Informant PZ 2001: Q. 3.4).

Takarazuka's so-called 'Violet Code' of unwritten taboos places restrictions on the representation of adult female sexuality on stage, so a *musumeyaku*'s womanly features are de-emphasised to a certain extent. In contrast to the quite suggestive costumes of the first Paris-style revue in 1927, one now sees no extremely plunging necklines or bulging breasts; midriffs and navels are almost always covered with flesh-coloured mesh; seemingly-bare legs are actually veiled in flesh-coloured or fishnet stockings; and leotards with high-cut legs are always worn over thick tights. A *musumeyaku*'s womanliness is most obvious in her shoulders, arms and neck, for these are the parts most often displayed bare, while those of her male-role counterpart are swathed in costume. A *musumeyaku* is also likely to sew extra padding to the bodice of her costumes, if she believes that her breasts are too small.

The female bodies of *otokoyaku* also must be disguised for them to play their roles convincingly, and, in some cases, to give such performers a feeling of security as they dare to impersonate a male before thousands of spectators, according to Ōura Mizuki (cited in Zimmerman 1989: 7). Players' frames are often slight, and must be considerably augmented by the judicious use of padding incorporated in specially-cut costumes, to compensate for their narrow shoulders and often bony chests. Former writer/director Kamura Kikuo notes that a mannish upper body shape (known as an 'upside-down triangle') was achieved in the early years of the Revue by use of broad shoulder pads, combined with a corset to hide the bulge of breasts and pull in the buttocks. A high waistline also contributed to what Kamura describes as 'an attractive silhouette like that of a Western male' (Kamura 1984: 68). Large-breasted *otokoyaku* flatten their chests by binding them, or wearing a tight, specially-made sleeveless undergarment of calico-like fabric, known in Takarazuka jargon as a *gakuya juban* (dressing-room undershirt). I was shown one example which was sewn and subtly embroidered by the owner's principal fan; it overlapped across the chest and fastened with ties at the waist.

It is interesting that a Caucasian model of masculinity, epitomised by the dandy gentleman in an evening suit, should have been chosen in preference to a Japanese model, which would have meant wearing a kimono. This is perhaps due to a perception by performers and their audiences that Japanese men appear less masculine than Western men because of their comparatively slight build, and the fact that the basic shape of the kimono, a gown-like garment, is similar irrespective of the sex of the wearer (see Takeda 1994: 217–51). When Takarazuka *otokoyaku* do play Japanese men in kimono, they achieve an illusion of masculinity by tightly binding their breasts, and padding their midriffs so they can wear their *obi* sash low on their hips. They may also augment their height by wearing so-called 'secret *tabi*,' a variation on the traditional split-toed socks, with the addition of subtly built-in heel lifts. In Western-style productions, on the other hand, high-heeled boots are the most common footwear for *otokoyaku*. The boots combine masculine and feminine elements, covering the instep in a mannish way, but with far slimmer heels than regular men's footwear. These heels, though, are in turn cleverly camouflaged by high-waisted trousers cut longer at the back than at the front – a style originally devised by early *otokoyaku* star Kasugano (1987: 98) – and stirrups which pass under the heel prevent the trousers from riding up, further ensuring a long, smooth line. However, as men are stereotypically taller than women, ironically, it is often the *otokoyaku* who wears the higher heels, while her *musumeyaku* partner, if relatively tall herself, usually resorts to wearing flat pumps, or even to bending her knees when the pair is standing together.

Sounding the part: voice *kata*

The first male-role player in the 1914 debut of the Girls' Opera surely did not imagine that her successors would win such public adulation for their portrayal of masculinity on stage. She may have made a swashbuckling impression as the folk-tale hero, Momotarō (Peach Boy), but she reportedly sang in soprano. The early performers were very young, and their voices were correspondingly immature, so even the *otokoyaku* used their own girlish pitch for singing and speaking. Until the introduction of microphones in 1934,[3] there was an additional acoustic reason for male-role players to sing in a much higher key than their modern-day counterparts: without mechanical amplification, women's low singing voices apparently lacked the volume to carry to the back of the third-floor seats in the Grand Theatre, according to Kasugano (1987: 96). One ex-*onnayaku* informant comments that popular *otokoyaku* from the 1930s–50s such as Kasugano, Ashihara Kuniko (1928–39), Akashi Teruko (1945–62) and Yodo Kaoru (1947–66) indeed all sang in high 'operatic' voices (*uragoe*) (Informant SS 2001: Q. 3.11).

By the 1960s, however, male-role stars such as Nachi Wataru (1953–68) and Uchinoe Noboru (1954–67) were using their so-called 'chest voice (*jigoe*),'[4] suppressing its tendency to change into falsetto on higher notes, and most *otokoyaku* now force their voice into as low a register as possible. This process is often destructive and irreparable, as it is achieved by such harsh means as cigarette-smoking and drinking copious amounts of alcohol (both technically illegal until the age of twenty, but apparently widespread even among younger Takarazuka performers, especially *otokoyaku*) (Ichiro, cited in Singer 1996: 177; Hyuga 1992: 110–20); deliberate shouting and growling; or not resting the larynx when the performer has a cold or throat infection. Kasugano (1987: 102), for one, found her voice irreparably 'broken' due to overuse during an illness affecting her throat. *Otokoyaku* Mori Keaki found that her over-used throat eventually baulked at producing the 'beautiful/clean voice' (*kirei-na koe*) of which she had formerly been proud, so she then decided to concentrate upon conveying the 'heart' of the lyrics rather than worrying about the compromised musical quality of her singing (Mori 1993: 58). Unlike in real opera, a 'broken' or unpolished voice in a Takarazuka *otokoyaku* is not necessarily a great disadvantage to her career, as it probably contributes to the illusion of masculinity she tries to project. Female-role players, on the other hand, must usually sing in an extra high register to compensate for the limitations of their male-role counterparts' voices. This, too, can be hard on the throat, but they cannot afford to 'crush (*tsubusu*)' their voices as can the *otokoyaku*. The renowned mezzo-soprano Sasa Junko (1959–74), for example, apparently kept a humidifier running while she slept at night to prevent dry air from damaging her throat, presumably during the winter months (cited in Ueda 1974: 69–70).

There are occasions, however, when specialists in one stage gender are called upon to sing in a register usually expected of the opposite gender, although this is generally limited to supporting players or veterans rather than current or upcoming stars. An *otokoyaku* with a powerful, 'uncrushed' voice and large vocal range such as current *senka* member Itsuki Chihiro (1973–), for example, sometimes is assigned to provide 'womanly' sung accompaniment to dance numbers. A few female-role specialists have the chance to develop their lower register after their stage gender has become fixed, such as one informant still in the Company, who chose to specialise in female roles because she had learned to sing as a soprano, but has recently discovered her ability to sing low; she now realises that she could have been an *otokoyaku* if she had received the appropriate training early on (Informant WF 2001: Q. 2.9). Another female-role player with exceptional vocal skill, Izumo Aya (1983–), even sang a comic 'duet' with herself on stage in 1993, taking male and female parts in alternate verses (cited in *Kageki* 1993: 82–83). Temporary gender-switching based upon voice *kata*, as in the above examples, is thus employed for particular dramatic effect, or to showcase individual versatility.

Gender in language: sociolinguistic *kata*

Another important method of portraying gender on the Takarazuka stage is through the selective use of linguistic devices available to speakers of Japanese. By calling upon the audience's familiarity with stereotypes of 'women's language' or 'men's language,'[5] writer/directors and performers can signal the gender of the person speaking or singing, as well as the latter's relationship to characters with whom 'he' or 'she' interacts. Such gender-marking linguistic elements underlie and reinforce the physical, external *kata* of femininity and masculinity adopted by the players. From the very beginning of the rehearsal period, when the cast gathers for the first reading of the script, gender divisions among characters are clear-cut in terms of speech, as the Japanese dialogue can employ a number of devices, including syntactical elements; vocabulary; levels of directness, politeness, intonation and so on, to signal the gender of the speaker and her/his status vis-à-vis other people to whom the words are addressed, or to whom they refer. Even if male-role players do not use particularly low voices, therefore, their very words will incorporate clues to the gender they are performing.

The gender-marked language incorporated by Takarazuka writer/directors into their scripts thus contributes significantly to the artificial representation of gender by Takarasiennes. Such writers' original intentions are sometimes subverted, however, by the unauthorised ad-libbing that often creeps into performances, especially at the final performance of a season, usually to the delight of audiences, who enjoy the often gender-bending subterfuge of such moments, when, for example, a supposedly male character momentarily assumes a girlish voice and uses feminine-sounding Japanese, or vice versa, to provoke laughter. 'Masculine' language features in Japanese include pronouns marked in contemporary standard Japanese as 'rough,' or at least not very polite, such as *ore/boku* for 'I' (feminine *atashi*, gender-neutral/humble *watashi/watakushi*), and *kisama/omae/kimi* for 'you' (feminine *anata*, which often has the added nuance of 'dear,' or use of a name plus title); the frequent use of plain verb forms instead of polite, honorific or humble forms, as in *iku* (to go) in place of *ikimasu/irasshaimasu/mairimasu*, respectively; sentences ending in the copula *da* (feminine *na no*), the question tag *ka* after a plain-form verb (feminine *no* or –*te* verb ending, with rising intonation), the sentence-final particles *zo, ze, nā* (feminine *wa, yo, ne*); and vocabulary items such as *kuu* (to eat) and *umai* (tasty/skilful) instead of the neutral words *taberu* and *oishii/jōzu*.[6]

Sociolinguistic features that indicate gender, which intrinsically tend to position males as superior to and more direct than females, are employed in all Takarazuka scripts, irrespective of the geographical setting and the supposed ethnicity of the characters. Thus, even when the characters are portrayed as 'American' and are assumed to be speaking 'English,' for example, their body language follows Japanese custom (such as pointing to the nose when meaning 'I,' and bowing in greeting) and the dialogue itself is in Japanese. Accordingly, there are many nuances particular to the Japanese stereotypical view of gender-appropriate language and behaviour. In *Bei shiti burūsu* (Bay city blues, 1993), for instance – an original musical set in a fictional American metropolis, by in-house writer/director Koike Shūichirō – most lines can be readily identified as spoken by male or female characters, as shown in the following (Koike 1993: 26), with gender-specific elements indicated in bold type:

> Leonardo: *Sō **ka**? **Omae** interi **da** kara **nā**. Anmari kangae-sugin **na** yo.* (You don't say? You're a nerd, that's why. Don't think too hard!)

In the above brief speech, the speaker has advertised his masculinity, familiarity and superior status to the listener by a string of features: the omission of a copula before the interrogative particle *ka*, the familiar copula *da*, the rough, condescending or familiar second-person referent *omae*, the final particle *nā*, truncated negative ending of *sugin*, brusque imperative *na*, and familiar final particle *yo*, which softens the force of the imperative.

By contrast, a female character still projects femininity when she is trying to stop a fight between her husband and stepson, this time with female linguistic features emphasised (from Koike 1993: 36):

> Gloria: *Yamete! **Anata**. Hābī ayamaru **no yo**.* (Darling, stop that! Harvey, you will apologise.)

Here, Gloria employs the feminine imperative *-te* (instead of masculine *-ro*), the familiar, feminine *anata* for 'you, dear,' and the feminine particles *no yo* (masculine equivalent *n da*).

Similar gendered language appears in Takarazuka productions with historical settings, whose scripts have a certain antiquated 'flavour,' yet are written for a general audience. In a 'musical romance' set in the late Tokugawa period, *Wakaki hi no uta wa wasureji* (I'll never forget the songs of the days of our youth),[7] one exchange between the young protagonists Bunshirō (male) and Fuku (female) proceeds as follows, when Fuku attempts to help Bunshirō pull a cart bearing his executed father's corpse up a slope (see Ōzeki 1993a: 68):

> Bunshirō: *Sonna koto o sureba, **omae** no kazoku made utagaware**ru** **zo**.* (If you do such a thing, even your family will come under suspicion.)

Fuku: *Bunshirō-**sama** hitori de wa, ano sakamichi o noborikire**nai** **wa**. (You won't be able to climb that hill all by yourself, Bunshirō.)

Bunshirō: *Ii kara yose!* (I'll be all right, so stop it!)

Fuku: **Fuku** *wa ojisama ni kawaigatte* **itadaita** *n desu mono. Onegai! Tetsudawasete!* (I always enjoyed Uncle [=Bunshirō's father]'s affection, so please let me help!)

Bunshirō: **Suman**. (Can't thank you enough.)

In the above conversation, Bunshirō's masculinity and his slightly superior status (derived from being male and a little older than Fuku, who is of similar class background) is expressed by his use of *omae* (masculine, rough, condescending or familiar: 'you'), *zo* (masculine emphatic particle), *yose* (masculine, plain imperative), and *suman* (masculine, truncated form of negative *nai*). On the other hand, Fuku's femininity and subordinate status are revealed by her substitution of personal names for pronouns, as well as her use of the honorific title *-sama*, the final particle *wa* (feminine, signifying certainty), *itadaita* (humble, 'received a favour'), *desu* (polite copula), and *tetsudawasete* (feminine imperative using the *-te* form of the verb in final position). Her familiarity with Bunshirō, however, is revealed in her use of the plain form negative, *nai*. She speaks of herself in the humble third person, *Fuku* (given name only, minus title) whereas Bunshirō, in other scenes, uses the rough, masculine self-referent *ore*. Later in the play, Fuku becomes a high-ranking official's wife, and Bunshirō is in the position of a subordinate. He then uses extremely humble and polite language to Fuku, but she, in turn, employs polite *-desu/-masu* forms in sentence-final position instead of the plain forms that a male superior would be likely to use to a person of lesser rank (see Ōzeki 1993b: 36).

In typical fashion for girls growing up in Japan, as discussed in the Introduction to this book, most Takarasiennes are taught from childhood to use 'ladylike' language as part of their socialisation. As members of the Revue, they need further to sharpen their awareness of how their choice of words and intonation conveys gender identity, in order not only to reinforce their portrayal of femininity or masculinity on stage, but also to create their own fan-oriented off-stage persona. In the case of many *otokoyaku*, this means incorporating certain masculine elements in their off-stage speech, though most stop well short of sounding brusque or coarse. Mastery of standard Japanese, based on the speech of Tokyo and its hinterland, is essential for all performers in their stage roles, and each Takarasienne is also expected to be able to speak in an appropriately polite, feminine manner in Standard Japanese when representing the Revue upon formal occasions, irrespective of her stage gender. In separate interviews with me, Informant TH (2001: Q. 2.1), and Informant AA (2001: Q. 3.2), both ex-Takarasiennes from a non-standard dialect area, cited the task of mastering Standard Japanese as one of the difficulties they faced as Takarasiennes.

Observing and imitating real/reel-world gender

Takarazuka's repertoire of plays includes many one-off productions for which no precedent exists. In the creation of a new role, each performer will work towards establishing her own original interpretation of her character, with varying degrees of input from the writer/director. While the emulation of seniors is vital for the handing down of stylised *kata* in order to portray the 'ideal' males and females of Takarazuka tradition, Revue performers, like all actors, nevertheless base many of their characterisations upon real people. *Otokoyaku* Mori Keaki, in her first year out of the Music School, was assigned the role of a man who did a lot of running around on stage. Determined to 'become as close as possible to an authentic man,' Mori (1993: 27) consequently began keenly observing how men ran, by staring down at male joggers from her balcony and stopping to observe every detail of the movements of each running man she encountered. One of my interviewees, many decades Mori's senior, also stresses the importance of personal observation, and of building up the skill to play various roles through daily effort:

> If I were given an *otokoyaku* part as a drunkard, for instance, then I'd be on the lookout even when I was walking along the street, to see how drunkards behaved…I was constantly studying [people] (Informant PP 2001: Q. 2.7).

The same speaker goes on to repeat the maxim that actors are *kojiki-bukuro*, literally 'beggar's bags,' in which all the minutiae of life are stored, ready to be pulled out and used when necessary.

Female-role players also look outside the Revue for inspiration in the creation of their characters. 1940s star Otowa Nobuko, for example, was cast in the role of a lively teenaged girl, Midori, in Takarazuka's 1943 dramatisation of Higuchi Ichiyō's 1885–86 short story, 'Takekurabe (Comparing heights).' Otowa apparently had agonised over how to play the part until she observed a female passenger in a suburban train who seemed 'the perfect model' on which to base her characterisation. Otowa went out of her way to follow her 'Midori' for a great distance, even changing trains when her subject did, in order keenly to observe her movements, facial expressions and gestures until satisfied that she had a clear image of how her own version of Midori should look and behave (cited in Ueda 1974: 34–35).

Films, television and the commercial stage also seem to provide much inspiration for players of either stage gender, especially in cases where an appropriate role model cannot be found either in the Takarazuka archive or in the general community. Most Takarasiennes are avid theatre- and film-goers for this reason. Kasugano Yachiyo (debut 1929), one of Takarazuka's definitive *otokoyaku*, writes that Western films were the predominant source of the masculine image she sought for creating her much-adored romantic male persona, after she switched from being a female-role player in her mid-teens (cited in Kōbe Shinbun Hanshin Sōkyoku 1984: 33–34). She also admired the Japanese film actor Hasegawa Kazuo, as a model of 'elegance coexisting with manliness' (Kasugano, cited in Ueda 1971: 64).

Conversely, decades later, the film *The Last Emperor* gave one now-retired informant some idea of how to tackle the challenging role of a Chinese eunuch. The cinematic example was still not sufficient, she said, and no amount of limp-wristed (*nayonayo*) posturing in her regular rehearsal clothes enabled her sufficiently to evoke the character's atmosphere, so she purchased a complete Chinese outfit, including a hat, plus some Western clothes she deemed suitable for the part. As a result, she was reportedly able to 'discard' herself, and 'completely *become* (*narikiru*)' her role (Informant DP 2001: Q. 3.4). Clothing, here, proved to be the crucial element in her characterisation, however stereotyped it may have turned out to be.

Even films with overtly sexual content, which would seem taboo for Takarasiennes because of their contravention of the Revue's tradition of 'purity,' have sometimes provided performers with inspiration for certain roles. Such films as Kurosawa Akira's celebrated *Rashōmon* (1951) and Shima Kōji's *Jūdai no seiten* (Teenagers' Sex Manual, 1953), as well as other sexually explicit films, apparently were avidly watched by one young *otokoyaku*, Uchinoe Noboru, in preparation for her part as a juvenile delinquent in Takarazuka's *Kōkō san-nensei* (High-school senior, 1958). Uchinoe claimed to have had her eyes 'glued to the cinema screen, in order to research the actions of adult men,' and her portrayal of a 'bad boy' gained her 'overwhelming popularity,' at least according to Takarazuka analyst Suzuki Tazuko. The production itself became controversial, Suzuki records, because of a violent lynching scene and an implied sexual assault (1976: 136–37).

Gender switching on the internal and external stage

Ambivalent attitudes seem to exist among performers, the Revue Administration and fans towards the 'true' gender of Takarasiennes.[8] The fact that all of the latter are anatomically female is taken by the majority as enabling each performer to look and behave as a feminine woman off the stage if she wishes, irrespective of her stage gender; and on this basis, it is expected that most performers will eventually retire from the Company, marry and bear children, according to the societal norm for an adult heterosexual woman. This is also reassuring for general audiences, who may not be comfortable with the idea that Takarasiennes might have unconventional sexuality in their personal lives. As Judith Halberstam observes in her discussion of Drag Kings, female entertainers who parody stereotypical masculinity:

> [M]ainstream audiences are interested and fascinated [by women performing masculinity on stage] as long as they are assured that there is a beautiful woman with femininity intact beneath the drag[,] [b]ut when the Drag King is a butch [lesbian], powerful and attractive to straight women as well as to dykes[,]…then those same audiences get rather nervous (Volcano and Halberstam 1999: 138–39).

While most roles in Takarazuka are played 'straight,' some parts call for the parodying of stereotypical masculinity, known in Takarazuka parlance as *kiza* (high-camp) or *kusai* (literally 'reeking') acting by *otokoyaku*, and, more rarely, the comedic mimicry of male appearance and mannerisms by female-role specialists in outlandish costumes and false facial hair, in the occasional revue-type show. Apart from the latter, Takarazuka's *musumeyaku* never take male roles, nor play cross-dressed female characters like the boyish Oscar in *The Rose of Versailles* – Oscar's masculinity apparently can

Plate 3: Martial lovers, Oscar and Andre, in The Rose of Versailles. The cross-dressed Oscar, front right, and her lover Andre, front left, prepare to fight to the death for their ideals. © Takarazuka Revue Company

only be effectively portrayed by a trained *otokoyaku*. The opposite situation sometimes arises, however, when strong, charismatic female characters are required, and *otokoyaku* are cast in such parts. The Revue Administration undoubtedly also capitalises upon the popularity of starring *otokoyaku* by casting them in the most prominent roles, even if this means they play women.

When an *otokoyaku* plays a female role, she must consciously prepare for a metaphorical 'sex change.' When rehearsing to play Scarlett O'Hara in *Gone with the Wind*, for instance, popular *otokoyaku* Migiwa Natsuko (1964–80) apparently began her preparation 'from external appearances' by dressing in colourful long skirts she had had made specially for the part. She was chagrined to be told that she was standing with her feet planted sturdily wide apart during a love scene with a male character, unaware of her mannish stance which had become second nature through years of practice ('Seitenkan ni daiseikō' 1979: 95). Some *otokoyaku* make a permanent switch to female roles. Interestingly, many of them have become top *musumeyaku* stars, examples including Hatsukaze Jun, Wakaba Hiromi and Sugata Haruka. While there are many examples of successful *musumeyaku* who specialise in female roles from the start of their training, the number of ex-*otokoyaku* who become leading female-role players is in fact significant. This suggests that intensive training in male gender portrayal later helps such performers to play a convincing woman, by teaching them to identify and emulate gender stereotypes, in a way that surpasses *musumeyaku* training. *Musumeyaku*, on the other hand, very rarely make the permanent switch to playing male roles. One fairly recent example is that of Asazora Riho (1991–96), who revealed to me that she had kept growing after joining the Company and became too tall to play female roles. Indeed, as recorded in the Revue's yearbooks, her height increased from 165 centimetres in the year of her debut to 167 centimetres three years later, after Asazora became an *otokoyaku* (*Takarazuka otome* 1991: 117; *Takarazuka otome* 1994: 121).

Occasionally, Takarasiennes are permitted by the Administration to perform with other companies on stage, on television or in film, but their participation is strictly controlled by the Takarazuka Company, which benefits from the advertisement value of having its name linked with that of the performer in programme notes and cast lists, which reach a much wider audience than its own regular patrons. These external appearances usually involve playing female roles with a mixed cast, necessitating a different acting style from that which the performer herself employs on the Revue stage, whether she is usually a female- or male-role player. Sometimes, such appearance in a television series is a precursor to rapid promotion to top star status within Takarazuka for female-role players, although not, interestingly, for male-role performers, as we will see below. In at least two examples from past decades, those of Haruka Kurara and Ayu Yūki, a temporary departure from the Takarazuka stage for television work marked young performers' transition from *otokoyaku* to *musumeyaku*. I suggest that the comparatively naturalistic character of their television roles – Haruka playing a school-teacher, Ayu an aspiring pop singer – probably enabled them to shift their acting style from the exaggeratedly 'masculine' voice and mannerisms they would have begun to assume for their Takarazuka roles back towards their 'normal' selves as young women (which could also be called constructs, but were probably less *consciously* constructed than the *otokoyaku* role). From this platform, they could then start to aim for the overdetermined femininity required of a Takarazuka *musumeyaku*.

When well-known *otokoyaku* appear in television series, usually in a female role among a mixed cast, they are not always successful in portraying sufficient femininity to suit the director, as in the case of Kō Nishiki (1960–74), who is now the manager of the new Tokyo Takarazuka Theatre under her real name of Ogawa Katsuko. Male-role specialist Kō recalls how difficult it was for her when acting in a mainstream television drama to suppress the *otokoyaku* habits she had acquired through years of practice. She describes feeling as stiff as if she had 'a wire in [her] back,' earning a scolding from the television director, who said, 'Your face may look like a woman's, but your movements are a man's.' 'In our time,' she explains, 'it was said that it would take ten years after retiring from Takarazuka for an *otokoyaku*'s body to become a woman's.' Ogawa also remarked that *otokoyaku* now seem able to slip easily into female roles, speculating that modern performers might be more 'versatile (*kiyō*)' than those of her generation (cited in Takubo 2001).[9]

At least for the duration of a performance, a Takarasienne is simultaneously two (or more) people: the character(s) she plays, which may include animals or inanimate objects; and her private and public self. Some spectators may attend the theatre to see only the fictitious characters represented by the actors, while others may be more interested in the performers than the performance. As the next chapter will show, among Takarazuka fans, there is a strong tendency towards the latter type, and certain performers will consciously play to such members of the audience, dropping their character at certain moments to assert their own personality, even when this involves switching genders for a short time. The audience is effectively watching two people in one body, and this adds to the potentially alternative, 'subversive' subtext underlying Takarazuka performances, as Robertson suggests (1998b: 60–61).

The role of surrogate families and affectionate relationships

In Takarazuka, the techniques of gender portrayal are learned not only by formal means, but also through the emotional bonds among performers, such as solidarity, rivalry, mentoring, friendship and love. These bonds characterise Takarazuka as a kind of extended family that gives performers a framework in which to learn and practise their gender portrayals. The open *expression* of sexuality is strictly repressed by the Company's tradition of secrecy. I suggest, however, that this tradition itself is a kind of *tatemae*, a polite fiction which overlies the interplay of a gamut of feelings and practices, from platonic admiration to dating, intimate relationships and even cohabitation with lovers. Adrienne Rich (1980: 631–60) calls such a

wide range of close, affectionate relationships among women, even
without overtly sexual elements, as a 'lesbian continuum,' though
the Revue Administration would undoubtedly be uncomfortable
with this term as potentially threatening its position on 'purity.' An
apparent 'moratorium' on mental growth which will be discussed
below might also be seen as justifying, or at least facilitating,
same-sex attraction, if the performers believe that such feelings
(as well as any sexual acts stemming from them) are a natural
part of adolescence: to be expected, if not necessarily encouraged.
Some performers also show fan-like sentiment towards other
Takarasiennes, especially vis-à-vis the more senior stars.

The extended family is frequently used as a metaphor for the
Takarazuka organisation, and its members often find themselves
assuming 'brotherly' or 'sisterly' status in relation to others, with
its concomitant gendered nuances. Writer/director Okada Keiji, in
paying homage to a retiring female-role player in late 1973, cited
her qualities of 'never losing her individuality, but always defending
and showing compassion for her juniors, while maintaining a
spirit of respect for her seniors' as a model of 'family-ism, in
which members' hearts were responsive to each other's (*kokoro to
kokoro ga kayoiatta kazoku shugi*).' This 'family-ism,' he suggests,
is what constitutes the 'splendid tradition of Takarazuka' (Okada
1973: 34).

As Chapter Three has shown, each Takarasienne learns her
place in the hierarchy from the time she enters the Music School,
first among her peers, as measured by her examination results,
and subsequently by comparison with other year-groups, senior
(*jōkyūsei*) and junior (*kakyūsei*), who correspond to older and
younger siblings, respectively.[10] As *otokoyaku* who are being
groomed for stardom tend to remain in the Company longer than
their *musumeyaku* counterparts, they can become like admired
'big brothers' to most of their troupe, both in terms of length
of experience and the heavy responsibility they bear to attract
audiences. As their success at the latter directly contributes to the
financial prosperity of the Company, they are in the position of
a family's main breadwinner, stereotypically male. However, no
performer can ever usurp the position of Kobayashi Ichizō himself
as the patriarch of the Takarazuka household, thanks in no small
part to the self-promotion of Kobayashi during his lifetime as the
loving father of all Takarasiennes. In one essay penned in 1953,
he describes his fantasy that each Takarasienne would 'come
back to him' even after retirement, a different career or marriage,

like a bride making a homecoming (*satogaeri*) trip to see her 'unforgettable' original home, where she can enjoy herself with her family group because that is the only place where she can 'be indulged (*amaeru*)' (Kobayashi 1955: 541).

The gender roles learned by Takarasiennes for their stage performances sometimes appear to affect their relationships with other performers on a private level. Strong relationships of affection among performers may seem to exceed the boundaries of ordinary friendship or pseudo-sibling ties. Each Takarasienne strives to create a superbly attractive, markedly gendered stage persona, deserving of the adoration of the opposite-gendered characters against whom she performs, in addition to the approval of the audience. Many *otokoyaku* hasten to emphasise that they are 'regular females' offstage, by which I assume they are laying claim to fundamental heterosexuality. However, my observation of and conversations with many current and past performers provide evidence that the gender-specific features of the personality, appearance and behaviour of Takarasiennes, especially the male-role players, are more fluid than those of other women of their age in the general community. In numerous instances, gender seems to be constantly fluctuating along a continuum of masculinity and femininity. It is not surprising, therefore, that performers' calculated charm should also captivate fellow members of the Company, with whom they frequently seem to form 'romantic friendships,' with or without sexual involvement. Indeed, the ability of an *otokoyaku* to inspire romantic sentiments among other women, especially those in her troupe who know her best, might even be interpreted as an indicator of her mastery of male gender portrayal.

As we have seen, Takarazuka is organised like a school, with senior 'students' (*senpai*) being made responsible for overseeing the behaviour of their juniors (*kōhai*), as well as for teaching them traditional techniques of portraying gender. As *otokoyaku* tend to be older and more experienced than their onstage *musumeyaku* partners, the former are usually in a position to coach the latter when they are rehearsing scenes together. This reflects the stereotypical gendered division of roles in mainstream society, in which men are expected to lead, and women to follow. According to one Company-sanctioned illustrated guide to Takarazuka, a leading female player in such a position is often called the top male-role star's '*o-yome-san* (bride)' (PHP Institute 1991: 53). Certainly, the tenderness with which some leading male-role stars appear to regard their opposite numbers can give the impression of romantic love.

In one example, 1970s *otokoyaku* Ōtori Ran frankly speaks of how
her juniors, when singing and dancing with all their might, seemed
'so adorable that she wanted to stroke their heads,' but she appeared
to reserve special consideration for her young *musumeyaku* partner
Haruka Kurara, who made her debut in 1973 when Ōtori was already
an established star (cited in Suzuki 1979: 177–78). In her role as the
freedom fighter Robert Jordan in the 1978 Takarazuka adaptation
of Hemingway's *For Whom the Bell Tolls* (*Ta ga tame ni kane wa
naru*), Ōtori did indeed daily ruffle the short hair of Haruka,[11] who
was cast in the role of a rape victim, Maria, with whom Jordan fell in
love. Television announcer Suzuki Haruhiko, who often interviewed
Takarasiennes on his programmes, observes that Ōtori appeared
completely taken with Haruka, who in turn needed the protection
of the older star in order to bear jealous attacks from more senior
rivals, who would have resented the Company's choice of Haruka
as Ōtori's fixed partner (Suzuki 1979: 301–02).

The love and admiration of a junior *musumeyaku* for her senior
otokoyaku stage partner may encourage the former to make greater
efforts to learn her feminine role. *Otokoyaku* may cultivate this
affection, which is especially important for the 'chemistry' of each
troupe's leading pair, known as its '*toppu konbi* (top combination).'
1990s *otokoyaku* star Maya Miki apparently asked her female-
role opposite whenever their paths crossed, 'Do you love me?
(*Aishiteru?*)' (cited in *Takarazuka gurafu* 1998: 6). Maya's Music
School contemporary Kuroki Hitomi, who was chosen in her second
year with the Company to play opposite the popular *otokoyaku* star
Daichi Mao, also describes how she would listen in silence with
downcast eyes to the star's advice, because she 'respected' and
was 'in love with (*aishiteru*)' Daichi, the affection evolving from
the respect. 'I was fond (*suki*) of her, but afraid of her, too, because
she was strict,' explains Kuroki. 'But I think I was able to perform
on stage because Mao-*san* really taught me [what to do] without
giving up on me. She always had an answer when I was floundering.'
Upon retiring from Takarazuka at the same time as Daichi, Kuroki
keenly felt that she had lost someone who would teach her and
make decisions (*handan*) on her behalf (cited in *Takarazuka gurafu*
1998: 6).

(Im)maturity and the mastery of gender portrayal

For the duration of their membership of the Revue, however long,
Takarasiennes must depend largely upon vicarious experience

and stylised *kata* to create their roles, because, in a way, they are prevented from 'growing up' or learning how to take on an adult female gender role in daily life, as they would be expected to do in mainstream society. In her limited period of training (now two years, but as short as one in the immediate post-war period), each Music School student must master the rudiments of the physical aspects of stagecraft – singing, movement, and Western and Japanese dance – to satisfy the Company's immediate need for a large chorus to fill the back of the stage behind the starring performers. Having come directly from junior or senior high school herself, and probably never having even taken a part-time job because of practice for the entrance examination, the typical Takarasienne thus has had little time or opportunity to learn about the adult world, with its obsessions including matrimony, mortgages and motherhood. Once within the female milieu of the Revue, she is first socialised to become an exemplary Takarasienne, then taught the techniques for performing as a *musumeyaku* or *otokoyaku*, but is not expected to behave as a typical adult woman would in a mixed-sex environment.

Many Takarasiennes who remain with the Company continue to dress and behave like teenaged girls well into their twenties, thirties or beyond, becoming what might be described as 'virtual *shōjo* (girls),' adult in body but childish in spirit. Novelist Tanabe Seiko, a fan since childhood, recalls a male teacher at her school during the war years sneering at the 'absurdity' of the Revue's pre-1940 nomenclature, Takarazuka shōjo kagekidan (Takarazuka Girls' Opera Company), which included mature women past thirty. Tanabe claims, however, that while they continue performing on the Revue stage, Takarasiennes are all 'girls (*shōjo*),' youthful because of their 'girlish sensitivity and steel-strong, limber bodies.' 'Trivial things like physical, biological age are blown away,' she adds (Tanabe and Sasaki 1987: 22). The childlike, or childish, nature which performers supposedly retain is valued by the Administration and Takarasiennes alike as contributing to their purported 'purity' – evil in Japan, as elsewhere, generally being associated with adults, and the adult word being seen as corrupting the 'originally pure and good nature of children' (Boocock 1991: 110; see also Simmons 1990: 100–01).

Mental immaturity is an important issue in Takarazuka because it means that adult gender must be learned in ways other than through personal experience. The very youth of the girls who join the Revue means that their identities are, as Susan Napier indicates in her discussion of strong, young female characters in Japanese animated films, 'seemingly still amorphous, ... embody[ing] the potential for unfettered change and excitement' (Napier 2000: 119). Many Takarasiennes apparently believe that their mental age stops rising after their entrance to the 'dream world' of Takarazuka, as evidenced by a *Kageki* (1992d) magazine survey of 286 Takarasiennes aged at least twenty, excluding *senka* members and first-year performers not yet assigned to a troupe. Only forty-one performers (fourteen percent) out of the entire sample felt that their real and mental ages were equivalent, while 147 (fifty-one percent) rated their mental age as between sixteen and twenty, markedly lower than their physical age. A great number of respondents in the same survey commented that their emotional maturation had 'stopped at the moment of entry to the Music School,' somewhere between the ages of fifteen and eighteen (*Kageki* 1992d: 146). As 'students' not only during training but also for as long as they remain with the Company, they are isolated by their 'teachers' (the Revue staff) from 'the pleasures and vices of the adult world,' like the Japanese high-school students described by Cyril Simmons (1990: 108). Takarasiennes' self-reported mental youthfulness may also be part of a ploy to win fans, however, for, as Sandra Buckley (2002: 207) remarks, 'apparent agelessness' is also one of the characteristics of popular female singing idols (*aidoru*) in Japan.

Apart from the need to concentrate upon performing and practising, to the exclusion of all other activities, another probable reason for Takarasiennes' mental immaturity is that they do not need to fend for themselves in their daily, off-stage lives. The performers' situation is somewhat comparable to that of young, unmarried female workers in non-career-oriented, white-collar jobs in Japan: the 'single aristocrats' (Jolivet 1997: 141–42) who live with their parents while in paid employment, have little or no responsibility for running the household, and are able to spend much of their income on themselves. The employment of Takarasiennes is virtually guaranteed until the end of their seventh year with the Company even if they exhibit no great talent. They are cast in every full-scale production undertaken by their troupe (although they may be disappointed at the insignificance of their roles); they do not have to pay an agent to represent them in order to secure work; they can take advantage of the great variety of free, in-house classes in all aspects of the performing arts offered by the Company; and they can pay a nominal fee to live in the Company dormitory and dine in its refectory if they wish, which removes the need to pay utility bills or buy and prepare food.

Although there are exceptions, performers' parents, or sometimes a wealthy patron, usually subsidise their accommodation if they live outside the dormitory. In addition, as will be elaborated in Chapter Six, responsibility for housekeeping, food preparation and other quotidian tasks is eagerly assumed by fans, especially in the case of popular *otokoyaku*, thus removing the opportunity for Takarasiennes to learn the household skills that other Japanese women acquire in the course of their home life. The Company's longest-serving *otokoyaku*, Kasugano Yachiyo, for example, once admitted that she was 'no good at any women's work' (cited in *Takarazuka gurafu* 1973: 29). One of my informants, another veteran performer who took both male and female roles, laughingly confessed that she was 'too scared to use a kitchen knife,' and was thus useless in the kitchen, so she relied upon someone else to cook for her in her post-retirement years (Informant PP 2001: Q. 2.11). Some other performers, though, even some male-role stars, do make a conscientious effort to manage various household tasks for themselves when they can. One, Todoroki Yū, who has been promoted to the status of *riji* (Board member) while still quite young, explains that she cooks her own meals for the sake of having control over at least one facet of her life – her nutritional intake (cited in *Takarazuka gurafu* 2001: 27). Another informant declares that Takarasiennes are 'pretty womanly' off stage, even if they do specialise in male roles in the Revue, and thus should not be expected to behave as stereotypical men (who cannot or will not do housework) in private life (Informant PZ 2001: Q. 3.4).

Once admitted to the Company, Takarasiennes can also rely upon a certain degree of social prominence, regardless of their own talent or effort. Jane Condon (1985: 211–12) observes that Japanese 'office ladies' who perform menial tasks for large corporations acquire prestige from their company's renown. In a similar manner, even the most junior Takarasienne automatically acquires the glory of the Takarazuka name. An ex-*musumeyaku* informant claims that the greatest advantage of having joined Takarazuka was the fact that people always afforded her more respect (*ichimoku okareru*) just for being a former Takarasienne than they would have if she had graduated from any famous university, or had been active in show business outside Takarazuka (Informant AA 2001: Q. 4.13).

Takarasiennes have thus been likened to 'hot-house flowers,' or, as writer/director Ueda Shinji (cited in Mizuho 1977: 218) prefers to say, 'hydroponically-grown vegetables,' sheltered from the challenges of wider society and the competitive world of commercial entertainment, which they can view through the 'glass' which surrounds them, but cannot join. As paid entertainers, their position is certainly more secure than that of independent actors, dancers and singers, who may suffer periods of unemployment and have to pay for any classes they attend, often need to audition for parts, and must constantly advertise their faces and abilities through an agent, Ueda adds (cited in Mizuho 1977: 218). On the other hand, makeup, costume jewellery and off-stage clothing are significant expenses for a Takarasienne, while gifts to creative staff in anticipation of, or in gratitude for, favouritism in casting, and fees and gifts to various teachers for private lessons, are also reputed to incur enormous sums which most performers, bar the most popular stars earning exceptional salaries, can ill afford.[12] Forced to rely upon the financial aid of parents for these less advertised expenses, such Takarasiennes are again thrust into the position of dependent daughters, irrespective of their age.

This chapter has illustrated how genders represented by *otokoyaku* and *musume/onnayaku* in Takarazuka are not re-creations of their counterparts in society in general, but rather constitute unique creations valid only in the fantasy realm of the Revue. The various permutations of behaviour, appearance and demeanour involved in performing masculinity and femininity by an *otokoyaku*, in particular, are chosen and utilised depending upon whether she is on stage, in the company of fans, or among her private friends and family. On a theoretical continuum of stereotypical traits of masculinity and femininity as exhibited by the general population, Takarazuka female-role players on stage would perhaps occupy a position closer to the 'very feminine' end of the continuum than the average woman, but be more gender-neutral than their stage persona when not in the public eye. Their male-role counterparts, on the other hand, would usually be more 'masculine' on stage than a significant proportion of men, yet much closer than most men, and perhaps even many women in general, to the 'feminine' end of the continuum when off-stage. Thus there is often quite a discrepancy between Takarasiennes' stage gender portrayals and their off-stage personae, with some *otokoyaku* said to be 'extremely feminine,' and some *musumeyaku* becoming 'quite boyish' when they are not performing for fans. Performers' gender, therefore, is fluid, not fixed, and various markers of gender can be consciously chosen and utilised by individuals to suit the purposes of each situation. Takarasiennes' deliberate performance of gender is, as the following chapter will show, one of the main attractions of the Revue for its fans, who both consume and help to construct Takarazuka performers' versions of gender.

5 Pleasures and Permutations of Takarazuka Fandom

The Takarazuka Revue, being a commercial enterprise, depends largely upon the support of its 'customers' – the millions of people annually who pay to attend its performances, buy its merchandise and subscribe to its publications. Many, if not most, of these individuals doubtless see themselves as 'fans' of Takarazuka, whose devotion is vital to the continued operation of the Revue in numerous ways. It is principally in order to satisfy fans – to cater to their 'dreams'[1] – that Takarazuka performers, creative staff and the Revue Administration collaborate to manipulate gender representations, as discussed in the previous two chapters. The overwhelming popularity of male-role players indicates that fans are engaged far more by the *otokoyaku*'s deliberate separation of gender and biological sex, than they are by a reproduction or exaggeration of orthodox gender.

The stereotypical model of fans of popular culture in general portrays fans as passive, ignorant and immature, as comprising the 'lowest and least critical segments of the population,' who are 'simply incapable of recognising that the culture they enjoy is actually being used to dupe and exploit them' (Grossberg 1992: 51). In this chapter, however, it is argued that many Takarazuka fans are not merely passive consumers of the Revue's productions and the 'gender gymnastics' of the performers on- and off-stage, but in fact are active participants in the production of distinct notions of gender, cooperating in the construction and manipulation of gendered roles as fans, vis-à-vis the Revue and each other, through their engagement in a variety of practices. These practices contribute to the fantasy world that has developed around the Takarazuka Revue, where sex and gender do not necessarily coincide, and orthodox concepts of hetero- and homosexuality seem not to apply. The chapter focuses upon the relationship between the stage gender of performers, which may differ from their biological sex, and the sex and gender of their fans. I show that though female fans of *otokoyaku* now appear to predominate, Takarazuka fans have always been diverse in sex,

gender and preference for particular types of performers; and fans'
engagement with the Revue takes many forms.

The attraction of Takarazuka for fans undoubtedly involves gender
issues and some kind of 'love,' probably lying somewhere between
the thesis suggested by Robertson (1998b: 145): that Takarazuka
inspires 'unaligned erotic play' for its fans, and is not specifically
hetero- or homo-sexual, but is nevertheless sexual in nature; and
the opposing view put forward by Nakamura and Matsuo (2003:
59–76): that sexual or erotic elements are absent from most fans'
attraction to Takarazuka, and that the Revue provides them instead
with a non-sexual environment to enjoy. I propose that the Revue's
motto, with its emphasis upon 'purity,' indoctrinates fans to the
extent that they are unwilling or unable to recognise sexual desire
as a facet of their fandom, even should it exist. While knowing that
all Takarasiennes are biologically female, fans obviously delight in
performers' defiance of conventional assignment of gender, within
temporal and spatial limits that do not (usually) threaten the social
order. Female fans, especially, enthuse over the beautiful, woman-
directed version of masculinity provided by the *otokoyaku*.

Many facets of Takarazuka fandom are in fact closely linked
with issues of gender: the composition of its fan base; the practices
in which its fans participate; and the stage gender of the performers
whom they idolise. This chapter focuses upon the social implications
of fandom: the mutually-dependent relationship enjoyed by the Revue
and its fans; and the dividends gained from diverse practices that both
increase the pleasure of spectatorship for fans, and encourage and
nurture performers. The chapter also applies the theoretical concept
of 'the gaze' to Takarazuka fandom, demonstrating that the interplay
of gazes involving audience members and the players on stage forms
a significant part of the pleasure of a Takarazuka performance, and
underlines the relative importance afforded to the different genders
on each side of the proscenium arch. The final section of the chapter
discusses the antithesis of fandom – the phenomenon of antipathy
towards the Revue professed by many people, even if they have
never seen a performance. Such antipathy, I contend, often arises
because of the low esteem afforded in Japan as elsewhere to women
and women's activities in general.

Fans and audiences in theoretical perspective

In this volume, I define a 'fan' of Takarazuka as a person who
makes a strong emotional investment in the Revue or in a particular

performer, irrespective of whether the fan actually attends performances. The stereotypical Takarazuka fan of today, as portrayed by the media, would probably be a female, somewhere between her early teens and middle age, who dresses in a T-shirt or trainer top emblazoned with the nickname of her favourite performer, and spends many hours attending performances and/or waiting at the stage door. Nevertheless, as this chapter will show, the characteristics of the 'typical' fan have not been static over the Revue's history, and even now, there are many permutations within the amorphous group of individuals who call themselves Takarazuka fans.

Jennifer Robertson extensively discusses fan behaviour and social attitudes to Takarazuka fandom (Robertson 1998b: 2–4, 139–215), though without explicitly defining what constitutes a fan. While she takes pains to point to the different genders and wide variety of ages and occupations of fans, she mostly deals with female fans, especially those categorised as *shōjo*: girls or unmarried women. Drama scholar Zeke Berlin, on the other hand, differentiates 'fans' from 'audience' by limiting the former to girls and women who 'wait at the stage entrance and in front of the rehearsal hall' (Berlin 1988: 177–78), and seems not to consider male fans at all. Karen Nakamura and Hisako Matsuo (2003), too, focus upon married, middle-aged women who belong to Takarazuka fan clubs, describing them as 'professional' fans, a term coined by Erving Goffman (1963: 108). The latter two definitions underplay or deny the existence and dedication of countless male fans, and the importance of the numerous other female supporters who are not 'stage-door Jills.'

In this chapter, the word 'audience' is used to denote all people who attend Takarazuka theatres – a mixture of dedicated fans and other, less committed individuals who simply happen to have obtained a ticket. For some people in the latter category, watching a Revue performance is a mere diversion, readily interchangeable with other diversions that are available. A proportion of these people may have unwillingly accompanied true fans to the theatre, with the result that some fall asleep from boredom, while others are captivated by Takarazuka as a whole or by a particular performer and consequently become 'fans' themselves.

Fans of theatrical groups and stage performers in Japan, as in other countries, share certain features with fans of other genres of popular culture such as popular music, film or television, but are also distinct because of the unusual degree of influence their live presence has upon performances. Numerous theorists have commented upon the significant role of audiences and/or fans in general in live theatre – in Japan, for example, the fifteenth-century actor Zeami advised the would-be actor that he (all professional actors at that time were male) 'must always be aware of and respond to the mood of the spectator, see[ing] himself as the audience sees him (*riken no ken*), and adjust[ing] his performance accordingly' (Zeami 1984: 100-02). As Susan Bennett points out, an audience's interpretation is an important, if often critically neglected, part of the theatrical process in the West, as well (Bennett 1990: 4; also Styan 1960: 7). Undeniably, Takarazuka fans have an even larger impact upon performers and performances than do the patrons of most other forms of live theatre.

The concept of 'the gaze' is important to an understanding of Takarazuka, where the interplay of gazes is a significant element in creating an emotion-charged atmosphere. Foucault first discussed the issue of 'the gaze' as all-penetrating or all-seeing, in medical and correctional contexts, respectively.[2] The predominance of females in today's Takarazuka audience, and the all-female cast (not all playing female roles), pose a challenge to pioneer theorists in the field of popular culture such as John Berger (1972) and Laura Mulvey (1989), who have argued respectively that 'the gaze' is necessarily male in art and film.[3] In a similar vein, feminist scholar Mieke van Schermbeek writes, 'It can generally be assumed that in theatre ... the organisation of the gaze serves male pleasure; the representation of women is considered to be an image seen through the eyes of men' (van Schermbeek 1995: 90). Until the 1990s, all Takarazuka writer/directors were men, and their masculinity doubtless influenced the way characters were written. Irrespective of the intentions of such writer/directors, however, performers and female fans have been an important force in ensuring that the Takarazuka experience has been tailored to women's tastes for the greater part of its history. Takarazuka spectators know that the 'men' they see on stage are biologically female, but what they perceive with their eyes is an attempt to belie this knowledge. Reproduced images of Takarazuka on television, video/Digital Versatile Disk (DVD) and the Internet, on the other hand, undermine the gender ambiguity of the live performance, as close-up shots of the faces of *otokoyaku* clearly reveal their use of coloured lipstick, eye-shadow and false eyelashes, which a biologically male actor usually would not be expected to apply.

Fandom, by its very nature, suggests an indulgence in fantasies or 'dreams,' and an obsessive enthusiasm which functions as an attempt to address an incompleteness or dissatisfaction in the fan's own self or life. Stephen Hinerman argues that fantasies operate 'much like a "suture" that a doctor uses to close a "gap" in a wound,' especially when 'desire is blocked by prohibition' (Hinerman 1992: 115-16). According to this reasoning, fantasy enables fans to transcend the boundaries of gender, sexuality or other potentially problematical or taboo areas, as a means of striving for wholeness. The 'dreams' which Takarazuka claims to sell function admirably in this way, as the discussion below will show.

Nakamura and Matsuo argue that the actor-fan relationship in Takarazuka creates a 'special type of asexual and agendered fantasy space,' in which 'both female and male fans, regardless of their sexual orientations, can temporarily transcend their everyday gender expectations and roles'; they conclude that Takarazuka's version of female masculinity generates this asexual space, and that fans of either gender 'suture' themselves to the empowered subjects (almost always the *otokoyaku*) they see on stage, making those characters into their own alter ego (Nakamura and Matsuo 2003: 59, 65). My own research and informal observations, however, suggest that other mechanisms are also at work, and Takarazuka is not as 'asexual' as they propose.

Apart from the work of the scholars cited above, English-language materials on Takarazuka fandom are few. Two notable treatments are Ingrid Sischy's *New Yorker* article (Sischy 1992: 84–103), and the 1993 British documentary film, *Dream Girls*, directed by Kim Longinotto and Jano Williams. Both create a composite picture of the typical Revue fan as female, often immature for her years, emotionally unfulfilled by 'real' men (or, in Sischy's version, perhaps a lesbian), and sufficiently affluent and leisured to be able to spend much of her time attending performances and participating in structured activities dictated by the fan club to which she belongs. The homosexual angle aside, this model resembles the image of fans projected by the mainstream Japanese media. It is clear from my own research, however, that there is a much broader range of Takarazuka fans than this view suggests.

Getting to know the fans

It should be noted that many sources on Takarazuka fandom, especially those published by the Revue Company or endorsed by it, are written by men, though girls and women certainly comprise an overwhelming majority of Revue fans nowadays, and female

fans' personal services are of inestimable worth to the performers
(see Robertson 1998b: 164). The Administration itself actively
encourages prominent fans to publish on Takarazuka, in order
to create publicity for stars and performances. Male fans' public
declaration of their fandom, particularly in the case of men in
influential positions, whose corporate financial contributions to
the Company's endeavours are probably considerable (Robertson
1998b: 171–72), is apparently seen by the Administration to have
better publicity value than that of female fans, based upon the sexist
assumption that things which appeal only to women and girls are of
lesser worth than those which are enjoyed also, or primarily, by men
and boys. Male celebrities such as writers, actors and politicians are
often invited to contribute written comments to the Revue's official
publications, or to talk about Takarazuka on television programmes
such as the national broadcaster NHK's 'specials' or regular
Takarazuka programmes made for satellite transmission. Moreover,
NHK's occasional gala telecasts of Takarazuka performances
are always introduced by a male announcer, either alone or
accompanied by a considerably younger female announcer who is
an obvious second to her male colleague. The blessing of celebrities,
especially male ones, probably does lend an air of legitimacy to
Takarazuka fandom.

Many female fans have in fact published their opinions on the
Revue, both in scholarly and in purely subjective format, but, as
noted above, the Company Administration seems to have regarded
their writings as less important than those of men. One 1976 book,
for example, purporting to be 'for the sake of people who aspire to
become "model" fans,' has a female author, but cites the opinions
of fourteen 'lovable uncles,' including politicians such as the late
Sakurauchi Yoshio and Harada Ken, and novelist Yashiro Seiichi,
whose own daughter entered the Music School in 1978 and performed
under the stage name of Mariya Tomoko until her retirement in
1985 (Suzuki 1976: 35, 44–101). The only women whose voices are
represented in that book, apart from performers, female members of
the Revue staff and the author herself, are three *tsukibito*, selected
fans that function as performers' personal assistants, and who until
recently were allowed to enter the dressing-rooms at the Tokyo
Takarazuka Theatre to help with dressing, run various errands and so
on. These three *tsukibito*, themselves atypical fans in the sense that
they were afforded entrée to the usually hidden backstage world of
Takarazuka and were expected to keep the details of that world secret
from other fans, were identified only by nicknames and by naming

the 1970s *otokoyaku* stars they served: 'Gata' was the *tsukibito* of Haruna Yuri, 'Hoi' of Ōtori Ran and 'Tomoko' of Anna Jun (Suzuki 1976: 256–60).

One notable exception to the Administration's apparent tendency to prioritise male fans' opinions is Natori Chisato, a married woman who has written copiously about Takarazuka in recent years in numerous publications, some issued by the Revue itself. She is obviously afforded access to performers for interviews, and her transcripts and interpretive comments are invariably flattering to the individuals concerned and to the Revue, to the extent that she seems to be an unofficial mouthpiece for the Revue Administration. Natori's series of 'Fairy Interviews,' for example, written for an independent monthly magazine of mixed content called *With Takarazuka*, give prominence to a number of *otokoyaku* whom the Administration is grooming for future stardom. Through such articles, the Revue obviously wishes to promote these performers among the general community as well as among already-committed Takarazuka fans (see Natori 2001–2007). The popular novelist Tanabe Seiko is another woman whose fondness for the Revue is actively courted by the Administration. She has woven Takarazuka into some of her fictional works, as well as writing a non-fiction book and some articles dedicated to the Revue, as in Tanabe and Sasaki (1987); and Tanabe (1995: 42–48).

A valuable insight into the workings of fan organisations may also be gained from the newsletters produced by fan clubs, which range from hand-written, hand-sketched pamphlets circulated among small numbers of enthusiasts to sophisticated, professionally printed and bound publications available in bookshops or by subscription, such as *Yume no hanataba* (Bouquet of dreams), a regular magazine edited by the Waseda daigaku Takarazuka kageki o aisuru kai (Waseda University 'We Love Takarazuka' Club), abbreviated in Japanese as Sōhōkai. Three former members of this club also edited an 'unofficial handbook' about Takarazuka, which contains specific instructions for would-be fans of all types (Waseda daigaku Takarazuka kageki o aisuru kai OG 1999).

Fan demographics, gender and the significance of fandom

The gender composition of audiences at Takarazuka performances certainly has changed with the years, reflecting to a considerable extent the changing tastes and circumstances of men and women in Japanese society. As previously noted, at the time of his

Plate 4: *Female fans emerge from Takarazuka's theatre complex.*
The daytime schedule of most performances excludes
the majority of males from the Takarazuka audience.
(Photograph courtesy of Terence Martin)

establishment of the Girls' Opera, Kobayashi identified middle-
class families, especially women and children, as a hitherto
unexploited potential audience. Moreover, due to a general dearth
of entertainment or spectacles specifically for young people at that
time, Takarazuka's development filled a niche, and was apparently
welcomed by this segment of the population (Takagi 1983: 57).

There are contradictory opinions as to the proportions of male
and female patrons at performances in the first decades after
Takarazuka's foundation. No official statistics seem to exist, as a
single entrance fee was charged to the 'Paradise' leisure facility,
and visitors attending the Girls' Opera situated within it were
not counted separately. It is certain, however, that in comparison
to today, a much greater number of boys and men once attended
performances, demonstrating considerable fervour for productions
and performers, as evidenced by archival photographs and the
reminiscences of various individuals. Overall, Takarazuka seems
to have appealed mainly to people who had the money and time

to travel a considerable distance from their homes in Osaka or its environs, and who were interested in live theatre performed by supposedly chaste young women.

In recent decades, especially, the typical Takarazuka audience, especially at weekday performances, probably has not truly represented the range of sex, age and occupation of people who consider themselves Takarazuka fans. The gender composition of the audience is strongly influenced by the performance schedule, which makes it much easier for female audience members to attend than males. The system of advance reservation of seats, the starting times of performances and, in the Kansai case, the location of the Takarazuka theatre complex combine to make it very difficult for most fully-employed persons to join the Takarazuka audience. Most shows take place during daylight hours, forcing weekday workers to compete with schoolchildren and families for the limited seats available at weekends or on public holidays. Men are more likely than women to have full-time jobs, to work overtime and to have business-related commitments in the evenings or at weekends. Such busy workers cannot queue for hours or even days outside a box office or ticket agency to obtain tickets for a forthcoming season, or spend time punching and re-punching the redial button on their telephones in an attempt to make a booking.

The very location of the Takarazuka Grand Theatre, unlike its Tokyo counterpart, which is in the middle of the capital city, is another factor in shaping its audience demographic. The municipality of Takarazuka itself has largely become a dormitory suburb serving nearby commercial and industrial centres such as Osaka, Kobe and Amagasaki. Even if Takarazuka performances were to begin in the early evening, as is the case at major theatres in Tokyo and Osaka, it would still be difficult for most workers to travel into Takarazuka for a five-thirty or six-o'clock start. The reliance of the majority of urban workers on public transport between home and workplace, and the increasingly long period of commuting for many city employees, mean that even if Takarazuka's evening performances were to start at seven-thirty or eight o'clock, as they usually do in countries like Australia, the United Kingdom and the United States, it is unlikely that many workers would attend because of the late hour of their homeward journey, with related transport problems.

Even among female fans, there seems to be an over-representation at weekday performances of post-secondary students, young unmarried adults and more mature married women whose children

are at school or have left home, for whom the Revue's daytime
entertainment schedule is extremely convenient, with performances beginning at one and ending at four in the afternoon. Some
of these women have a part-time job, and some are employed in
retailing, which usually means that workers take one or more
weekday holidays per week but work on weekends, while others
do not participate in paid employment. Takarazuka fans need to be
fairly affluent to attend performances, however, as even the cheap-
est tickets cost more than twice a premium cinema ticket, though
somewhat less than tickets to mainstream theatre productions of
similar scale. The Hankyu-owned Umeda Arts Theatre in Osaka,
for example, currently charges 4000 to 12000 yen for seats at its
mainstream theatrical shows (Umeda Arts Theatre 2007), while
similar seats in the Takarazuka Grand Theatre cost between 2000
(for same-day tickets for remaindered upstairs rear seats) and 10000
yen (Takarazuka Kageki 2007b). Particularly sought-after tickets,
however, may fetch many times that in private auctions which are
not condoned by the Revue administration.

   Dreams of romance with the stage characters played by Takarazuka *otokoyaku* seem to be used by middle-class women as a respite
from the usual motherly and housewifely duties through which
they are usually seen to contribute to society, while for Japanese
men, by contrast, 'escape from the habits of labour' might mean
casual sexual encounters with bar-workers and prostitutes, at least
according to Anne Allison (1996: xv). One youngish widow living
in Takarazuka, for example, whose mother-in-law was apparently
very strict, confessed to me in February 2001 that Takarazuka
was her 'safety valve (*iki-nuki*),' although she had to attend
performances in secret, on the pretext of going shopping. Husbands
of avid Takarazuka fans may be unaware of their wives' fervent
interest in the Revue and/or a particular performer, and if the
family purse-strings are controlled by the wife, as is typical, then
her expenditure upon theatre tickets, gifts for her idol and fan-club
membership may be hidden from her husband. On the other hand,
some husbands are accepting of their wives' fandom. Hashimoto
cites the example of a matriarchal line of Takarazuka fans in which
the grandmother, mother, daughter and granddaughter were all
without brothers to continue the family name, a husband being
consequently adopted into the family for each of them: 'We've
had adopted husbands (*yōshi*) for generations,' declared the
grandmother, 'We don't adopt men who don't understand about
Takarazuka' (cited in Hashimoto 1988: 109).

In addition to its function as a source of enjoyment for Revue enthusiasts of either gender, Takarazuka fandom fulfils an important economic role which benefits the Revue itself, its parent company, Hankyu, and many other enterprises of various sizes. Fans purchase theatre and train tickets, Revue-related merchandise such as fan magazines, related books, Compact- and Digital Versatile Disks, and other miscellaneous goods bearing Takarazuka logos. Fans probably also patronise Hankyu's department stores and hotels around Japan, where Hankyu's link with Takarazuka is made obvious by the prominent display of posters and panels bearing pictures of Revue stars. In central Takarazuka, and to a lesser extent in Tokyo's Yurakucho, adjacent to the Tokyo Takarazuka Theatre, many bars, restaurants, florists, other retail stores and service outlets look to fans for much of their custom. The horticultural industry, for which the city of Takarazuka itself is one of the three largest producing areas in the country, also profits greatly from fans' purchase of cut or potted flowers to present to their favourite stars, to the extent that fans' purchases allegedly influence the national wholesale price. Many such businesses located in Takarazuka choose not to open on Wednesdays, when the Grand Theatre is usually closed. These establishments, in turn, provide numerous individuals with employment. Fans also support media services including a dedicated satellite television channel, 'Takarazuka Sky Stage,' which was opened in July 2002 to cater specifically to Revue fans, who pay to view its programmes (Yabushita 2002b; Takarazuka Sky Stage 2002–2004). Now, there is even 'Takarazuka *karaoke*,' launched in October 2003 for '*i*-mode' telephone customers of a large telecommunications company (Takarazuka Revue 2003). In all, Takarazuka fans thus comprise a considerable force as consumers.

Male fans

As orthodox notions of gender construct an attraction for members of the opposite sex as 'natural,' most male fans of Takarazuka probably feel no need to justify their enthusiasm for Revue performers, who are all female, irrespective of their stage gender. However, as noted above, male fans do appear to have been far more numerous during the first three decades of the Revue's existence, in the heyday of the *musumeyaku*, than at present. Hōjō Hideshi, a member of the Girls' Opera staff from around 1930 who remembers its beginnings, recalls that although teenaged girl students in Osaka were the first section of the population to become 'excited' over Takarazuka, their enthusiasm in turn infecting 'respectable [middle-class] wives (*ryōke no fujin*),' a passion for Takarazuka then 'spread like wildfire to all the [boys'] middle schools in the Osaka–Kobe area' (cited in Sakata 1983: 253). Recess-time talk among Hōjō's own classmates at the all-male Tennōji Commercial School in Osaka around 1919 was apparently monopolised by discussion of Takarazuka, and Hōjō himself boasts of achieving considerable celebrity at school, among relatives and the neighbourhood girls while still aged about seventeen, when his prize-winning submission to a Takarazuka script-writing competition was staged in the summer of 1920 as an operetta entitled *Koronbusu no ensei* (The expedition of Columbus) (cited in Sakata 1983: 255).

Other young male fans included the students of a private boys' college, Kwansei Gakuin, which moved in 1929 to a site near the Hankyu train line linking Takarazuka with Nishinomiya-kitaguchi, a railway junction halfway between Osaka and Kobe. In anticipation of encountering Takarasiennes, Kwansei Gakuin students would crowd the last carriage of the Hankyu trains, where performers and Music and Opera School pupils were obliged by Kobayashi's rules to ride standing up, near the conductor's booth (symbolically the humblest position in the train), clad in their distinctive uniforms. School rules forbade trainees and performers alike to speak to men in public, especially the students of private universities such as Kwansei Gakuin and Kyoto's Dōshisha, who were apparently most eager to make the acquaintance of Takarasiennes. One of my informants mentions her own embarrassment at being hailed by her cousins from Kwansei Gakuin, when she was a trainee in the late 1930s. She could not reply for fear of having marks docked from her school record (Informant MH 2003: Q. 2.10). Vivacious, dancing gracefully, singing sweetly and sometimes scantily clad on stage, yet silent, demure and modestly-dressed in their dark green *hakama* over an economy-grade kimono in the intimate confines of the train carriage, these pre-war Takarasiennes must have seemed like tantalising 'forbidden fruit' to the male students.

Even primary school boys participated in Takarazuka-worship. Lyricist and writer Sakata Hiroo, for one, confesses to being a 'Takarazuka maniac' in his boyhood around 1935, although he had only seen one performance at that time, and he estimates that two-thirds of his all-male primary school classmates in the fifth grade were Takarazuka fans. At the age of eleven or twelve, he boned up on personal details of Takarazuka stars by surreptitiously studying back issues of the magazine *Shōjo no tomo* (Girls' companion) in order to impress his school friends; he also recalls 'being immersed in joyful feelings' in 1943, when he heard that the younger sister of his cousin's fiancée was a Takarasienne (Sakata 1992: 68–69, 73). Sakata himself dreamed of becoming a Takarazuka writer/director, and many years later, as the father of two girls, he encouraged his younger daughter to enter the Music School – she becoming Ōura Mizuki, a leading *otokoyaku* in the late 1980s.

Not only young boys, but married men, too, were fans. Television personality Suzuki Haruhiko, for example, writes that his family in the 1930s was 'unusual' in that his father was more besotted (*muchū*) with both Takarazuka and Kabuki than his mother, travelling far and wide to see various performances and buying many performing arts and film magazines, and taking his five-year-old son to see Shirai Tetsuzō's Takarazuka production *Hana shishū* (Flower anthology) in 1934; Suzuki himself, who had no sisters, used to dream of having a 'gentle older sister,' and after becoming familiar with the faces of Takarasiennes from his father's magazines, he often imagined scenes in which those Takarasiennes fulfilled that role, joining him in play, telling him fairy tales and showering him with gifts (Suzuki 1979: 96, 98–99). In the opinion of writer/director Kamura Kikuo, the romantic mood and melodies of Paris, as reinvented on the Takarazuka stage, seem to have been particularly captivating to male fans, for when the 1930 Shirai Tetsuzō revue *Parisette* smashed attendance records set by *Mon Paris* three years previously, the number of male student fans in the Kyoto–Osaka–Kobe area reputedly doubled (Kamura 1984: 68). Kamura also observes that male fans were in the majority because as late as the early 1930s, it was not considered proper for girls to attend the theatre alone, or even in groups with female friends, such behaviour courting disapproval from families and both public and private girls' schools (Kamura 1984: 68).

For many men about to face the harshness of military service during the war, the dream world of Takarazuka, with its 'pure, righteous and beautiful' women, became a place of final pilgrimage, as described in Chapter One, but the post-war Revue may have become less enticing, or less accessible, to men and boys. Kobayashi lamented in the 1950s that young people had 'conspicuously gone off the rails (*me ni amaru dassen-buri*)' in the immediate post-war years, due to the proliferation of mixed dance halls, tea parties and dating in couples (*abekku*), without the supervision of other family members (Kobayashi 1955: 507). The establishment of co-educational public secondary schools to replace single-sex middle-

and high schools and girls' higher schools also enabled adolescent
boys and girls in the post-war period to associate with each other
on a daily basis, thus probably removing much of the mystique that
had surrounded the opposite sex.

Other reasons, too, probably contributed to the post-war fall
in male attendance at the Revue. Widespread poverty and the
necessity to concentrate upon the realities of rebuilding homes
and livelihoods, especially in the bombed cities fringing the Osaka
Bay area, from which the Revue had drawn much of its patronage,
probably made entertainment such as the Revue unaffordable for
many people, including many men who had formerly frequented it.
Moreover, the post-war lifting of the school-leaving age to fifteen
in Japan meant that new entrants to the Music School were several
years older than the majority of pre-war and wartime recruits had
been at commencement of their training. Some male fans who had
enthused over the very young stars of former decades might have
been disappointed at the greater maturity of this new generation
of Takarasiennes, and turned to other avenues to satisfy their taste
for girls. While the official Revue fan organisation, Takarazuka
tomo no kai (Takarazuka friendship club), founded in 1934 as a
club restricted to girls and women, opened its ranks to males in
1951, men and boys have never comprised a large proportion of its
membership, and make up a mere one-tenth of registered members
now.[4] My observations, however, suggest that this figure somewhat
underestimates the true popularity of Takarazuka among men,
many of whom are 'dormant' fans without any fan club affiliation,
who may never actually attend performances.

Men have probably been attracted to Takarazuka for a variety of
reasons. Actresses had appeared on the professional stage in Japan
for only a few years when Takarazuka was founded, and the all-male
Kabuki was probably more familiar to regular theatregoers of either
sex. To boys and men attracted by (representations of) femininity,
especially, the relatively unpolished stage skills and smooth,
youthful faces and limbs of Takarazuka performers, as well as their
girlish off-stage appearance, must have seemed delightfully fresh in
comparison to the highly stylised refinement of the cross-dressed
Kabuki *onnagata*, who were beloved of theatrical connoisseurs but
who may have been quite ugly, elderly, balding or wrinkled without
their makeup and costumes. Kobayashi Ichizō, for example, was
apparently revolted as a child to find that a swarthy, pockmarked
male actor had played the part of the beautiful, enchanting princess
in a play he had seen (Sakata 1983: 15–16).

Many male fans probably continue to enjoy the exaggerated femininity of the female-role players. In the presence of such a 'woman,' even the least 'masculine' of men could feel manly. Indeed, many might wish that the women with whom they associated in real life were as purely feminine, graceful, subservient and beautiful. Up till the mid-1940s, productions gave prominence to female-role players, and the large number of male fans in the audience during that period suggests that the *musumeyaku* were especially attractive to them. The female-role players also won more approval from patriarchal authorities and the media.[5] Moreover, as the previous chapter has shown, until after the war even the *otokoyaku* sang in high 'operatic' voices that reminded the audience of their female physiology, and men and boys thus may have found them more alluring than their more masculine, present-day counterparts.

It is hard to concur with Nakamura and Matsuo's argument that Takarazuka is 'asexual,' given the apparent fervour of many male fans (if not female ones, as well): after all, it is assumed that every Takarasienne is anatomically female, and most, if not all, embody such qualities as beauty, talent and charisma. Even the most masculine-looking of them will not possess male genitalia beneath their costumes, and are not 'men' in their off-stage moments. It thus seems plausible that heterosexual men might become enamoured of a certain Takarazuka performer (rather than the characters she plays) to the extent of desiring a romantic or sexual relationship with her, even if this is destined to remain a fantasy. Male fans have an advantage over female fans in one respect – they can publicly aspire to marry their favourite Takarasienne. One such man, Nagata Masakazu (1976), a film company employee, recalls being a 'real fan' at the age of about twenty, when he went to Takarazuka on his days off every week from around 1925 (Nagata 1976: 86). In those years, he claims, all young men in the Kyoto–Osaka–Kobe area used to tell each other that they would 'get a wife from Takarazuka'; and many members of what Nagata calls '*modan na renchū* (the fashionably modern set),' including professional baseballers, newspaper reporters and the like, apparently did marry Takarasiennes. 'It used to be much more romantic, fifty years ago, than it is now,' he alleged in the mid-1970s, while acknowledging that 'fashionable' men still sought Takarazuka performers as wives (Nagata 1976: 86).

Revue writer/director Takagi Shirō records the case of Okitsu Namiko, one of Takarazuka's first stars, who reputedly had many male admirers and suitors, among them wealthy and influential men, but finally married Takarazuka director Shirai Tetsuzō

(Takagi 1983: 92). Many other directors have since married Takarasiennes, for whom the Revue's creative staff-members are often the only adult males with whom they have regular contact, considering the long hours the performers work, which preclude much socialising away from their female colleagues; single-sex dormitory accommodation for many; and, nowadays at least, the predominantly female composition of their fan networks. Another male fan, writer Yazaki Yasuhisa, whose father was also a Takarazuka fan who often took the young Yazaki to see the Revue in pre-war years, boldly challenges the platonic, sexless image of Takarazuka by writing of finding *otokoyaku* 'extremely sexy.' The charm of Takarazuka for his father's contemporaries in the 1930s and 1940s, too, Yazaki surmises, lay in a 'sexual, sort of perverted (*tōsakuteki*)...somewhat strange (*ippū kawatta*) eroticism,' which he suggests these men felt in relation to the cross-dressed performers (Yazaki 1976: 95).[6] How typical such an attitude as Yazaki's might be, however, is unknown – certainly, one would expect the Revue administration sternly to discourage blatantly sexual nuances in fans' words or behaviour towards its performers.

Marriage to a performer seems not to be the only possibility on lusty male fans' minds. One predatory male acquaintance of mine in the late 1980s who enjoyed Takarazuka, for example, bragged that he would mingle on purpose with the crowd leaving Revue performances, and approach lone female fans whose flushed faces and dreamy eyes suggested sexual arousal. He claimed to be occasionally successful in persuading such a woman to accompany him to a so-called 'love hotel' for sex, after having encouraged her to talk fervently about her favourite *otokoyaku* star. Irrespective of the veracity of his boastings, his identification of Takarazuka as a trigger for a sexual response in women runs counter to the cult of purity promoted by the Revue itself, and the findings of Nakamura and Matsuo. I propose that the experience of watching a Takarazuka performance may give rise to a diffuse feeling of warmth and excitement in women's bodies which they cannot, or are reluctant to, identify as sexual arousal – unlike men, in whom physical arousal is usually unmistakeable and undeniable. Even given prior sexual experience, a girl or woman may hesitate to attach 'unladylike' sexual meanings to physiological changes she detects in her own body, especially when she is in the 'pure' environment of Takarazuka where overt sexuality seems to be taboo.

Not all male fans of Takarazuka are heterosexual, nor is male interest in Takarasiennes necessarily directed at the performers for the sole reason that they are women. As Nakamura and Matsuo (2003) suggest, Takarazuka may offer male fans a space in which to indulge in fantasies that transcend gender and (perceived) sexuality. Some gay men and male-to-female transgendered or transsexual people who are attracted to masculinity, for instance, might find the 'ideal male' represented by the cross-dressed *otokoyaku* just as attractive as many women in the audience claim to do. I refute Robertson's assertion that male transvestites find Takarazuka *musumeyaku* attractive as 'models for cross-dressing' (Robertson 1998b: 198). The photograph she uses to illustrate her argument – that of the female-role player Yashioji Mari on the cover of the December 1969 issue of *Takarazuka gurafu*, in heavy makeup and blonde wig, clad in a tight, lamé gown which makes her breasts look false – is atypically showy for a Takarazuka magazine. Here, Yashioji indeed more closely resembles a drag queen than an ordinary woman, whereas other covers of similar vintage featuring female-role players picture them in a less 'artificial' light.[7] While I agree that the stereotypical femininity performed by most *musumeyaku* is overdetermined, I have observed long-haired male-to-female transgendered or transsexual individuals, who appeared to be professional female impersonators, enthusing wildly over a particular *otokoyaku* at the Takarazuka Grand Theatre, rather than over the female-role players.

Fan behaviour differs considerably according to the gender of the fan. Male fans are seldom observed waiting outside the stage door, for example, and they cannot associate publicly with individual performers because of the unwritten rule forbidding Takarasiennes from open, one-to-one association with males. There are also numerous famous, rich or powerful men who are acknowledged by the Administration and performers alike as valuable supporters of the Revue, who might in any case be too busy to attend performances, or too proud or well-known to join the official fan club or gaze at performers from afar as 'stage-door Johnnies.' Some are able privately to arrange 'group dates' with their favourite Takarasiennes, and thus do not need to wait outside the stage door with the crowd. Novelist Nosaka Akiyuki, for example, boasts of enjoying 'totally innocent' meetings with selected Takarazuka stars at supper clubs in Tokyo together with his male friends, including writer Ei Rokusuke and musician Izumi Taku (Nosaka 1977: 58). Such occasions are usually off-limits to other females, presumably because the male hosts want their Takarasienne guests to behave as women at such gatherings, irrespective of the performers' stage gender. The presence of female fans would likely dictate that an *otokoyaku* maintain some vestige of her 'professional' gender, thus competing with the men in terms of masculinity rather than projecting her feminine persona for their gratification, while a *musumeyaku* might regard other females present as her own rivals.

Some powerful male fans seem also to make their enthusiasm for Takarazuka into an opportunity for homosocial bonding. A number of high-ranking politicians and business leaders, for instance, make a public declaration of their interest in the Revue by membership of exclusive fan clubs such as the Aihōkai (We love Takarazuka club), founded in 1955 and headed for many years by a former Cabinet minister, the late Sakurauchi Yoshio,[8] or the Kansai-based group of business leaders called Takarazuka kageki o kōen shi gekirei suru kai (Club to support and heartily encourage the Takarazuka Revue), formed in 1960.[9] Some of these influential men apparently have such a 'soft spot' for Takarasiennes that they will readily grant any request made by other men whose prestige is sufficient to command the presence of Revue performers. The memoir of Tomogane Nobuo, mayor of Takarazuka from 1971 to 1991, records three separate instances of remarkably successful petitions to high-ranking bureaucrats, one of whom was certainly Sakurauchi, for public works funding. Said mayor was accompanied on his visits to request funding from the ministries concerned by Takarazuka stars, who sang Takarazuka's signature tune or chatted informally with ministry officials (Tomogane 1993: 45–51).

Female fans

The conspicuous and highly organised nature of the expression of female fandom in Takarazuka today renders male fans almost invisible. Certainly, female fans seem to have much more time to spend on fan-related activities than do boys or men. Moreover, their current preference for the male-role players markedly differentiates them from male fans.

Female fans, like their male counterparts, know that the 'men' they see on the Takarazuka stage are anatomically female, but women, especially, seem to highly appreciate the *otokoyaku*'s skilful simulation of many aspects of masculinity, while simultaneously undervaluing the artistry of the *musumeyaku*. Female fans themselves may be accustomed to acting out stereotypical femininity on a daily basis, and thus may assume that this comes naturally to all women.

Alternatively, they might also feel jealousy, even strong animosity, towards the female-role player being romanced on stage by their favourite *otokoyaku*. On public toilet walls at the Grand Theatre, for example, I have seen graffiti urging a certain female-role player to 'drop dead,' accompanied by the intimation that she was an inappropriate on-stage partner for a particular *otokoyaku*, whom the graffiti-writer apparently followed.

Although comparatively few, there are some girl or woman fans who support female-role players. They are more likely to see their favourite rise to top stardom in only a few years after her debut, unlike the performer's male-role peers who usually spend a decade or more in supporting roles. Wieringa (2007: 37) asserts that Takarazuka performers 'arouse same-sex (but not same-gender) erotic desire in their fans,' but my observations suggest that this is not necessarily the case, as it seems common for *musumeyaku* to have feminine-looking female fans, also. Admittedly, some female fans who become a personal assistant (*tsukibito*) to a *musumeyaku* may dress in somewhat masculine clothing, perhaps in order to emphasise their idol's femininity, or to function as an 'escort' – the *tsukibito* of a *musumeyaku* friend of mine, for example, always dressed in mannish clothing, but was allegedly just waiting for the performer to retire so that she herself could 'go back to being a girl' and marry her fiancé.

It is accepted that most female Revue fans seem to prefer the *otokoyaku*, but what attracts them? Women quizzed in magazine and television interviews regularly echo the answer often publicised by the Company itself: the *otokoyaku* are 'ideal men (*risō no dansei*),' embodying such qualities as delicacy, handsomeness, long legs, gentleness, and the ability to speak romantic phrases without embarrassment. Malcolm Davies adds that the *otokoyaku* 'create the ideal man whom Japanese women really want,...in particular lacking the blind and narrow devotion to the work ethic which characterises so many real husbands in late twentieth-century Japan' (Davies 1995: 152). One of my informants, a veteran ex-performer, declared that people paid money to come and see Takarazuka precisely because its *otokoyaku* were a charming 'fabrication (*esoragoto*).' 'Nobody would come if they were the same as real men,' she said. She further asserted that married women would return from the theatre after having swooned over the tall *otokoyaku* star Asami Rei (1970-85) in her swallowtail coat, take one look at their 'short-legged husbands' and sigh to themselves, 'It would have been better not to have come home!' (Informant PZ 2001: Q. 3.7). Nobody would dare suggest, however, that these 'ideal men' might be regarded as ideal by very reason of their physical impotence – they can romance a woman with honeyed words, caresses and passionate kisses, but lack the organs by which to impregnate her.

The words of popular female cartoonist Kihara Toshie, a regular member of the Takarazuka audience, encapsulate typical fan opinion. In a journal interview, Kihara explains:

> Takarazuka gathers together and shows on its stage everything that girls must discard from their everyday lives. On stage, the *otokoyaku* say lines that girls would really like to hear, but which would sound too affected and set hearers' teeth on edge if they came from the mouths of men of flesh and blood, especially inarticulate Japanese men who would rather die than say such things...The *otokoyaku*, like the epitome of ideal images, speak those...lines with utmost seriousness; there is beautiful music playing in the background, flowers are falling from above, and the lights are shining beautifully upon them. Would one call it a 'non-space (*a-kūkan*),' perhaps? The entire audience is a dream state (*uttori*)...I think that the founder of Takarazuka was a genius (cited in *Subaru* 1987: 89).

Kihara's expression '*a-kūkan*' suggests Nakamura and Matsuo's 'fantasy spaces' (2003: 1), and Robertson's use of the term 'space off,' which she borrows from Teresa de Lauretis (1987: 26) to describe how the Revue and its fan clubs function as a separate space from daily life and regular life cycles (Robertson 1998b: 175).

I propose, however, that Takarazuka is a shared fantasy of not only the fans, but of the performers, too, who 'live' the dream of portraying beautiful people in their everyday work, and even perpetuate this fantasy after the curtain is down, in an environment considerably removed from regular society. In the evening, for example, in bars and restaurants near the Grand Theatre in Takarazuka and at similar establishments in fashionable parts of Tokyo, many Takarasiennes – usually dressed to reflect their stage gender, as they might be observed by outsiders to the Revue – relax and socialise with each other and with fans, while other women of their age are more likely to be engaged in domestic chores,[10] if not overtime work in offices or factories. Contemporary off-stage *otokoyaku*, in particular, represent flesh-and-blood examples of women largely unbound by orthodox gender roles, at least until they retire, and may thus seem as attractive to fans as the strong female characters found in fantasy comics and animation, as discussed by Susan Napier (1998: 91–109).

While male fans' adoration of Takarasiennes, singly or as a group, has been regarded as an expression of 'normal' sexuality, the attitudes and behaviour of female Revue fans have long been the target of debate and censure by such 'experts' as social critics, psychologists and sexologists, in the mass media and in academic publications. Such criticism was especially prevalent in the 1930s, such as in *Asahi shinbun* (1935: 7), after *otokoyaku* adopted short hair. Female fandom was considered pathological and indicative of homosexual leanings, though Robertson notes that some Japanese psychologists were of the opinion that homosexuality in 'feminine' women (not 'butch' or mannish types) was a transient (*kari*) condition, constituting a temporary period of 'spiritual hedonism' curable by marriage (Robertson 1999: 22). One 1930s medical doctor, however, comments that girls' revue fandom was not surprising, given that girls often felt a strong yearning or admiration (*dōkeishin*) for the abilities and status of males (and, arguably, for the females who emulated them on stage); and he regards the 'masculinisation of adult women (*fujin danseika*)' as an inevitable 'phase of the times' (Sugita 1935: 277).

Not only academics and social commentators, but some fans and others evidently connect the attraction of Takarazuka with sexuality and eroticism, abetted by tabloid journalism that deliberately rumour-mongers about same-sex relationships between fans and performers, or between performers themselves. In the 1930s, for example, there were reports of a love relationship between the famed Shinpa actress Mizutani Yaeko and the Takarazuka *otokoyaku* Nara Miyako (1919–39), of whom Mizutani was a professed enthusiastic fan (*Fujin kōron* 1935: 297, cited in Robertson 1998b: 149–51).

I take issue with the strong emphasis upon eroticism through much of Robertson's work, largely based on published sources such as those above, and also exacerbated by her particular interpretation of certain Japanese-language terms relating to love, for example. Thanks to the efforts of Hori Chieko, the translator of Robertson's 1998 book, who hunted down many of the original quotations cited (see Robertson 2000: 352), it is often possible to reach different conclusions about the material from those of Robertson. In one salient example, Robertson translates '*koi*' as 'sexual love,' whereas 'romantic love' is probably more apt. Robertson's choice of nuance casts a strongly erotic slant upon the paragraphs below, which recount one girl's experience of 'first love (*hatsukoi*).' The original Japanese version, taken from a privately-published fan magazine, is as follows:

Aru hitori no jūnanasai ni naru jogakusei ga koi o shiyō to omoimashita.
Kanojo wa isei to kōsai shite, sono hi kara de mo seppun o shidekasu
yō na yūki no aru o-jōsama de wa arimasen. Kanojo wa hitori
nayamimashita. ...Kanojo wa futo kangaemashita. Dangakusei
to kōsai sureba, hōken-teki na katei ga kyoka suru hazu ga naku...
(Takarazuka fuan 1955: 7, cited in Robertson 2000: 246).

Robertson's English version of the above runs:

One seventeen-year-old student thought about making [sexual] love.
She got together with a boy, but didn't have the courage to follow
through. Disappointed, she became lost in her thoughts...She thought
about how if she actually got together with a male, she would become
trapped in a feudal household system (Robertson 1998b: 185).

In the original Japanese, though, far from being on the verge of
losing her virginity, the girl merely fantasises about romance. I
would translate as follows:

One seventeen-year-old female student decided to fall in love. She was
not the type of young lady who would have the courage to date someone of the opposite sex, and flagrantly kiss him from that very first day.
She agonised in secret... Suddenly, she had a thought. Were she to date
a male student, her feudalistic family would be unlikely to allow it...

Moreover, later in the same passage, the original text tells of the
hapless girl deciding that a Takarazuka *otokoyaku* would be the
most suitable target for her yearnings. After having saved up to
visit Takarazuka, she queues up to meet the *otokoyaku* star she
admires, then:

Yatto purezento o o-watashi suru koto wa dekimashita ga, kanojo wa
hitokoto mo kuchi ga kikemasen deshita...Kō shite kanojo no hatsukoi
wa yaburete shimaimashita (Robertson 2000: 246–47).

In my English translation of the above:

She was finally able to hand over her gift, but could not utter a single
word...In this way, her first love ended in defeat.

Robertson, on the other hand, has the star, rather than the fan,
uttering 'not a word' (of thanks for the gift, presumably), and writes
that 'the experience frustrated the fan' (Robertson 1998b: 185).

Overt same-sex relationships have long been the target of disapproval by both the Takarazuka Administration and modern Japanese society in general, and homophobia seems rife among fans, at least at the level of lip-service. Nonetheless, in the present day, it is possible to infer from observation of behaviour and conversations with some of the parties concerned that many female fans long to have an exclusive personal relationship with a performer (as friends, sisters or even as lovers), and that certain individuals indeed do engage in mutual romantic and sexual relationships with Takarasiennes, though their behaviour in private is really their own business. While documentary evidence is almost non-existent, anecdotal evidence for this argument is plentiful and persuasive. One ex-*musumeyaku* informant, a long-serving member of the Revue from pre- to post-war years, suggests that *otokoyaku*, in particular, are 'safe' targets for female affection, in that however besotted (*muchū*) a female fan became with an *otokoyaku*, there would not be any 'mistakes' (Informant MH 2001: Q. 3.2). In this informant's eyes, the risks inherent in heterosexual coupling, such as pregnancy and sexually-transmitted disease, make same-sex relations a more desirable alternative for female fans, about whose welfare she obviously cares.

While many Japanese women acknowledge that they feel strong emotional attraction towards other women, and some also admit to feeling physical attraction, a comparative few seem to identify this as a manifestation of a lesbian *identity* as known in the West. Wim Lunsing (1997: 285) points out that sexual preference in Japan is 'generally not seen as a feature that determines one's personhood more than partially,' an idea echoed by Mark McLelland (2001).[11] In turn, Kawasaki Kenko calls the sexual identity of Takarazuka performers and their fans 'de-heterosexual (*datsu-iseiai-teki*),' which, she claims 'cannot be reduced to a lesbian/feminist identity' (Kawasaki 2005: 153). Moreover, Nakamura and Matsuo (2003: 65) argue that being a Revue fan and identifying as a lesbian are distinctly separate issues even among fans who admit to both. In my own discussions with numerous female Takarazuka fans and a few performers, I have found very strong resistance towards the labelling of intimate feelings, sexual behaviour or close interpersonal relationships with other women as 'lesbian,' even though many of the individuals in question did inform me that they were living with or 'dating' women. One Takarasienne and her female partner, a staunch supporter of Takarazuka who was well known to Revue staff, performers and fans alike, had been a couple for more than a decade, but the performer was taken aback when I broached the subject of lesbianism, and quickly reassured me, during a private conversation around 1990, that she herself wasn't 'that way.'

On the other hand, while homoeroticism in the sense of lesbian desire may not be openly acknowledged as one of the attractions of Takarazuka for its fans, an interesting permutation of this seems to exist, involving imagined 'gay male' romances between the characters played by *otokoyaku*. Writer/directors may even deliberately include ambiguous elements that invite the construction of such subplots. A dance scene in the 1995 revue *Mega Vision*, for example, featured a beautiful Greek youth (Maya Miki) being tenderly embraced by a 'god' (Anju Mira) in the guise of an (apparently) male swan. The mythic setting did nothing to dispel the homoerotic mood of the piece, as the audience would have been aware that both performers habitually played male roles.[12] Doubtless writers and directors are aware of the popularity among Japanese women of comics (*manga*) based on the theme of gay male love, or 'boy love (*shōnen ai*),' which proliferated in the 1970s and enjoyed a boom at least until the late 1980s (Tanigawa 1989: 195–206; McLelland 2001b). At a restaurant frequented by Takarazuka devotees in about 1991, I overheard fans gleefully suggesting that the two leading 'male' characters in a certain Takarazuka production, whose on-stage friendship was supposedly platonic, had an erotic male-to-male relationship which was conducted in an imagined space and time off-stage.

The practice of fandom

One of the most conspicuous features of the contemporary Revue is the extraordinary number of female fans who participate in organised fan activities. Many fan practices are in themselves equally enjoyable to fans of either gender, but most fan clubs now have a predominantly female membership, and some activities, such as chauffeuring or house-cleaning for a performer, are off-limits for males because they involve the possibility of close contact with a beloved performer in the private space of a car or dwelling. The following discussion, therefore, will concentrate upon fan culture as practised exclusively or mainly by female Takarazuka fans.

As we have seen, female fans know that their *otokoyaku* idol is not really a man, but may still feel free to enjoy the make-believe that 'he' is – after all, fantasy is the 'commodity' purveyed by the huge Takarazuka organisation, and it is offered unreservedly to all who care to consume that fantasy. Its consumers need not justify their liking for the Revue, for the Company urges them in many ways simply to indulge in it to their hearts' content. The constantly reiterated motto: '*Kiyoku, tadashiku, utsukushiku* (Purely, righteously, beautifully)' may be interpreted as both prescriptive and proscriptive, in setting the boundaries of behaviour and thought for both performers and fans. From an opposite point of view, though, the motto also works to give respectability to a variety of activities and emotions which, in a different context, might be seen as anything from merely frivolous to 'perverted.'

The behaviour of some fans resembles that of stalkers: obsession with a performer to the extent of loitering in the same place every day to observe her ingress and egress; regularly thrusting letters full of praise and/or criticism into her hand; photographing her at every opportunity; and showering her with unsolicited bouquets and gifts. Yet if the waiting and the exchange of letters, gifts and flowers takes place outside the stage door of a Takarazuka theatre, and especially if not one, but scores of individuals engage in identical behaviour towards their favourite, then it apparently is not considered untoward. On the contrary, such mass adulation, signified principally by numerous bouquets and the provision of lavish lunches in lace-trimmed baskets, is usually welcomed by the recipient as a measure of her popularity, and allegedly taken into account by the Company when choosing which performers to promote to top stardom. Certainly, however, uninvited encroachment by fans into the private lives of performers, and especially any action by a commercial enterprise apart from Hankyu or the Revue itself to profit from fans' curiosity about their off-stage activities, is deemed reprehensible. This is evidenced by court action mounted by the Revue Administration against publishing company Rokusaisha in December 1996 to suppress the sale of a book giving details of performers' real names and hints as to where to find their homes.[13] Clearly unfazed, the publishers also brought out two more similar, updated versions of their 'stalkers' handbooks' in the early 2000s (Takarazuka Kageki Kenkyūkai 2002, 2003).

Takarazuka fandom is thus seen as something safe to practise in groups, where members regulate the extent of each other's personal involvement with the performers. The Administration is probably glad of this self-regulatory function of the various fan clubs, though it officially recognises only one organisation, the Takarazuka tomo no kai (Takarazuka Friends' Club), which does not profess exclusive loyalty to any particular performer or troupe. Within a year or two of her debut, nearly every Takarasienne – or, at least, every

otokoyaku – probably has attracted sufficient fans to form a 'club.'
With approximately half of the Company's performers being male-
role players, this would mean that at least two hundred clubs would
exist at any one time, with membership numbers ranging from a
handful of individuals to a thousand or more, in the case of stars.
Sakuragi Seiko, herself an ex-Takarasienne, offers evidence on her
Internet site, which lists links to a multitude of Takarasiennes' fan
clubs (Sakuragi 2004).

On the periphery of Takarazuka fandom lies a different kind of
fan club from those established to support a particular performer or
one of the various troupes – the all-female, 'Takarazuka copycat'
theatre groups (*modoki gekidan*), of which there are several in both
the Kansai and Tokyo areas, as noted by Robertson (1998b: 172–76,
179) and Waseda daigaku Takarazuka kageki o aisuru kai OG (1999:
230–31). Many of their participants are would-be Takarasiennes,
usually past the age of possible entry to the Music School, who wish
to simulate the experience of their idols by mounting their own all-
female musical theatre productions, often adaptations of Takarazuka
scripts. Moreover, in recent years, largely through the medium of the
internet, Takarazuka seems to have inspired numerous individuals
and groups even outside of Japan to copy its stage costumes and
indulge in 'cosplay.' A simple online search yields a range of
examples, including video clips of non-Japanese cosplayers miming
and dancing to Takarazuka songs, or showing off their faithful
reproductions of Takarazuka characters at cosplay contests.

Trouble can arise when individual fans attempt to transgress
the boundaries set by fan clubs and seek a one-to-one relationship
with their idol, even occasionally resorting to criminal acts (such
as embezzlement of funds from their workplace) in order to
impress their favourite with expensive gifts, which may extend to
apartments, jewellery or cash.[14] Undisciplined fans can also cause
inconvenience to performers, and even instil fear in them. During
the boom ignited by *The Rose of Versailles*, for example, fans tore
at stars' hair and clothing to obtain a 'souvenir,' according to a
television interview with one of the performers involved, Ōtori Ran
(NHK Osaka 1992b). Even earlier, Kasugano Yachiyo, a star in both
pre- and post-war periods, records that some fans would place 'all
sorts of things' into her kimono sleeves; 'I had my hair pulled, and
my handbag slashed,' she reminisces (Suzuki 1976: 193–94).

Many Takarazuka fans engage in particular fan activities
on a regular basis, indulging in multiple viewings of the same
production,[15] frequent stage-door vigils, letter-writing, rostered

lunch preparation for their idol, mandatory queuing for tickets and so on. This behaviour is seldom self-regulated by individuals, however, for organised fan clubs make and enforce rules regarding their members, each of whom has a certain place and function in the club hierarchy. Members are reminded that they have a responsibility to their idol and to the group, which makes their fandom not simply a self-indulgent pastime. The fan club uniform, usually a short- or long-sleeved cotton top, erases differences in taste and markers of social status, as well as disciplining the wearers, who cannot engage in non-sanctioned activities (such as eagerly looking at performers other than the club's idol) without being recognised.

The frequency of participation in fan activities is in fact one external measure of the degree of a fan's dedication. Takarazuka often assumes central place in the lives of serious fans, whose family, school and/or work responsibilities become secondary. At a 'tea party' (*ochakai*) I attended in the late 1970s with Japanese and American friends, held by the fan club of Daichi Mao, one fan declared proudly that she had seen the current production starring Daichi *five* times. To the embarrassment of the fan and the merriment of the assembled crowd, Daichi retorted, '*Sukunai!* (Not enough!).' There are even cases in which fans endure repeated viewings of a production they find boring or distasteful, in order to show their support for a specific performer, irrespective of the play in which she appears, or to demonstrate loyalty to a fan club which has been left with too many unsold tickets for an unpopular play.

Some fan habits verge upon the ritualistic, and the physical discomfort of some practices, such as standing waiting in the open air for hours, in all kinds of weather, in order to glimpse an idol or purchase tickets, is akin to the ascetic. Though performances are held in the daytime, fans who participate in the practice known in Takarazuka parlance as *de-machi* (waiting for a performer's exit from the stage door, as opposed to *iri-machi*, waiting for the star's arrival at the theatre) must wait for an hour or more after regular audience members have left, in order to see their idol emerge. Rehearsals may extend fans' wait until late evening. Any action by the Administration or by the performers themselves to reduce opportunities for fans' indulgence in the pleasurable pastimes of *iri-machi* and *de-machi* would be unpopular, as evidenced by the controversy stirred by 1990s star Amami Yūki, who was thought arrogant because she apparently issued an edict to her fans that they were to go home if she had not emerged from the stage door or rehearsal hall by ten o'clock at night (Sumire uotchāzu 1996:

48). Takarazuka fandom and religious piety are thus somewhat similar – the more often a fan proves her devotion by engaging in such behaviour in the prescribed manner, the more respect she gains from the larger group of Takarazuka fans, as well as from the performer whom she supports.

The social aspect of fan activities is also attractive to most – especially, it seems, to full-time housewives who perhaps would otherwise be socially isolated in the daytime. Watching a telecast or DVD of a Takarazuka performance alone at home may be physically comfortable and more economical of both money and energy, but it is emotionally less satisfying because of the lack of opportunity to converse and otherwise interact with others who share the fan's enthusiasm.

The hierarchical structure of the Revue, with its glorification of male-role players, is also reproduced among the hundreds of non-official fan clubs dedicated to individual performers. Although the choice of which performer to support is usually quite arbitrary, the implications of choosing a particular performer differ according to that Takarasienne's stage gender, seniority and level of popularity. Firstly, a performer's number of years of stage experience, rather than her star status, dictates to whom respect must be paid by her fans, and from whom they can expect to receive respect, meaning that fans of a young player on the rise to stardom, for instance, irrespective of their own age and social status, are still expected to bow and use polite language towards fans of more senior performers, even though the latter may be by-players with far fewer supporters. Within each fan club, there are various types of members. Apart from attending performances, many ordinary members actively help the group as a whole by queuing for tickets to contribute to the club pool of seats; others join merely to be allowed to attend tea-parties, receive newsletters containing information about their idol, and so on. Long-serving club members are usually afforded considerable respect by those joining later, and given greater responsibility within the organisation. They may even share some of the performer's glory through their direct contact with her. This envied position can give them power over sometimes hundreds, or even thousands, of members, some of whom may curry favour with the club's officials in the hope of gaining privileged access to, or otherwise undisclosed information about, the performer they support. This power can be occasionally misused, and misappropriation of club funds by officials has occurred, as suggested by Sischy (1992: 99). To my knowledge, women lead all Takarazuka fan clubs, bar the few mentioned above which are organised by groups of powerful men. Organisations in society in general probably seldom offer women the kind of status afforded by Takarazuka fan club leadership.

Another factor differentiating the status of the various fan clubs relates to a kind of sexism that now seems to operate in the fan community, relegating fans of female-role players to the periphery, even though the performers in question are supposedly of equal rank to *otokoyaku* from the same Music School graduating class. Just as males have always dominated the leading administrative and creative staff positions in the Company, and male-role players have grown to almost monopolise fans' affection, fans of stage 'men' also seem to assert themselves more than supporters of stage 'women,' and advertise their presence more confidently than the latter by such means as matching clothing. The sheer numerical superiority of *otokoyaku* fans is evidenced by the crowds which mob the male-role players outside the stage door, while only a few people accompany, or even glance at the female-role players as they enter or exit. Typical fans, it seems, are attracted and assured by a performer's very popularity. Female fans of *musumeyaku* or *onnayaku* today perhaps are embarrassed to be members of a minority, as their liking for a particular female-role performer might be disparaged by other fans for going against the norm. Fans who find fault with the *musumeyaku* paired with their favourite *otokoyaku* may even direct their scathing criticisms at supporters of the female-role player concerned. Another possible reason for the lesser popularity of players of female roles among female fans is the frequent failure of *musumeyaku* to provide female spectators with a positive model of female agency, due to their dependent and subordinate status vis-à-vis their male-role opposites. Moreover, women who profess support for a *musumeyaku* cannot use the excuse reiterated by female fans of *otokoyaku*, namely that their idol is attractive because (s)he is an 'ideal man,' and thus may be uncomfortable with the fact that they are drawn to a fellow female.

The Revue Administration obviously prefers unobtrusively heterosexual fans who enjoy Takarazuka performances in general, irrespective of which troupe is performing, and do not concentrate their adoration upon one particular star, because such fans are less likely to cut their ties with Takarazuka when a favourite performer retires.[16] Many fans of *otokoyaku* lose interest in their idol when she sheds her masculine persona upon retirement, as she can no longer fulfil their fantasies of the 'ideal man,' or continue to be a role model for women who dislike stereotypical femininity.

However, a frequent pattern is for fans to transfer their allegiance from a retiring to a current performer, often a younger, promising *otokoyaku* whose career they can follow for a number of years, and whose rise to stardom will give them growing personal satisfaction, plus a measure of prestige among other performers' fans if their new favourite eventually achieves top billing.

It must be remembered that, as Chapters Two and Three have shown, a large proportion of performers themselves have been fans before joining Takarazuka, and the practice of fandom thus forms an especially meaningful part of their lives. As previously discussed, the *akogare* (adoration/platonic yearning/desire to emulate) which such entrants felt towards the Revue in general, and frequently towards one star in particular, is often considered by them to have bolstered their determination to succeed at their Music School training and become good performers themselves, in spite of the considerable physical and emotional hardship involved. After their retirement, too, performers themselves usually continue to support the Revue as fans. While most simply enjoy occasional trips to the theatre, some become unpaid mentors or paid instructors to promising juniors, as will be discussed in Chapter Six. A number of retirees become 'second-wave' fans, zealously attending performances and promoting the careers of young Takarasiennes who may be many years their juniors in the Company hierarchy, and are therefore obliged to show them respect. The alumnae status of these women affords them access to the back-stage world of Takarazuka, where they can chat to or watch current performers at close hand. This behaviour is not always welcomed, however: one of my informants, in an aside to her interview, named a particular ex-Takarasienne as a 'nuisance' in the dressing rooms because of her fan-like attitude and incessant chatter (Informant SS 2001).

Many retirees belong to the official alumnae association, Hōyūkai (Takarazuka friends' association) or other groups, such as Juhōkai ('Tree treasure club'), an organisation made up of female 'old fans,' once headed by former star Ashihara Kuniko, which awards annual prizes for excellence to selected performers.[17] These associations allow them close contact with stars of the past whom they might have idolised in their own youth. Moreover, a number of 'old girls' occasionally join together to stage amateur performances for charity, or even participate in professional productions whose casts comprise retirees, sometimes with the addition of a couple of current Takarazuka members as 'guest' stars. Such performances enable retirees to relive their stage days by recreating their *musumeyaku* or *otokoyaku* personae. This simulation of Takarazuka performance practices is similar to that of the amateur 'copycat' theatre groups described above, showing that close parallels do exist between fans and performers, and also that fans' enjoyment of Takarasiennes' skilful manipulation of gender does not necessarily cease when performers retire.

As we have seen, fans are not merely passive consumers of Takarazuka, but also involve themselves actively in the creation of the total experience that centres on the Revue. Fans can also wield a measure of power over their idols, and the Revue itself, through various means. By supplying performers with food, drink, clothing and other gifts, for example, individual fans not only nourish and care for their idols, but also can dictate to a certain extent what the performers consume, wear and use, if the recipients are willing to cooperate. One 1990s star gained a reputation for arrogance by refusing all such favours (Amami 1995: 132), because other performers usually graciously accepted fans' gifts and services, even if they ultimately passed unwanted items on to others. Accepting a gift usually creates an obligation to reciprocate in some way, and Takarasiennes accomplish this by such means as sending New Year and midsummer greeting cards to fans, wearing presented clothing and accessories in magazine photographs or at public appearances, and publicly thanking their supporters in speeches and interviews. I remember eagerly awaiting the postal delivery on 1 January each year, anticipating a few words of personal greeting on New Year's cards from Takarazuka acquaintances to whom I had taught English diction.

Fans have also been able to attempt to influence different aspects of Takarazuka by writing critiques of performers, productions, Revue policy and so on, addressing their letters to the Takarasienne(s) concerned, the Administration, or various fan-oriented publications. Most recently, the forum for such opinion has increasingly been Internet chat rooms or Websites. The anonymity and privacy afforded by cyberspace could be considered especially valuable to female fans that might otherwise be reticent about engaging in open discussion. As Junko R. Onosaka notes, 'the effectiveness of the Internet for accomplishing a variety of goals' has been rapidly discovered by women (Onosaka 2003: 95).

Another avenue by which fans' favouritism can be signalled is the giving of ostentatious bouquets of flowers to particular performers at the theatre, where they are prominently displayed. One day in early 2001, for example, in the corridor beside the Takarazuka

Grand Theatre's stage door, I counted more than a hundred potted butterfly orchid plants sent by fans, each plant costing perhaps twenty or thirty thousand yen. Due to limited space backstage at the new Tokyo Takarazuka Theatre, however, bouquets are now forbidden. Conversely, fans' disapproval of particular stars, troupes or productions is starkly communicated to the Administration by the number of tickets left unsold, or the empty seats at performances which appear to be sold out, but whose ticket-holders baulk at attending.

When the nature of theatrical productions dictates that characters on stage interact only among themselves, audience members in general are more or less relegated to the status of onlookers or voyeurs beyond the 'fourth wall' of the proscenium arch. In Takarazuka theatres, however, fans frequently reject this role and draw attention to their own presence, influencing performers' mood, timing and ability to stay in character by pronounced applause, laughter, weeping or calling out of the nicknames of their favourites. Such activity is probably more common and more influential than it is among audiences at other forms of live theatre in Japan and elsewhere, though there are some similarities with Kabuki audiences. Even silence on the part of the Takarazuka audience can communicate tension, hostility or other emotions for the players to interpret.

Applause in moderation may be welcomed by the Revue Company, but not other fan practices which could disturb the flow of a performance or indicate excessive adulation of one player, to the detriment of her fellow Troupe members. One such practice now discouraged is the use of *kakegoe*, in which fans, singly or in unison, called out the nickname of their favourite player whenever she made an entrance or at some other appropriate juncture in her performance, such as immediately before a song or when she assumed a particularly striking pose. As early as 1964, and again in the early 1970s (when ear-splitting, chorused *kakegoe* punctuated every performance that I saw), the Revue Company attempted to enforce a prohibition, still officially current, upon such name-chanting.[18] The Takarazuka ban was apparently imposed because of the disruptive effect of the loud cries, which often rendered other performers' songs and dialogue inaudible, but a well-timed *kakegoe* may sometimes be heard even now, when a Takarazuka star is making her farewell appearance before retirement, for instance. Haruna Yuri recalls her elation at hearing her name called from the audience by Music School classmate Gō Chigusa, a retired star with an unmistakeable voice, when Haruna was performing for the last time (Haruna 1993: 176).

Fans as audience: 'the gaze'

One vital part of the relationship between fans and players in Takarazuka is encapsulated in the concept of 'the gaze,' which plays a major role in creating and sustaining pleasure for those involved and in forming interrelationships (however ephemeral) between performers and spectators. As we know, the spectacle of Takarazuka, which is certainly calculated to please the eye of its beholders, consists of a combination of a large stage, numerous cast members, bright lights, huge sets, colourful costumes and spot-lit stars, who usually wear white, silver or gold spangles during the finale, thus ensuring that they reflect the maximum amount of light. On this issue, Kawasaki comments:

> The audience gazes at the stars, who seem almost to be generating light themselves because of the reflection of all the illumination upon them. There is an illusion shared both by those up on stage and those down in the auditorium that the constantly-gazing audience is being gazed at in turn by the performers on stage. Fans rejoice that their 'eyes locked' with a star's on stage. For the spectators, the performers on stage are not only playing against each other [but also playing to and for the audience]. The Revue Company's theatrical space is made complete only when it envelops this give-and-take exchange of gazes (Kawasaki 1999: 17).

Kawasaki further explains that, unlike other contemporary theatre in which the stage action is self-contained, and audience members are cut off from each other in the darkness, the 'excessive brightness' of Takarazuka stage-lighting blurs the boundary between stage and audience, filling the theatrical space with a sense of 'symbiosis (*kyōsei*) and unity (*yūgō*)': old-time Kabuki fans apparently say that to be stared at by an actor is to 'have one's demons exorcised,' and Takarazuka, also, seems to generate something akin to or substituting for a sense of sacredness (*seisei*) (Kawasaki 1999: 17–18). Nosaka similarly asserts that Takarazuka is 'like a sacred place for girls' (Nosaka 1977: 118).

The mutuality of the gaze is most palpable during the finale parade, in which a combination of downlights, footlights and spotlights is used. It is no accident that these are the very scenes in

which performers are most likely to be looking directly out into the
auditorium, returning the gaze of the audience. The way in which
stars use this as an opportunity to capture the loyalty of new fans
and gladden existing ones was demonstrated in one light-hearted
television variety programme shown during the New Year period
(NHK Television 2001). In one segment of that programme, 1970s
star Ōtori Ran gave 'instruction' in various *otokoyaku* techniques or
kata. Among these techniques was an eye-sweep that encompassed
the entire auditorium, to give each member of the audience the
illusion that s/he was 'being looked at' by the performer.

Spectators may also imagine themselves as a performer's lover
during romantic scenes in which the male- and female-role players
on stage are embracing. One of the pair is usually facing out into
the auditorium, suggesting that his/her 'true lover' is the spectator,
not the character in his/her arms. Arguably, Takarazuka fans have
paid money for tickets to 'possess' the performers with their eyes,
in similar manner to the male 'spectator-owner' of a painting of a
woman with her male lover, about whom John Berger has written in
his analysis of the ways people perceive art (Berger 1972: 56).

Research published in the journal *Nature* shows that returned eye
gaze from an attractive face, irrespective of the gender and sexual
orientation of each party, may engage the brain's central reward
systems (and thus, it may be deduced, produce feelings of pleasure);
correspondingly, avoiding the gaze of an unattractive face may
also produce a reward (manifested as a feeling of relief), and not
having one's gaze returned by an attractive face, moreover, leads to
feelings of disappointment (Kampe et al 2001: 589). In terms of the
Revue, this hypothesis may offer an explanation as to why women
who do not identify as lesbian and who have no sexualised, same-
sex relationships outside the context of adoration for a Takarazuka
otokoyaku still seem to derive so much pleasure from looking at, and
being seen by, that performer. The eye of a female fan's favourite
otokoyaku is perhaps a kind of mirror in which the fan longs to see
herself reflected, either as the fantasy lover of, or the body-double
for, the performer.

In Takarazuka, this mirror function would usually only work
during parts of a performance when cast members were actively
engaged in communicating with the audience, such as during the
vocal numbers of a typical finale. A lack of opportunity for such
communication would lessen the popularity of a production among
regular fans, in spite of any other merits the production might have.
The Revue Administration thus has had to seek permission from the

copyright-holders of some imported musicals to add a finale. This permission was apparently not granted for Takarazuka's première seasons of *Oklahoma* and *West Side Story*, and these productions were not very popular.[19] The Revue Administration seems to have learnt from this experience, for later imports have been better received, partly because of a wiser choice of script, as in *Me and My Girl*, whose cheerful 'Lambeth Walk' song-and-dance sequence, introduced at the end of Act One and reprised in the finale, certainly contributed to its success by encouraging the audience to clap along with the rhythm, and enabled cast members to step down into the aisles.

The power of the gaze of Takarazuka performers as they beam out across the audience is significantly enhanced by their makeup conventions, which create gendered faces that are considerably different from faces in mainstream society. As we have seen in the previous chapter, contemporary Takarazuka eye makeup – especially that used in productions with a non-Japanese setting – creates an illusion of very large eyes, somewhat similar to those typical of characters in comics aimed at a female readership (*shōjo manga*). *Otokoyaku* are the ones most likely to face out into the auditorium to capture and return the gaze of spectators during 'show' songs, soliloquies and dramatic asides, as well as in the finale, while *musumeyaku* tend to look towards *otokoyaku*, and are seldom on stage alone. Any gaze directed at a female-role player from the audience would tend to be rerouted towards her male-role opposite – in other words, deflected rather than returned. One reason for the lesser popularity of *musumeyaku* may be that audience members are frequently frustrated by this lack of reciprocity, and come to prefer the *otokoyaku* who appear to return their gaze even for an instant.

Multiple viewings of the same performance enable fans to anticipate at which moment eye exchanges can take place. Where there is a choice of seating, a fan might pick a position from which s/he expects to enjoy an exchange of gazes. Photographs and videos of such moments are eagerly taken by some fans, who employ various ingenious means to disguise the appearance of and muffle any noise produced by the devices in order to evade the vigilance of ushers, who seem to spend most of their time while the curtain is up scrutinising the audience, in an attempt to enforce the Administration's prohibition upon the use of cameras and electronic recording devices of all kinds during performances.[20] The reflection of stage lights upon a camera lens would make the position of photographers visible to performers, who may even play to these cameras, knowing that their fans are likely to proffer copies of their best shots, often suitably enlarged or cropped, to the performer. Fans' photographs and videos are also frequently copied and distributed among fellow devotees.

While a reciprocated gaze is tantalising for some fans, it is anathema to others. I have observed members of the Takarazuka audience attempting to hide from certain performers' view at particular moments by lowering their heads and hunching down in their seats. Three differing explanations could be offered for this phenomenon: the fans are so strongly attracted to the performer in question that they anticipate a level of pleasure too great to bear and therefore actively seek to avoid the return of their gaze; they know the performer well but are painfully shy; or else they dislike the performer for some reason and crave the relief that would stem from avoiding eye contact with her. I have also seen one woman putting her fingers into her ears to shut out the sound of a particular performer's singing voice, thus signalling her acute displeasure to those around her, and perhaps even sending a silent but visible insult to the performer on stage. Some *otokoyaku* also seem to enjoy the fervent gaze of the females in the audience: ex-star Mine Saori, for example, once described bathing in that gaze as 'sheer pleasure...better than anything' (cited in *Subaru* 1987: 86–97).

The antithesis of fandom

As a counterpoint to the preceding discussion, which focuses upon lovers of Takarazuka and the gender issues involved in their fandom, it is necessary also to recognise the antipathy harboured by some people towards the Revue, as the latter, too, seems to involve stereotypical notions of gender, which include the frequent assignment by society of lesser value to activities by and for females, in comparison to those by and for males. The attitudes of Takarazuka's detractors often involve a gender bias. One commentator on women's issues in popular culture, Nimiya Kazuko, offers the opinion that Takarazuka is denigrated mainly because of the idea held by some people that 'women are idiots, so it is natural to make fun of all things that women enjoy' (Nimiya 1995: 18). She remarks that despite what she sees as societal acknowledgement of the economic significance of the 'culture of cuteness (*kawaii bunka*)' [21] enjoyed by many women and children, such culture still tends to be regarded as something that has 'absolutely no [intrinsic] value' (Nimiya 1995: 194). Takarazuka, in this view, was given more credence in the pre-war and wartime years, when boys and men made up a much larger proportion of the audience than in recent decades, and openly expressed their liking for it. According to Takagi, the intelligentsia (*shikisha*), who were mostly men, also showed great interest in the original Girls' Opera, especially in its foundation years (Takagi 1983: 57).

Anti-Takarazuka articles in the media of the mid-1930s, soon after short hair for *otokoyaku* had become the norm, were often concerned with warning of the dangers of homosexuality, while those of the war years tended to criticise the Revue for the frivolous lifestyle of its performers during a time of austerity and national emergency (see Robertson 1998b: 146–47, 164). Although trousers are no longer regarded as garments exclusively for males in contemporary Japan, and hair length is no longer a strict indicator of gender identity, the calculatedly androgynous appearance of the male-role performers may still disturb some people who believe that gender roles are immutable, that men should be manly and women womanly (or girlish), and therefore regard 'cross-dressing' as 'abnormal.'

On the other hand, many feminists object to what they see as the glorification of masculinity on the Revue stage, with female-role players existing only as a mirroring moon to the male-role players' sun, reflecting back their brilliance (Cline and Spender 1988). The feminist Sasaki Toshiko (1985) writes that when engaged in her own tug-of-war between Takarazuka and Women's Liberation philosophy as a university student in the 1970s, she longed for Takarazuka all the more when she became increasingly aware of the structure of discrimination against women and the disheartening realities of women's situation in male-centred society. After attending a Women's Liberation meeting, Sasaki would almost always watch a Takarazuka performance, Takarazuka becoming for her 'a place to relax and escape.' As she came to understand through the feminist movement that the root of discrimination against women lay in fixed gender roles, she changed her view of Takarazuka, where old-fashioned andocentric gender relationships were still played out on stage. Torn between her new awareness and her fondness for the Revue, Sasaki nevertheless chose to continue patronising Takarazuka (Sasaki 1985: 123–34).

By contrast, many Japanese lesbians – especially those who actively promote gay pride and the recognition of sexual minority rights – express enmity towards the Revue Company's denial of any lesbian basis to female fans' same-sex attraction towards the *otokoyaku*, except in the context of 'normal' female attraction to an individual of the 'opposite' gender (who is usually a biological male, but is a 'fantasy male' in the case of a Takarazuka *otokoyaku*). I posit that so strongly-entrenched is homophobia even among many Takarazuka fans that an 'out' lesbian could find herself ostracised from the fan community because of her flagrant transgression of the 'Purely, righteously, beautifully' motto. To speak of platonic love towards a shared idol, to joke about an imagined 'gay male' relationship between certain stage characters played by *otokoyaku*,[22] or even to indulge in rumour-mongering and speculation about the love life of various performers may be permissible, or even expected among fans, but to openly declare one's lesbianism, with the inherent nuance of anticipating a sexual relationship with a particular Takarasienne, would mark one as either dangerous, or at least risible. One long-time fan told me of a woman who was notorious among the stage-door crowd for coming every day, dressed in her most alluring clothes, with the apparent hope that her favourite star would invite her on a date that evening. Lesbians, then, often feel alienated from Takarazuka, and those who continue to participate in fan activities probably keep their sexual orientation secret from most fellow fans. Some undoubtedly also keep their fan activity secret from other lesbians.

Again, from the point of view of aesthetics, many anti-Takarazuka individuals probably have found the strident stage makeup repugnant, especially when viewed in close proximity, as in the publicity posters displayed at Hankyu-affiliated facilities and on theatre programmes. The covers of some issues of the official fan magazine *Takarazuka gurafu* also formerly featured exaggerated makeup, but adverse reactions to these cover portraits probably lessened when the renowned photographer Shinoyama Kishin took charge of posing and photographing performers in naturalistic makeup from the January 1998 issue onwards.

This chapter has provided a wide-ranging overview of fan practices and attitudes from the past nine decades of Takarazuka's existence. Fan behaviour or demographics may change in the twenty-first century, however, if women continue to seek ever-higher levels of education; if marriage and childbearing are postponed or even rejected completely; or if the structure of paid work for both women and men undergoes significant change. If women gain more economic power, and in doing so become more 'androgynous,' will the *otokoyaku* still be so popular? Perhaps some men also will move closer to an androgynous ideal, and thus answer some of the yearnings of the women who flock to Takarazuka because of their disillusionment with flesh-and-blood males. These issues certainly deserve further observation.

Next, I will examine, among other issues, how fans react to their idol's retirement from the uniquely gendered world of Takarazuka to marry or pursue a new career, and what place gender roles play in that final stage of a Takarasienne's life.

6 Life after Takarazuka

On 19 October 2007, Takarazuka's most senior performer, Kasugano Yachiyo, known to her fans as the 'Prince of the White Rose,' danced with stately grace in a masculine topknot wig and a dapper pair of 'young man's' *hakama* culottes over a black kimono, in a special Japanese classical dance performance staged to commemorate the hundredth anniversary of the founding of the Hankyu railway (Yabushita 2007b).

The octogenarian Kasugano has never married, instead devoting her life since her early teens in 1928 to the endless pursuit of perfection in the performing arts, and she symbolises the pinnacle of Takarazuka's moral and artistic tradition. Kasugano's life as a Takarasienne is atypical, however, as most performers have left the company within ten or fifteen years of graduating from the Takarazuka Music School. Orthodox societal views on the 'proper' life cycle of women are often used by the Administration and the performers' relatives as a rationale for encouraging performers to quit the Company while they are still in their twenties or early thirties. For these young retirees, a new challenge awaits when they step down from the Takarazuka stage: to rejoin mainstream society, whose notions of gender can be considerably different from those played out in the all-female Revue.

Takarazuka teaches its members to observe, manipulate and modify orthodox gender roles for their own purposes, and ex-Takarasiennes take this knowledge with them as they rejoin the everyday world, where different versions of masculinity and femininity are played out. This chapter examines the issues affecting Takarasiennes as women in Japan in their post-performing lives, showing how their training in gender portrayal for the Revue stage enables some to adapt readily to new circumstances and form new relationships after quitting Takarazuka, while their lack of formal education and experience of life apart from the stage impedes the entry to employment, or leads to an unhappy marriage, for others. The chapter first discusses performers' reasons for leaving the Company and the traditional attitude of the Takarazuka Revue to marriage, which is shaped by the philosophy of the founder. Secondly,

Plate 5: Kasugano Yachiyo, pinnacle of Takarazuka's hierarchy.
© *Takarazuka Revue Company.*

I examine the rationale for the Revue's ban upon married performers, which is supported by most Takarasiennes. Thirdly, I explore Kobayashi's claim that Takarazuka is a 'school for brides,' and that playing male roles on stage, especially, equips performers to become superior wives. Fourthly, the chapter examines the adjustments, if any, deemed necessary by retired performers to adapt to society at large, especially in regard to learning and unlearning gender roles. Here, a variety of other career choices made by former Takarasiennes is discussed, revealing the efforts made by selected individuals to compensate for a lack of formal educational qualifications. Finally, the chapter outlines the functions fulfilled by retired performers in providing diverse services to current members of the Revue, staff and fans, and in training would-be recruits. Overall, the chapter will show that for Takarasiennes, at least, the process of learning and relearning gender is actually a continuing one, certainly not confined only to the years they spend on the Revue stage.

Sayonara, Takarazuka: reasons and rules

It is difficult to gain a comprehensive view of Takarasiennes' reasons for retirement, as few retirees are the subject of media attention, apart from the most popular *otokoyaku* stars who pursue a show business career, and details of the post-Takarazuka lives of others are seldom publicised. Nevertheless, my research shows that in spite of efforts by the Administration to represent retired Takarasiennes as fitting particular, narrow moulds of womanhood – as either lifelong entertainers, or wives and mothers – the women themselves cannot be stereotyped. While impending marriage is still a common reason for retiring, many leave the Company to develop their performing skills in a new environment, to pursue a different avenue of employment, or simply to rest and regain control over their lives, which were regimented by the Company for so long.

With or without a formal limit being set upon the length of their membership of the Revue, few Revue performers have stayed with the Company throughout their adult lives, Amatsu Otome being the first 'career Takarasienne,' remaining a member for sixty-two years until her death in 1980. Accident and illness have claimed the lives of a small number of serving performers, but the majority of others have left the Company while comparatively young to pursue other activities, for reasons both internal and external to the Revue.

There was originally no set limit on the number of years a Takarasienne could stay with the company if she did not marry, unless she committed some criminal or morally-reprehensible act. Even among the initial group of recruits making their debut in 1914, there were five who remained for between fourteen and eighteen years, and several performers who debuted in the 1920s remained for more than two decades (see Hashimoto 1994: 178). Now, however, there is definite cut-off point: the mandatory retirement age, set at fifty-five in 1972, now extends to sixty (Fujino 1990: 169). The two exceptions are Kasugano Yachiyo and, apparently, also her immediate junior, Matsumoto Yuri (debut 1957), an accomplished Japanese classical dancer, who are both members of the Company's executive Board (*riji kai*) as well as performers. For some years now, biographical details accompanying the photographs of these two most senior performers in the annual *Takarazuka otome* (2007: 5) omit the year of their debut – information usually provided – from which their ages could be guessed. Other Board members over sixty, such as Imanishi Masako (stage name Hayama Michiko), deputy principal of the Takarazuka Music School, have remained in senior positions within the organisation after retirement from performing.

While death or infirmity may be the only reasons for an elderly Kabuki actor to quit the stage, a senior Takarasienne evidently is seen not so much as an artiste whose maturity is to be treasured, but as a commodity with a fixed 'shelf-life.' In the words of one of my informants, herself retired by Company policy, Takarazuka is unique among performing arts companies in not allowing any 'flagrant display of the ugliness of old age' to mar its stage (Informant PP 2001: Q. 4.3). Many Takarasiennes declare that they wish to quit the stage while they still have *hana*, which not only means 'flower' but also refers to superlative skill in a stage performer, as described by the actor Zeami (1363-1443) (see Umesao 1995: 1167). The modern usage of the term in a theatrical context alludes to attractiveness and charisma. This metaphorical 'flower' can fade as a performer passes her artistic prime. The Revue Administration, especially in recent years, also seems intent upon rejuvenating the Company by hastening the retirement of top stars, sometimes less than a year after promotion, to make way for promising youngsters (Informant IN 2001: Q. 3.16). Takarazuka audiences are known for their generosity in overlooking the immaturity of performers' skills as long as they exude youthful energy and charm, and one Company executive emphasises the need for constant renewal:

> Takarazuka has continued for eighty-something years, thanks to a certain extent to its steady 'metabolism' by which its members keep

on retiring, not only for marriage but also for various other reasons.
I think that the constant replacement of members has been vital
(Informant IN 2001: Q. 3.16).

The stage gender of performers has some bearing on when they will
retire, as 'men' on the Revue stage, and males in society in general,
are typically older and more mature-looking than their female
partners. Most *otokoyaku* stars retire in their late twenties or early
thirties, before their *hana* becomes 'full-blown.' *Musumeyaku* stars
tend to retire even earlier, perhaps while they are still 'budding,' as
they are often paired with a more senior *otokoyaku*. The on-stage
partnership of particular leading *otokoyaku* and *musumeyaku* is
often so strong that they retire at the same time. In 2006, Cosmos
Troupe pair Waō Yōka and Hanafusa Mari, for example, not only
left simultaneously, but continued to perform together (Yabushita
2007c). On the other hand, one ex-Takarasienne film and television
actress, Kuroki Hitomi, felt that her dreams had been fulfilled after
four years on the Takarazuka stage, three of them playing opposite
the dashing Daichi Mao. Kuroki and Daichi left together in 1985, and
both have since successfully combined acting careers with marriage
(though Daichi divorced in late 2003). Kuroki has a daughter, but
continues to work (Ioi 1999: 76). Other *musumeyaku* may bow to
subtle, or overt, pressure from the Administration to make way for
a promising junior who is seen as better complementing a chosen
ascendant *otokoyaku*. Conversely, Shiraki Ayaka, top *musumeyaku*
of the Star Troupe for five years until 1997, apparently felt that her
full potential was still unrealised at the time of her first partner's
retirement. Shiraki later decided to quit when she found herself no
longer 'challenged' by her roles (Tsuji 1997:65). Shiraki's second
male-role opposite was then assigned a different *musumeyaku*
partner.

In terms of retirement protocol, Takarazuka can be compared
with other cultural and sporting traditions. Ōtori Ran (1964-79)
likened Takarazuka top stars to sumo grand champions, for both
must start considering retirement from the moment they reach the
top (cited in Shimose 1994: 32). Sumo, in turn, has been compared
by Yamaguchi Masao with Kabuki theatre, in this and other respects
(Yamaguchi 1998: 20). The retirement of stars of Kabuki, sumo
and Takarazuka is marked with a degree of pomp commensurate
with the individual's fame. Some professional baseball players, for
example, become national idols whose final moments on the field
are usually seen by millions. Former *otokoyaku* Tsurugi Miyuki

(1974-90, now a stage actress) claims to have had 'no blueprint at all' for retirement until she watched baseball star Nakahata Kiyoshi hit a solo home run in the last game of his career in 1989. At that instant, struck with admiration at this triumphant final act, Tsurugi resolved to retire from Takarazuka (Tsurugi 1992: 24–25).

Burnout, too, seems to be a strong reason for retirement for many Takarasiennes. Irrespective of age, it is difficult for popular performers to take proper nutrition and sufficient rest. The physical demands of performing are great for the often slight figures of Revue members, and years of punishing performance schedules may lead to illness. One retiree, who battled poor health after quitting, 'exhausted in mind and body,' speaks of now enjoying the luxury of relaxing after a meal instead of having to rush back onstage (Informant PZ 2001: Q. 4.9).

In order to capitalise upon the popularity of its top *otokoyaku*, the Company tries to maximise their exposure to audiences by casting them not only in regular full-troupe performances but also in recitals, small-scale musicals and dinner shows; as guest performers at special events; and on television and radio, meaning that the stars have so little respite that they may long to escape. Extremely popular male-role star Amami Yūki (1987-95), for one, apparently shocked many with her audacity in requesting a reduction in her work. Amami writes: 'From the time I started to be treated as Number Three from the top, I felt as if my life were rapidly moving out of my own hands' (Amami 1995: 274). Upon her promotion to the Moon Troupe's top position in 1993, Amami was shown a long-term production schedule, and promptly decided she would retire two years hence, in December 1995. She had initially won acclaim in her first year with the Company as the lead in a 'New Faces' performance of the imported musical *Me and My Girl*, and hoped to reprise that role before she retired. She compared her own experience of being born and raised in a downtown (*shitamachi*) area of Tokyo before entering the 'high-class' atmosphere of Takarazuka with that of her character, Bill, the illegitimate son of an English lord, raised in London's seedy Lambeth but groomed in adulthood to join the British aristocracy: Amami, like Bill, wanted to end her Takarazuka career with the line, 'I'm going back to Lambeth' (Amami 1995: 268, 272). Her wish was granted, in spite of Company efforts to persuade her to remain, and she has since pursued a busy film and television career.

The early thirties are a challenging time for many Takarasiennes. Not only are these years often the most productive, but they also constitute the most physically and mentally demanding time of a performer's career, especially in the case of a popular *otokoyaku*. Takashio Tomoe (1972–87), for example, suffered from intermittent loss of voice after damaging her throat at about the age of thirty-four, one year before retiring (Usami and Obata 1987: 19). Takashio's successor, Ōura Mizuki, called 'Takarazuka's answer to Fred Astaire' because of her dancing prowess, sustained a serious knee injury due to overuse six months before her scheduled promotion to leading *otokoyaku*, at the age of about thirty. After surgery and lengthy rehabilitation, Ōura began four years in top position. As she informed me in 1992, it was not until after she quit the Company that she was able to strengthen her damaged leg fully. Now, more than fifteen years after quitting Takarazuka, Ōura continues to perform, often dancing with more junior retirees with similar talent who held her in considerable awe, including Shibuki Jun and Asami Hikaru (see *Theater Guide* 2007). Similarly, recent retirees Emao Yū and Takumi Hibiki (1987–2002) each quit after one season as top stars, having also suffered illness and injury in their early thirties (*Sports Nippon* 2002; *Sankei Sports* 2002). At a press conference, Emao hinted that her retirement was not voluntary, speaking frankly of her disappointment at being offered only one season as top star: 'It's a pity, but I suppose the Revue Company has its own agenda, too. As a member of the Company, I simply obeyed their ruling' (Yabushita 2002a). Both Emao and Takumi announced their intention to become 'actresses (*joyū*),' signalling an end to male impersonation.

Until the recent trend in Japan for women to postpone marriage until their late twenties or early thirties, or even to eschew marriage entirely,[1] it was generally assumed that all women should wed, ideally by the age of twenty-five, and that a daughter's duty to her parents would not be fulfilled until she took a husband. The verb often used to describe a daughter's marriage, *katazuku*, likens an unmarried daughter to a mess that needs to be 'tidied away.' Even if the daughters themselves were less than eager to wed, parents, relatives or matchmakers traditionally busied themselves finding suitable men for formal introduction as marriage candidates when the daughters approached marriageable age.[2] It will be remembered that one of the unique features of Takarazuka is that its cast is composed entirely of unmarried women, so a Revue performer must quit upon impending marriage, never to return, except perhaps as a guest in a special 'homecoming' performance. This rule has not been challenged successfully in the past, and seems likely to remain, in spite of increasing social acceptance of women's right to continue paid employment after marriage and childbearing.

The majority of Takarazuka performers are certainly expected by the Company, and probably also by their own families, eventually to leave the public domain of theatrical life. This means jettisoning their stage names and rejoining the non-theatrical community. Indeed, marriage was formerly seen as the only respectable reason for a Takarasienne's retirement, and resigning performers' farewell salutations in the Revue magazines *Kageki* and *Takarazuka gurafu* even as late as the 1970s invariably included one of two reasons for quitting: 'marriage' (for those with a prospective groom in mind), or 'preparation for marriage' (for all others, who may or may not have actually intended to wed). Such wording ensured that the public was continually exposed to the rhetoric that Takarazuka performers were all heterosexual women ready to become wives and mothers, while, in fact, domesticity has been but one of many life-paths chosen by ex-Takarasiennes.

From the Company's point of view, this system encourages a turnover of performers and a constant infusion of rising stars, who, in turn, attract new fans. In its early decades, the Company apparently wrote to parents of unpromising students (rather than approaching the performers themselves), suggesting husbands be found for them. Yoshioka notes that Kobayashi certainly put the onus upon families to steer their daughters towards an early marriage if sufficient talent were not evident, as Kobayashi declared:

> There are some who are late bloomers, but generally one can guess where each girl is headed after two or three years on the boards, so I believe that it is necessary for her parents or guardians to orient her in the right direction according to her prospects, be it as a stage performer, or as a housewife (Yoshioka 1994: 105).

Apart from encouraging them to marry, though, no formal system for 'weeding out' the less attractive or less talented existed until the current 'talent (*tarento*) contract system' was inaugurated in 1977. Under this system, each new graduate of the Music School joins the Company as a 'female performing artist (*joshi gigeiin*)' and is automatically given roles in all productions of her troupe; unless she quits in the meantime for some reason, her place in the Company is guaranteed for a maximum of seven years, at the end of which she and all her remaining year-group members are 'retired' simultaneously and re-hired on an annual contractual basis, with renewal options, pay and conditions subject to individual negotiation with the Administration.[3] Young women of today, according to one informant of mine who joined Takarazuka around 1980, are apt to quit anyway after only two or three years on stage if not assigned interesting roles, whereas in her generation it was sheer love of Takarazuka that had made them persevere as long as the Company would have them (Informant NK 2001: Q. 2.11). The alternatives of early marriage, or other employment as essentially unskilled labour, also probably seemed to those earlier performers so unappetising that even the less talented nevertheless stayed for the entire seven years, playing minor characters while enjoying Takarasienne status, which often ensured them preferential treatment in society.

The Company's rationale for the seven-year rule is that the retirement age in question coincides with a woman's *tekireiki*, the age said to be most suitable for marriage. Under current entrance rules for the Takarazuka Music School, a performer would be aged between twenty-four and twenty-seven at this point. At the time of contract renewal in this or subsequent years, the Company can tempt performers whom it considers a liability to retire, perhaps with the promise of a meaty role prior to farewell, though the Administration has stated that no performer who fervently wishes to remain will be forced to leave (see Kishi 2000: 146–50; Miki 1994: 142). The performers' enterprise-based union, known as *Joshikai* (Women's Association), has been 'rendered toothless' by this system, according to one informant (Informant PZ, interview, Q. 2.3). The latter comment suggests that members probably hesitate to use the union to criticise the Administration or make suggestions for improvement, lest they be considered troublemakers and their contracts not be renewed.

Top stars whose popularity guarantees sold-out performances, and those who are being groomed for future stardom, may be offered more monetary incentives than their classmates to encourage them to remain in Takarazuka after the seven-year mark, but other performers may have to quit for financial reasons because they lack aid from parents or patrons to maintain a lifestyle in which they are under constant public scrutiny. Some parents baulk at supporting a daughter beyond the age of university graduation, for example, and insist that she quit Takarazuka to marry or to seek other employment unless she is prepared to earn her own keep after her early twenties, according to one *musumeyaku*, Sen Hosachi (Ishii 2000: 189).

Most literature on the Revue fails to indicate that graduates have not always been disqualified from returning to the Takarazuka stage

should their marriages fail. In the early decades of the Takarazuka
Girls' Opera, for example, some performers reportedly rejoined the
company after having quit for marriage, then having divorced. One
informant, who began her Takarazuka career before 1930, confirms
that such women were reaccepted 'without anyone thinking
anything of it' (Informant PP 2001: Q. 3.16). There were many
defacto (*naien*) marriages in that period in Japan, and therefore
some, or all, of these performers' failed 'marriages' may actually
have been informal liaisons. The Company may have had good
reason to welcome them back: recruits were paid even during the
training period, when they learned most of their stage skills from
the most basic level (unlike the well-prepared applicants of today,
whose parents pay Music School fees). Stage-ready performers
would thus have represented an investment of time and money that
the Company was probably loath to waste. For many decades now,
however, Takarasiennes have been obliged to leave the Company
if they wish to wed, however regretted their departure (Ishii 2000:
87). When president of the Hankyu Corporation, Kobayashi's son
Yonezō considered the idea of allowing married women to remain,
but this was reportedly quashed by director Utsumi Shigenori
(Amano 1994: 147). The retirement-upon-marriage rule still stands
in Takarazuka, in spite of the April 1999 enactment of the Basic
Law for a Gender-Equal Society (Danjo kyōdō sankaku kihon hō),
a revised version of the 1986 Equal Employment Opportunity Law,[4]
which includes a ban upon the discriminatory practice of forcing
women to quit work upon marriage.

The mystique of Takarazuka, with its emphasis on 'purity' and
'innocence,' which also can be equated with lack of sexual experience
with men, seems so thoroughly to pervade the consciousness of
Company members that the 'iron rule' of retirement upon impending
marriage is supported in almost every opinion expressed in printed
or oral sources. There seems to be widespread aversion to the idea
of Takarasiennes (especially *otokoyaku*) marrying while continuing
to perform in Takarazuka. My interviewees indicate that they find
repugnant the demonstration by a fellow performer of mature
female (hetero-)sexuality; this reinforces the notion that the private
behaviour of a Takarasienne cannot be truly private, but is always
an extension of her public self, which is always under moral scrutiny.
One informant spells it out: 'I might be a bit biased, but I think
Takarasiennes have innocence; an *otokoyaku* cannot be on the
Takarazuka stage if she marries and carries on a regular family life.
If she wants to do that, she ought to become an actress.' It will be

remembered that the word 'actress (*joyū*)' is not usually applied to Takarazuka performers; '*seito* (student)' is used instead. An 'actress' can be a wife and/or a mother in addition to making herself an 'art object' (Blair 1981: 208) – essentially different from a Takarasienne, who seems to exist for herself, her fellow performers, and her fans, but never for a husband, a male lover, or children.

One of my informants, a stage veteran who remained until mandatory retirement age, denies any *otokoyaku* the right to claim her place in both the conjugal and the theatrical spheres: 'If she has a husband waiting at home, she mustn't be wearing a tailcoat herself.' Her warning is extended to *musumeyaku*, also: 'Don't perform opposite a fictitious *otokoyaku* character when there's a real husband waiting for you! If you're going to marry, then I'd prefer you to hurry up and quit the Company' (Informant PZ 2001: Q. 3.16). Another informant explains that Takarazuka is 'a special world, a drama in which *otokoyaku* really become men and fall in love with the women played by *onnayaku*' (Informant RX 2001: Q. 3.16). Biological males presumably have no place in such a world. This blurring of the boundaries between an *otokoyaku*'s stage character, her created persona as a Takarasienne and her identity as a private individual is also indicated by Robertson, who writes that the *otokoyaku* are 'able to operate as hinge figures whose very bodies mediate the fantasies of the stage with the realities of everyday life' (Robertson 1998b: 85). Thus, an *otokoyaku* must be seen to be 'available' so that her fans can indulge their fantasies of a romance with the characters she portrays – or with the performer herself.

Only one interviewee of mine dares to dispute the retirement-upon-marriage rule, saying: 'I think that it should be all right for a *senka* member, at least, to marry...after a certain age, even if she stays in the Company' (Informant KT 2001: Q. 3.16, Q. 3.17). Her reasoned statement shows an understanding of the difference between the young troupe members, who are highly conspicuous because they perform and rehearse all year, and most of those belonging to the so-called 'Superior Members' (*senka*) group, who, with the exception of versatile character players including Ebira Kaoru and the now-retired Kishi Kaori, perform so seldom that their existence is all but forgotten by most fans. As a *senka* member's pay is likely to be as low as her stage appearances are infrequent, marriage could give her added financial security. Arguably, the average Takarasienne imagined by objectors to the idea of a performer having a husband and children is a young, fertile woman, completely unlike the seasoned veterans of *senka*, who frequently play elderly, dastardly or unkempt characters of either sex, far removed from the stereotypical *otokoyaku* and *musumeyaku* who embody the Takarazuka 'dream.'

Issues of women's fertility, and especially the assumption that matrimony automatically leads to childbirth, underlie further arguments for the upholding of the Company marriage policy which were offered both by my informants and by other Takarasiennes, in spite of the fact that, at least since the post-war legalisation of abortion and the popularisation of various contraceptive methods, Japanese women have demonstrated a marked ability to control their fertility. The Japanese are bearing fewer children than ever before; the proportion of childless couples is rising for various reasons; and population statistics show that the Japanese birth-rate is among the lowest in the world.

Nevertheless, an incompatibility between the masculine image of an *otokoyaku* and the unmistakably feminine physicality of breast-feeding is cited as one reason why Takarazuka performing should not be combined with motherhood, which is assumed to follow marriage. One informant expresses her distaste at the idea of a lactating *otokoyaku*: 'If an *otokoyaku* were to breast-feed a baby, it would be like destroying the dream. Even if [a Takarasienne] could return to the stage after having babies, I think it would be better for her not to play male roles if she intended to raise the children herself' (Informant NK 2001: Q. 3.16). The 'dream' metaphor recurs in the comment of another informant, now with adult children, who admits that she and her colleagues would have liked to continue performing even after marriage, yet argues: 'If performers brought their children into the dressing-rooms, or were seen walking about with the children, things would be awkward. After all, Takarazuka relies on its fans, and in those situations, fans' dreams would be shattered' (Informant EF 2001: Q. 3.16). One current performer, she herself single and childless, as one would expect, also speculates:

> If, for example, such an *otokoyaku* had a child, I think it would be possible for her to arrive backstage after having attended to the baby, to put on her makeup and to perform as an *otokoyaku*, but if people found out about it, not only the spectators, but her fellow performers in the play, too, would probably grow somewhat cold towards her (Informant RX 2001: Q. 3.16).

This same informant further expressed a wish to marry and have children after leaving Takarazuka, but not to become a full-time

housewife, presumably because she imagined her abilities to be
better exercised by working outside the home.

Other endorsements of the retirement-upon-marriage rule refer
to a 'homey appearance' and 'worldly odour' allegedly acquired
by performers when they retire (Informant AA 2001: Q. 3.16;
Informant SS 2001: Q. 3.16). One interviewee says:

> There are some male actors who don't give off any whiff of family
> life, even if they are married and have children at home, aren't
> there? They can do it, even if they have children, but it's different
> for women – when they marry, they always exude that 'family smell
> (*shotai-kusasa*).' In fact, there are a few ex-Takarasiennes who have
> changed to a puzzling degree when I see them now in rehearsal or on
> stage [outside Takarazuka]. I don't know whether it's their attitude, but
> those Old Girls are completely different from the single ones of the
> same age who are still with the Company. It's a funny thing. There's
> that smell of daily life about them (Informant DP 2001: Q. 3.16).

The 'odour' these interviewees imagine is surely the taint of worldly
experience – perhaps a smell to do with sex, or money, or male
sweat, or domestic cleaning products, or a whiff of babies' napkins,
or of breast milk.

Matrimony could also have undesirable aesthetic ramifications, so
it seems. The orthodox on-stage body shape of a male-role performer,
for example, which has assumed the status of a stereotyped *kata*, may
also be jeopardised by the changes in physique that can result from
marriage, or at least from heterosexual activity – namely pregnancy,
childbirth and lactation. The ideal, boyish figure of an *otokoyaku* can
only be maintained through the strenuous daily exercise of dancing
and through the various methods she employs to disguise her
breasts. According to another informant, this regimen would become
difficult or impossible after marriage. 'When most marry, they are
too busy with childrearing to do any [dance] practice,' she says
(Informant TH 2001: Q. 3.16). In this definition, corporeal beauty
for a Takarasienne is thus partly dependent upon the body showing
no evidence of adult sexual experience, either to the audience or to
other Revue members. As Takarazuka theatre dressing rooms and
bathing areas are communal, the naked or near-naked body of a
performer is frequently exposed to the eye of fellow Takarasiennes.
It would therefore be impossible for a performer to hide for long the
physical signs of pregnancy or lactation.

In terms of time management, as well as other issues of gender, marriage is seen as not feasible because of Takarasiennes' busy round of company classes, rehearsals and performances. No provision is made for family commitments in performers' long work days, which sometimes last twelve hours, and even the female-role players 'would like to have a wife,' according to one informant (Informant MH 2001: Q. 2.11). While the stereotype of absolute loyalty to one's work, typified by the 'corporate warrior' image, is usually applied to male company workers, it is obviously alive in Takarazuka as well, and the belief that 'the show must go on' even keeps performers from the deathbed of family members. Otowa Nobuko's father, for instance, sent a telegram calling her home to Kobe as her grandmother was near death, a fortnight before the end of her Tokyo performance run. The grandmother, however, sent another telegram immediately afterward, forbidding Otowa to return. After closing night, Otowa hurried home, her grandmother reportedly dying in her arms after bidding her welcome and seeing her granddaughter's face (Ueda 1974: 35–36). Fear of missing an ailing parent's final moments was a compelling reason for the retirement of one informant whose family lived near Tokyo, and whose seniority would have made it difficult to rush home from Takarazuka in an emergency (Informant NK 2001: Q. 3.22).

On the other hand, wives and mothers are generally expected to strive for the happiness and stability of the home, and this time-consuming responsibility is not to be taken lightly, as another informant admonishes. Her advice to one performer, Hatsukaze Jun, who consulted with her on marriage and motherhood, was that 'acting work would have to be [just] a hobby, or else her family would disintegrate, and child-rearing would be a disaster...She would have to devote seventy per cent of her time to her family, and limit her "hobby" to thirty per cent' (Informant TH 2001: Q. 3.16). Hatsukaze apparently heeded this advice in her post-retirement years. She had played Marie Antoinette in the original cast of *The Rose of Versailles* in 1974, and one of her memorable lines had been a proud declaration that she was queen of France. Fifteen years later, however, at a special event prior to the 1989 revival of that same musical, Hatsukaze boasted that she had become 'queen of the kitchen' and 'queen of the tricoloured packed lunch (*sanshoku bentō*),' adding that she had prepared and left her son(s) a boxed meal to eat while she was away in Takarazuka (cited in Haruna 1993: 182–83). Personal experience of marriage, and work during

pregnancy, childbirth and child-rearing, has similarly informed
another interviewee's response:

> Since I quit [Takarazuka], I've realised that, in actual practice,
> combining motherhood with performing would be impossible, time-
> wise. Even without children, a Takarasienne would have no time to
> spend with her husband, because the Takarazuka schedule is incredibly
> hard. It might be all right if her husband were the type to say she
> needn't do any housework, but I doubt that she would be able to prepare
> even two or three meals a week (Informant NK 2001: Q. 3.16).

As such comments show, Takarasiennes themselves echo standard
gender-role expectations in relation to married life, however
unorthodox their life as members of the Revue may have been. The
above informant is the only one to mention the possibility of a wife
not having to 'keep house,' but this is seen as dependent upon the
generosity of her spouse. The husband is otherwise absent from
the domestic scenario, and there is no suggestion that childcare or
housework could be entrusted to professionals, or even to members
of a woman's extended family, to enable her to continue performing
if she wished. If Takarazuka is any guide, it is plain that, despite new
laws, there have as yet been limited results from the recent national
and local government campaigns to encourage gender equality in
Japan, especially as regards the sharing of family responsibilities
across gender lines.[5]

The above arguments for retention of the retirement-upon-
marriage rule hinge, above all, upon the performers being female.
In an all-male company, a skilled performer would certainly not be
expected to retire on marriage or fatherhood. In Kabuki, for example,
to which Takarazuka is often compared, practitioners have a
responsibility to reproduce, in both the biological and artistic sense:

> In Kabuki, it's a matter of heredity, so Kabuki actors have to have a
> family and children, don't they? The family's artistic tradition (*ie no
> gei*) is handed down that way, involving the sons, so the actors are
> in an embarrassing position if they don't have sons. So the boy has
> his first formal stage appearance in a child's role, whether he's the
> family's adopted son or their real son, and by properly conducting
> that debut, the family shows to society at large that their art is being
> transmitted to the next generation. The actor's wife has to be a hostess:
> her job is to entertain fans, so an actor is in trouble if he has no wife
> and children (Informant SS 2001: Q. 3.16).

Several Takarasiennes have married Kabuki actors,[6] including Kotobuki Hizuru (1973–82), who quit the Company on the eve of top stardom to marry a Kabuki star, Bandō Yasosuke (later known as Mitsugorō X). Kotobuki devoted her married life to her husband's career and the raising of their three children, but after the marriage ended due to her husband's infidelity, she promptly returned to the musical theatre stage, caring for the children nonetheless (*Sankei Sports* 2000; *Theater Guide* 2001).

Marriage seems to be a hazy concept to most Takarasiennes, who are prevented by the Violet Code from public discussion of sexual matters, as we have seen in previous chapters, and may have little opportunity to develop strong feelings towards a specific man. The pseudo-romantic bond between a performer and her fans would also be jeopardised by the existence of a tangible male rival. Some performers, however, are outspoken in their determination to marry: the ethnically Chinese *otokoyaku* Ōtori Ran, for example, whose 'exotic' appearance and masculine acting reputedly earned her the nickname *hitozuma kirā* (lady-killer) because of her popularity among married women, long professed a strong desire for marriage, starting in her twenties, and voiced disapproval of Women's Liberation (Ōtori 1971: 62). She eventually married and produced two daughters, but then divorced, boasting gleefully from the stage at a charity concert I attended at Nihon Seinenkan Hall, Tokyo, on 7 July 2000: 'I'm recommending divorce to everyone!'

Takarazuka: a school for brides?

Kobayashi Ichizō actively promoted his opinion that Takarazuka graduates made the best wives and daughters-in-law, and this notion seems to have become a cliché, even though the Revue provides its performers with no opportunity to learn most practical domestic skills, and, in fact, deliberately places most of its members into a totally non-domestic context. Apart from guarding its residents' chastity, the only way in which the Sumire (violet) dormitory could be construed as preparing its residents for a good marriage is through its system of hierarchical discipline, which retired Takarasiennes often claim was later useful in maintaining harmony in their marital home. Having learnt that it is expedient to look and sound as if one agrees, even when a senior says something contrary to either common sense or one's own inner convictions, Takarasiennes apparently find placating mothers-in-law and husbands easy. *Otokoyaku* Amachi Hikari (1983–96), for example, anticipated that she would handle married life well, saying: 'I cultivated both physical and mental strength in Takarazuka, so I'm confident that I won't founder at some trivial problem. One cannot go on stage in a depressed condition. Through my experience of daily acting in live theatre, I have developed the ability to bounce back even if I am feeling down' (cited in Minakaze and Natori 1997: 144–45).

Dormitory life does not teach household management, for its inhabitants only need keep their own clothes clean and the shared bedrooms tidy. Meals are provided, no utility bills need to be paid, and the resident supervisor, the only male allowed on the premises, handles security and building maintenance. When water and gas mains were cut for several weeks following the 1995 Hanshin earthquake, most residents who remained at the dormitory reportedly left the task of carrying well-water for washing and for flushing their own toilets up to a small group of volunteers among their number (Kishi 2000: 214). Yet even a Takarasienne who lives in her own apartment is still largely absolved from the responsibility of running a household, thanks to the enthusiastic ministrations of fans, especially the *tsukibito* whose role was examined in Chapter Five, or to family assistance: the mother of *musumeyaku* Sen Hosachi, for example, made the long drive from south of Osaka each day to her daughter's apartment to leave prepared meals, so that the busy Takarasienne could have a balanced diet (cited in Ishii 2000: 88).

To take their place as women in regular society, and especially if they intend to marry, retiring Takarasiennes may have to master all kinds of domestic skills which they do not learn in Takarazuka. The labour-intensive cleaning regimen from Music School days may make Takarasiennes sticklers for cleanliness, but does not teach them how to use modern appliances. One *otokoyaku*, Shizuki Asato, did list 'cleaning' as her hobby among other biographical details in the 1999 yearbook (*Takarazuka otome* 1999: 112), yet such a domestic bent seems rare in a Takarasienne: Kōzuki Noboru, for example, claimed in 1969 that her culinary skill was limited to making *miso* soup (*Takarazuka gurafu* 1969: 59). Another confession of domestic ineptness was made by an interviewee who had retired to marry after decades of performing. As a newlywed, before the couple had hired home help, she had prepared a variety of dainty dishes to feed her husband's guests, but she neither thought to cook rice, nor knew how to wash and steam it, even though she was vaguely aware that there was an electric rice-cooker in the house.

The guests, all men, ended up having to cook the rice for her, and the interviewee recalls being so mortified that she 'bawled [her] eyes out' (Informant MH 2001: Q. 4.6). Not all Takarasiennes are bad cooks, however, and the monthly fan magazines occasionally carry performers' favourite recipes. Haruna Yuri, *otokoyaku* heartthrob of the 1970s, even publicised her own gourmet tastes and culinary prowess, saying: 'I am often told that if I can cook this well, then I'll be fine if I get married...but in spite of my cooking skill, there is no prospective groom in sight, so marriage is out of the question, after all' (cited in Suzuki 1979: 157).

Rather surprisingly, it is not the female-role players in Takarazuka who are reputed to make better wives, but the male-role players. Certainly, the latter must make the larger adjustment to life after performing, and it may be that, by taking nothing for granted, *otokoyaku* successfully re-socialise themselves as adult females, whereas *musumeyaku* perhaps underestimate the adjustment they need to make to relate to an actual man rather than an *otokoyaku*, and to function normally as a woman rather than act out the Takarazuka version of exaggerated femininity. The theatrical experience, training and emulation of various models of masculinity are thought to enable *otokoyaku* both to support and to manipulate their post-retirement male partners. While female-role players of old are said to have 'looked after' *otokoyaku* in various ways, male-role players in more recent decades, such as those in the 1968 Music School graduating class, are said to be the more diligent (*komame*) in responding to others' needs, for whatever reason, according to *otokoyaku* Shinjō Mayumi (cited in Suzuki 1979: 254–55). One interviewee of mine describes female-role players as 'sloppy' and 'impertinent,' while claiming that male-role players are more 'delicate' in their sensibilities, and tend to be even more solicitous to senior *otokoyaku* than are their *musumeyaku* counterparts (Informant CL 2001: Q. 4.8). The manner in which Takarasiennes treat each other, however, should not be taken as indicative of how they would behave to people outside the Takarazuka milieu. One ex-*musumeyaku* guffawed at the suggestion that she might treat actual men in the same worshipful way as she had treated *otokoyaku* (Informant CL 2001: Q. 4.8).

An *otokoyaku* doubtless appreciates the feeling of being looked up to and adored. Especially if she has been a star, she has tasted the ego-boosting concentration of energy focused upon her by fellow performers and fans, especially as she descends the grand staircase in the moments before each final curtain. The top male-role star is, after all, the unifying element in each troupe, and as such must cultivate and retain the love, loyalty and cooperation of all her *kumiko* (troupe members). The leading *otokoyaku* must be a charismatic 'boss,' [7] though she herself must answer to the more senior *kumichō* (troupe head) and her deputy, who function as surrogate parents. Having received such adulation, a retiring *otokoyaku* might well try to reproduce it to make life very 'comfortable' for her husband or male lover, if she served him as she herself had been served (Informant SS 2001: Q. 4.8). Initially, however, seeing one's husband basking in so much loving attention may be discomfiting, as in the case of popular *otokoyaku* Sumi Hanayo (1948-63), who was taken aback and envious when her actor husband was mobbed by female fans who ignored Sumi, making her realise that it was now time for her to 'pull back, in order to back him up' (cited in Suzuki 1976: 121).

In private life, many retirees may realise that various habits acquired for the portrayal of their stage gender are hard to break. One former *otokoyaku* interviewee claims that since her marriage, there had been occasions when it was 'like having two men in the house' – she and her husband. Her small daughter would exclaim, 'It's like having two daddies!' when the same hair-setting gel was used by both of her parents, or when her mother scolded the child in her low voice. This interviewee continues to wear trousers after marriage, for comfort and convenience, and keeps her hair short; she has also been unable to 'cure' herself of sitting in the *otokoyaku* manner, with knees apart, as she had sat for years in the Takarazuka rehearsal studio, even though the habit now apparently embarrasses her. 'Every *otokoyaku* says the same thing,' she asserts (Informant NK 2001: Q. 3.4).

Careers after Takarazuka

Whatever their post-retirement plans, Takarazuka retirees leaving the insular world of the Revue are immediately confronted with the gender norms and biased attitudes of mainstream society, which restrict the range of careers and life-courses these women can follow. Those who wish to work are thus likely to be concentrated in areas which value their sex and their performing background. As I have shown, Takarazuka provides attractive young women with comprehensive training and practical experience in numerous aspects of acting, singing and dancing, yet implements policies that encourage most of its performers to leave the Company within ten years of graduating from the Music School. It is natural, therefore, that many of its retiring members should seek employment in commercial theatre, film and television, while enjoying comparative freedom to choose roles and genres, to pursue further artistic development, and to marry and/or bear children.

As Chapter One has noted, the world of films was an early magnet for popular Takarasiennes, to the chagrin of the Takarazuka Administration. Standing on stage at the Revue's fortieth anniversary celebration in 1954, backed by rows of smiling Takarasiennes lined up like wares on sale, Kobayashi appealed to the audience to come to Takarazuka to choose a bride instead of 'head-hunting' his performers for motion pictures (NHK Osaka 1992b). Kobayashi, as a father figure, may also have had a personal objection to his 'daughters' appearing in films outside of Takarazuka's jurisdiction, unrestricted by the Revue's requirement for 'wholesomeness.' Both then and now, the prospect of seeing a former Takarasienne on screen exhibiting more daring behaviour (especially overt sexuality) or more bare flesh than in her Revue days draws a large audience, not only of curious fans, but also of men who probably would not patronise the Revue or sympathise with its stated moral philosophy. A nude scene, for instance, was featured in the screen debut of Kuroki Hitomi in 1987 (Kuroki 1999: 75–76). The contrast between Kuroki's cheerful but chaste portrayals in Takarazuka revues and her screen role in steamy scenes opposite a male actor underlines not only the marketing skill of her new employers, but also Kuroki's own desire to make a complete break from Takarazuka and to expand her artistic skills.

The specific forms of gender portrayal that are deemed necessary for acting in Takarazuka productions must be adapted to a considerable extent when Takarasiennes quit the Revue, especially for a career in theatre, films or television. This mainly involves shedding various mannerisms peculiar to the Takarazuka stage. For *otokoyaku*, it usually also means learning how to act and sing convincingly as a woman, while for *musumeyaku* and *onnayaku*, it may mean adopting a less exaggeratedly 'feminine' manner, including a more natural speaking voice than the squeak employed by many female-role Takarasiennes. For many *otokoyaku*, retirement in fact spells a chance to try to reclaim their original singing voice, which may have been soprano before years of forced lowering. The high soprano demanded by the title role in the Japanese mixed-cast premiere of the Viennese musical *Erizabēto* (Elisabeth), for instance, proved a challenge to former *otokoyaku* Ichiro Maki

(1982-96), who spent a year preparing her voice (*Myūjikaru* 2000: 14–15). This was necessary because Ichiro's final Takarazuka role four years previously had been as Elisabeth's low-voiced, androgynous suitor from the underworld, Death.

Once an *otokoyaku* has learned how to play a masculine role, however, this skill may remain dormant in later life until needed. In one instance, sixteen years after leaving Takarazuka, Ōtori Ran played both male and female roles in the play *Angel*, and comments that it was still easier for her to be an *otokoyaku* because she was originally trained to play male roles: 'It was as if I were pure white, and *otokoyaku* was the first colour that I was dyed.' The director of *Angel* also told her that she was 'natural' acting as a man but awkward as a woman (Ōtori, cited in Ōno 1995: 200). It must be noted, on the other hand, that not all the adjustments that ex-performers have to make for a career in mainstream entertainment are necessarily concerned with gender portrayal. The sheer scale of the Takarazuka Grand Theatre stage and auditorium, where players must act, sing and dance for up to three thousand spectators at one performance, and the dazzling spotlight which illuminates the stars, are usually absent from the venues at which ex-Takarasiennes perform. Ōura Mizuki, for example, speaks of having to learn how to perform in a small space, without special lighting, but claims that it was easier for her to scale down her presentation than it would have been to build it up (cited in Ōno 1995: 202).

In the case of an *otokoyaku* moving into films or mainstream theatre, a sudden transition from a manly to a markedly feminine role may alienate fans. Filmmakers thus may choose to cast a newly retired *otokoyaku* in a fairly androgynous role at first, in order to prime her fans for a later transition to typically female characters. One such performer, Amami Yūki, made her 1996 film debut as a swashbuckling female police detective, with bobbed hair, trench-coat and trousers, in the action movie *Christmas Apocalypse*. Moreover, Amami later reprised her *otokoyaku* persona as Shining Prince Genji in a lavish film, *Sennen no koi: hikaru Genji monogatari* (A thousand-year romance: the tale of shining Genji), transporting the representation of this beautiful, fictitious male by a female actor outside the confines of Takarazuka (where stars such as Kasugano Yachiyo and Haruna Yuri have played the role) into a performance by a mixed cast. The choice of Amami for the part is not particularly surprising, considering that Genji is, after all, constructed in Japanese literary and romantic tradition as an 'ideal male,' in a setting far removed from present-day life, and is thus an appropriate role for a Takarazuka *otokoyaku*. One reviewer comments:

[Amami] is masculine in every look and movement, while embodying the Shining Prince as an androgynous ideal of beauty and grace – a trick a mere man, straight or no, would find hard to pull off. *The absence of erotic charge* in her lovemaking is, given the film's gauzy romanticism, hardly a defect; the intrusion of real male sexuality would break the delicately wrought spell (Schilling 2001; emphasis added).

The male reviewer obviously cannot imagine the kind of 'frisson'[8] that is perhaps enjoyed by Amami's female fans as they fantasise themselves as one of Genji's female lovers.

A post-Takarazuka career on the live stage is arguably a natural choice for many retirees, who can rely upon the 'old girl network' of horizontal and vertical relationships in the Revue hierarchy to gain entrée into further employment in the performing arts, where their sex is no impediment, and their comprehensive training makes them versatile cast members. In fields of endeavour unconnected to show business, however, retired Takarasiennes may be at a disadvantage when seeking employment. The recruitment practices of Japanese firms, especially prestigious large enterprises, have until recently been very rigid and discriminatory against females, mature-aged individuals of either sex and members of ethnic or social minorities. While legislation such as the Equal Employment Opportunity Law has in theory removed or lowered barriers to satisfying careers for many in the above groups, Takarazuka retirees are still likely to be hampered in their search for employment outside the entertainment industry, by reason of their sex, their lack of formal education, and the relatively late age at which they seek to join the general labour force. In addition, they may have difficulty finding jobs because of a perception on the part of some employers that Takarasiennes are somehow too idiosyncratic or haughty to fit in with the regular staff. As the examples below will suggest, however, numerous ex-Revue performers have found, or created, fulfilling job opportunities for themselves through imagination, boldness or tenacity, taking advantage of the adaptability produced by their training in portraying different genders.

There is little data on the post-performing lives of the majority of Takarasiennes, as the relative few who have been the subject of media reporting have either been popular stars, or have pursued some line of work considered especially noteworthy. The public seldom learns of the rest, most of whom have blended once more into the general population, and hide their distinctive label of 'ex-Takarasienne,' with its complex connotations. Nevertheless, the experience these women gained in Takarazuka, both in an artistic and a personal sense, has evidently been very significant in the establishment of their new lives. Retirees' professional occupations encompass many fields, such as theatrical production and multilingual translation agency management, in the case of Hashizume Kishiko[9] (Takaoka Nachiko, 1953–58) (Kōbe Shinbun Hanshin Sōkyoku 1984: 103–05); writing novels and musical theatre scripts, in the case of Yamazaki Yōko (Hatagumo Akemi, 1955–58) (Natori and Takeichi 1996a: 192–205); and the practice and teaching of calligraphy and the tea ceremony, in the case of Nakayama Kyōko (Asanagi Mifune, 1952–65) (Kōbe Shinbun Hanshin Sōkyoku 1984: 100–02). One of the more unusual occupations, perhaps, is that of the late Sakura Hisako (1930–40), who, after many years of stage and film acting, became a Buddhist nun of the Nichiren sect. Her religious activities included conducting memorial services for the souls of departed Takarasiennes at her temple atop Mt Hachiman in Shiga Prefecture (Kōbe Shinbun Hanshin Sōkyoku 1984: 76–78).

Work involving women's affairs, or in a field where female gender is an advantage, has figured in some ex-Takarasiennes' second careers. Now an accredited 'wedding producer,' Wada Chikako (Kozue Manami, 1980–91), for one, was encouraged by her husband to find an occupation that would supplant Takarazuka as a target for her passions, for Wada says: 'I had loved Takarazuka so excessively that my husband worried I would be an empty husk when I quit' (cited in Natori and Takeichi 1996b: 72). Kamo Miyaji (1937–44), on the other hand, the pioneer of professional fashion-modelling in Japan, launched her catwalk career at Osaka's inaugural post-war fashion show in 1947, while still a dressmaking student. She formed the Osaka Fashion Model Union, and reportedly trained more than two hundred professionals herself (Natori and Takeichi 1996b: 241; Kōbe Shinbun Hanshin Sōkyoku 1984: 88–90; Kamo and Sakaba 1996).

Gender has been a considerable impediment to involvement in politics for many Japanese women, as universal female suffrage was not achieved until after Japan's 1945 defeat, and far fewer women than men have become members of parliament,[10] yet a few Takarazuka retirees have become members of the Diet. One of the most powerful women in Japan, recently-retired House of Councillors member Ōgi Chikage (real name Hayashi Hiroko), twice a Cabinet minister, and a former leader of the New Conservative Party (Hoshutō), is an ex-Takarasienne who became the first female President of the Upper House. Ōgi reportedly had originally wished to further her education after leaving girls' high school, but entered Takarazuka when blocked by her father's fierce opposition to her academic aspirations. She acted in films and television, married a Kabuki and film actor, reared two sons, and entered politics in 1977.[11] In May 2007, she announced her retirement from politics, saying, 'I've spent 30 years in politics, and before that I worked 25 years as an actress. I've been working all my life, and I need some time to relax' (cited in *Japan Times Online* 2007). In other cases, active involvement in the lay Buddhist organisation, Sōka Gakkai, led to the political candidacy of Tajima Kumi and Matsu Akira, both former *otokoyaku*. Matsu successfully ran as a New Progress Party (Shinshintō) candidate for the House of Councillors in 1995, while her husband simultaneously entered the House of Representatives (Matsu 2001). Similarly, Tajima (Hayashi Kumiko), a renowned dancer and deputy troupe leader in Takarazuka, also entered the Diet for one term in 1995, after working as a fitness instructor (Natori and Takeichi 1996a: 136–47).

An interest in caring for the elderly, a field typically associated with women in Japan, as elsewhere, apparently inspired a change of career for male-role star Shion Yū (1976-1994), who is reputed to be the only top *otokoyaku* to have neither married nor pursued a career in entertainment after retirement (Tsuganezawa and Natori 2001: 28–29). Now, Shion (real name Watanabe Natsuko) also teaches a weekly drama class at the Takarazuka Music School. For her, lifelong work is important, as it enables her to live without depending on a man for financial support. Shion explains:

After I quit, nobody that I liked enough to marry appeared, so I worked hard and bought an apartment so that I could be independent (*jikatsu*). And once I did that, marriage was no longer necessary, in the sense of having somebody keep me. It would be okay to live with someone if I found a person I liked and wanted to be with forever. If you live alone for a long time, you have a selfish side, and you definitely want free time. I originally had a precocious desire to marry in senior high school, but now, it is easier to be alone (cited in Tsuganezawa and Natori 2001: 28).

In some cases, however, the erotic or morally questionable nature of certain retirees' new occupations conflicts with the 'pure, righteous and beautiful' image of the Takarasienne. Those who engage in such occupations are usually too ashamed to divulge the true nature of their work to Revue acquaintances or former fans. Hamai reports one example, that of a senior whom she identifies only as 'S,' whom she visited at the Kobe dance hall where 'S' worked as a dance partner to Occupation troops in 1948 (Tamai 1999: 106). Nor is there any publicity about ex-performers who cross-dress as males in private life, and who choose women, not men, for their life partners, such as several ex-Takarazuka bar-owners and bar employees of my acquaintance, who make their living as professional male impersonators known as *bōisshu* (boyish) or *onabe*.[12] One of my informants criticises several *otokoyaku* of similar type from around the war years, who have continued to behave as men in private life since retirement: 'They cannot go on being stars for ever. Takarazuka is Takarazuka, so when they retire, they should stop [such behaviour]' (Informant TH 2001: Q. 4.7).

Making up for interrupted education

During their girlhood, Takarasiennes are affected by gender norms relating to education, but joining Takarazuka has often further resulted in Revue performers receiving fewer years of academic education than their female peers in the general Japanese population, especially since the final decades of the last century. As Chapter Two has noted, girls in Japan now enjoy a similarly high rate of completion of senior high school as boys, though at post-secondary level, a far greater proportion of boys than of girls attends four-year universities, many girls choosing two-year junior colleges instead. Among Revue performers, there are probably many women whose high intelligence and excellent pre-Takarazuka scholastic achievements would have enabled them to attend university and enter a profession, had they had not been stage-struck or opposed by parents. As retirees, who have spent any number of years away from formal education, some of them yearn to return to school, or enter university, to study towards a new goal. Faced with the prospect of earning a living as women, they may feel under-qualified for the second career to which they aspire.

The first need for some such retirees is to compensate for a truncated secondary education. One of the most recent leading players to leave the Takarazuka stage, 174-centimetre-tall Kozuki Wataru, announced at her retirement press conference that she would be fulfilling a promise made long ago to her father that she would attend university (*Sponichi Takarazuka* 2006: 6). Another, Nishida Yōko (*musumeyaku* Hana Yōko, 1985–93), had found herself barred from applying even for part-time jobs because she had quit high school one year short of graduation. 'I suddenly realised that although I knew plenty about Takarazuka, I knew too little about society,' she said, further confessing that she did not even know how to catch a public bus (cited in Natori and Takeichi 1996b: 28). After a year of night-school to attain secondary graduation, Nishida pursued university studies by correspondence, majoring in English. However, in spite of transient dreams of studying overseas or involving herself in welfare work for people with disabilities, her subsequent career veered back towards performing on stage and television, and singing (*Osaka nikkan supōtsu* 2000a; also see *Shōwa Production* 2004).

There have even been some ex-Takarasiennes who have gained admittance to the most difficult of university courses: medicine and dentistry, which traditionally have attracted far more male applicants than female. One ex-*musumeyaku*, real name Masutani Takiko, apparently became aware, 'through conversations with men,' of a lack of intellectual depth in her life in the single-sex world of Takarazuka (cited in Natori and Takeichi 1996a: 129). She quit the Revue in 1970 at the age of twenty-five after having played opposite a leading *otokoyaku*, and it took her twelve more years of study to gain national accreditation as a dentist. She now runs a clinic in Takarazuka, and reportedly counts many performers and Music School students among her patients. Though some retirees may awaken to the world outside Takarazuka like the folk-tale character Urashima Tarō, to find that they have nothing to show for their years of comfort, Masutani claims that the time she spent in Takarazuka was also 'necessary' for her in order to become a dentist (cited in Natori and Takeichi 1996a: 130). Arguably, this was because she learned many things there, including self-discipline and the importance of the quest for excellence. In the same vein, one veteran informant advises young Takarasiennes and Music School students to store plenty of knowledge and experience in their own 'treasure chest,' in order to cope with the vicissitudes they may face after quitting (Informant PP 2001: Q. 4.10).

As Kobayashi, the Takarazuka Administration and perhaps other observers have seemed to assume that marriage is the only alternative for Takarazuka retirees who do not seek employment as entertainers, a Takarasienne's choice of a post-performing career which requires numerous years of further academic study

is deemed newsworthy by the media, irrespective of the former
popularity or status of the performer. There was a media flurry
when ex-otokoyaku Mitsuya Nao, who had joined Takarazuka
after junior high school, gained admittance to the Vocal Music
course at Tokyo National University of Fine Arts and Music upon
her first attempt in 1996 (Mitsuya 2007). Newspapers also eagerly
reported the story of Mekari Miyo (Mei Karen; 1994–97), the first
Takarazuka graduate to enter medical school (e.g. *Sponichi Annex*
2001). Unlike the dentist Masutani, already a senior high school
graduate when joining Takarazuka, Mekari had completed only
ten years of schooling before entering the Music School. Later, the
'selfless dedication' of a social worker at an aged-care facility where
Mekari and her fellow Takarasiennes performed reportedly inspired
Mekari to follow a career in geriatric medicine. A mere four months
after quitting Takarazuka, she passed the high school equivalency
examination (*daigaku kentei shiken*), enrolled in a preparatory
school for would-be medical students, and finally began university
four years later, in 2001.[13]

Back to Takarazuka

While numerous retirees have found new occupations in fields quite
different from performing, and moved away from Takarazuka,
many others continue to live in the vicinity, probably because of
the emotional, and sometimes the material, support to be gained
from closeness to the 'extended family' that is the Revue. Some
marry and raise a family in Takarazuka; some commute to a job
in Osaka or Kobe; and yet others establish a new livelihood on the
periphery of the Revue community. Fellow performers, Company
staff, fans and local service-providers form an audience for their
cultural activities or a client-base for their businesses, which fall
into several broad areas: the teaching of current performers and
would-be Takarasiennes; creative work as Revue staff members; and
the operation of various retail and service outlets, cosy restaurants
and intimate bars. Though the 'village' atmosphere of Takarazuka
is not shared by Tokyo, the latter and its environs also are home
to a large community of ex-performers who support each others'
endeavours and band together as a close-knit family in times of
need, such as their fund-raising efforts after the 1995 earthquake
which hit Takarazuka. Some retirees' restaurants in Tokyo, however,
including 'Weak Point,' run by Shioji Asako (1963–76); and
'Yoshizumi,' operated by Honami Makoto (1971–73), are reputedly

very popular among visiting performers and Tokyo fans alike (Natori and Takeichi 1996b: 114–15).

The Revue Company itself is a place where the talents of women have long been recognised, not only as performers, but also as instructors and mentors who can perpetuate or improve upon Takarazuka's techniques of gender portrayal and are familiar with its off-stage discipline. The position of in-house writer/director, however, has only been open to women for about a decade, beginning a few years after the implementation of the Equal Employment Opportunity Law, and no retirees have successfully applied for such a position; for one thing, university graduation is mandatory. Hibino Momoko (Misato Kei, 1968-81) was hired as a trainee on a trial basis for five years in the early 1980s, but apparently gave up, exhausted (Informant PZ 2001: Q. 3.15; Natori and Takeichi 1996a: 108–09).

On the other hand, the Administration has employed numerous retirees as choreographers, as specialist instructors at Company classes, or as Violet Dormitory supervisors. Tsukasa Konomi (1960–73), for one, was sent by Takarazuka to study dance in the United States even while still performing (Ueda 1974: 88), and became a Company choreographer.[14] Sha Tamae (Hayabusa Amiri, 1971–75), another choreographer who studied dance and directing in New York, and Yō Shukubi (Aomi Ren, 1984–86), a vocal coach who studied opera in the United Kingdom, have worked on specific Takarazuka productions; while Chiaki Shin (1983–98), who apparently used to spit blood when gargling in the morning during her *otokoyaku* years, due to strain on her throat, went on to study to become a voice trainer at a US music school, reportedly in order to save other Takarasiennes from suffering throat damage from forcing their voices unnaturally low (or high, presumably) in order to portray their stage gender (*Osaka nikkan supōtsu* 2000b). Another former *otokoyaku*, Kei Chibune (1966–72), whose professional name is now Hanayagi Hagi, coaches Takarasiennes to diploma level in classical Japanese dance (*Nihon buyō*),[15] and choreographs for Takarazuka productions, taking advantage of her thorough familiarity with the styles of both 'women's dance (*onna-mai*)' and 'men's dance (*otoko-mai*).'

The grooming of teenaged girls in readiness for the Takarazuka Music School entrance examination is another occupation that offers many retirees an avenue for utilising performing skills which can be combined with marriage, thus enabling them to fulfil a typical female gender role as well as work outside the home. As Chapter Three has noted, many ballet and singing schools in both the Tokyo and Osaka/Takarazuka areas are owned or staffed predominantly by ex-Takarasiennes: Okada Taiko (Wakana Yuki 1964–68), the wife of Revue writer/director Okada Keiji, runs a children's musical theatre school, Nonnon Ballet Studio (*With Takarazuka* 1992; Natori and Takeichi 1996a: 160–69). Another retiree, Kojima Kie (Nangō Kie, 1981–85), juggled caring for her infant son with the operation of K.I.E. Musical School, which also employed several other ex-Takarasiennes to teach Takarazuka aspirants.[16]

This chapter has continued the argument introduced in preceding chapters, that Takarasiennes are a very diverse group of individuals, whose attitudes and experiences in relation to the portrayal of gender and the gender issues affecting them as women in Japan are similarly varied, in their post-performing lives as well as on-stage during their tenure with the Revue. Takarazuka training is credited with developing resilience to hardship, a willingness to learn new skills in a short time, an ability to 'act' appropriately to ensure smooth interpersonal relationships, and a determination to pursue dreams that carries over into such life-stages as marriage, motherhood and further careers. The naivety of some performers, though, means that these dreams sometimes remain unfulfilled in the multi-gendered, real world outside the 'stage full of dreams' that Takarazuka purports to be.

Conclusion

The production and consumption of the emphatically-gendered fantasy world of Takarazuka extends far beyond its stage into the private lives of performers, creative staff and fans alike. As this volume has shown, all who are involved, both individually and collectively, approach it with preconceived notions of masculinity and femininity derived from the socialisation they receive at home, at school and as members of society in general; from images of gender roles in Japan and elsewhere which are projected by the media, the arts and popular culture; and from their own imagination and biases. Nonetheless, Takarasiennes are still adolescents when they join Takarazuka (or even younger children, in the Revue's early decades), and I have thus argued that their grasp of orthodox gender roles is inadequate for them convincingly to portray adult females, let alone males. Accordingly, it is necessary for them to learn, through formal instruction, imitation of their revered seniors, and other methods, how to perform Takarazuka's particular versions of gender, which, to varying extents, reflect, amend or subvert the gender norms of wider society.

My examination of Takarazuka's history, augmented by many examples of the words and activities of numerous Takarazuka performers, their supporters of both sexes, and the Revue's creative staff, as well as others' interpretations of such examples, both informal and scholarly, has suggested that pervasive stereotypes of Japanese womanhood (and manhood) fail to encompass the true breadth of variation in attitude and experience that exists in the gendered lives of actual people in contemporary Japan. In my exploration of the on- and off-stage lives of Takarazuka performers, and of the *otokoyaku*, in particular, I have reasoned that it is possible for a trained individual (here, anatomically female) successfully to assume a gendered persona which does not necessarily correspond to her biological sex, for a specific purpose and for a particular period, without this necessarily challenging her basic gender identity.

Clearly, the distinctiveness and appeal of Takarazuka, for its performers, creative staff and audience alike, depend largely upon its specialised representation of contrasting genders, performed entirely by a female cast. We have seen that the Revue's idealised version of masculinity, which approximately half of its members are groomed to perform, markedly differs in many respects from that expected of actual males in Japanese society, because it is largely a romantic fiction, developed by the collective imagination of countless women and men over many decades, mainly for the sake of other women. For many female fans of the *otokoyaku*, especially, this fantasy masculinity appears to be a preferred alternative to the rougher, more physical, less sensitive masculinity of the real men they encounter outside Takarazuka, with whom many women seem disappointed. I have shown that male impersonation by Takarasiennes, within the parameters of what is considered by performers and fans alike to be 'beautiful,' is usually rewarded with fame and public adulation. Takarazuka's fantasy males, and the performers who portray them, have become commodities which are eagerly consumed by its female fans, earning considerable fame (if not revenue) for the Revue Company and for its owners, the Hankyu Corporation. The Revue's male-role players, whose portrayal of 'ideal men' is supposedly limited to the duration of their on-stage performances, may appear somewhat androgynous off-stage, but are presented in the Revue's public relations material as 'normal' females in private life. They thus enjoy a widespread social acceptance that is commonly denied cross-dressed individuals, especially those suspected of homosexual orientation.

The elegantly-constructed masculinity of the *otokoyaku* un-doubtedly has been the most significant factor in the Revue's enduring popularity. Fans' dramatic withdrawal of support for a well-loved *otokoyaku* who retires from Takarazuka and continues her theatrical career by playing female roles in mainstream show business indicates that it is largely her assumed masculinity, framed within the fantasy world of the Takarazuka stage and its environs, that attracts these fans, rather than the intrinsic personality and talent of the performer herself. It is clear, however, that fellow performers, too, believe that the *otokoyaku* exists to fulfil the romantic fantasies of women, including other Takarasiennes. Repugnance for the overt (hetero-)sexuality implied by marriage and childbirth clearly underlies performers' overwhelming support for Takarazuka's 'retirement-upon-marriage' rule – in particular, it seems, in the case of *otokoyaku*, of whose underlying female physiology they do not wish to be reminded.

Given the current overwhelming popularity of the *otokoyaku*, the importance of the female-role players, the *musumeyaku* and *onnayaku*, is often under-emphasised by fans, by the general populace and in general scholarship on the Revue, probably because female-role players are assumed to be acting 'naturally,' simply utilising their own feminine persona. Their existence commonly is seen to have little intrinsic value, bar that of reflecting the male-role players' glory. Such an attitude echoes the inferior status afforded by society in general to women and women's activities, in comparison to those of men – a reason also underlying many people's apparent antipathy towards Takarazuka itself. Moreover, the lesser popularity of *musumeyaku* and *onnayaku* among female fans, especially, probably derives from the latter's displeasure at being reminded of society's low estimation of their own worth, and of the wiles to which women are expected to resort in order to flatter and serve others. I have shown that the exaggerated femininity of the female-role player's performance is as much a specialised technique that must be learned as that of the *otokoyaku*, and that the contribution of a *musumeyaku* or *onnayaku* is vital to counterbalance the assumed 'maleness' of her stage partner playing the opposite gender. Irrespective of their stage gender, all Takarasiennes are equally important for the creation and maintenance of Takarazuka's fantasy world, in which gender manipulation is the principal focus of attention. I have asserted that the Revue absolutely reveals the artifice of gender, because Takarasiennes constitute living examples of how gender can be seen not as a 'natural' consequence of having a male or female body, but as a repetitive 'act' which requires frequent rehearsal and reinforcement.

Morally-problematic aspects of gender impersonation by women have been addressed by the male founder and his successors in the Revue Administration by such means as the formulation and popularisation of the Company motto, 'purely, righteously, beautifully,' to construct and project the image of all performers, irrespective of stage gender, as chaste, feminine, heterosexual women in private life, who will probably leave the Company to marry and bear children while still comparatively young. My examples have illustrated, however, that there is actually considerable diversity in the timing of and motivation for performers' retirement from Takarazuka, and in their post-retirement activities. Obviously, marriage and motherhood as an exclusive occupation do not constitute the only life-course for Takarasiennes who quit the stage.

Male administrators in Takarazuka, including Kobayashi, also have imposed written and unwritten rules to govern Takarasiennes' everyday conduct and their interactions with the rest of society, especially with their fans, in accordance with the same chaste image as the motto prescribes. This is emphasised in the case of male-role players, arguably in order to allay suspicions of lesbianism, though open discussion of such a topic is, in any case, proscribed by the unwritten code of conduct now known as the Violet Code. We have seen, however, that rules are not always followed, and that the Company motto is actually a kind of veil, used, for example, to hide or disavow the sexual aspects of feelings, behaviour and interpersonal relationships among members and fans, and to suppress the open discussion or publication of other potentially controversial matters relating to the Revue.

Takarazuka's ethos, performance practices and audience demographics have been significantly affected by the historical context in which the Revue was founded and developed. Takarazuka and its rival all-female revue companies created a new genre of popular culture in the early decades of the twentieth century, of which Takarazuka is now the only thriving survivor, and the clearest example among them of the appeal of performances whose main aim is to highlight gender impersonation. However, in spite of its commercial success, its longevity, its artistic merit and the talent of many of its performers, Takarazuka is dismissed by many people as trivial or amateurish, based again on the premise that female endeavours are by definition of less value than those of males, especially if those endeavours are directed at a largely female public. This view was reinforced by Kobayashi Ichizō's attitude to girls and women, whose theatrical activities, he believed, were best kept at an amateur level, as their ultimate career should be marriage and motherhood.

While creating a fantasy world of its own in the imagination of each of its participants, Takarazuka has nevertheless been part of the larger community, and, as such, has been affected by social, economic and historical developments on a local, national and global scale. It was founded when professional acting was a new and controversial occupation for women, and Takarazuka's development was shaped by its founder's response to the societal assumption that the stage was no place for respectable females. In pre-war years, as we have seen, government policies and campaigns had a direct impact upon the content and style of productions, and Takarasiennes' status as patriotic, gendered citizens was emphasised by their participation in nationalistic propaganda efforts and mobilisation for war work, along with other women in the general population. Since the war's end, while state control has been lifted, Takarazuka's repertoire and performance practices have reflected, to some extent, various changes in the sexual mores of wider society in Japan, and have been influenced by the boom in girls' comic books and animation featuring cross-dressing and same-sex love, and by the hiring of guest directors and choreographers from the West. Such elements have introduced new ideas on gender and sexuality, which sometimes have conflicted with the 'wholesome' traditions that Takarazuka claims to uphold. Amendments to laws relating to gender equality and education also have had some impact upon Takarazuka's training and hiring protocols, though the Company continues to encourage performers to retire at an age deemed appropriate for marriage, in spite of the escalating trend in Japanese society for women to marry late or to remain single.

My exploration of the link between Takarazuka and gender issues relating to teenaged girls' self-determination, in such matters as education, training, occupation and marriage, has shown that girls' ability and desire to pursue their own goals varies considerably among individuals. Some girls' Takarazuka aspirations are so strong that they are prepared to go to great lengths to fulfil them, even in defiance of opposition from parents and others, which is often based upon orthodox notions of suitable education and careers for women. In other cases, relatives and mentors urge girls to join the Revue, often in anticipation of vicariously enjoying the Takarazuka experience through the girl's success, or of transcending the limitations of their own gender through close contact with Takarazuka's fantasy world.

The Takarazuka Music School is the site where future Takarazuka performers are taught the basics of stagecraft, and begin to learn gender-performance techniques. A largely unwritten, but similarly important, moral curriculum indoctrinates the students with the ethos of purity, righteousness and beauty: qualities which, in combination, are typically expected of females in Japanese society. The strict cleaning regimen imposed upon first-year students and the inclusion of the tea ceremony in the Music School timetable further echo the stereotype of diligent, cultured females, ready to be good wives (if not wise mothers, as well). Juniors are taught to assume their place in the Revue hierarchy, which means learning the rituals involved in demonstrating, or at least feigning, subservience towards and respect for seniors. In turn, they also learn how to assert psychological domination over others, and to guide their juniors by a combination of intimidation and example. This training is reportedly useful when Takarasiennes rejoin society, for handling their husbands and mothers-in-law, and, perhaps, for controlling their daughters-in law in later life.

The real task of mastering gender portrayal, as I have shown, is undertaken once performers have graduated from the Music School and made their stage debut, with a new identity symbolised by their professional name. The length of their hair, and, to a lesser extent, the masculine or feminine ring of their stage name, signals their intention to specialise in a particular stage gender. Once inducted into the Company proper, Takarasiennes emulate the example of their seniors during rehearsals and performances in order to learn the established techniques for portraying gender, as well as incorporating notions of masculinity and femininity from the outside world. They also learn how to project the accepted image of the model Takarazuka *musumeyaku* or *otokoyaku* off-stage, as well, for their fans and for the general public. Those performers who refuse to comply with the stereotypes developed over many decades by their seniors may be criticised by fellow performers and by fans, who expect their idols to uphold Takarazuka 'traditions'. Fans also object to any performer's attitude or action which reduces fans' opportunity to participate in pleasurable practices of fandom, such as being able to watch the ingress and egress through the stage door of their favourite Takarasienne in her off-stage attire.

Takarazuka is by no means a company that pursues its own artistic aims in isolation from its audience. The scale of its productions and the number of on- and off-stage employees it engages require its 2,500-seat theatres to be well-patronised throughout the year. Its creative and administrative staff thus attempt to cater to the perceived tastes of the majority of its fans. Fandom is a well-established and well-organised phenomenon in Takarazuka, with its own history of differing gender composition and practices. The economic and social significance of fans is great, for the Revue and the Hankyu Railway, and for the peripheral communities whose existence depends largely upon the patronage of Takarazuka supporters and would-be Takarasiennes. The membership of many of the hundreds of fan clubs dedicated to individual performers numbers in the thousands, and some exclusive fan clubs, such as those formed by male leaders of industry, commerce and politics, have high status within mainstream society. For some women, fan clubs can provide an outlet for leadership and organisational ability, and afford them the control over others that their position as females in Japan may otherwise deny them. This book has discussed the importance to fans of an awareness of gender and an enjoyment of performers' manipulation of gender roles, and, to a more limited extent, of fans' own juggling of masculinity and femininity, as well.

As my examples illustrate, erotic sexuality cannot be ignored or denied as one significant element in many fans' attraction towards Takarazuka, in spite of the insistence of the Revue Administration and numerous fans that the appeal is non-sexual, if somehow connected with fervent admiration (*akogare*) and fantasy romance. Male fans' expressed longing to marry a Takarazuka performer can surely be taken as encompassing sexual desire. Unlike female fans, men do not need to justify a liking for Takarasiennes as being based on anything but 'normal' heterosexuality, on the understanding that all performers are biologically female, irrespective of their stage gender, and are therefore the natural targets for male affection and sexual interest. However, female fans who certainly worship Takarasiennes with no less fervour than do males, and spend much time and money supporting their favourite, are discouraged by the homophobic attitudes of society and by the Revue ethos itself from acknowledging the possibility of any (homo-)sexual basis to their fandom. They are thus likely to insist that their love for *otokoyaku* is platonic and directed towards the imagined male gender of the player, not her anatomical sex.

Playing with gender, especially when it is obvious that such play is not merely a public exaggeration of the performer's own persona, is, after all, very entertaining, both for the players and for the spectators. The illusion of intimacy which is constructed between Takarazuka performers and their fans, through such means as an exchange of gazes during performances; the dissemination, through magazine articles penned by Takarasiennes themselves, of myriad details about their own background and everyday experiences, as well as backstage gossip; and off-stage personal appearances at fan gatherings, also enables dedicated fans to recognise when players drop in and out of character, and thus to take delight in the gender gymnastics that this usually involves. Fans feel personally acknowledged when they receive greeting cards from their idols, even if hundreds, or thousands, are issued twice yearly by each performer. In addition, fans actively contribute to the construction and manipulation of gender portrayal on- and off- stage, by aspiring to become performers themselves; by writing scripts or letters to performers and the Administration; by nurturing performers as surrogate mothers/fathers, friends or even lovers; by engaging in 'copycat' theatricals; or by encouraging girls to join or coaching them for the Music School entrance examination.

Once they have decided to marry, pursue a different career, or are edged out of the Company by its retirement policies, most Takarasiennes face the challenge of engaging with the world outside the 'hot-house' environment of the Revue and its immediate vicinity, in which they are protected and nurtured. We have explored various retirees' experiences, which frequently involve the necessity to adapt both behaviourally and attitudinally to a new gender role or roles, in professional and private life alike. It apparently takes some time to unlearn various stage-gender-specific mannerisms, such as sitting with legs wide apart in the case of *otokoyaku*. It is clear, too, that some ex-Takarasiennes yearn to reprise the gender portrayal for which they were once trained – and therefore take the opportunity to participate in charity performances and so forth, recreating their former stage persona with its uniquely Takarazuka-oriented appearance and acting technique. Even former female-role players who pursue an acting career in mainstream theatre, films or television usually play a woman's part opposite actual males, and therefore no longer act as they did in Takarazuka, opposite an *otokoyaku*. Yet the proliferation in recent years of all-female performance groups composed of retirees from Takarazuka and similar revue companies, who can continue to recreate their *otokoyaku* and *musumeyaku* roles on stage to the evident delight of fans, old and new, suggests that these artistic representations of gender no longer need to be abandoned once their players quit their original companies. The internet, with its ability to publicise players' activities to a potential audience and provide a forum for fans' discussion and exchange of information, has surely played a major role in the growth of this phenomenon. Moreover, the anonymity afforded by cyberspace will perhaps facilitate a freer discussion of such topics as sexuality, and especially same-sex attraction, which have been such touchy subjects among fans and the performers they idolise. This may, in turn, contribute to determining their respective self-identity in a way that face-to-face interaction has discouraged.

Though the tenets of patriarchy are upheld by various Revue policies, the experiences and opinions of performers and their supporters I have noted in this volume have suggested that alternative models of female existence are often just as attractive to women as orthodox life-courses – if not even *more* attractive, seeing that marriage is considered by some to be 'life's graveyard,' in the words of one of my informants. After all, joining Takarazuka was such an enjoyable experience for many Takarasiennes that they often encourage their own daughters, female relatives and other promising girls to aspire to the Revue stage, where they would uphold Takarazuka's tradition of exquisite gender performance. So long as Japanese society continues to offer women fewer opportunities for self-determination than it offers men, and the range of experience open to young women who choose to remain within broadly respectable bounds is still restricted, Takarazuka will surely remain a popular medium which caters to the otherwise unfulfilled dreams of countless women, whether as performers or as fans, by affording them the chance vicariously to participate in a wider world not dependent upon their own sex, gender or ethnicity. On the other hand, though, I have also argued that the gendered structure of work and leisure in post-war Japan has enabled Takarazuka to profit greatly from middle-class women's pursuit of daytime entertainment, as it is now such women, not men, who have the leisure time and the financial leeway to seek pleasure in live theatre. In this sense, the contemporary Revue very much reflects the social changes which have taken place in Japan over the past several decades.

Many questions remain to be answered in relation to Takarazuka. Will future social and legal developments that impact upon the status and role of women and men in Japanese society, and around the globe, also influence the Revue's performance practices and the imagined masculinity and femininity it enacts, or will Takarazuka's 'traditions' remain aloof from the world? In spite of the hiring of female writer/directors and orchestra conductors by the Revue in response to Equal Employment Opportunity legislation, there seems to be no further suggestion of recruiting male performers, as the exclusively single-sex format seems to be so successful, and ensures that Takarazuka caters to a niche market that mainstream theatre cannot satisfy. Its long-time rival company, SKD, for example, did not repeat attempts in the 1980s to stage musicals with mixed casts.

As an organisation employing some four hundred female performers, Takarazuka is likely to respond in other ways to challenges to prevailing gender stereotypes, posed by such factors as the falling marriage- and birth-rates; rising educational levels and more choice of curriculum content; expanded employment opportunities outside traditionally single-gender occupations;

social attitudes to sexual diversity; and advances in reproductive technology. As the Takarazuka Revue anticipates celebrating its centennial in less than a decade, a significant factor in its ongoing prosperity will be how it deals with a variety of gender issues, both on and off its colourful 'stage of dreams.'

Notes

Introduction

1 This sobriquet was devised in the late 1920s by analogy with Parisienne, as a referent for Takarazuka performers, by writer/director Shirai Tetsuzō, who apparently coined the term as a replacement for the often-used epithet, *'Zuka gāru* ([Takara]'zuka girl). On the meaning of 'girl (*gāru*)' as an occupational referent with erotic overtones, see Sato (2003: 120–21).

2 See Robertson (1989, 1991, 1992a, 1992b, 1992c, 1995, 1998a, 1998b, 1999, 2000, 2001).

3 On various 'invented' traditions of Japan, see Vlastos (1998).

4 On Japanese classical theatrical forms, see, e.g. Bowers (1974); Kawatake (1971); Nishiyama (1997); Pound and Fenollosa (1959).

5 On gender performance, also see Butler (1999: 173–80); Halberstam (1998); Volcano and Halberstam (1999).

6 See, for example, Smith (1987: 1–25); Condon (1985); Eccleston (1989: 162–210).

7 See Mochizuki (1999: 12–13); also Smith (1983: 70–84).

8 Though Takarazuka was founded a decade before the identification of the Modern Girl phenomenon, Robertson (1998b: 27) erroneously cites the 'excessive and unfeminine charisma of the Modern Girl' as one reason why Kobayashi initially established an all-female revue.

9 Female students at universities and colleges in general predominate in subjects such as domestic science, early childhood education and humanities, and are significantly underrepresented in fields such as science and engineering, though the proportion of girls attending four-year universities is growing markedly, and the range of subjects studied by girls is diversifying. The proportion of female students in postgraduate studies has also risen to an all-time high of 7.2 per cent (Gender Equality Bureau 2007).

Chapter 1

1 On Sadayakko, see Downer (2003); Kano (1999: 46–48; 2001: 39–122); Gilbert-Falkenburg (1985: 35–36).

2 The Taishō era, falling between the Meiji and Shōwa eras, extended from 1912 to 1926.

3 By the *kazoedoshi* system, babies were deemed to be one year old at birth, turning two at New Year, when all Japanese became one year older. By Western calculation, therefore, the first recruits would have ranged in age between eleven and fourteen, one to two years younger than the *kazoedoshi* figure.

4 On the introduction and popularisation of Western music in Japan, see Eppstein (1994).

5 For a history of the Takarazuka Symphony Orchestra which grew from this amateur musical group, see Kondō (1997: 153–55).

6 Kobayashi's pen name of Ikeda Hatao refers to the location of his home, which lay amid fields (*hata*) in the municipality of Ikeda. Hatao literally means 'man of the fields.'

7 This nomenclature reflects the Japanese expression used as a traditional metaphor for beauty, *setsugekka* ('snow, moon [and] flowers,' spelt *yuki*, *tsuki* and *hana*, respectively, when the characters are used in isolation). Subsequent additional troupes (*kumi* or *-gumi*) were also named in like manner: Yuki-gumi (Snow Class/Troupe) in 1924; Hoshi-gumi (Star Class/Troupe) in 1933 (disbanded in 1939 when company numbers fell; reinstated in 1948 when numbers again swelled). In 1998, a competition was held to choose the name of the newest troupe, Sora-gumi (Cosmos Class/Troupe). It employs a non-standard reading of a character meaning 'space; cosmos,' pronouncing it as the native word for 'sky.'

8 A male pit chorus was engaged as a temporary measure in 1940, and boys were again admitted to the Music School in 1947, but none of these attempts culminated in mixed casts performing on Takarazuka's main stage.

9 After a fire in 1935 destroyed the theatre's interior, fewer seats were installed. The size of each seat was enlarged post-war, and the final seating capacity remained static at 2,865 from 1968 until late 1992, when the structure was demolished to make way for a new theatre which opened in January 1993. In the pre-1993 theatres, audience capacity could be expanded by the selling of hundreds of *tachimi* (standing-room) tickets, which were available at cheap prices after all seats were filled, usually on weekends and holidays. The current Grand Theatre has only two levels, seating a total of 2,500 (*Kageki* 1992b: 55).

10 See Sugahara (1996: 155), for a description of Mizunoe in 1930 as the first 'beautiful woman in men's clothes (*dansō no reijin*)' in Japan's revue history.

11 The original version of this song, written in German, was *Wenn der weisse Fliedder wieder blüht* (When the white lilacs bloom again), with words by Fritz Rotter and music by Franz Doelle. Shirai probably became acquainted with a French-language version during his sojourn in Paris. In Shirai's Japanese translation of the lyrics, the lilacs became violets (*sumire*).

12 For a more comprehensive analysis of Japanese wartime cinema, see High (2003).

13 Radio listeners in Mongolia, China, Thailand, India and Burma who perhaps missed seeing such live performances could listen to broadcasts of selected Takarazuka productions such as *Pekin* (Peking, 1942): see Hagiwara (1954: 141).

14 For photographs of wartime costumes, see, for example, Hashimoto (1994: 54–58). On wartime civilian wear, see Havens (1986: 18).

15 The all-female revue companies OSSK and SSKD, established in the 1920s in Osaka and Tokyo by the theatrical organisation Shōchiku, also

jettisoned the word '*shōjo*' in 1943 and 1945, becoming OSK (Osaka Shōchiku kagekidan) and SKD (Shōchiku kagekidan), respectively (Sugahara 1996: 126; 164). In the OSK case, at least, Sugahara suggests that this was because the age-range of performers now extended far beyond girlhood (1996: 126).

16 There is discrepancy in the number of entrants according to different sources. The name lists compiled by Hashimoto (1994: 184) show fifty-three entrants in 1939, forty-seven in 1940, thirty-three in 1941, and eighteen in 1942. The final intake before the war's end, in 1943, was again thirty-three. On the other hand, Kobayashi's table (1955: 556) for the years 1938–54, for example, shows sixty-two admitted out of 681 aspirants in 1939; fifty out of 520 in 1940; fifty-five out of 295 in 1941; forty out of 279 in 1942; and fifty-one out of 387 in 1943.

17 On the wartime mobilisation of women, see, for example, Mitchell (1986).

18 Continuing membership of the Revue in the war years provided some air-raid victims with a safe haven, and a steady trickle of homeless Takarasiennes took up residence at the Company's dormitory. Tamai records that dormitory rooms originally meant for four persons eventually had to accommodate five or six (Tamai 1999: 39; also see Fujino 1990: 129–30). A four-storey, concrete dormitory for Takarazuka students and performers was erected in 1944, replacing three separate facilities ('Danshi kinsei' 1980: 144).

19 Shirai had been promoted by Kobayashi to Chief Executive Officer in the Revue administration, in order to prevent his defection to the rival theatrical organisation, Shōchiku, and this, apparently, also caused resentment among other employees. Although his critics later retracted their accusations of lack of patriotism, Shirai quit the Company after the 1943 revue, *Uta no hanakago* (Flower-basket of songs). He rejoined the staff in September 1947 (Takagi 1983: 239).

20 For details of Allied restrictions upon Kabuki, see, for example, Okamoto (2001).

21 On the male recruits' subsequent careers, see Tsuji (2004), the book which inspired a musical theatre production staged in 2007, entitled *Takarazuka Boys*.

22 Otowa apparently quit the Revue because she disliked what she termed the 'feudalistic (*hōkenteki*)' atmosphere inside Takarazuka (Honchi 1977: 40).

23 Kobayashi descendants have largely monopolised senior positions in the giant Hankyu Corporation, which embodies many elements of a hereditary family company – Yonezō's son Kōhei is current Chair (*kaichō*) of Hankyu and Principal of the Music School, while Kobayashi's great-grandson Kōichi is the latest appointee as Chief Executive Officer (*rijichō*) (Sponichi Annex Osaka 2004). Dorinne Kondo's work on Japanese family businesses is a useful tool in understanding the dynastic nature of these organisations. See Kondo (1990).

24 A well-known example is that of popular singer Koyanagi Rumiko, who left Takarazuka in 1970 to make her recording debut soon after graduating from the Music School, taking the stage name Natsukawa Rumi.

Chapter 2

1 For statistics on the activities of graduates of various levels of secondary and tertiary education in Japan, see, for example, *Monbukagakushō* (2003).

2 The ages given here are approximate, having been recorded respectively as twelve and nineteen by *kazoedoshi* reckoning: see *Kageki* (1974a: 110). Higher elementary school graduates could obtain a licence to teach lower primary grades after four years' study at normal school (Newell 1997: 23).

3 The railway was later renamed several times, but finally became Hankyu, part of the overarching company now known as Hankyu-Hanshin Holdings, Incorporated, which advertises the Revue wherever it has business interests. See *Hankyu Hanshin Holdings Incorporated Web Site* (2007).

4 Takarazuka posters emblazon every Hankyu/Hanshin station and affiliated subway stations in the Osaka/Kyoto/Kobe area, as well as hanging inside every train.

5 See Kobayashi (1955: 455). Scripts written by in-house writer/directors, including dialogue, lyrics and commentary, are now incorporated in the playbills sold at each performance, unless copyright reasons prevent this, and several anthologies of works by veteran staff members such as Shibata Yukihiro and Ueda Shinji have been published in recent decades.

6 The first Takarazuka CD, produced by an affiliated company, Takarazuka ongaku shuppan (Takarazuka music publishing), was launched in August 1987 (Hashimoto 1994: 277). The pastime of trying to emulate idols by singing their songs to karaoke accompaniment is practised not only by would-be Takarasiennes, but also by Japanese people in general. See Ogawa (1990: 32); Kelly (1998: 77–78).

7 An amateur theatrical group to which I briefly belonged in Kansai in the late 1980s also used Takarazuka videos to choreograph its own versions of *shōjo manga* (girls' comics) such as *The Rose of Versailles*. For a description of a similar theatre group, 'Sister,' see Robertson (1998b: 172–74).

8 Sugahara (1996) offers a comparison of Takarazuka with the Shōchiku-affiliated companies latterly known as SKD and OSK.

9 Rural girls probably had little chance to be inspired by such films, as touring projection units usually showed only old, silent films in the countryside during the 1930s and 1940s. See Anderson and Richie (1982: 146).

10 For a synopsis, see 'Bangumi shōsai: Takarazuka fujin (Programme details: *Takarazuka wives*),' in *Takarazuka Sky Stage Web Site* (2002).

11 For descriptions of acting in Takarazuka films in the 1950s, see Yachigusa (1999: 53–58, 272); also, Kishi (2000: 41, 44–49). According to film and stage actress Sawamura Sadako, studios (other than Takarazuka's) neither trained their actresses nor properly rehearsed scenes before filming (Sawamura 1969: 203).

12 On the stigma associated with film-acting, according to one non-Takarazuka actress, see Sawamura (1969: 77).

13 The telecast of the wedding of the then Crown Prince in 1959, the introduction of colour broadcasts in 1960, and the 1964 Tokyo Olympic

Games each are claimed to have spurred television purchases, resulting in a corresponding drop in cinema audience numbers. See Partner (1999: 173–75); also, Ivy (1993: 248).

14 A telecast of Takarazuka's 1965 Paris performance, produced by West German Bavaria Atelier Television, was apparently shown all over Europe (Tanimura 1971: 39). Several acquaintances also report having watched satellite telecasts of Takarazuka programmes in Hong Kong, Taiwan and Korea, more recently.

15 Overseas performances are not the only avenue by which applicants from outside Japan become aware of the Revue, however: Honolulu resident Yuki Reina (1970–78; second-generation Japanese-American) saw a Takarazuka performance during a sojourn in Japan; while Sachikaze Irene (1979–93; second-generation Japanese-Mexican) apparently missed Takarazuka's Mexico City season, but travelled to Japan to study performing arts, and applied successfully to the Music School (see Hashimoto 1988: 117–18).

16 Maori Yuki, cited in Nakamura (1994: 70). Maori apparently feared that her fervent admiration for Daichi, a woman, meant that she was a 'pervert,' but Maori was reassured by a female friend, who agreed that Daichi was indeed 'gorgeous (*suteki*)' (Nakamura 1994: 70).

17 Three *otokoyaku* stars from one graduating class is considered a large number, although a record of four 1985 graduates occupied top male-role position in their respective troupes in 1999 (see *Takarazuka otome 1999*: 19, 43, 67, 90).

18 The first Japanese talkie was a 1930 Shōchiku production entitled *Madamu to nyōbō* (The neighbour's wife and mine), directed by Gosho Heinosuke (see Nolletti 1992: 6).

19 Colour feature films were also imported from the West, but the 1939 Hollywood production of *Gone with the Wind*, for example, was not released in Japan until 1952 (see Koyama 2004: 63).

20 The Osaka shōchiku gakugekibu, for example, received 1,025 applications for sixty places in spring 1936. It performed both in Osaka theatres and at an amusement park in the Nara outskirts from the 1930s (see Kurata 1990: 96).

21 A small number of SKD members regrouped to put on sporadic performances for several years, including those with mixed casts and/or all-female casts with no *otokoyaku*, as a company renamed Shōchiku myūjikaru (Shochiku musical), between 1992 and 1996. See *Suna no ue no sanba* (1993). Other ex-SKD members have formed alternative groups (e.g. *STAS Official Web Site* 2003).

22 Several acquaintances of mine reported having attempted both examinations, but preferred Takarazuka in terms of scale, popularity, prestige and the quality of its staging facilities. In only one case that I know, a place at the Takarazuka Music School was declined in favour of OSK, in return for guaranteed rapid promotion to stardom.

23 Bungakuza (Literary Theatre) was formed in 1937; Mingei (Gekidan mingei), originally a Shingeki (New Drama) company called Minshū geijutsu gekijō (People's Arts Theatre), was relaunched in 1950; Haiyūza (Actors' Theatre) was formed in 1944 (see Umesao 1995: 661, 1705, 1936).

24 Daughters' earnings made a valuable contribution to the finances of many middle-class families in early decades of the last century (see Nagy 1991: 204). Now, however, it is common for middle-class, employed, single women living with their parents to pay little or no board, while enjoying the home-cooked meals and housekeeping services their mothers provide, and spending their income as they wish. One media term for such young women was '*Hanako-zoku* (Hanako tribe),' after a magazine, *Hanako*, which catered to their supposed tastes in travel, fashion, food and lifestyle. On such 'single aristocrats,' see Jolivet 1997: 141–42. Now, such unmarried adult offspring still living at home have become known as 'parasite singles' (Dales 2005).

25 Since the Meiji period, in rural communities, at least, it had been common practice for girls – especially those from poorer families – to leave their villages to labour as 'migrant workers (*dekasegi*)' to contribute to household finances and to save for their trousseau; see Tsurumi (1990: 9–10).

26 This thinking was echoed in a comment I heard from a child psychologist and counsellor when a drama department was established in 1985 at a prefectural upper-secondary school, Takarazuka North Senior High School (Takarazuka kita kōtō gakkō). In the speaker's opinion, a boy should not consider such fields of study as dance and drama, for his chances of entering a 'good' university and obtaining a 'proper' job would be jeopardised if he did so. For statistics on the further education, training and employment of Takarazuka North Senior High School graduates from the period 1988–93, see Yamazaki (1993: 246–49).

27 Also see Hashimoto (1994: 178–81, 184–89, 192–97). The records in Hashimoto's volume indicate the year of entry to training (*nyūgaku*) for each recruit until 1938, and the year of joining the company proper (*nyūdan*), thereafter.

28 On the eugenic efficacy of chairs, see Robertson (2001: 23).

29 For an excerpt from *The Rose of Versailles* referring to Oscar's upbringing and gender socialisation, see Robertson (1998b: 74–76).

Chapter 3

1 For descriptions of two such schools, see Matsuo (1998: 129–132); Natori and Takeichi (1996a: 105, 109–13).

2 From 1946 to 1957, however, as a measure to build up company numbers depleted during the war years, training consisted of only one year at the School, and entrants were consequently free from seniors' supervision until they joined the Company proper (e.g. Kishi 2000: 25–26).

3 The numbering system for intakes and graduating classes is complex, as there were multiple intakes in some years, none in others: see Hashimoto (1994: 178–84).

4 On the concepts of receiving and giving indulgence, *amae[ru]* and *amayakasu*, see Doi (1986); Lebra (1976).

5 For a comprehensive treatment of *tatemae* and *honne*, see Doi (1986).

6 For a humorous account of this task, see Maya (1994: 161–66).

7 According to my own observations and the comments of acquaintances in OSK, its disciplinary practices, hierarchy and cleaning regimen seem to

have been broadly similar to those of Takarazuka. Some US arts academies have enforced similar rules: see Robertson (1998b: 218, n. 16).

8 On *jigoe*, see the account of a performer famed for her vocal prowess, Fukamidori Natsuyo (*With Takarazuka* 1993: 3).

9 On Takarasiennes' nicknames, see Nimiya (1994: 79–81).

10 On Takarasiennes' names in general, see Izumi (1987: 71–72).

11 Biographical details show Koshiro as born in Dadong, Shanxi. Other Takarasiennes who were born in China during Japan's colonial period include: Miyama Shinobu (debut 1945) and Rijō Mariko (1954), both born in Dalian (Dairen), and Mizu Hayami (1962), born in Xinjiang (Shinkyō) (*Takarazuka otome 1970*).

12 In the five-year period from 1912, while approximately sixty-six per cent of all Japanese girls' names ended in -*ko*, more than ninety per cent of Takarazuka stage names used it. Among the general population, the popularity of -*ko* names rose to near eighty-five per cent by 1927, not dropping until after 1942. Takarazuka *geimei*, on the other hand, moved against this convention, with -*ko* names comprising some thirty per cent less than in Japanese society as a whole by about 1932. See Izumi (1987: 74–75).

13 See Hashimoto (1994: 178–95). The official yearbook, *Takarazuka otome 2006*, listed only six names ending with -*ko* out of almost 470 current Company members.

Chapter 4

1 On *kejime*, see Bachnik (1992: 152–72).

2 On group loyalty in Japan, see, for example, Kondo (1990).

3 Fixed microphones were first installed in 1934 for the performance of *Jabu jabu konto*, apparently at the instigation of staff member Umemoto Rikuhei, who had seen them in use in the United States during a study tour in 1931. See Sugahara (1996: 207, 210).

4 The 'chest voice,' otherwise known as the 'chest register,' 'chest tone' or 'heavy mechanism,' is of low or medium pitch, and is thought to be produced by resonance in the chest, giving it a 'thicker' quality than its opposite, the 'head voice,' which has high pitch, a lighter, 'thinner' quality, and apparently resonates in the head. In the case of male voices, the latter is also called falsetto.

5 On gender stereotyping in Japanese, see Takeda (1991: 53–62); Okamoto (1995: 297–325); Maree (2003).

6 On masculine and feminine Japanese, see, for example, Jorden (1983a: 250–51, 1983b: 124–25); Shibamoto (1985); Endō (1987, 1997); Cherry (1987); and Kurihara (1990: 72–82).

7 The script was adapted by in-house writer/director Ōzeki Hiromasa from the 1986–87 serialised novel, *Semishigure* (A chorus of cicada song), by Fujisawa Shūhei.

8 I have no data from which to formulate any suppositions about the performance of gender among the few young men who received Takarazuka training. In their performances, which, it will be remembered, took place not at the Takarazuka Grand Theatre but at a smaller venue, they played (presumably heterosexual) male roles on stage, opposite Takarasiennes cast

in female roles, presumably producing a markedly different atmosphere from the usual all-female Revue.

9 Ogawa (cited in Takubo 2001) reports that many Takarazuka stars made television appearances during her years with the Revue. This was possibly a deliberate attempt by the Revue to boost Takarazuka's popularity, which had dipped prior to the staging of *The Rose of Versailles* in 1974.

10 It will be remembered, however, that seniority by birth order does not necessarily apply in Takarazuka. A 'junior' who began training at eighteen, the upper age limit for application to the Music School, for example, may be up to three years older than her 'senior' who joined at the minimum age, immediately after graduation from junior high school. This parallels the practice in university clubs, especially those specialising in martial arts or sports such as baseball, in which those students whose entrance to university was delayed for a year or more are treated as subordinates by peers who proceeded directly from high school to tertiary education.

11 Haruka's hair was short probably because Maria was her first female role since Haruka switched from an *otokoyaku* to a *musumeyaku*, and her hair had not yet grown long.

12 The custom of presenting gifts to superiors and others whose favour is sought at mid-year and year-end, termed *o-chūgen* and *o-seibo*, respectively, has become institutionalised in Japanese society.

Chapter 5

1 'Dream' is the most often-used word in Japanese advertising, particularly when women are the target audience, according to Merry White (1995: 265).

2 On the 'clinical gaze,' see Foucault (1994); on the normalising, 'inspecting gaze' of gaols, see Foucault (1995).

3 For a discussion of female spectatorship, as revealed by letters and questionnaires written by cinema fans of the 1940s and 1950s, see Stacey (1994, 1995); also, Gamman and Marshment (1988); Walters (1995: 50–66).

4 For illustrated details of the Takarazuka tomo no kai, see PHP Institute (1991: 84–85).

5 For examples of a 1938 legal measure against non-pro-natal journalism in women's magazines, as well as a 1939 Osaka Prefecture ban on *otokoyaku*, see Robertson (1998b: 63).

6 See Robertson (1998b: 198) for an analysis of Yazaki's further comments about female bottoms and his excitement at 'finding the woman in the man.'

7 A cover photograph of similar vintage, showing *onnayaku* Hatsukaze Jun in the December 1973 issue of *Takarazuka gurafu*, for example, shows the latter in regular makeup, with her own hair loose.

8 See Robertson (1998b: 171). The late Sakurauchi Yoshio, former Speaker of the House of Representatives, retired from parliament in 2000 at eighty-eight after eighteen terms in office spanning fifty-one years, beginning in 1947. His positions included Minister of International Trade and Industry, Minister of Foreign Affairs and Secretary-General of the Liberal Democratic Party. He died in July 2003.

9 For a photograph of the president of this club, Abe Kōjirō, awarding certificates and prizes for merit to Takarasiennes, see *Kageki* (1973: 44).

10 On the home as women's physical space, see Blair (1981: 194–98). On the lives and issues of same-sex attracted people in Japan, see, e.g. Kakefuda (1992); Sasano (1995); Summerhawk et al (1998); Ito and Yanase (2001).

12 See synopsis in *Kanashimi no Korudoba / Mega Vijon* (1995: 72).

13 The volume in question, Kannazuki (1996), is out of circulation. The case, mounted a month after publication, was eventually settled out of court, with all copies withdrawn from sale, but Rokusaisha then published its version of the events surrounding the case, replete with copies of complainants' statements, in a further volume, Takarazuka Kageki Kenkyūkai (1999a).

14 On the prosecution of one such fan in the early 1970s, see Berlin (1988: 177–78).

15 Except for a few hits, such as *Elisabeth* and *The Rose of Versailles*, Takarazuka productions are seldom re-staged after one season each at the Takarazuka Grand Theatre and Tokyo Takarazuka Theatre, and perhaps a provincial tour. Unlike Kabuki fans, who can become familiar with the repertoire over years of attending various versions of the same piece, and enjoy comparing the performances of different actors, Takarazuka fans can usually only frequent a production during the ten or so weeks of its limited run, deriving pleasure from their perception of subtle daily differences in performance. The 'New Faces' performance (*shinjin kōen*) held once or twice during each season, and occasional interchanges of cast (such as guest appearances by stars from other troupes, or a 'gender change' when players swap roles), also enable fans to compare the talent and charisma of various performers.

16 A pen pal of mine in the early 1970s wrote that she would never set foot in Takarazuka again after the retirement of her favourite star, Gō Chigusa, who retired for marriage.

17 This organisation was formerly known as Ryokuhōkai ('Green treasure club'), which Robertson (1998b: 165–66) translates as 'Green Praise.' In the various clubs' names, the *hō* syllable, meaning 'treasure,' is written with the same Chinese character as is used to spell Takara[zuka].

18 Kabuki performances continue to feature such calls, however, and these are understood to form an integral part of the theatrical experience of Kabuki fans. See Shively (1978: 20); Kawatake (1971: 55). Oddly, Arnott (1969: 250) approves of *kakegoe* in Kabuki but disparages the same practice in Takarazuka.

19 Guest director Alan Johnson apparently appended a finale for the 1999 Takarazuka version of West Side Story, after its finale-less run with a different cast in 1998 had not been popular with fans (Takarazuka Kageki Kenkyūkai 1999a: 51). The later version was probably better appreciated as it enabled cast members to commune directly with the audience during the finale in their capacity as Takarasiennes, rather than as the character they had performed in the body of the musical.

20 The Takarazuka Administration frequently reminds patrons of its prohibition of any unauthorised recording or photography during performances through posters displayed in the theatre lobby, its public address system and its Web site.

21 'Cuteness' indeed has proved to be a very popular and marketable commodity, as various studies have shown. See, for example, McVeigh (2000: 135–181); Kinsella (1995: 220–54); Schomer and Chang (1995: 54–8).

22 As briefly mentioned previously, male homosexual love is sometimes represented on the Takarazuka stage, although it is rare to see such overt expressions of it as in a kiss, even simulated, between two men.

Chapter 6

1 Official statistics show that the average age for first marriage was 28 for females in 2005, a 3.3-year rise over the figure for 1975, and just over four years higher than the 1950 figure of 23.59 (*Kōseirōdōshō* 2007a). The celibacy rate is also rising: over 5% of women aged fifty or less had never married in 1995, as compared to a mere 1.35% in 1950 (Nipponia 1999: 11).

2 So-called 'arranged marriages (*miai kekkon*),' which comprised 69% of all marriages in 1935, dwindled to a mere 6.4% in 2005, while 'love marriages (*ren'ai kekkon*)' grew from 13.4% in 1935 to 87.2% of total marriages in 2005 (*Kōseirōdōshō* 2007b).

3 A Takarazuka fan of my acquaintance reported the gist of a conversation with her favourite star, who had said that the Company Administration had sworn the performer to absolute secrecy as to the terms of her contract. The fact that she was forbidden to divulge details of her pay offer, especially to her 'classmates' from the Revue, suggests that each performer was offered a different amount, according to the eagerness of the Company to extend her employ.

4 See Buckley (1997: 326, 328, 341); also Public Policy (1997).

5 See *Cabinet Office Gender Information Site* (2004).

6 Takarazuka–Kabuki couples include Suzuka Yumiko (1930–35) and Kawarasaki Kunitarō V; Yamaji Sayuri (1943–57) and Sawamura Sōnosuke; and Hana Kuniko (1961–68) and Onoe Kikunojō II. Kabuki actor Yorozuya Kinnosuke seemingly had a remarkable taste for all-female revue graduates as wives, sandwiching his 1966–87 marriage to ex-SKD performer Awaji Keiko between marriages to two different Takarasiennes: Arima Ineko from 1961 to 1965; and Kō Nishiki from 1990 until his death in 1997.

7 '*Shachō* (boss)' was the actual nickname affectionately used by Flower Troupe members in the late 1980s and early 1990s for their top star, Ōura Mizuki (1974–91).

8 Robertson (1998b: 3–4) employs this term to describe the wave of 'eroticised energy' she perceived at a Takarazuka performance.

9 Hashizume also produced the play, *Boys in the Band* (Japanese title: *Mayonaka no pātī*), which deals with gay male issues (see Hashizume 1984: 103–05).

10 During Meiji, female participation in political activities was banned under Article Five of the Chian keisatsu hō (Public Peace Police Law) of 1890, though some engagement in political gatherings was afforded to women from 1922, when the 1890 law was amended (see Mackie 1997: 130). In 1931, a limited bill for women's suffrage, to allow women 'civic rights' to

vote and stand for office in city, town and village assemblies (albeit with
their husbands' permission), was passed by the Lower House, but was
rejected by the Upper House (see Nolte 1986: 690–714; Garon 1997: 116,
134–40; Mackie 1997: 131, 143). By contrast, universal suffrage had been
granted in 1925 to most Japanese males over the age of twenty-five.

11 For biographical details on Ōgi, see *Koizumi Cabinet Home Page* (2001).
12 On *onabe*, see Longinotto and Williams (1995).
13 On Mekari's first year at university, see *Campal.net* (2001).
14 Other prominent ex-Takarasienne choreographers include Ai Erina,
Hayama Kiyomi and Shō Sumire.
15 Hanayagi Hagi's famous students include top stars Mori Keaki (1979–93)
and Kōju Tatsuki (1986–2003); moreover, her Mexican-born student,
Sachikaze Irene (1981–93), has achieved coveted *shihan* (teacher/master)
rank, under the guidance of the veteran Takarasienne Fujino Takane (dance
name Hanayagi Rokuharu). On Sachikaze, see Iida (2000).
16 K.I.E. was one of several preparatory schools I visited during fieldwork.
For examples of other schools, see such web sites as those of Kawaji
Masa Ballet Studio (2007), which boasts of having had 'more than 100
ex-students join Takarazuka; and the singing school, Niji-no-kai (2007).

Appendix: Survey Questionnaire

This questionnaire aimed to elicit responses which would reveal a variety of experiences in the upbringing, education and career of girls and women in twentieth-century Japan, with a focus upon graduates of the Takarazuka Music School who were performing at the time of the interviews in early 2001, or had previously performed with the Takarazuka Revue Company. The questions were translated into Japanese by the author, and face-to-face interviews conducted in private with only the author and the interviewee present. Interviews were tape-recorded and later transcribed, concealing the identity of informants as required by research ethics protocol. Random initials, chosen by the informants themselves or assigned by the researcher, are used in lieu of names throughout this book to indicate each informant's responses.

Part 1 (Early influences)

Q. 1.1. Please describe your family structure.

Q. 1.2. What kind of examples of differing gender roles did you see in your family? (e.g., were the girls treated the same or differently from the boys?)

Q. 1.3. In your family, were you expected to behave a certain way because you were a girl?

Q. 1.4. How did you react to such expectations?

Q. 1.5. Did you attend a co-educational or single-sex junior and/or senior high school?

Q. 1.6. At that school, were you expected to behave in a certain way because you were a girl?

Q. 1.7. How old were you when you became interested in (joining) Takarazuka?

Q. 1.8. (a) Were you a "fan" before entering the Music School? If so,

(b) what did you like most about Takarazuka?

(c) what did you think of the *otokoyaku/musumeyaku*?

Q. 1.9. Why did you want to become a Takarasienne?

Q. 1.10. If you had not entered Takarazuka, what might you have done?

Part 2 (School training)

Q. 2.1. When you were a first-year, how did the strict rules make you feel?

Q. 2.2. When you were a second-year, how did you feel about administering the discipline?

Q. 2.3. What use do you think the strict discipline is/was?

Q. 2.4. Did you feel more like a female as a first-year than as a second-year?

Q. 2.5. Did you choose to become a *musumeyaku* or an *otokoyaku* while studying at the Music School? At what point did you decide?

Q. 2.6. Why did you choose that stage gender?

Q. 2.7. What kind of specialised training did you receive at the Takarazuka Music School for the stage gender you chose?

Q. 2.8. Was there anything especially difficult about training for the stage gender you chose?

Q. 2.9. Would you have preferred to take the other stage gender? Why?

Q. 2.10. Was Takarazuka's reputation as a "brides' school" influential in gaining your parents' consent to send you to the Music School?

Q. 2.11. Do you think that Takarazuka deserves its reputation as a "brides' school"?

Part 3 (Life as a performer)

Q. 3.1. In which stage gender did you ultimately specialise (*otokoyaku* or *musumeyaku/onnayaku*)?

Q. 3.2. How do/did you prepare for that stage gender?

Q. 3.3. Have you had to perform the opposite stage gender, also? If so, did you make any special efforts?

Q. 3.4. Does/Did your stage gender influence your appearance and behaviour off-stage? (e.g. clothing, hairstyle, makeup, tone of voice, posture, way of movement, home interior decoration, etc.)

Q. 3.5. Do/Did you behave differently to your family and pre-Takarazuka friends compared to people you met after joining Takarazuka?

Q. 3.6. Do/Did you find your stage gender limits/limited your freedom in any way? If so, what do/did you wish you could have done if that limitation were not present?

Q. 3.7. How similar do you think an *otokoyaku* is to a "real" male?

Q. 3.8. Which do you prefer, and why?

Q. 3.9. How similar do you think a *musumeyaku/onnayaku* is to a "real" female?

Q. 3.10. Which do you prefer, and why?

Q. 3.11. Do you think that Takarazuka *otokoyaku* and *musumeyaku* have changed much during the time you have known the Revue? If so, in what way?

Q. 3.12. Do you think that men and women in society have changed much in the same period? If so, in what way?

Q. 3.13. Which change has been greater in your opinion, 3.11 or 3.12?

Q. 3.14. Do you think that the attitudes of writer/directors about women's and men's place in society strongly influence the way females and males are portrayed on the Takarazuka stage?

Q. 3.15. Do you think that female writer/directors have made a difference to the way males and females are portrayed in Takarazuka?

Q. 3.16. Do you think that the rule about compulsory retirement of Takarazuka performers before marriage should be changed? Why (not)?

Q. 3.17. Are there any aspects of Takarazuka that you would change, if you could?

Q. 3.18. Is/Was there anything in your life as a performer which is/was especially important to your happiness and peace of mind? (e.g. interesting roles on stage, friendship, family, pets, hobbies, religious faith, volunteer activities, etc.?)

Q. 3.19. Do/Did your family or any others urge you to marry?

Q. 3.20. Do/Did you yourself want to marry?

Q. 3.21. Do/Did you yourself want children?

Q. 3.22. What post-Takarazuka plans do/did you have?

Part 4 (Post-Takarazuka experience (asked only of retirees)

Q. 4.1. When did you quit Takarazuka?

Q. 4.2. What was the main reason for your retirement?

Q. 4.3. Would you have liked to remain with the Company longer?

Q. 4.4. What main activities did you pursue after retirement?

Q. 4.5. Has your Takarazuka experience been directly useful to your post-Takarazuka life?

Q. 4.6. Did you have to un-learn your Takarazuka stage gender or learn a new gender for stage performance or in private life? If so, was that difficult?

Q. 4.7. Do you behave/ Have you behaved towards males the way *musumeyaku* and *onnayaku* behave towards otokoyaku?

Q. 4.8. Do you agree that *otokoyaku* understand the male psyche better than other women do?

Q. 4.9. Do you feel that you have more freedom now than when you were a member of Takarazuka? Why (not)?

Q. 4.10. Would you recommend that a daughter of your own, or any other girl, consider entering Takarazuka now? Why (not)?

Q. 4.11. If you were fifteen years of age now, do you think you would want to enter Takarazuka?

Q. 4.12. Did you miss out on anything that you strongly desired because you entered Takarazuka?

Q. 4.13. What was the greatest thing you gained from having been a Takarasienne?

Part 5 (Optional)

Q. 5.1. Please add any comments you may have about the above topics.

Bibliography

Note: Unless otherwise indicated, the place of publication for Japanese works is Tokyo. Macrons are not used in well-known place-names, except where these form part of a company name.

Allison, Anne (1996), *Permitted and Prohibited Desires: Mothers, Comics, and Censorship in Japan*, Boulder, Colorado: Westview Press.

Amami, Yūki (1995), *Ashita fuku kaze no tame ni* (For the wind that will blow tomorrow), Kōdansha.

——————— (1996), *Kurisumasu mokushiroku* (Christmas apocalypse), Wani Books.

Amano, Ikuo (1992), 'The Bright and Dark Sides of Japanese Education,' *Japan Foundation Newsletter*, no. 19, pp. 3–6.

Amano, Michie (1994), *Takarazuka no rūru* (The rules of Takarazuka), Asahi Shinbunsha.

AMPO – Japan Asia Quarterly Review (ed.) (1996), *Voices from the Japanese Women's Movement*, Armonk, New York; London: M.E. Sharpe.

Anderson, Benedict (1991), *Imagined Communities: Reflections on the Origins and Spread of Nationalism*, revised edition, London: Verso.

Anderson, Joseph L. and Donald Richie (1982), *The Japanese Film: Art and Industry*, Princeton: Princeton University Press, expanded edition.

Anju, Mira (1993), *Sugao no enzeru* (Barefaced angel), Soirée Books.

Aoyama, Tomoko (2005), 'Transgendering *Shōjo Shōsetsu*: Girls' Intertext/Sex-uality,' in Mark McLelland and Romit Dasgupta (eds), *Genders, Transgenders and Sexualities in Japan*, Oxford: Routledge.

Ardener, Edwin (1972), 'Belief and the Problem of Women,' in J. La Fontaine (ed.), *The Interpretation of Ritual: Essays in Honour of A.J. Richards*, London: Tavistock Publications, pp. 135–58.

——————— (1975), 'The "Problem" Revisited,' in Shirley Ardener (ed.), *Perceiving Women*, London: Malaby Press, pp. 19–27.

Ardener, Shirley (1978), 'Introduction: The Nature of Women in Society,' in Shirley Ardener (ed.), *Defining Females*, New York: Halsted, pp. 9–48.

Arnott, Peter D. (1969), *The Theatres of Japan*, London; Melbourne; Toronto: Macmillan.

Asahi Shinbun (1935), 'Kore mo jidaisō ka (Is this, too, a phase of the times?),' Tokyo morning edition, 30 January, p. 7.

Asaji, Saki and Susumu Fukaya (1997), 'Taidan: yume ni iki, yume o ataeru (Dialogue: living in dreams, and giving dreams),' interview, in Toshihiro Tsuganezawa and Chisato Natori (eds), *Takarazuka beru epokku: kageki + rekishi + bunka = Takarazuka*, Kobe: Kōbe Shinbun Sōgō Shuppan Sentā, pp. 64–79.

Asanagi, Rin (1997), *Takarazuka: kindan no sono wa mitsu no aji* (Takarazuka: the forbidden garden tastes of honey), Nippon Bungeisha.

Ashihara, Kuniko (1985), *Takarazuka monogatari* (Takarazuka tales), Kokusho Kankōkai.

Aston, Elaine and George Savona (1991), *Theatre as Sign-System: A Semiotics of Text and Performance*, London and New York: Routledge.

Bachnik, Jane (1992), 'Kejime: Defining a Shifting Self in Multiple Organisational Modes,' in Nancy R. Rosenberger (ed.), *Japanese Sense of Self*, Cambridge: Cambridge University Press, pp. 152–72.

——————— (1994), 'Uchi/Soto: Authority and Intimacy, Hierarchy and Solidarity in Japan,' in Jane M. Bachnik and Charles J. Quinn Jr (eds), *Situated Meaning: Inside and Outside in Japanese Self, Society, and Language*, Princeton: Princeton University Press, pp. 223–43.

Benedict, Ruth (1989), *The Chrysanthemum and the Sword: Patterns of Japanese Culture*, Boston: Houghton Mifflin.

Bennett, Susan (1990), *Theatre Audiences: A Theory of Production and Reception*, London and New York: Routledge.

Berger, John (1972), *Ways of Seeing*, London: British Broadcasting Corporation and Penguin Books.

Berlin, Zeke (1988), 'Takarazuka: A History and Critical Analysis of the Japanese All-Female Performance Group,' unpublished Ph.D. dissertation, New York University, University Microfilms International.

——————— (1991), 'The Takarazuka Touch,' *Asian Theatre Journal*, vol. 8, no. 1, Spring, pp. 35–47.

'Berusaiyu no bara (The rose of Versailles)' (1994), in *Mainichi gurafu bessatsu, Takarazuka: karei naru hachijūnen; nijūisseiki e no tabidachi* (Mainichi Graphic supplement, Takarazuka: eighty magnificent years; setting off for the twenty-first century), Mainichi Shinbunsha, pp. 82–88.

Bessatsu Takarajima no. 64, Onna o aisuru onnatachi no monogatari (Takarajima special edition, no. 64: a tale of women who love women) (1987), JICC Shuppankyoku.

Birnbaum, Phyllis (1999), *Modern Girls, Shining Stars, the Skies of Tokyo: 5 Japanese Women*, New York: Columbia University Press.

Blair, Juliet (1981), 'Private Parts in Public Places: The Case of Actresses,' in Shirley Ardener (ed.), *Women and Space: Ground Rules and Social Maps*, London: Croom Helm, pp. 205–28.

Boocock, Sarane Spence (1991), 'The Japanese Preschool System,' in

Edward R. Beauchamp (ed.), *Windows on Japanese Education*, New York: Greenwood Press, pp. 97–125.

Bowers, Faubion (1974), *Japanese Theatre*, Rutland, Vermont; Tokyo, Japan: Charles E. Tuttle Co.

Brandon, James R. (1989), 'A New World: Asian Theatre in the West Today,' *TDR (The Drama Review): A Journal of Performance Studies*, vol. 33, issue 2, Summer, pp. 25–51.

Brandon, James R., William P. Malm and Donald H. Shively (1978), *Studies in Kabuki: Its Acting, Music and Historical Context*, East-West Center, Honolulu: The University Press of Hawai'i.

Brau, Lori (1990), 'The Women's Theatre of Takarazuka,' *Drama Review*, vol. 34, no. 4, Winter, pp. 79–95.

Breakwell, Ian (1995), *An Actor's Revenge*, London: British Film Institute.

Buckley, Sandra (1993), 'Altered States,' in Andrew Gordon (ed.), *Postwar Japan as History*, Berkeley: University of California Press, pp. 347–72.

Buckley, Sandra (ed.), Morris Low et al. (associate eds) (2002), *Encyclopedia of Contemporary Japanese Culture*, London; New York: Routledge.

Buckley, Sandra, with Sakai Minako (1997), 'Chronology of Significant Events in the Recent History of Japanese Women (1868–1991),' in Sandra Buckley (ed.), *Broken Silence: Voices of Japanese Feminism*, Berkeley: University of California Press, pp. 303–41.

Burman, Erica (1995), '"What is it?" Masculinity and Femininity in Cultural Representations of Childhood,' in Sue Wilkinson and Celia Kitzinger (eds), *Feminism and Discourse: Psychological Perspectives*, London; Thousand Oaks, California; New Delhi: Sage Publications, pp. 49–67.

Buruma, Ian (1988), *A Japanese Mirror: Heroes and Villains of Japanese Culture*, London: Penguin.

Butler, Judith (1990), 'Performative Acts and Gender Constitution: An Essay in Phenomenology and Feminist Theory,' in Sue-Ellen Case (ed.), *Performing Feminisms: Feminist Critical Theory and Theatre*, Baltimore and London: The Johns Hopkins University Press, pp. 270–82.

——————— (1993), *Bodies That Matter: On the Discursive Limits of "Sex,"* New York: Routledge.

——————— (1999), *Gender Trouble: Feminism and the Subversion of Identity*, New York; London: Routledge.

——————— (2004), *Undoing Gender*, New York; London: Routledge.

Campal.net Web Site (2001), 'Takarazuka kara igaku no michi (From Takarazuka to the path to medicine).' Available from: <http://www.campal.net/hito/2001/1201.html, 1 December [16 August 2002].

Chalmers, Sharon (2001), 'Tolerance, Form and Female Dis-ease: The Pathologisation of Lesbian Sexuality in Japanese Society,' *Intersections: Journal of Gender, History and Culture in the Asian Context*, issue 6,

August. Available from: <http://wwwsshe.murdoch.edu.au/intersections/issue6/chalmers.html> [27 February 2002].

————— (2002), *Emerging Lesbian Voices from Japan*, London and New York: RoutledgeCurzon.

Cherry, Kittredge (1987), *Womansword: What Japanese Words Say About Women*, Tokyo and New York: Kodansha International.

Chiba, Junko (1996), *Takarazuka to ikiru hinto: utsukushiki koi, yūai, namida* (Hints for living with Takarazuka: beautiful romantic love, friendship and tears), Coara Books.

Chow, Cheryl (2002), 'Prurient Publication Peeps into Pretty Performers' Private Lives,' *Mainichi Daily News Mainichi Interactive*. Available from: <http://mdn.mainichi.co.jp/waiwai/0210/021012takarazuka.html, 12 October [17 December 2002].

Cline, Sally and Dale Spender (1988), *Reflecting Men at Twice Their Natural Size: Why Women Work at Making Men Feel Good*, Glasgow: Fontana/Collins.

Conboy, Katie, Nadia Medina, and Sarah Stanbury (eds) (1997), *Writing on the Body: Female Embodiment and Feminist Theory*, New York: Columbia University Press.

Condon, Jane (1985), *A Half Step Behind: Japanese Women Today*, Rutland, Vermont and Tokyo: Charles E. Tuttle.

Dales, Laura (2005), 'Lifestyles of the Rich and Single: Reading Agency in the "Parasite Single" Issue,' in Lyn Parker (ed.), *The Agency of Women in Asia*, Singapore: Marshall Cavendish Academic, pp. 133–157.

'Danshi kinsei no otome no o-shiro (The maidens' fortress forbidden to men)' (1980), in *Bessatsu ichiokunin no Shōwa shi, Takarazuka: karei naru butai to sutā o sodateta nanajū-nen* (Special edition, 100 million people's history of Shōwa – Takarazuka: the seventy years which nurtured the brilliant stage and stars), Mainichi Shinbunsha, pp. 144–45.

Davies, Malcolm (1995), 'Theocritus' "Adoniazusae",' *Greece & Rome*, vol. 42, no. 2, October, p. 152.

Debord, Guy (1990), *Comments on the Society of the Spectacle*, trans. Malcolm Imrie, London; New York: Verso.

————— (1995), *The Society of the Spectacle*, trans. Donald Nicholson-Smith, New York: Zone Books.

Devor, Holly (1989), *Gender Blending: Confronting the Limits of Duality*, Bloomington and Indianapolis, Indiana: Indiana University Press.

Doi, Takeo (1966) (1962), 'Amae: A Key Concept for Understanding Japanese Personality Structure,' in Robert J. Smith and Richard K. Beardsley (eds), *Japanese Culture: Its Development and Characteristics*, Chicago: Aldine Publishing Company, reprinted with corrections, pp. 132–39.

————— (1986), *The Anatomy of Self: The Individual Versus Society*, trans. Mark A. Harbison, Tokyo: Kodansha International.

Domenig, Roland (1998), 'Takarazuka and Kobayashi Ichizō's Idea of "Kokumingeki",' in Sepp Linhart and Sabine Früstück (eds), *The Culture of Japan as Seen through its Leisure*, Albany, New York: State University of New York Press, pp. 267–84.

Downer, Lesley (2003), *Madame Sadayakko: The Geisha who Seduced the West*, London: Review.

Eccleston, Bernard (1989), *State and Society in Post-War Japan*, Cambridge: Polity Press.

Eguchi, Nobuko (ed.) (1977), *Takarazuka: kaze to tomo ni ai no bōken ga* (Takarazuka: a love adventure [gone] with the wind), Gendai Shinsha.

Endō, Orie (1987), *Ki ni naru kotoba: Nihongo saikentō* (Words that bother me: a re-examination of the Japanese language), Nan'undō.

———— (1997), *Onna no kotoba no bunkashi* (A cultural history of women's language), Gakuyō Shobō.

Endō, Orie (ed.) (1992), *Josei no yobikata daikenkyū* (A grand study of words to call women), Sanseidō.

Eppstein, Ury (1994), *The Beginnings of Western Music in Meiji-Era Japan*, Lewiston, New York: E. Mellen Press.

Faderman, Lillian (1985), *Surpassing the Love of Men: Romantic Friendship and Love between Women from the Renaissance to the Present*, London: The Women's Press.

Ferris, Lesley (1990), *Acting Women: Images of Women in Theatre*, Basingstoke and London: Macmillan.

Foucault, Michel (1978), *The History of Sexuality*, vol. 1, trans. Robert Hurley, Harmondsworth: Penguin.

———— (1994), *The Birth of the Clinic: An Archeology of Medical Perception*, trans. A.M. Sheridan Smith, New York: Vintage Books. (Originally published in French, 1963).

———— (1995), *Discipline and Punish: The Birth of the Prison*, trans. Alan Sheridan, New York: Pantheon. (Originally published in French, 1975).

Freedman, Barbara (1990), 'Frame-Up: Feminism, Psychoanalysis, Theatre,' in Sue-Ellen Case (ed.), *Performing Feminisms: Feminist Critical Theory and Theatre*, Baltimore and London: The Johns Hopkins University Press, pp. 54–76.

Fujii, Tadatoshi (1985), *Kokubō fujinkai: hinomaru to kappōgi* (The Women's National Defence Association: rising sun flags and cooking aprons), Iwanami Shoten.

Fujii, Toshiko (1983), 'Women in the Labor Force,' in *Kodansha Encyclopedia of Japan*, vol. 8, Tokyo; New York: Kodansha Ltd, pp. 264–66.

Fujimoto, Yukari (1998), *Watashi no ibasho wa doko ni aru no? Shōjo manga ga utsusu kokoro no katachi* (Where do I belong? The state of mind reflected by girls' comics), Gakuyō Shobō.

Fujimura-Fanselow, Kumiko and Anne E. Imamura (1991), 'The Education of Women in Japan,' in Edward R. Beauchamp (ed.), *Windows on Japanese Education*, New York; Westport, Connecticut; London: Greenwood Press, pp. 229–58.

Fujin kōron (Women's review) (1935), 'Shōjo kageki o kataru: haha to musume no kai (Discussing the girls' revue: a mother–daughter meeting),' April, pp. 288–97.

Fujino, Takane (1990), *Konjaku Takarazuka: hanabutai itsumademo* (Takarazuka then and now: the flowery stage forever), Takarazuka: Takarazuka Kagekidan.

Fujita, Akira (illust.) (1971a), 'Zoku watashi no rirekisho: Sawa Kaori (My curriculum vitae, continued: Sawa Kaori),' *Kageki*, October, p. 108.

———————— (1971b), 'Zoku watashi no rirekisho: Jun Mitsuki (My curriculum vitae, continued: Jun Mitsuki),' *Kageki*, November, p. 109.

———————— (1977a), 'Shin watashi no rirekisho: Kazami Kei (The new my curriculum vitae: Kazami Kei),' *Kageki*, December, p. 119.

———————— (1977b), 'Shin watashi no rirekisho: Tamazusa Maki (The new my curriculum vitae: Tamazusa Maki),' *Kageki*, July, p. 127.

Fujitani, Atsuko and Kimio Itō (sup.), Japan Society for Gender Studies (ed.) (2000), *Jendāgaku o manabu hito no tame ni* (For students of gender studies), Kyōto: Sekaishisōsha.

Fukaya, Masashi (1998), *Ryōsai kenbo shugi no kyōiku* (Education for good wives and wise mothers), Reimei Shobō.

Fukuoka City Foundation for Arts and Cultural Promotion (1999), 'Risking it all on the Stage: Inoue Kocho's Dream – An All Girls' Opera to Showcase the Splendor of Performing Arts in Hakata,' *Magazine*. Available from: <http://www.ffac.or.jp/magazine/03/kocho_e.html> [20 September 2007].

Fukutake, Tadashi (1989), *The Japanese Social Structure: Its Evolution in the Modern Century*, trans. Ronald P. Dore, Tokyo: University of Tokyo Press, second edition.

Gamman, Lorraine and Margaret Marshment (eds) (1988), *The Female Gaze: Women as Viewers of Popular Culture*, London: The Women's Press.

Garon, Sheldon (1997), *Molding Japanese Minds: The State in Everyday Life*, Princeton: Princeton University Press.

Geinōshi Kenkyūkai (ed.) (1990), *Nihon geinōshi 7: kindai/gendai* (History of Japanese performing arts, vol. 7, recent times/contemporary period), Hōsei Daigaku Shuppankyoku.

Gender Equality Bureau, Cabinet Office (2007), *Gender Equality in Japan 2007*. Available from: <http://www.gender.go.jp/english_contents/index.html> [20 September 2007].

Gilbert-Falkenburg, Pamela (1985), *Women in Japanese Theatre*, (private publication), Elizabeth Vale, South Australia: P. Gilbert-Falkenburg.

Gluck, Carol (1985), *Japan's Modern Myths: The Ideology of the Late Meiji Period*, Princeton, New Jersey: Princeton University Press.

Goffman, Erving (1963), *Stigma: Notes on the Management of Spoiled Identity*, Englewood Cliffs, New Jersey: Prentice-Hall.

Gondō, Yoshikazu (1990), 'Geinō no hogo to hozon (Protection and conservation of performing arts,' in Geinōshi Kenkyūkai (ed.), *Nihon geinōshi 7: kindai/ gendai*, Hōsei Daigaku Shuppankyoku, pp. 355–71.

Grossberg, Lawrence (1992), 'Is There a Fan in the House?: The Affective Sensibility of Fandom,' in Lisa A. Lewis (ed.), *The Adoring Audience: Fan Culture and Popular Media*, London and New York: Routledge, pp. 50–61.

Hagiwara, Hiroyoshi (1954), *Takarazuka kageki yonjūnen shi* (The forty-year history of the Takarazuka Revue), Takarazuka: Takarazuka Kagekidan Shuppanbu.

Halberstam, Judith (1998), *Female Masculinity*, Durham and London: Duke University Press.

Hanes, Jeffrey E. (1998), 'Media Culture in Taishō Osaka,' in Sharon A. Minichiello (ed.), *Japan's Competing Modernities: Issues in Culture and Democracy 1900–1930*, Honolulu: University of Hawai'i Press, pp. 276–87.

Hankyu Hanshin Holdings Incorporated Web Site (2007). Available from: <http://holdings.hankyu-hanshin.co.jp/> [4 May 2007].

Hara, Goichi (1997), *Sumire no hana wa yoru hiraku: Takarazuka – okkake rokujūnen no* ashiato (Violets bloom at night: Takarazuka – footprints from sixty years of ardent pursuit), Nishinomiya: Rokusaisha.

Hara, Junsuke and Kazuo Seiyama (2005), *Inequality amid Affluence: Social Stratification in Japan*, trans. Brad Williams, Melbourne, Australia: Trans Pacific Press.

Hara, Minako (1996), 'Lesbians and Sexual Self-Determination,' in AMPO – Japan Asia Quarterly Review (ed.), *Voices from the Japanese Women's Movement*, Armonk, New York; London: M.E. Sharpe, pp. 71–73.

Haruna, Yuri (1976), *Ai no echūdo – Takarazuka ni ikiru seishun* (Love étude – [my] youth spent in Takarazuka), Futami Shobō.

————— (1993), *Toppu Haruna Yuri no 'Oh! Takarazuka'* (Top star Haruna Yuri's 'Oh! Takarazuka'), Osaka: Naniwasha.

Hashimoto, Masao (1988), *Sa se Takarazuka* (Ça c'est Takarazuka), Yomiuri Shinbunsha.

————— (1993), *Sumire no hana wa arashi o koete: Takarazuka kageki no Shōwa shi* (Violet blooms transcend the storms: the Shōwa history of the Takarazuka Revue), Yomiuri Shinbunsha, 1993.

————— (1999), *Subarashii Takarazuka kageki: yume to roman no hachijūgonen* (The wonderful Takarazuka Revue: eighty-five years of dreams and 'romans'), Takarazuka: Hankyu Books.

Hashimoto, Masao (ed.) (1994), *Yume o egaite hanayaka ni: Takarazuka Kagekidan hachijū-nenshi* (Sketching dreams, colourfully: a history of the eighty years of the Takarazuka Revue), Takarazuka: Takarazuka Kagekidan.

Hauser, William B. (1991), 'Women and War: The Japanese Film Image,' in Gail Lee Bernstein (ed.), *Recreating Japanese Women, 1600–1945*, Berkeley: University of California Press, pp. 296–313.

Havens, Thomas R.H. (1986), *Valley of Darkness: The Japanese People and World War Two*, Lanham, Maryland: University Press of America.

Hendry, Joy (1987), *Understanding Japanese Society*, London and New York: Croom Helm.

Hibino, Momoko (1986), *Yume no chizu* (Map of dreams), Chikuma Shobō.

High, Peter B. (2003), *The Imperial Screen: Japanese Film Culture in the Fifteen Years' War, 1931–1945*, Madison: University of Wisconsin Press.

Hinerman, Stephen (1992), 'I'll Be Here with You: Fans, Fantasy and the Figure of Elvis,' in Lisa A. Lewis (ed.), *The Adoring Audience: Fan Culture and Popular Media*, London and New York: Routledge, pp. 115–16.

Honchi, Eiki (1974), 'Tōkyō, Takarazuka sengo shōshi (shū): "Okurahoma!" de dai-ippo honmono myūjikaru jidai e (A little history of Tokyo and Takarazuka (final): one step toward the age of authentic musicals with "Oklahoma!"),' *Kageki*, December, pp. 30–32.

———————— (1977), 'Takarazuka sodachi no butai joyū (shū): Otowa Nobuko to geisha Otama (Takarazuka-raised stage actresses (final): Nobuko Otowa and the geisha, Otama),' *Kageki*, December, pp. 39–41.

Hyūga, Kaoru (1992), *Wa-ta-shi Hyūga Kaoru* (I, Kaoru Hyūga), Shinkō Music.

Ichikawa, Yasuo (1980), 'Takarazuka kageki: hachijū-nen no tenbō (The Takarazuka Revue: an overview of its eighty years),' in *Bessatsu ichiokunin no Shōwa shi, Takarazuka: karei naru butai to sutā o sodateta nanajū-nen*, Mainichi Shinbunsha, p. 102.

Ichiro, Maki (1996), *Shinjitsu* (Truth), Shūeisha.

Iida, Irene (2000), 'El Teatro de Revista Musical Takarazuka (The musical revue theatre, Takarazuka),' *El Patio*, vol. 7, July, *Japan Foundation in Mexico Web Site*. Available from: <http://www.fjmex.org/cgi-bin/elpatio.cgi?action=showcontenido&id_contenido=64&volume=7> [20 May 2001].

Ikeda, Kumiko (1999), *Sensei no rezubian sengen: tsunagaru tame no kamu auto* (Teacher's lesbian declaration: coming-out to join together), Kyōto: Kamogawa Shuppan.

Ikeda, Tomotaka (1980), 'Yume no machi, Takarazuka (Takarazuka, town of dreams),' in *Bessatsu ichiokunin no Shōwa shi, Takarazuka: karei naru butai to sutā o sodateta nanajū-nen*, Mainichi Shinbunsha, pp. 138–43.

International Foundation for Androgynous Studies (2003), 'Glossary of

Androgynous Terms.' Available from: <http://web.archive.org/web/ 20050616102028/www.ifas.org.au/index.cgi?article=content_8&menu= content_8_menu> [2 October 2004].

Ioi, Kenji (ed.) (1999), *Takarazuka Revue: nijūisseiki e no tabidachi* (Takarazuka Revue: setting out for the twenty-first century), Osaka: Hankyu Corporation.

Ishii, Keifu (2000), *Takarajennu no fearī tēru* (Fairytales of the Takarasiennes), M.Wave.

—————— (2003), 'Ishii Keifu no kōza Takarazuka: za kageki – yodan, hiwa, itsuwa, 21: Takarazuka ongaku gakkō saikō gōkaku bairitsusei no ima (Ishii Keifu's Takarazuka lectures: the Revue – digressions, unknown episodes, anecdotes, no. 21: what are the Takarazuka Music School students who passed the stiffest-ever competition for entry doing now?),' *Sankei Sports On Line*. Available from: <http://www.sanspo.com/geino/takara/ kouza/kouza_76.html> [21 December 2003].

Ishii, Takeshi (2002), 'Senzen no Takarazuka eiga mitsukaru (Pre-war Takarazuka films discovered),' *The Sankei Shimbun Online*. Available from: <http://www.sankei.co.jp/edit/bunka/takara0205/0830oldfilm.html, 30 August [20 September 2002].

Ishii, Tatsurō (1994), *Dansōron* (Theories on women's cross-dressing), Seikyūsha.

Ishii, Tetsuya (1993), *Takarazuka kenbunroku* (A chronicle of things seen and heard in Takarazuka), Seikyūsha.

—————— (1996), *Takarazuka fū'unroku: hanagumi, yukigumi hen* (A chronicle of Takarazuka's situation: Flower Troupe and Snow Troupe edition), Seikyūsha.

Ito, Satoru and Ryuta Yanase (2001), *Coming Out in Japan*, trans. F. Conlan, Melbourne: Trans Pacific Press.

Ivy, Marilyn (1993), 'Formations of Mass Culture,' in Andrew Gordon (ed.), *Postwar Japan as History*, Berkeley: University of California Press, pp. 239–58.

—————— (1995), *Discourses of the Vanishing: Modernity, Phantasm, Japan*, Chicago: University of Chicago Press.

Izumi, Yoshiko (1987), 'Takarazuka kagekidan seito no geimei (Stage names of Takarazuka Revue Company performers),' in Shinji Sanada (ed.), *Meimei no shosō: shakai meimeiron dēta shū* (Various thoughts on naming: a collection of data on theories of social naming), Osaka: Osaka Daigaku Bungakubu, pp. 71–72.

Izumo, Marou and Claire Maree (2000), *Love upon the Chopping Board*, trans. Claire Maree, North Melbourne, Victoria: Spinifex Press.

Japan Times Online (2004), 'Upper House gets first woman Speaker.' Available from <www.japantimes.co.jp/weekly/ news/nn2004/nn20040807a6.htm> 7 August [15 August 2004].

———————— (2007), 'Ogi to skip Upper House poll, retire from politics.' Available from: <http://search.japantimes.co.jp/rss/nn20070512a4.html> 12 May [1 June].

Jō, Haruki (1985), *Takarazuka: Waga ai no uta* (Takarazuka: my love poems) (private publication), Kōchi: Miyai Yuriko.

Johnson, Frank A. (1993), *Dependency and Japanese Socialisation: Psychoanalytic and Anthropological Investigations into Amae*, New York: New York University Press.

Johnston, Eric (2002), 'Hankyu to pull plug on its parks: Takarazuka Familyland, PortopiaLand fall victim to USJ,' *Japan Times Online*. Available from: <http://www.japantimes.co.jp/cgi-bin/getarticle.pl5?nn20020413b4.htm> 13 April [28 July 2002].

Jolivet, Muriel (1997), *Japan: The Childless Society?: The Crisis of Motherhood*, London and New York: Routledge.

Jorden, Eleanor H. (1983a), 'Feminine Language,' in *Kodansha Encyclopedia of Japan*, vol. 2, Tokyo; New York: Kodansha Ltd, pp. 250–51.

———————— (1983b), 'Masculine Language,' in *Kodansha Encyclopedia of Japan*, vol. 5, Tokyo; New York: Kodansha Ltd, pp. 124–25.

Kageki (1969), 'Amatsu Otome: sono gojūnen no rekishi (Amatsu Otome: a history of her fifty years),' September, pp. 32–33.

———————— (1973a), 'Kobayashi Ichizō sensei o shinobu (Honouring the memory of [our] teacher, Kobayashi Ichizō),' January, pp. 123–125.

———————— (1973b), 'Haha to musume: Natsuki Teru (Mother and daughter; Natsuki Teru),' November, p. 107.

———————— (1974a), 'Ima wa mukashi, Takarazuka kageki oitachi no ki (Now, and long ago: a chronicle of the early days of the Takarazuka Revue),' March, p. 110.

———————— (1974b), 'Kiyoku, tadashiku, utsukushiku: Tōkyō nyūgaku daiichigō, Amatsu Otome (Purely, righteously, beautifully: the first to enrol from Tokyo, Amatsu Otome),' June, pp. 62–64.

———————— (1991a), 'Haha to musume: Minoru Kō (Mother and Daughter: Minoru Kō),' January, p. 123.

———————— (1991b), 'Juri Misao, Ōtaki Aiko gōdō ressun happyōkai (Juri Misao and Ōtaki Aiko joint lesson showcase),' February, p. 136.

———————— (1991c), 'Haha to musume: Itsumine Aki (Mother and daughter: Itsumine Aki),' May, p. 123.

———————— (1992a), 'Konna koto ga shiritakatta 9: "Takarazuka konjaku 1" – daigekijō tanjō made no ashiato (I wanted to know such things, no. 9. Takarazuka now and then, 1: "Footprints leading to the birth of the Grand Theatre,' February, p. 54.

———————— (1992b), 'Konna koto ga shiritakatta 10 "Takarazuka konjaku 2": Taishō jūsan-nen, Takarazuka daigekijō tanjō (I wanted to know such things, no. 10. "Takarazuka now and then, 2": Takarazuka Grand Theatre is born, 1924),' March, pp. 54–55.

——————— (1992c), 'Hatsubutaisei zadankai: mirai e mukatte, habatake! (Stage debutantes' forum: flap your wings towards the future!),' May, pp. 131–32.

——————— (1992d), 'Takarajennu dai ankēto (Takarasiennes' big question-naire) part II,' December, pp. 142–46.

——————— (1993) 'Hoshigumi kōen "Utakata no koi", "Paparagi" gakuya shuzai (Star Troupe performance [of] *Mayerling* [and] *Papalagi* dressing-room news-gathering),' August, pp. 82–83.

——————— (1994), 'Hatsubutaisei zadankai: atsui omoi de ima tobitate! (Stage debutantes' forum: now take wing, with fervour),' May, pp. 130–33.

——————— (1995), 'Jiman no MY Family (My family, of whom I boast),' October, pp. 122–23.

——————— (1999), 'Takarazuka to watashi. Dai-ikkai: naki haha to mita Takarazuka (Takarazuka and I. No. 1: the Takarazuka I watched with my late mother),' September, pp. 56–57.

Kaji, Shigeo (2001), "Nichiyōbi no hiroin, no. 259: Tsure-chan akkerakan zachō (Sunday's heroine, no. 259: Tsure, the absent-minded troupe leader),' *Nikkan Sports News Web Site*. Available from: <http://www.nikkansports. com/news/entert/entert-etc3/2001/sun010401.html, 1 April [20 December 2002].

Kakefuda, Hiroko (1992), *'Rezubian de aru koto' to iu koto* (What it means to 'be lesbian'), Kawade Shobō Shinsha.

Kamiya, Setsuko (2004), 'Korean Love Story Heats up Japan,' *Japan Times Online*, 7 April. Available from: <http://www.japantimes.co.jp [20 August 2004].

Kamo, Miyaji and Tetsuko Sakaba (1996), *Oshare no kī to watashi: shōgai, gen'eki no moderu toshite tsutaeru koto* (The key to fashion, and me: advice from a lifelong working model), Osaka: Brain Center Shuppan.

Kampe, Knut K.W., Chris D. Frith, Raymond J. Dolan, Uta Frith (2001), 'Reward Value of Attractiveness and Gaze,' *Nature*, vol. 413, 11 October, p. 589.

Kamura, Kikuo (1981), 'Osaka bojō: Takarazuka no gen'ei (6) (Osaka affections: visions of Takarazuka, no. 6), *Kamigata geinō* (Kamigata performing arts), no. 70, April, pp. 52–58.

——————— (1984), *Itoshi no Takarazuka e* (To [my] beloved Takarazuka), Kobe: Kōbe Shinbun Shuppan Sentā, 1984.

Kanashimi no Korudoba; Mega vijon (The matador in Cordoba; Mega vision) (Takarazuka Grand Theatre performance programme) (1995), Takarazuka: Takarazuka Kagekidan.

Kannazuki, Rei (1996), *Takarazuka okkake mappu* (Takarazuka stalkers' map), Nishinomiya: Rokusaisha.

Kano, Ayako (1999), 'Visuality and Gender in Modern Japanese Theater: Looking at Salome,' *Japan Forum*, vol. 11, no. 1, pp. 43–55.

——————— (2001), *Acting Like a Woman in Modern Japan: Theatre, Gender, and Nationalism*, New York; Basingstoke: Palgrave Macmillan.

Kasugano, Yachiyo (1987), *Shiroki bara no shō* (Chapters on the white rose), Takarazuka: Takarazuka Kagekidan.

Katsuki, Miyo (1971), 'Zuihitsu: jūnigatsu ni yosete (Random notes for December),' *Kageki*, December, p. 78.

Kawabata, Yasunari (1930), 'Interview: "Kyōrakuchi mandan kai (A leisurely discussion about pleasure spots)",' *Kindai seikatsu* (Modern life), March.

Kawahara, Yukari (2000), 'Diverse Strategies in Classroom Instruction: Sex Education in Japanese Secondary Schools,' *Japanese Studies*, vol. 20, no. 3, December, pp. 295–311.

Kawaji Masa Ballet Studio Web Site (2007). Available from: <http://www. kawajiballet.net/> [20 September 2007].

Kawasaki, Kenko (1996), 'Niji no kanata ni: Takarazuka media ni okeru kuia seorī no jissen to shōmei (Over the rainbow: the practice and proof of queer theory in Takarazuka media),' *Yurīka: shi to hyōka* (Eureka: poetry and criticism), vol. 28, no. 13, pp. 174–79.

——————— (1999), *Takarazuka: shōhi shakai no supekutakuru* (Takarazuka: the consumer society spectacle), Kōdansha Sensho Mechie 147.

——————— (2005), *Takarazuka to iu yūtopia* (A utopia called Takarazuka), Iwanami Shoten.

Kawasaki, Kenko and Miwako Watanabe (eds) (1991), *Takarazuka no yūwaku: Osukaru no akai kuchibeni* (The temptation of Takarazuka: Oscar's red lipstick), Seikyūsha.

Kawasaki, Kenko, Satoshi Kotake, Mariko Tanaka, Sachio Mizoguchi and Mika Moriyama (eds) (2003), *Takarazuka Academia*, no. 19, Seikyūsha.

——————— (2005), 'Shōtokushū. Otokoyaku fairu: Yon-sama-do chekku (Mini special edition. *Otokoyaku* file: "Prince Yong"-ness check)', *Takarazuka Academia*, no. 23, Seikyūsha.

Kawatake, Shigetoshi (1959), *Nihon engeki zenshi* (Complete history of Japanese drama), Iwanami Shoten.

Kawatake, Toshio (1971), *A History of Japanese Theatre II: Bunraku and Kabuki*, Yokohama: Kokusai Bunka Shinkokai (Japan Cultural Society).

Kelly, Bill (1998), 'Japan's Empty Orchestras: Echoes of Japanese Culture in the Performance of Karaoke,' in D.P. Martinez (ed.), *Japanese Popular Culture: Gender, Shifting Boundaries and Global Cultures*, Cambridge: Cambridge University Press, pp. 75–87.

Kihara, Toshie (1980), 'Takarazuka sutā kānibaru '80 repōto (Takarazuka star carnival '80 report),' in *Bessatsu ichiokunin no Shōwa shi, Takarazuka: karei naru butai to sutā o sodateta nanajū-nen*, Mainichi Shinbunsha, pp. 106–07.

Kimoto, Kimiko (2005), *Gender and Japanese Management*, trans. Teresa Castelvetere, Melbourne, Australia: Trans Pacific Press.

Kinsella, Sharon (1995), 'Cuties in Japan,' in Lise Skov and Brian Moeran (eds), *Women, Media and Consumption in Japan*, Honolulu: University of Hawai'i Press, pp. 220–54.

Kishi, Kaori (2000), *Niji iro no kioku: Takarazuka, watashi no ayunda yonjūnen* (Rainbow-coloured memories: Takarazuka, my forty years' path), Chūōkōron Shinsha.

'Kiyoku, tadashiku, utsukushiku: Takarazuka ongaku gakkō (Purely, righteously and beautifully: the Takarazuka Music School' (1980), in *Bessatsu ichiokunin no Shōwa shi, Takarazuka: karei naru butai to sutā o sodateta nanajū-nen*, Mainichi Shinbunsha, pp. 146–53.

Kobayashi, Ichizō (1925), 'Nihon kageki gairon (An outline of Japanese opera),' in Ichizō Kobayashi (1962), *Kobayashi Ichizō zenshū* (The collected works of Kobayashi Ichizō), vol. 6, Daiyamondosha, pp. 3–145.

———— (1926), 'Takarazuka no jin'yō isshin: seito narabi ni hogosha shoshi e (Takarazuka's new battle formation: to all students and their guardians),' *Kageki*, no. 72, March, pp. 2–8.

———— (1940), 'Ran'in o shibaraku mitari (Briefly looking at the Dutch East Indies),' in Ichizō Kobayashi (1962), *Kobayashi Ichizō zenshū*, vol. 4, Daiyamondosha, pp. 313–62.

———— (1942), 'Shibai zange (Theatrical confessions),' in Ichizō Kobayashi (1961), *Kobayashi Ichizō zenshū*, vol. 2, Daiyamondosha, pp. 205–439.

———— (1953), 'Itsuō jijoden (An autobiography of old man Kobayashi),' Sangyō Keizai Shinbunsha.

———— (1955), 'Takarazuka manpitsu (Takarazuka jottings),' in Ichizō Kobayashi (1961), *Kobayashi Ichizō zenshū*, vol. 2, Daiyamondosha, pp. 441–575.

Kobayashi, Kōhei (1984), *'Hana no michi' shō: Takarazuka shishi* (A 'flower path' anthology: a personal history of Takarazuka), Kōdansha.

———— (1996), 'Hana no michi yori (From the flower path), no. 284,' *Kageki*, April, pp. 50–53.

———— (2003), 'Hana no michi yori, no. 371,' *Kageki*, July, pp. 58–59.

Kobayashi, Yonezō (2001), *Mita koto, kiita koto, kanjita koto: waga Takarazuka* (Things I saw, heard and felt: my Takarazuka), Osaka: Hankyu Books.

Kōbe Shinbun Hanshin Sōkyoku (ed.), (1984) *Ō, Takarazuka* (Oh, Takarazuka), Kobe: Kōbe Shinbun Shuppan Sentā.

Kōbo Opus (ed.) (2001), *Takarazuka! Kore zo entāteinmento* (Takarazuka! This is entertainment), Kōsaidō Shuppan.

Kodai, Mizuki (1997), 'Kodai Mizuki-san no baai (1979–1996) (The case of Ms Mizuki Kodai),' in Mai Minakaze and Chisato Natori (eds), *Takarajennu ni naritai!*, Japan Mix, pp. 69–86.

Koike, Shūichirō (1993), *Bei shiti burūsu* (Bay city blues) (unpublished playscript), Takarazuka: Takarazuka Kagekidan.

Koizumi Cabinet Home Page (2001). Available from: <http://www.kantei.go.jp/jp/koizumidaijin/010426/10oogi.html, 26 April [12 September 2002].

Kojima, Naoki (1983a), *Kisai jūō: hyōden – Kobayashi Ichizō* (The length and breadth of an awesome genius: a critical biography of Kobayashi Ichizō), vol. 1, Kyoto: PHP Institute.

Kojima, Naoki (1983b), *Kisai jūō: hyōden – Kobayashi Ichizō*, vol. 2, Kyoto: PHP Institute.

Kojima, Naoki (1983c), *Kisai jūō: hyōden – Kobayashi Ichizō*, vol. 3, Kyoto: PHP Institute.

Kokubungaku (1999), 'Tokushū: sekushuariti kakumei – kindai no (Special feature: the sexuality revolution – of modern times),' vol. 44, no. 1, January.

Koma Stadium Web Site (2004), 'Erizabēto (Elisabeth).' Available from <http://www.koma-sta.co.jp/kouen/osaka/11_kouen.html> [10 November 2004].

Komashaku, Kimi (ed.) (1985), *Onna o yosōu* (Dressing (as) women), Keisō Shobō.

Kondo, Dorinne K. (1990), Crafting Selves: Power, Gender and Discourses of Identity in a Japanese Workplace, Chicago: University of Chicago Press.

Kondō, Kumi (1997), 'Seiyō ongaku no madoguchi toshite no Takarazuka kageki (The Takarazuka Revue as a window to Western music),' in Toshihiro Tsuganezawa and Chisato Natori (eds), *Takarazuka beru epokku: kageki + rekishi + bunka = Takarazuka* (Takarazuka belle époque: opera + history + culture = Takarazuka), Kobe: Kōbe Shinbun Sōgō Shuppan Sentā, pp. 153–55.

Kōno, Kiyomi (1998), *Josei to shinri series no. 2: sekushuariti o megutte* (Women and psychology series, no. 2: on sexuality), Shinsuisha.

Kōsaka, Masaaki (1966), *Shiken kitai sareru ningenzō* (A private view: my anticipated human image), Chikuma Shobō.

Kōseirōdōshō (Ministry of Health, Labour and Welfare) *Web Site* (2002a), 'Heisei jūyonen jinkō dōtai tōkei no nenkan suikei (Annual estimate of population statistics, 2002).' Available from: <http://www.mhlw.go.jp/toukei/saikin/hw/jinkou/suikei02> 1 October [20 January 2003].

————— (2002b), 'Shussei ni kansuru tōkei no gaikyō: jinkō dōtai tōkei tokushu hōkoku (Special report on vital statistics: an outlook on statistics

relating to births).' Available from: <http://www.mhlw.go.jp/toukei/saikin/
hw/jinkou/tokusyu/syussyo-4/index.html> [3 April 2003].

———————— (2007a), 'Hyō 2: Otto/tsuma no heikin kon'in nenrei oyobi
nenreisa no nenji suii: Shōwa 50–Heisei 17-nen (Table 2: Yearly transitions
in husband/wife's average age at marriage and age differential).' Available
from: <http://www.mhlw.go.jp/toukei/saikin/hw/jinkou/tokusyu/konin06/
dl/gaiyou1.pdf> [30 September 2007].

———————— (2007b), 'Zu 1.2: Kekkon nenjibetsu ni mita, ren'ai kekkon, miai
kekkon kōsei no suii (Figure 1.2: Transitions in the composition of love
marriages and arranged marriages, seen by year of marriage).' Available
from: <http://www.mhlw.go.jp/shingi/2006/06/dl/s0630-4f2.pdf> [30
September 2007)

Koyama, Noriko (2004), 'Essē sukina serifu 58: "Asu wa mata, betsu no hi"
(Essay – favourite lines, no. 58: "Tomorrow is another day"),' *Kamigata
geinō*, no. 154, December, p. 63.

Kubota, Toshiko (2001), 'Kindai ongaku no ranshō: sōkyoku kyōiku no shūhen
(The beginnings of modern music: on the margins of *koto* music education),
Nara University of Education Web Site. Available from: <http://www.nara-
edu.ac.jp/LIB/material/topic4_3.htm, 6 March [22 December 2002].

Kumakura, Isao (1990), 'Geigoto no ryūkō (The boom in artistic accomplishments),' in Geinōshi Kenkyūkai (ed.), *Nihon geinōshi 7: kindai/gendai*
(History of Japanese performing arts, vol. 7, Recent times/contemporary
period), Hōsei Daigaku Shuppankyoku, pp. 221–38.

Kumono, Kayoko (1980), 'Gobusata shite imasu. Ima, watashi wa ..., 1
(It's been a long time. Now, I'm ..., 1,' in *Bessatsu ichiokunin no Shōwa
shi, Takarazuka: karei naru butai to sutā o sodateta nanajū-nen*, Tōkyō:
Mainichi Shinbunsha, p. 170.

Kurata, Yoshihiro (1990), '1. Asakusa to Takarazuka (Asakusa and Takarazuka),' in Geinōshi Kenkyūkai (ed.), *Nihon geinōshi 7: kindai/gendai*, Hōsei
Daigaku Shuppankyoku, pp. 75–100.

Kurihara, Yōko (1990), 'MANSWORD gokiburi hoi hoi (Mansword cock-
roach trap [sic]),' in *Joseigaku nenpō* (Annual report of Women's Studies
Society), no. 11, November, pp. 72–82.

Kuroki, Hitomi (1999), 'Takarazuka OG intabyū: Takarazuka to watashi.
Kuroki Hitomi-san (Takarazuka old girl's interview: Takarazuka and I. Ms
Hitomi Kuroki),' in *Takarazuka Revue: nijūisseiki e no tabidachi*, Osaka:
Hankyu Corporation, pp. 75–76.

de Lauretis, Teresa (1987), *Technologies of Gender: Essays on Theory, Film
and Fiction*, Bloomington, Indiana: Indiana University Press.

Lebra, Takie Sugiyama (1976), *Japanese Patterns of Behaviour*, Honolulu:
University of Hawai'i Press.

—————— (1984), *Japanese Women: Constraint and Fulfilment*, Honolulu: University of Hawai'i Press.

—————— (1992a), 'Gender and Culture in the Japanese Political Economy: Self-Portrayals of Prominent Businesswomen,' in Shumpei Kumon and Henry Rosovsky (eds), *The Political Economy of Japan*, vol. 3: *Cultural and Social Dynamics*, Stanford: Stanford University Press, pp. 364–422.

—————— (1992b), 'Self in Japanese Culture,' in Nancy R. Rosenberger (ed.), *Japanese Sense of Self*, Cambridge: Cambridge University Press, pp. 105–20.

Leheny, David Richard (2003), The Rules of Play: National Identity and the Shaping of Japanese Leisure, Ithaca: Cornell University Press.

Longinotto, Kim and Jano Williams (directors) (1993), *Dream Girls* (video documentary), London: Twentieth Century Vixen.

—————— (1995), *Shinjuku Boys* (documentary film, 16 mm), London: Twentieth Century Vixen; Uplink Tokyo.

Low, Morris (2003), 'The Emperor's Sons Go to War: Competing Masculinities in Modern Japan,' in Kam Louie and Morris Low (eds), *Asian Masculinities: The Meaning and Practice of Manhood in China and Japan*, London and New York: RoutledgeCurzon, pp. 81–99.

Lunsing, Wim (1997), 'Gay Boom in Japan? Changing Views of Homosexuality,' *Thamyris: Mythmaking from Past to Present*, vol. 4, no. 2, pp. 267–93.

Lyotard, Jean-François (1984), *The Postmodern Condition: A Report on Knowledge*, (*Theory and History of Literature*, vol. 10), trans. Geoff Bennington and Brian Massumi, Manchester: Manchester University Press.

Mackie, Vera (1997), Creating Socialist Women in Japan: Gender, Labour and Activism, 1900–1937, Cambridge: Cambridge University Press.

—————— (2003), *Feminism in Modern Japan: Citizenship, Embodiment, and Sexuality*, Cambridge; New York: Cambridge University Press.

Mainichi Interactive (2003), 'Ex-Lower House Speaker Sakurauchi dies at ninety-one.' Available from: <http://mdn.mainichi.co.jp/news/archive/200307/06/20030706p2a00m0dm010000c.html> 6 July [30 September 2003].

Malm, William P. (1971), 'The Modern Music of Meiji Japan,' in Donald H. Shively (ed.), *Tradition and Modernisation in Japanese Culture*, Princeton: Princeton University Press, pp. 257–300.

Maree, Claire (2003), '"Ore wa ore dakara (Because I'm me)": A Study of Gender and Language in the Documentary *Shinjuku Boys*,' *Intersections: Gender, History and Culture in the Asian Context*, issue 9. Available from: <http://wwwsshe.murdoch.edu.au/intersections/issue9/maree.html> 11 August [23 October 2003].

Martinez, D. P. (1998), 'Gender, Shifting Boundaries and Global Cultures,' in D.P. Martinez (ed.), *The Worlds of Japanese Popular Culture: Gender, Shifting Boundaries and Global Cultures*, Cambridge: Cambridge University Press, pp. 1–18.

Matsu, Akira (2001), 'Sawayaka tōku (Refreshing talk,' in *Matsu Akira Web Site*. Available from: <http://www.m-akira.com/sawayakatalk.html> 25 April [17 December 2002].

Matsuo, Hisako (1998), 'Onaji mokuhyō ni mukatteiru kara tanoshii! Ongaku gakkō juken o mae ni shite (It's fun because we're aiming for the same goal! Facing Music School entrance examinations),' in Mainichi Mukku Amyūzu (ed.), *Takarazuka '97–'98*, Mainichi Shinbunsha, pp. 129–32.

Maya, Miki (1994), *I Love Takarazuka*, Shōgakukan.

McLelland, Mark J. (2001a), 'Out on the Global Stage: Authenticity, Interpretation and Orientalism in Japanese Coming Out Narratives,' *Electronic Journal of Contemporary Japanese Studies*. Available from: <http://japanesestudies.org.uk/articles/McLelland.html> 10 October [27 September 2003].

———— (2001b), 'Why Are Japanese Girls' Comics Full of Boys Bonking?' *Intensities: the Journal of Cult Media*. Available from: <http://www.cult-media.com/issue1/CMRmcle.htm> issue 1, Spring/Summer [12 December 2003].

McVeigh, Brian J. (1996), 'Cultivating "Femininity" and "Internationalism": Rituals and Routine at a Japanese Women's Junior College,' *Ethos*, vol. 24, no. 2, pp. 314–49.

———— (1997), *Life in a Japanese Women's College: Learning to be Ladylike*, London; New York: Routledge.

———— (2000), *Wearing Ideology: State, Schooling and Self-Presentation in Japan*, Oxford; New York: Berg.

Miki, Akio (1977), 'Ano koro no watashi: Yuki Reina (Myself in those days: Reina Yuki),' *Takarazuka gurafu*, October, pp. 76–77.

Miki, Heisuke (1994), *Takarazuka kara sekai ga mieru* (From Takarazuka one can see the world), Tōkyō, Osaka, Nagoya: Shichiken Shuppan.

Minakaze, Mai and Chisato Natori (eds) (1997), *Takarajennu ni naritai!* (I want to become a Takarasienne!), Japan Mix.

Mindan Shinbun Online Community (2007), 'Kankoku no hokori mune ni: Takarazuka hoshigumi toppu Aran Kei-san (With Korean pride in her breast: Takarazuka Star Troupe top [star], Ms Kei Aran).' Available from: <http://www.mindan.org/shinbun/news_bk_view.php?corner=6&page=1&subpage=1471> 16 May [29 June 2007].

Mitchell, Jane (1986), 'Women, the State, and National Mobilisation in Prewar Japan,' unpublished B.A. (Honours) thesis, University of Adelaide.

Mitsuya, Nao (2007), *Mitsuya Nao Home Page*. Available from: <> [20 September 2007].

Miyata, Tatsuo (1981), 'Terebi no naka kara mita Takarazuka no miryoku (The charm of Takarazuka seen from within television),' *Kamigata Geinō*, no. 70, April, pp. 34–37.

Mizuho, Yōko (1977), *Abekobe no Takarazuka gaido* (Abekobe's Takarazuka guide), Kōsaidō Books.

Mizushiro, Tamamo (1969), 'Dai-jūnikai Tamamo taidan, gesuto: Gō Chigusa, kakkoyosa batsugun no kiza na nimaime! (Tamamo dialogue no. 12, guest: Chigusa Gō, a dandy romantic hero with outstanding good looks),' *Takarazuka Gurafu*, December, pp. 37–40.

Mochizuki, Mamor[u] (1959), 'Cultural Aspects of Japanese Girl' Opera,' in Hidetoshi Kato (ed.), *Japanese Popular Culture*, Tokyo: Charles E. Tuttle, pp. 165–74.

Mochizuki, Takashi (1999), 'The Evolving Institution of Marriage,' *Nipponia*, no. 9, pp. 12–13.

Modleski, Tania (ed.) (1986), *Studies in Entertainment: Critical Approaches to Mass Culture*, Bloomington, Indiana: Indiana University Press.

Monbushō (Ministry of Education) (1986), *Seito shidō ni okeru sei ni kansuru shidō: chūgakkō kōtō gakkō hen* (Instruction relating to sex in the teaching of students: junior [and] senior high school edition), Ōkurashō Insatsukyoku.

Monbukagakushō (Ministry of Education, Culture, Sports, Science and Technology) *Web Site* (2003), 'Chūō kyōiku shingikai daigaku bunkakai (dai-nijūsan-kai) giji shidai, shiryō 1: daigaku shikaku no danryokuka (an) (Central Council for Education, Subdivision on Universities (no. 23) agenda, datum 1: towards more flexible university [entrance] qualifications) (draft plan),' August. Available from: <http://www.mext.go.jp/b_menu/shingi/chukyo/chukyo4/gijiroku/001/03080701/001.htm> [12 January 2004].

—————— (2007a), 'Jūhassai jinkō oyobi kōtō kyōiku kikan e no nyūga-kusha-sū, shingaku-ritsu tō no ikō (Changing trends in population aged eighteen years and new enrolment numbers and advancement rates into higher education institutions, et cetera).' Available from: <http://www.mext.go.jp/b_menu/shingi/chukyo/chukyo4/gijiroku/015/06101201/003/001.pdf> [20 September 2007].

—————— (2007b), 'Shingakuritsu (School advancement rates).' Available from: <http://www.mext.go.jp/b_menu/toukei/001/06121219/005/004.xls> [20 September 2007].

Moore, F. Michael (1994), *Drag! Male and Female Impersonators on Stage, Screen and Television*, Jefferson, North Carolina; and London: McFarland and Company, Inc.

Moore, Henrietta L. (1994), *A Passion for Difference*, Bloomington and Indianapolis: Indiana University Press.

Mori, Keaki (1993), *120% no dārin* (120% darling), Soirée Books.

Morinishi, Mayumi (1991), 'OSK Osaka kōen (OSK's Osaka Performances),' in *Kamigata geinō techō: butai, hito, Osaka* (A Handbook of Kamigata Performing Arts: Stages, People, Osaka), Osaka: Kamigata Geinō Shuppan Sentā, pp. 97–100.

Morley, Patricia (1999), *The Mountain is Moving: Japanese Women's Lives*, Vancouver: UBC Press.

Morohashi, Taiki (1993), *Zasshi bunka no naka no joseigaku* (The culture of women's magazines: A Study of Gender Image), Akashi Shoten.

Morris-Suzuki, Tessa (1998), *Re-inventing Japan: Time, Space, Nation*, Armonk, New York: M.E. Sharpe.

Mulvey, Laura (1989), *Visual and Other Pleasures*, Bloomington: Indiana University Press.

'Mune odoru "honba no butai"' (Pari kōen) (The thrilling "home stage [of the Revue]") (Paris performance)' (1975), *Nikkan Supōtsu*, 30 November, p. 10.

Murakami, Yōko (1997), *Otokoyaku tte suteki! Takarazuka: shakunetsu no koi shūdan* (How gorgeous the male-role players are! Takarazuka: a community of burning romantic love), Nishinomiya: Rokusaisha.

Myūjikaru (Musical) (2000), 'Tōhō kōen myūjikaru "Erizabēto" de Erizabēto o enjiru Ichiro Maki (Maki Ichiro, who plays Elisabeth in the Toho performance of the musical "Elisabeth"),' vol. 185, June, pp. 14–15.

Nagata, Masakazu (1976), 'Sorya nan to itte mo Amatsu da na; Takarazuka no yomesan o morau n da to iu no ga seinenkan no ai kotoba da yo, kimi (Amatsu was undeniably [the best]; the catch-phrase among young men was that they'd get a wife from Takarazuka),' in Tazuko Suzuki, *'Zuka fan no kagami: Mon Pari kara Beru bara made*, Zero Bukkusu, p. 86.

Nagy, Margit (1991), 'Middle-Class Working Women During the Interwar Years,' in Gail Lee Bernstein (ed.), *Recreating Japanese Women, 1600–1945*, Berkeley; Los Angeles; Oxford: University of California Press, pp. 199–216.

Naikakufu (Cabinet Office) *Gender Information Site* (2002), '10. Danjo kyōdō sankaku o suishin shi tayō na sentaku o kanō ni suru kyōiku, gakushū no jūjitsu (10. The full implementation of education and learning which enable diverse choices and promote gender equality).' Available from: <http://www.gender.go.jp/koudou/part2-10.html> 5 April [12 January 2004].

——————— (2004). Available from: <http://www.gender.go.jp/index2.html> [17 June 2004].

Naikakufu (Cabinet Office) *Web Site* (1997), 'Heisei ku-nen kokumin seikatsu hakusho: hataraku josei, atarashii shakai shisutemu o motomete (1997 White Paper on national life: working women, seeking a new social system).'

Available from: <http://wp.cao.go.jp/zenbun/seikatsu/wp-pl97/wp-pl97-01401.html> [20 January 2003].

Nakagawa, Yoshizō (2003), 'Haru da! Odori da! Watakushi no haru da! (It's spring! It's dancing! It's my spring!),' in 'Tokushū: OSK no hachijūichinen to shinsei e (Special feature: to the eighty-one years of OSK and its rebirth),' *Kamigata geinō*, no. 149, September, pp. 46–47.

Nakamura, Akira (1994), 'NOVA de mattemasu! 2; Maori Yuki no baai (Waiting at NOVA! no. 2: The case of Yuki Maori),' *Takarazuka gurafu*, May, pp. 70–71.

Nakamura, Karen and Hisako Matsuo (2003), 'Female Masculinity and Fantasy Spaces: Transcending Genders in the Takarazuka Theatre and Japanese Popular Culture,' in James Roberson and Nobue Suzuki (eds), *Men and Masculinities in Contemporary Japan: Dislocating the Salaryman Doxa*, London and New York: RoutledgeCurzon, pp. 59–76.

Nakane, Chie (1970), *Japanese Society*, London: Weidenfield and Nicolson.

Nakanishi, Toyoko (ed.) (1988), *Karada: watashitachi jishin* ([Our] bodies, ourselves), Kyoto: Shōkadō.

Nakao, Akira (1991), *Tezuka Osamu* (Osamu Tezuka), Kōdansha Hinotori Denki Bunko, no. 75.

Napier, Susan J. (1998), 'Vampires, Psychic Girls, Flying Women and Sailor Scouts: Four Faces of the Young Female in Japanese Popular Culture,' in D.P. Martinez (ed.), *The Worlds of Japanese Popular Culture: Gender, Shifting Boundaries and Global Cultures*, Cambridge: Cambridge University Press, pp. 91–109.

——————— (2000), *Anime: From Akira to Princess Mononoke*, New York: Palgrave.

Narita, Ryūichi (1994), '"Sei" no chōryō: 1920-nendai no sekushuariti (The rampancy of "sex": sexuality in the 1920s),' in Wakita Haruko and Susan B. Hanley (eds), *Jendā no Nihonshi* (Gender and Japanese history), vol. 1, Tōkyō Daigaku Shuppankai, pp. 523–64.

Nasu, Shoichi (2003), 'The Show WILL GO ON,' *Daily Yomiuri*, 9 July, p. 15.

Natori, Chisato (1990), *Dorīmu shiatā* (Dream theatre), Osaka: Kansai Shoin.

——————— (1993), 'Kāten kōru no hitobito: chikyūgi ga suki (Curtain-call people: I love the Earth),' *With Takarazuka*, no. 83, March, pp. 8–10.

——————— (2001a), 'Takarazuka intabyū: enshutsuka, Ueda Keiko-san (Takarazuka interview: Ms Keiko Ueda, director),' *With Takarazuka*, no. 175, January, pp. 8–11.

——————— (2001b), 'Takarazuka intabyū: senka, Kasugano Yachiyo-san (Takarazuka interview: Ms Yachiyo Kasugano, of the Superior Members' group),' *With Takarazuka*, no. 178, May, pp. 6–8.

——————— (2001–2007), 'Fairy Interview,' With Takarazuka Web Site. Available from: <http://www.with-takarazuka.com/back/back.html> [20 September 2007].

Natori, Chisato and Chiaki Takeichi (eds) (1996a), Sumiretachi no dai-ni maku: Takarazuka sotsugyōseitachi wa, ima (The violets' second act: what Takarazuka graduates are doing now) (Original English title: The fairies' 2nd stage), Kōyū Shuppan.

——————— (1996b), Sumiretachi no dai-ni maku II: midori no hakama o nuide (The violets' second act, vol. 2: taking off the green hakama), Kōyū Shuppan.

Natsushiro, Rei (2001), 'Natsushiro Rei: Takarazuka no omoide (Rei Natsushiro: memories of Takarazuka),' in Toshihiro Tsuganezawa and Chisato Natori (eds), Takarazuka beru epokku II: Takarazuka modanizumu wa seiki o koete (Takarazuka belle époque II: Takarazuka modernism transcends the century), Kobe: Kōbe Shinbun Sōgō Shuppan Sentā, pp. 41–44.

New OSK Official Web Site (2007). Available from: <http://www.sakura-saku-kuni-osk.net/> [20 September 2007].

Newell, Susan (1997), 'Women Primary School Teachers and the State in Interwar Japan,' in Elise K. Tipton (ed.), Society and the State in Interwar Japan, London: Routledge, pp. 17–41.

NHK Osaka (1992a), BS Special: Natsukashi no eizō de tsuzuru Takarajennu sutā gurafiti pāto 1 (Takarasienne star graffiti spelled out in nostalgic images, part I) (television documentary).

——————— (1992b), BS Special: Natsukashi no eizō de tsuzuru Takarajennu sutā gurafiti pāto 2 (part II) (television documentary).

NHK Television (2001), Kin'yō no sutēji: futari no biggu shō; Ōtori Ran to Umezawa Tomio (Friday stage: a big show by the duo, Ōtori Ran and Umezawa Tomio), television 'special' telecast 12 January.

Nihon Fujin Dantai Rengōkai (ed.) (1997), Fujin hakusho 1997: 2000-nen – danjo byōdō shakai e (Women's white paper 1997: the year 2000 – towards a society with male/female equality), Horupu Shuppan.

Niji-no-kai Web Site (2007). Available from: <http://www2s.biglobe.ne.jp/~seigaku/> [20 September 2007].

Nikkei Net (2004), 'Iki iki kenkō – tokushū: susumu shōshika. Gōkei tokushu shusshōritsu, Tōkyō wa hajimete 1.0 waru (Lively health – special series: plummeting fertility. Tokyo's birthrate drops below 1.0 per woman for the first time),' 11 June. Available from: <http://health.nikkei.co.jp/special/child.cfm> [20 June 2004].

——————— (2007), 'Iki iki kenkō – tokushū: susumu shōshika. 06-nen no shusshōritsu, 30,144-nin zō, roku-nen-buri purasu. (Lively health – special series: plummeting fertility. 2006 birthrate increases by 30,144; first positive figure in six years),' 7 September. Available from: <http://health. nikkei.co.jp/special/child.cfm?&i=2007090708430p4> [10 September].

Nikkei Net Kansai (2004), 'Takarazuka Kagekidan, jiki rijichō ni Kobayashi Kōichi-shi (Mr Kōichi Kobayashi to be next Takarazuka Revue Company Chair),' 20 June. Available from: <http://www.nikkei.co.jp/kansai/ news/20263.html, 20 June [27 June 2004].

Nimiya, Kazuko (1994), *Honto no Takarazuka ga wakaru hon* (A book for understanding the real Takarazuka), Tōkyō, Kōsaidō Shuppan.

————— (1995), *Takarazuka no kōki: Osukaru kara posutomodanizumu e* (The fragrance of Takarazuka: from Oscar to post-modernism), Kōsaisha.

Nipponia (1999), 'Statistical View of Marriage in Japan,' no. 9, pp. 10–11.

Nishikawa, Yūko and Miho Ogino (eds) (1999), *Kyōdō kenkyū: danseiron* (A joint study: on men), Kyōto: Jinbun Shoin.

Nishina, Yuri (1996), 'Nishina Yuri,' in Takarajennu kyatto fan kurabu (ed.), *TAKARA-JENNE Cats Fan Club*, Seibundō Shinkōsha, pp. 74–77.

Nishiyama, Matsunosuke (1997), *Edo Culture: Daily Life and Diversions in Urban Japan, 1600–1868*, trans. and ed. Gerald Groemer, Honolulu: University of Hawai'i Press.

Nolletti, Arthur, Jr (1992), '"Woman in the Mist" and Gosho in the 1930s,' in Arthur Nolletti, Jr, and David Desser (eds), *Reframing Japanese Cinema: Authorship, Genre, History*, Bloomington and Indianapolis: Indiana University Press, pp. 3–32.

Nolte, Sharon and Sally Ann Hastings (1991), 'The Meiji State's Policy toward Women, 1890–1910,' in Gail Lee Bernstein (ed.), *Recreating Japanese Women, 1600–1945*, Berkeley; Los Angeles; Oxford: University of California Press, pp. 151–74.

Nolte, Sharon H. (1986), 'Women's Rights and Society's Needs: Japan's 1931 Suffrage Bill,' *Comparative Studies in Society and History*, vol. 28, no. 4, pp. 690–713.

Nosaka, Akiyuki (1977), *Watashi no Takarazuka* (My Takarazuka), Kyōto: Shinshindō Yunikon Karā Sōsho.

Nozoe, Yasuo (1997), 'Waga chichi, Hori Seiki no omoide (Memories of my father, Seiki Hori),' in Toshihiro Tsuganezawa and Chisato Natori (eds), *Takarazuka beru epokku: kageki + rekishi + bunka = Takarazuka* (Takarazuka belle époque: opera + history + culture = Takarazuka), Kobe: Kōbe Shinbun Sōgō Shuppan Sentā, pp. 93–104.

Obata, Masanori and Masashi Usami (1993) (1989), *Takarazuka graffiti*, Osaka: Osaka Shoseki.

Ochiai, Emiko (1989), 'Kindai kazoku to Nihon bunka: Nihonteki boshi kankei o tokiguchi ni (The modern family and Japanese culture: an approach through Japanese mother-child relationships),' *Joseigaku nenpō*, no. 10, October, pp. 6–15.

Ogawa, Hiroshi (1990), "'Idol Industry" Hits the Skids,' *Pacific Friend*, vol. 18, no. 1, p. 32.

Ohnuki-Tierney, Emiko (1984), *Illness and Culture in Contemporary Japan: An Anthropological View*, Cambridge: Cambridge University Press.

Ohzasa, Yoshio (1997), 'Shingeki's Restless Century,' *Unesco Courier*, November, p. 19.

Okada, Keiji (1973), 'Koko ga ii no da!! Hatsukaze Jun no maki (This is what I like!! On Jun Hatsukaze),' *Takarazuka gurafu*, December, p. 34.

Okamoto, Shigeko (1995), '"Tasteless" Japanese: Less "Feminine" Speech among Young Japanese Women,' in Kira Hall and Mary Bucholtz (eds), *Gender Articulated: Language and the Socially Constructed Self*, New York: Routledge, pp. 297–325.

Okamoto, Shirō (2001), *The Man who Saved Kabuki: Faubion Bowers and Theatre Censorship in Occupied Japan*, trans. Samuel L. Leiter, Honolulu: University of Hawai'i Press.

Ōkawa, Takehiro (1995), 'Chō kakumei teki danshi dai dōin keikaku (A super-revolutionary huge plan for male mobilisation),' in Waseda daigaku Takarazuka kageki o aisuru kai (ed.), *Ai no hanataba* (Bouquet of love): *We love Takarazuka*, KK Besuto Serāzu, pp. 10–19.

One's Co. Ltd (ed.) (1996), *Jenne* (Takarasiennes) *Vol. 1, Actress File Extra*, Soirée Books.

Ōno, Satomi (ed.) (1995), *Fantasutikku Takarazuka* (Fantastic Takarazuka), Geibunsha.

Ortolini, Renito (1990), *The Japanese Theatre from Shamanistic Ritual to Contemporary Pluralism*, Leiden; New York, København, Köln: E.J. Brill.

Osaka nikkan supōtsu (2000a), 'Takarazuka mangekyō no. 35. Hachinen no "shakai benkyō" hete butai fukki (Takarazuka kaleidoscope, no. 35. Returning to the stage after eight years of "studying society"),' 28 November. Available from: <http://osaka-nikkan.com/lib/oet/kaleido/001128.html> [17 November 2002].

—————— (2000b), 'Takarazuka mangekyō, no. 37. Boisu torēnā to shite "seikan": taidan chokugo NY shugyō e (Takarazuka kaleidoscope, no. 37. Back as a voice trainer: straight to New York training after quitting),' 12 December. Available from: <http://Osaka-nikkan.com/lib/oet/kaleido/001212.html> [15 July 2002].

OSK sonzoku no kai (2004). Available from: <http://www.sakura-saku-kuni-osk.net> [22 February 2004].

Ōta, Tetsunori (2001), 'Takarazuka ongaku gakkō no sōritsu to hensen (The founding and vicissitudes of the Takarazuka Music School),' in Toshihiro Tsuganezawa and Chisato Natori (eds), *Takarazuka beru epokku II: modanizumu wa seiki o koete*, Kobe: Kōbe Shinbun Sōgō Shuppan Sentā, pp. 111–17.

Ōtori, Ran (1971), 'Yonjūroku-nen ni yonjūroku no shitsumon (Forty-six questions for 1971),' *Takarazuka gurafu*, May, pp. 60–63.

Ōura, Mizuki (1993), *Natsume de gojaimasu* (My nickname is 'Natsume'), Shōgakukan.

——— (1991), *Yume* Takarazuka* (Dream* Takarazuka), Shōgakukan.

Ozaki, Hirotsugu (1969), 'Han-seiki ni wataru butai (Stage [performances] spanning a half-century),' *Kageki*, September, pp. 30–31.

Ōzasa, Yoshio (1985), *Nihon gendai engekishi* (A history of modern Japanese theatre), vol. 1, Hakusuisha.

——— (1986), *Nihon gendai engekishi*, vol. 2, Hakusuisha.

——— (1990), *Nihon gendai engekishi*, vol. 3, Hakusuisha.

——— (1993), *Nihon gendai engekishi*, vol. 4, Hakusuisha.

Ōzeki, Hiromasa (1993a), *Wakaki hi no uta wa wasureji* (I'll never forgot the songs of the days of our youth), part 1 (unpublished playscript), Takarazuka: Takarazuka Kagekidan.

——— (1993b), *Wakaki hi no uta wa wasureji*, part 2 (unpublished playscript), Takarazuka: Takarazuka Kagekidan.

Pacific Friend (1975), '"Zuka" Shows Win Public Acclaim,' April, vol. 2, no. 12, pp. 17–21.

Partner, Simon (1999), *Assembled in Japan: Electrical Goods and the Making of the Japanese Consumer*, Berkeley, California; London: University of California Press.

Pharr, Susan J. (1981), *Political Women in Japan: The Search for a Place in Political Life*, Berkeley: University of California Press.

PHP Institute, Inc. and Takarazuka Revue Company (eds) (1991), *(Zukai) Viva Takarazuka!* (Viva Takarazuka!) (Illustrated), PHP Institute.

Pound, Ezra and Ernest Fenollosa (1959), *The Classic Noh Theatre of Japan*, New York: New Directions.

Poynton, Cate (1985), *Language and Gender: Making the Difference*, Geelong: Deakin University Press.

Public Policy (1997), 'Overhauling the Equal Employment Opportunity Law,' vol. 36, no. 3, 1 March. Available from: <http://www.jil.go.jp/bulletin/year/1997/vol36-03/04.htm> [20 August 2004].

'Rajio, terebi e no tōjō (The advent of radio and television)' (2004), in *Takarazuka kageki kyūjū-nenshi: sumirebana toshi o kasanete*, Takarazuka: Takarazuka Kagekidan, p. 204.

Rebyū sanka, Takarazuka (A paean to the revue, Takarazuka), (1977), Takarazuka: Takarazuka Kagekidan.

Rich, Adrienne (1980), 'Compulsory Heterosexuality and Lesbian Existence,' *Signs: Journal of Women in Culture and Society*, vol. 5, Summer, pp. 631–60.

Robertson, Jennifer (1989), 'Gender-bending in Paradise: Doing "Female" and "Male" in Japan,' *Genders*, no. 5, Summer, pp. 180–207.

————— (1991), 'Theatrical Resistance, Theatres of Restraint: The Takarazuka Revue and the "State Theater" Movement,' *Anthropological Quarterly*, vol. 64, no. 4, pp. 165–77.

————— (1992a), 'Doing and Undoing "Female" and "Male" in Japan: The Takarazuka Revue,' in Takie Sugiyama Lebra (ed.), *Japanese Social Organisation*, Honolulu: University of Hawai'i Press, pp. 165–93.

————— (1992b), 'The "Magic If": Conflicting Performances of Gender in the Takarazuka Revue of Japan,' in Laurence Senelick (ed.), *Gender in Performance: The Presentation of Difference in the Performing Arts*, Hanover, New Hampshire: Tufts University/University Press of New England, pp. 46–67.

————— (1992c), 'The Politics of Androgyny in Japan: Sexuality and Subversion in the Theater and Beyond,' *American Ethnologist*, vol. 19, no. 3, August, pp. 419–42.

————— (1995), 'Mon Japon: Theater as a Technology of Japanese Imperialism,' *American Ethnologist*, vol. 22, no. 4, November, pp. 970–96.

————— (1998a), 'The Politics and Pursuit of Leisure in Wartime Japan,' in Sepp Linhart and Sabine Früstück (eds), *The Culture of Japan as Seen through its Leisure*, Albany, New York: State University of New York Press, pp. 285–301.

————— (1998b), *Takarazuka: Sexual Politics and Popular Culture in Modern Japan*, Berkeley: University of California Press.

————— (1999), 'Dying to Tell: Sexuality and Suicide in Imperial Japan,' *Signs*, vol. 24, no. 1, Autumn, pp. 1–35.

————— (2000), *Odoru teikokushugi: Takarazuka o meguru sekushuaru poritikusu to taishū bunka* (Dancing imperialism: sexual politics and popular culture surrounding Takarazuka), trans. Chieko Hori, Gendai Shokan.

————— (2001), 'Japan's First Cyborg? Miss Nippon, Eugenics and Wartime Technologies of Beauty, Body and Blood,' *Body & Society*, vol. 7, no. 1, pp. 1–34.

Rodd, Laurel Rasplica (1991), 'Yosano Akiko and the Taishō Debate over the "New Woman",' in Gail Lee Bernstein (ed.), *Recreating Japanese Women, 1600–1945*, Berkeley: University of California Press, pp. 175–98.

Roden, Donald T. (1990), 'Taisho Culture and the Problem of Gender Ambivalence,' in J. Thomas Rimer (ed.), *Culture and Identity: Japanese Intellectuals during the Interwar Years*, Princeton: Princeton University Press, pp. 37–55.

Rosenberger, Nancy R. (1994), 'Indexing Hierarchy through Japanese Gender

Relations,' in Jane M. Bachnik and Charles J. Quinn Jr (eds), *Situated Meaning: Inside and Outside in Japanese Self, Society, and Language*, Princeton: Princeton University Press, pp. 88–112.

Sakata, Hiroo (1983), *Waga Kobayashi Ichizō: kiyoku tadashiku utsukushiku* (Our Kobayashi Ichizō: [with] purity, righteousness and beauty), Kawade Shobō.

———— (1992), *Ō Takarazuka: shai fazā, musume o kataru* (Oh Takarazuka: a shy father talks about his daughter), Bungei Shunjū.

Sakuragi, Seiko (2004), 'Takarazuka Fan,' *All About Web Site*. Available from <http://allabout.co.jp/entertainment/takarazukafan/subject/msub_sAll. htm> [2 February 2004].

Sand, Jordan (1998), 'At Home in the Meiji Period: Inventing Japanese Domesticity,' in Stephen Vlastos (ed.), *Mirror of Modernity: Invented Traditions of Modern Japan*, Berkeley and Los Angeles: University of California Press, pp. 191–207.

Sankei Sports (2000), 'Kotobuki Hizuru, "adakataki" Sato-san ni dōjō (Hizuru Kotobuki, sympathy for "arch-rival," Sato),' 29 June. Available from: <http://www.sanspo.com/geino/g0006/top2000062902.html> [17 September 2003].

———— (2002), 'Takarazuka kenkyūka Tōfū no gekipen, no. 18, Yukigumi Tōkyō kōen, myūjikaru roman "Tsuioku no Baruserona" (Takarazuka researcher Tōfū's dramatic pen, no. 18. Snow Troupe Tokyo performance, musical romance "The Barcelona I remember").' Available from: <http://www.sanspo.com/geino/takara/gekipen/gekipen_18.html> 22 September [16 December 2002].

Sanspo Com (2003), 'Go-kumi-me no futago shimai ga gōkaku: Takarazuka on-gaku gakkō kyūjūikkisei (Fifth pair of twin sisters pass [exam]: Takarazuka Music School ninety-first intake).' Available from: <www.sanspo.com/geino/top/gt200303/gt2003040116.html> 1 April [20 December 2003].

Sasaki, Toshiko (1985), 'Onna ga zubon o haku toki (When women don trousers),' in Kimi Komashaku (ed.), *Onna o yosōu* (Dressing (as) women), Keisō Shobō, pp. 116–56.

Sasano, Michiru (1995), *Coming OUT!*, Gentōsha.

Sato, Barbara Hamill (2003), The New Japanese Woman: Modernity, Media, and Women in Interwar Japan, Durham, NC: Duke University Press.

Sawachi, Hisae (1989), 'The Political Awakening of Women,' *Japan Quarterly*, no. 36, pp. 381–85.

Sawamura, Sadako (1969), *Kai no uta: ikitekita michi* (Shell song: my life's path), Kōdansha.

Schilling, Mark (ed.) (1997), *The Encyclopedia of Japanese Popular Culture*, New York: Weatherhill.

Schilling, Mark (2001), 'My heart will go on...for 1,000 years,' *Japan Times*

Online, 26 Dec. Available from: <http://search.japantimes.co.jp/cgi-bin/ff20011226a2.html> [6 May 2003].

Schermbeek, Mieke van (1995), 'Women in the Limelight: Feminist Theatre Studies,' in Rosemary Buikema and Anneke Smelik (eds), *Women's Studies and Culture: A Feminist Introduction*, London: Zed Books, pp. 66–81.

Schomer, K. and Y. Chang (1995), 'The Cult of Cuteness,' *Newsweek*, 28 August, pp. 54–8.

'Seitenkan ni daiseikō (Great success in sex change)' (1979), in *Migiwa Natsuko no sekai: Kageki, Takarazuka gurafu yori* (The world of Migiwa Natsuko: From *Kageki* and *Takarazuka Gurafu*), Futami Shobō, p. 95.

Senelick, Laurence (2000), *The Changing Room: Sex, Drag and the Theatre*, London and New York: Routledge.

Shibamoto, Janet S. (1985), *Japanese Women's Language*, Orlando: Academic Press.

Shiki Theatre Company (2007). Available from: <www.shiki.gr.jp> [14 September 2007].

Shimizu, Miyabi (1957), *Kobayashi Ichizō ni oshierareru mono* (Lessons from Kobayashi Ichizō), Osaka: Umeda Shobō.

Shimose, Naoko (1994), *Takarazuka: eien no toppu sutā* (Takarazuka: top stars forever), Rippū Shobō.

Shion, Yū (2001), 'Intabyū: Shion Yū – taidango no koto (Interview: Shion Yū – about post-retirement)' (2001), in Toshihiro Tsuganezawa and Chisato Natori (eds), *Takarazuka beru epokku II: Takarazuka modanizumu wa seiki o koete*, Kobe: Kōbe Shinbun Sōgō Shuppan Sentā, pp. 26–40.

Shirai, Tetsuzō (1967), *Takarazuka to watashi* (Takarazuka and I), Nakabayashi Shuppan.

———— (1980) 'Eien ni ikiru Kobayashi Ichizō (Kobayashi Ichizō, who will live forever),' in *Bessatsu ichiokunin no Shōwa shi, Takarazuka: karei naru butai to sutā o sodateta nanajū-nen*, Mainichi Shinbunsha, pp. 110–11.

Shiraishi, Yūji (1980), 'Otokoyaku, musumeyaku o sodateta nanajū-nen (Seventy years that nurtured *otokoyaku* and *musumeyaku*),' in *Takarazuka: karei naru butai to sutā o sodateta nanajū-nen*, Mainichi Shinbunsha, pp. 120–27.

Shively, Donald H. (1978), 'The Social Environment of Kabuki,' in James R. Brandon, William P. Malm and Donald H. Shively, *Studies in Kabuki: Its Acting, Music and Historical Context*, Honolulu: The University Press of Hawai'i, pp. 1–61.

Shōwa Production Co. Ltd (2004). Available from: <http://www.showapro.com/home/profile/hana.html> [24 June 2004].

Sievers, Sharon (1983), Flowers in Salt: The Beginnings of Feminist Consciousness in Modern Japan, Stanford: Stanford University Press.

Silverberg, Miriam (1991), 'The Modern Girl as Militant,' in Gail Lee Bernstein (ed.), *Recreating Japanese Women, 1600–1945*, Berkeley; Los Angeles; Oxford: University of California Press, pp. 239–66.

Simmons, Cyril (1990), *Growing up and Going to School in Japan: Tradition and Trends*, Milton Keynes; Philadelphia: Open University Press.

Singer, Jane (1996), 'The Dream World of Takarazuka,' *Japan Quarterly*, vol. 40, no. 2, pp. 162–81.

Singer, June (2000), *Androgyny: The Opposites Within*, York Beach, Maine: Nicholas-Hayes.

Singleton, John (1967), *Nichū: A Japanese School*, New York: Holt, Rinehart and Winston.

Sischy, Ingrid (1992), 'Onward and Upward with the Arts: Selling Dreams,' *New Yorker*, September 28, pp. 84–103.

Smethurst, Richard J. (1978), 'The Army, Youth, and Women,' in Edward R. Beauchamp (ed.), *Learning to be Japanese: Selected Readings on Japanese Society and Education*, Hamden, Connecticut: Linnet Books, pp. 137–66.

Smith, Robert J. (1983), 'Making Village Women into "Good Wives and Wise Mothers" in Prewar Japan,' *Journal of Family History*, vol. 8, no. 1, Spring, pp. 70–84.

————— (1987), 'Gender Inequality in Contemporary Japan,' *Journal of Japanese Studies*, vol. 13, no. 1, Winter, pp. 1–25.

Soireé (1997), 'Soirée Excellent Gallery: Amami Yūki,' vol. 39, March, pp. 6–11.

Spender, Dale (1990), *Man Made Language*, second edition, London: Pandora.

Sponichi Annex (2001), 'Moto Takarajennu igakubu gōkaku (Former Takarasienne accepted into medical school).' Available from: <http://www.sponichi.co.jp/entertainment/kiji/2001/02/11/01.html> 11 February [16 August 2002].

Sponichi Annex Osaka (2004), 'Yume wa Burōdowē shinshutsu: Kobayashi Kōichi shin rijichō ni kiku ([Our] dream is to advance onto Broadway: asking new CEO, Kōichi Kobayashi' at: www.sponichi.co.jp/osaka/ente/takarazuka/backnumber/040703/takarazuka.html, 3 July [6 August 2006].

Sponichi Takarazuka Kageki tokushū gō (Sports Nippon Takarazuka Revue special edition) (2006), 'Omoide itsumademo (Memories for ever),' 3 August, p. 6.

Sports Nippon Osaka (2002), 'Takumi Hibiki, sekitsuien datta! Hanagumi Tōkyō kōen mo tōmen wa kyūen (Hibiki Takumi had spinal-cord inflammation! out of Flower Troupe Tokyo run indefinitely),' 28 April. Available from: <www.sponichi.com/ente/takarazuka/backnumber/020428/takarazuka.html> [14 May 2002].

Stacey, Jackie (1994), Star Gazing: Hollywood Cinema and Female Spectatorship, London: Routledge.

————— (1995), 'The Lost Audience: Methodology, Cinema History and Feminist Film Criticism,' in Beverley Skeggs (ed.), *Feminist Cultural Theory: Process and Production*, Manchester: Manchester University Press, pp. 97–118.

STAS Official Web Site (2003). Available from: <http://skd-og-stas.pave.jp/index2.html> [9 September 2007].

Stickland, Leonie Rae (2004a), 'Gender Gymnastics: Performers, Fans and Gender Issues in the Takarazuka Revue of Contemporary Japan,' unpublished Ph.D. dissertation, Murdoch University Digital Theses. Available from: <http://wwwlib.murdoch.edu.au/adt/browse/view/adt-MU20050310.103233> [5 May 2005].

————— (2004b), 'Romanchikku-na Nihon bunka toshite: kaigai kara mita Takarazuka kageki (As romantic Japanese culture: the Takarazuka Revue seen from overseas,' *Kamigata geinō*, no. 154, December, pp. 25–28.

Styan, J. L. (1960), *Elements of Drama*, Cambridge: Cambridge University Press.

Strinati, Dominic (1995), *An Introduction to Theories of Popular Culture*, London & New York: Routledge.

Subaru (1987), 'Torikaebaya ibun: Takarazuka otokoyaku kō (Strange tales of changelings: thoughts on Takarazuka *otokoyaku*),' May, pp. 86–97.

Sugahara, Midori (1996), *Yume no rebyū shi: sumire no sono Takarazuka, sakura saku kuni OSK, SKD* (A History of the Revue of [our] Dreams: The Garden of Violets, Takarazuka, [and] the Lands where Cherries Bloom, OSK [and] SKD), Tōkyō Shinbun Shuppankyoku.

Sugimoto, Yoshio (1997), *An Introduction to Japanese Society*, Cambridge: Cambridge University Press.

Sugita, Naoki (1935), 'Shōjo kageki netsu no shindan (Diagnosis of fever for girls' opera),' *Fujin kōron*, no. 4, pp. 274–78.

Sumi, Hanayo (1999), 'Hajimete no josō de ashi o dasu no ga hazukashikute (Embarrassed at showing my legs in female costume for the first time),' in Ioi Kenji (ed.), *Takarazuka Revue: nijūisseiki e no tabidachi*, Osaka: Hankyu Corporation, p. 51.

Sumire Society (1994), *Fushigi no hanazono Takarazuka no himitsu* (The secrets of Takarazuka, garden of mystery), Bunka Sōsaku Shuppan.

Sumire tomo-no-kai (ed.) (1993), *Ōru zatto Takarazuka: shunran gōka miwaku no sutēji no subete* (All that Takarazuka: all about that gorgeous, colourful, enchanting stage), Nippon Bungeisha.

Sumire uotchāzu (Violet watchers) (1996), *Amami Yūki to Takarazuka no nazo* (The mysteries of Yūki Amami and Takarazuka), Coara Books.

Summerhawk, Barbara, Cheiron McMahill and Darren McDonald (eds) (1998), *Queer Japan*, Victoria, Canada: New Victoria Publishers.

Suna no ue no sanba (Samba on the sand): *Dance Dance SKD* (Shochiku Musical performance programme) (1993), vol. 1.

Suwa, Ai (1980), *Mayonaka no Takarazuka* (The midnight Takarazuka [sic]), Sōbunsha.

————— (2002), *Mayonaka no Takarazuka Part II: shinguru mazā funtōki* (The midnight Takarazuka, part II: the chronicle of a single mother's struggles) (private publication), Kyoto: Suwa Ai Musical School.

Suzuki, Akira (2002), 'Nihon no gendai buyō: seiritsu haikei to genjō (Japanese contemporary dance: foundation, background and current situation),' *Japan Performing Arts Net Web Site*. Available from: <http://www.jpan.org/cdance.html, 22 January [5 December 2002].

Suzuki, Atsuko (2007), 'Introduction: Micro–Macro Dynamics,' in Atsuko Suzuki (ed.), *Gender and Career in Japan*, trans. Leonie R. Stickland, Melbourne, Victoria: Trans Pacific Press, pp. 1–32.

Suzuki, Haruhiko (1979), *Takarazuka ni ai o komete* (To Takarazuka, with love), Gakken.

Suzuki, Tazuko (1976), 'Zuka fan no kagami: Mon Pari kara Beru bara made (Model 'Zuka fans: from Mon Paris to The Rose of Versailles), Zero Bukkusu.

Takagi, Shirō (1976), *Takarazuka no wakaru hon: butai ura no Takarajennu* (A book for understanding Takarazuka: Takarasiennes behind the curtain), Kōsaidō Shuppan.

————— (1983), *Revyū no ōsama: Shirai Tetsuzō to Takarazuka* (The king of revues: Tetsuzō Shirai and Takarazuka), Kawade Shobō.

Takagi, Tadashi (2003), 'Marriage and divorce in the Edo Period,' *Japan Echo*, October, pp. 58–62.

Takahara, Kanako (2004), 'Takarazuka Groupies Do It by the Book: Hard-Core Fans of All-Female Troupe Follow Etiquette, Pecking Order,' *Japan Times Online*. Available from: <http://www.japantimes.co.jp/cgi-bin/getarticle.pl5?nn20040507f1.htm, 7 May [26 June 2004].

Takarajennu kyatto fan kurabu (ed.) (1996), *TAKARA-JENNE Cats Fan Club*, Seibundō Shinkōsha.

Takarazuka fuan (Takarazuka fan) (1973), 'Shoshun taidan: Koshiro Miyako, Hatsukaze Jun. Takarazuka wa onshitsu, gaibu no sekai wa kibishii (Early spring interview: Miyako Koshiro [and] Jun Hatsukaze. "Takarazuka is a hot-house, [and] the outside world is harsh"),' no. 311, January, p. 5.

Takarazuka Garden Fields (2007). Available from: <http://www.gardenfields.jp/> [20 September 2007].

Takarazuka Grand Theater (1993), Osaka: Hankyu Corporation (Public Relations Office).

Takarazuka gurafu (1969), 'Sutā jiten; Kōzuki Noboru (Star's encyclopaedia: Kōzuki Noboru),' December, p. 59.

———————— (1973), 'Sutā komyunitī: mukashi mo ima mo Takarazuka no shinboru, Kasugano Yachiyo (Star community: Kasugano Yachiyo, symbol of Takarazuka, back then and now),' December, pp. 28–29.

———————— (1998), '*Gurafu* supesharu Session [sic]: Maya Miki vs Kuroki Hitomi-san ([*Takarazuka*] *Gurafu* special session: Maya Miki versus Kuroki Hitomi),' January, pp. 5–8.

———————— (2001), 'Great! Todoroki Yū,' March, p. 27.

Takarazuka kageki gojū-nen shi (The fifty-year history of the Takarazuka Revue), (1964), Takarazuka, Takarazuka Kagekidan.

Takarazuka Kageki Kenkyūkai (ed.) (1995), *Takarazuka: himitsu no hanazono* (Takarazuka: Garden of Secrets), Nishinomiya: Rokusaisha.

———————— (1999a), *Takarazuka: seikimatsu no hanazono* (Takarazuka, the fin-de-siècle flower garden), Nishinomiya: Rokusaisha.

———————— (1999b), *Takarazuka: yume no butai no mukō-gawa* (Takarazuka: beyond the stage of dreams), Nishinomiya: Rokusaisha.

———————— (2002), *Takarazuka okkake mappu Again* (Takarazuka stalkers' map again), Nishinomiya: Rokusaisha.

———————— (2003), *Takarazuka okkake mappu 2003* (Takarazuka stalkers' map 2003), Nishinomiya: Rokusaisha.

Takarazuka kageki kyūjū-nen shi: sumirebana toshi o kasanete (The ninety-year history of the Takarazuka Revue: violet flowers year on year), (2004), Takarazuka: Takarazuka Kagekidan.

Takarazuka kageki no nanajūnen (Seventy years of the Takarazuka Revue), (1984), Takarazuka: Takarazuka Kagekidan.

Takarazuka Music School (1999), (pamphlet), Takarazuka: Takarazuka ongaku gakkō.

Takarazuka Music School (2000), 'Year 2000–2001 curriculum and school calendar,' (photocopy).

Takarazuka ongaku gakkō (Takarazuka Music School) (1994), (pamphlet), Takarazuka: Takarazuka Kagekidan.

Takarazuka ongaku gakkō 1985 (1985), (pamphlet), Takarazuka: Takarazuka ongaku gakkō.

Takarazuka ongaku gakkō (2007), 'Nyūgaku annai (School admittance guide).' Available from <http://www.tms.ac.jp/annai.html> [17 May 2007].

Takarazuka otome 1970 (Takarazuka maidens 1970) (1970), Takarazuka: Takarazuka Kagekidan.

Takarazuka otome 1991 (1991), Takarazuka: Takarazuka Kagekidan.

Takarazuka otome 1994 (1994), Takarazuka: Takarazuka Kagekidan.

Takarazuka otome 1999 (1999), Takarazuka: Takarazuka Kagekidan.

Takarazuka otome 2006 (2006), Takarazuka: Takarazuka Kagekidan.

Takarazuka otome 2007 (2007), Takarazuka: Takarazuka Kagekidan.

Takarazuka Revue 2006 (2006), Takarazuka: Hankyu Communications Co., Ltd.

Takarazuka Revue Official Web Site (2003), 'Keitai denwa (*i* mōdo) de karaoke ga tanoshimeru shin sābisu "Takarazuka karaoke" tōjō! (Advent of new service, "Takarazuka *karaoke*," enabling enjoyment of *karaoke* on mobile telephones' *i*-mode).' Available from: <http://kageki.hankyu.co.jp> 3 October [15 October 2003].

———— (2007a), 'Hanagumi shuen otokoyaku Haruno Sumire taidan kisha kaiken (Flower Troupe leading otokoyaku Sumire Haruno retirement press conference).' Available from: <http://kageki.hankyu.co.jp/news/detail/19b5ab816ae220138d75598b506f4ff1.html> 7 June [12 June 2007].

———— (2007b), 'Tōjitsuken jōhō (Information on same-day tickets).' Available from: <http://kageki.hankyu.co.jp/aticket/day.html> [27 August 2007].

Takarazuka Sky Stage Web Site (2002), 'Bangumi shōsai: Takarazuka fujin (Programme details: *Takarazuka wives*).' Available from: <http://www.so-net.ne.jp/takarazuka-skystage/Prgm/Detail/20.html> [20 January 2003].

———— (2002–2004). Available from: <www.skystage.net> [7 April 2004].

Takarazuka-shi kankō hyakunen kinen jigyō kyōkai (ed.) (1988), *Takarazuka: Takarazuka-shi kankō hyakunen (kaitō hyakunen) kinen* (Takarazuka: commemorating a century of tourism in Takarazuka City (the centennial of the tapping of the spa), Takarazuka: Takarazuka-shi onsen ryokan kumiai.

Takashio, Tomoe (1989), *Kiyoku, tadashiku, utsukushiku* (Purely, Righteously, Beautifully), Hinode Shuppan.

———— (1977), 'Waga hai wa Pei de aru!! (I am Pei),' *Kageki*, December, pp. 92–93.

Takeda, Haruko (1990), 'Gengo seisa no sutereotaipu: "Imada Yūko" e no "shikisha" no komento o yomu (Stereotypes of gender difference in language: reading the comments of "intellectuals" on "Imada Yūko",' *Joseigaku nenpō*, no. 11, November, pp. 29–39.

Takeda, Sachiko (1994), 'Dansō, josō: sono Nihonteki tokushitsu to ifukusei (Male and female cross-dressing: special Japanese characteristics and sartorial regulations),' in Wakita Haruko and Susan B. Hanley (eds), *Jendā no Nihonshi*, vol. 1, Tōkyō daigaku Shuppankai, pp. 217–51.

Takigawa, Sueko (1974), 'Rokujūnen o Takarazuka to tomo ni (Sixty years with Takarazuka),' *Kageki*, May, pp. 34–36.

Takubo, Ōko (2001), 'Yōkoso gekijō e: Tōkyō Takarazuka gekijō shihainin,

Ogawa Katsuko (Welcome to the theatre: Katsuko Ogawa, manager of Tokyo Takarazuka Theatre),' *Sankei Shimbun Web Site* Available from: <http://www.sankei.co.jp/edit/bunka/takara/011210_ogawa_1.html> 13 December [21 May 2002].

Tamai, Hamako (1999), *Takarazuka ni saita seishun* (A youth that blossomed in Takarazuka), Seikyūsha.

Tanabe, Seiko (1995), 'Konna ni tanoshii Takarazuka, shirazu ni iru no wa mottai nai koto (Takarazuka is worth knowing: it is so much fun),' in Ōno Satomi (ed.), *Fantasutikku Takarazuka*, Geibunsha, pp. 42–48.

Tanabe, Seiko (text) and Keiko Sasaki (photography) (1983), *Yume no kashi o tabete: waga ai no Takarazuka* (Eating dream candy: our beloved Takarazuka), Kōdansha.

Tanabe, Setsurō (1994), *Takarajennu e no michi* (The path to becoming a Takarasienne), Kōdansha.

Tanaka, Mariko (1998), *Takarazuka yo, doko e iku* (Oh, Takarazuka, where are you headed?), Seikyūsha.

Tanigawa, Tamae (1989), 'Josei no nanshoku shikō ni tsuite – sono imi to shinsō (Women's liking for homosexual men's love – its implication and the depth of their consciousness),' *Joseigaku nenpō*, no. 10, October, pp. 195–207.

Tanimura, Hideshi (1971), 'Terebijon to Takarazuka (Television and Takarazuka),' *Kageki*, July, pp. 38–39.

Tasker, Yvonne (1993), Spectacular Bodies: Gender, Genre and Action Cinema, London: Routledge.

Theater Guide (2001), 'Bandō Mitsugorō,' February, pp. 17–20.

Theater Guide Web Site (2007), *DANCIN' CRAZY* seisaku happyō (*Dancin' Crazy* production announced),' 12 June. Available from: <http://www.theaterguide.co.jp/pressnews/2007/06/12.html> [20 June 2007].

'Tokushū: isō no erochishizumu (Special feature: the eroticism of cross-dressing)' (1987), *Subaru*, May, pp. 86–110.

'Tokushū: OSK no hachijūichi-nen to shinsei e (Special feature: to the eighty-one years of OSK and its rebirth)' (2003), *Kamigata geinō*, no. 149, September, pp. 1–68.

Tomogane, Nobuo (1993), *Aishite aishite Takarazuka* (Loving and loving Takarazuka) (private publication), Takarazuka: Yū kikaku.

Tong, Rosemarie (1995), *Feminist Thought: A Comprehensive Introduction*, London: Routledge.

Torii, Hiroshi (1997), 'Eko-bacha (Auntie Eko),' in Toshihiro Tsuganezawa and Chisato Natori (eds), *Takarazuka beru epokku: kageki + rekishi + bunka = Takarazuka*, Kobe: Kōbe Shinbun Sōgō Shuppan Sentā, pp. 10–18.

TOYRO Library Web Site (2002), 'Eiga no machi Takarazuka, Nihon no eiga shi o kazaru machi: katsute sutā ga fudangi de aruiteita machi ni eigasai ga yatte kuru (Movie town, Takarazuka: a town adorning Japanese film history; film festival coming to the town where stars once strolled in everyday clothes).' Available from <http://www.toyro.co.jp/library/kikou/no_10.html> [30 August 2003].

Tsubouchi, Shikō (1977), *Koshikata kyūjū-nen* (How I have spent ninety years), Seiabō.

Tsuganezawa, Toshihiro (1991), *Takarazuka senryaku: Kobayashi Ichizō no seikatsu bunkaron* (The Takarazuka strategy: the life-culture theories of Kobayashi Ichizō), Kōdansha gendai shinsho 1050.

Tsuganezawa, Toshihiro and Chisato Natori (eds) (1997), *Takarazuka beru epokku: kageki + rekishi + bunka = Takarazuka* (Takarazuka belle époque: opera + history + culture = Takarazuka), Kobe: Kōbe Shinbun Sōgō Shuppan Sentā.

———— (eds) (2001), *Takarazuka beru epokku II: Takarazuka modanizumu wa seiki o koete* (Takarazuka belle époque II: Takarazuka modernism transcends the century), Kobe: Kōbe Shinbun Sōgō Shuppan Sentā.

Tsuji, Norihiko (1997), 'That's Takarazuka: kenmei ni noboritsuzukeru "kewashii yama," Erizabēto yaku ni ikiru shiawase! (The joy of living the role of Elisabeth, a "steep mountain" she keeps climbing with all her might),' *Soirée*, March, pp. 64–65.

———— (2004), *Otokotachi no Takarazuka: yume o otta kenkyūsei no hanseiki* (The men's Takarazuka: the half-century of trainees who pursued their dreams), Kobe: Kōbe Shinbun Sōgō Shuppan Sentā.

Tsurugi, Miyuki (1992), *Merīgōrando no yō ni* (Like a merry-go-round), Tōhō eizō jigyōbu.

Tsurumi, E. Patricia (1990), *Factory Girls: Women in the Thread Mills of Meiji Japan*, Princeton: New Jersey: Princeton University Press.

TV Osaka (1993), *Onna no shiro: daremo shiranai Takarazuka urabutai* (The women's castle: the stage-behind-the-stage of Takarazuka that nobody knows) (television documentary).

Ueda, Shinji (1997), *Takarazuka, waga Takarazuka* (Takarazuka, my Takarazuka), Hakusuisha.

———— (2002), *Takarazuka, hyakunen no yume* (Takarazuka, dreams of a century), Bunshun shinsho.

Ueda, Yoshitsugu (1971), 'Otokoyaku no engijutsu: nimaime no bigaku (The acting techniques of male-role players: the aesthetics of the romantic lead),' *Takarazuka gurafu*, May, p. 64.

———— (1974), *Takarazuka sutā: sono engi to bigaku* (The acting and aesthetics of Takarazuka stars), Osaka: Yomiuri shinbunsha.

———— (1986), *Takarazuka ongaku gakkō* (The Takarazuka Music School), Yomiuri raifu.

Umeda Arts Theatre Web Site (2007), 'Kōen annai (Performance guide).'

Available from <http://www.umegei.com/m_lineup.html> [27 August 2007].

Umehara, Riko (text) and Ai Otohara (illustrations) (1994), *For Beginners Series no. 68: Takarazuka*, Gendai Shokan.

Uno, Kathleen (1993), 'The Death of "Good Wife, Wise Mother"?' in Andrew Gordon (ed.), *Postwar Japan as History*, Berkeley: University of California Press, pp. 293–322.

Usami, Tadashi, 'Takarazuka no kōgengaku: "Berubara" izen/igo (The modernology of Takarazuka: pre- and post- "The Rose of Versailles"),' *Kamigata geinō*, no. 70, April 1981, pp. 4–28.

Usami, Tadashi (text) and Masanori Obata (photographs) (1987), *Takarazuka dokuhon* (Takarazuka reader), Osaka: Osaka Shoseki.

Utsumi, Shigenori (1980), 'Takarazuka kageki, junan no kūhaku jidai: jūku-nen daigekijō heisa kara nijūichi-nen saikai made (The Takarazuka Revue: its blank period of suffering: from the Grand Theatre's closure in 1944 to its reopening in 1947),' in *Bessatsu ichiokunin no Shōwa shi, Takarazuka: karei naru butai to sutā o sodateta nanajū-nen*, Mainichi Shinbunsha, pp. 166–67.

———— (2000), *Watashi ga aishita Takarazuka kageki* (The Takarazuka Revue that I loved), Takarazuka: Hankyu Books.

Vlastos, Stephen (ed.) (1998), *Mirror of Modernity: Invented Traditions of Modern Japan*, Berkeley and Los Angeles: University of California Press

Vogel, Ezra F. (1978), 'The Gateway to Salary: Infernal Entrance Examin-ations,' in Edward R. Beauchamp (ed.), *Learning to be Japanese: Selected Readings on Japanese Society and Education*, Hamden, Connecticut: Linnet Books, pp. 213–39.

Volcano, Del Delagrace (foreword and photography), and Judith 'Jack' Halberstam (text) (1999), *The Drag King Book*, London: Serpent's Tail.

Wakaba, Hiromi (1996), 'Wakaba Hiromi no ojama shimasu! Dai-san-kai: Tsurugi Miyuki (Wakaba Hiromi's "Pardon my disturbing you": no. 3): Tsurugi Miyuki,' in One's Co. Ltd (ed.), *Jenne* (Takarasiennes) *Vol. 1, Actress File Extra*, Soirée Books, pp. 141–46.

Walters, Suzanna D. (1995), *Material Girls: Making Sense of Feminist Cultural Theory*, Berkeley: University of California Press.

Waseda daigaku Takarazuka kageki o aisuru kai (ed.) (1995), *Yume no hanataba* (Bouquet of dreams): *We Love Takarazuka*, KK besuto serāzu.

Waseda daigaku Takarazuka kageki o aisuru kai OG (1999), *Takarazuka hikōshiki handobukku* (Takarazuka unofficial handbook), Kōdansha.

Waswo, Ann (1996), *Modern Japanese Society 1868–1994*, Oxford: Oxford University Press.

Wetmore, Kevin J., Jr (2006), 'From *Scaretto* [sic] to *Kaze to tomo ni sarinu*:

musical adaptations of *Gone with the Wind* in Japan,' in David Jortner, Keiko McDonald and Kevin J. Wetmore Jr (eds), *Modern Japanese Theatre and Performance*, Lanham, Maryland: Lexington Books, pp. 247–49.

White, Merry Isaacs (1993), *The Material Child: Coming of Age in Japan and America*, New York: Free Press.

————— (1995), 'The Marketing of Adolescence in Japan,' in Lise Scov and Brian Moeran (eds), *Women, Media and Consumption in Japan*, Honolulu: University of Hawai'i Press, pp. 255–273.

————— (2002), *Perfectly Japanese: Making Families in an Era of Upheaval*, Berkeley: University of California Press.

Wieringa, Saskia E. (2007), 'Silence, Sin, and the System: Women's Same-Sex Practices in Japan,' in Saskia E. Wieringa, Evelyn Blackwood and Abha Bhaiya (eds), *Women's Sexualities and Masculinities in a Globalising Asia*, New York: Palgrave Macmillan, pp. 23–45.

Wilson, Sandra (2001), 'Rethinking the 1930s and the "15-year War" in Japan', *Japanese Studies*, vol. 21, no. 2, pp. 155–164.

With Takarazuka (1992), *'With* intabyū: Okada Yasuko-san (*With* interview: Ms Yasuko Okada),' no. 78, October, pp. 4–5.

With Takarazuka (1993), *'With* intabyū: Fukamidori Natsuyo-san (*With* interview: Ms Natsuyo Fukamidori),' no. 88, August, pp. 2–3.

With Takarazuka (1996), 'Interview in Takarazuka Special: Anju Mira,' no. 117, March, pp. 2–4.

Yabushita, Tetsuji (2002a), 'Asami, Sena ga Sukāretto kyōen. Takarazuka hachijūhasshūnen kinen kōen, "Kaze to tomo ni sarinu"; Yukigumi toppu, Emao Yū ga taidan happyō (Asami, Sena to compete in Scarlett role [in] Takarazuka's eighty-eighth anniversary performance of *Gone with the Wind*; Snow Troupe top star Yū Emao announces retirement),' *Sports Nippon Osaka Web Site*, 21 April. Available from: <http://www.sponichi.com/ente/takarazuka/backnumber/020421/takarazuka.html> [3 October 2002].

————— (2002b), '"TCA supesharu 2002," hikken bangumi zokuzoku: Takarazuka kageki sen'yō channeru iyoiyo kaikyoku (*TCA Special 2002*, a succession of must-see programmes: dedicated Takarazuka channel opening soon),' *Sports Nippon Osaka Web Site*, 16 June. Available from: <http://www.sponichi.com/ente/takarazuka/backnumber/020616/takarazuka.html> [29 August 2002].

————— (2003), 'Shin senka dai-ikki sei, Iori Naoka no taidan (Retirement of Naoka Iori, inaugural member of New Superior Members),' in Kotake Satoshi, Tanaka Mariko, Mizoguchi Sachio, Moriyama Mika (eds), *Takarazuka Academia*, no. 19, Seikyūsha, pp. 75–78.

————— (2007a), 'Eri Miyuki-ra jitsuryoku-ha ga taidan o happyō (Miyuki Eri and other capable players announce retirement),' *Sponichi Osaka Web Site*, 30 June. Available from: <http://www.sponichi.co.jp/

osaka/ente/takarazuka/backnumber/070630/takarazuka.html> [2 August 2007].

———— (2007b), 'Kasugano Yachiyo, yūga-na mai o hirō: *Dai-yonjūhakkai Takarazuka buyōkai*, daigekijō de kaisai, (Yachiyo Kasugano displays graceful dancing: *Forty-eighth Takarazuka [Japanese] dance meet* held at Grand Theatre,' *Sponichi Osaka Web Site*, 20 October. Available from: <http://www.sponichi.co.jp/osaka/ente/takarazuka/backnumber/071020/takarazuka.html> [25 October 2007].

———— (2007c), '"Shinsei Waō" o apīru: konsāto, *NEW YOKA~ROCKIN' Broadway~*, Tōkyō de kaisai (Promoting the "reborn Wao": concert held in Tokyo),' *Sponichi Osaka Web Site*. Available from: <http://www.sponichi.co.jp/osaka/ente/takarazuka/backnumber/070818/takarazuka.html> [9 September 2007].

Yachigusa, Kaoru (1999), *Yasashii jikan* (Gentle times), Sekai bunkasha.

Yamaguchi, Masao (1998), 'Sumo in the Popular Culture of Contemporary Japan,' in D.P. Martinez (ed.), *The Worlds of Japanese Popular Culture: Gender, Shifting Boundaries and Global Cultures*, Cambridge: Cambridge University Press, pp. 19–29.

Yamamoto, Kumiko (ed.) (1995), *Takarajennu to kōhī bureiku* (A coffee break with Takarasiennes), Takarazuka: Takarazuka Kagekidan.

Yamazaki, Masakazu (1993), *Kōkō engeki-ka* (Senior high school drama department), Kobe: Kōbe Shinbun Sōgō Shuppan Sentā.

Yamazaki, Yōko (1992), *Ano..., desu kara, Takarazuka: Takarazuka seishun monogatari* (Um..., so you see, [I'm off to] Takarazuka: a tale of my youth in Takarazuka), Shōgakukan.

Yano, Christine R. (1998), 'Defining the Modern Nation in Japanese Popular Song, 1914–1932,' in Sharon A. Minichiello (ed.), *Japan's Competing Modernities: Issues in Culture and Democracy 1900–1930*, Honolulu: University of Hawai'i Press, pp. 247–64.

Yazaki, Yasuhisa (1976), 'Boku no Takarazuka imēji: boku wa amachuarizumu ga suki; otokoyaku ni wa erotishizumu o kanjiru naa; waisetsu na no ka naa (My image of Takarazuka: I prefer amateurism; I feel eroticism from the otokoyaku; Am I lewd, I wonder?),' in Tazuko Suzuki, *'Zuka fan no kagami: Mon Pari kara Beru bara made*, Zero Bukkusu, pp. 94–98.

Yomiuri Online (2006), 'Tsuki-gumi, Seijō Kaito: Shinjin kōen de kanroku no Kaesaru (Moon Troupe's Seijō Kaito: a mature Caesar in the New Faces performance).' Available from: <http://osaka.yomiuri.co.jp/takarazuka/tk60607a.htm> 7 June [9 September 2006].

Yomiuri On-Line Kansai (2002), 'Otokoyaku kara joyū e hitosuji ni: joyū, Ōtori Ran (1) (Straight from a male impersonator to an actress: Ōtori Ran, actress, no. 1).' Available from: <http://osaka.yomiuri.co.jp/kousai/020107.htm>, 7 January [13 January 2003].

Yoshida, Kiyomi (1988), 'Onna no ikikata o kangaeru: kōkō kokugo de no jugyō jissen (Thinking about women's way of living: putting it into practice in senior high school Japanese classes),' *Joseigaku nenpō* (Annual report of Women's Studies Society), no. 9, October, pp. 74–83.

Yoshihara, Yukari, 'A Transvestite Caliban Rules over Kowloon – *The Tempest in Kowloon*: A Takarazuka Adaptation of Shakespeare's *Tempest*,' Workshop 11: Cultural translation, Adaptation and Resistance: The multicultural transformation and the imperialism in modern East (sic), *Lingnan University*. Available from: <www.ln.edu.hk/eng/staff/eoyang/icla/submittion%20copy %20Workshop%2011%20-%20Yukari%20Yoshihara%20.doc> [16 January 2007].

Yoshioka, Noriaki (1994), 'Les Jeunes Filles: Takarazuka ongaku gakkō (The young girls: Takarazuka Music School),' in *Mainichi gurafu bessatsu, Takarazuka: karei naru hachijū-nen; nijūisseiki e no tabidachi*, Mainichi Shinbunsha, pp. 102–05.

Yuki, Reina (1972), personal communication, Takarazuka.

Zeami, Motokiyo (1984), *On the Art of the Nō Drama: The Major Treatises of Zeami*, trans. J. Thomas Rimer and Yamasaki Masakazu, Princeton: Princeton University Press, pp. 100–02.

Zimmerman, Eve (1989), 'On the Dreamy Stage with the Takarazuka Revue Company,' *Japan Society Newsletter*, October, pp. 4–7.

Interview informants

Note: Dates of joining and retiring are approximate, to protect confidentiality. Status is as at time of interview.

Informant AA (2001), interviewed in Tokyo, 18 January. AA joined in the early 1990s, retiring in the mid-1990s; played only female roles; was single at the time of the interview.

Informant AB (2001), interviewed in Tokyo, 29 January. AB joined around 1980, retiring in the early 1990s, exclusively playing female roles; married; childless.

Informant CL (2001) interviewed in Takarazuka, 13 February. CL joined around 1970, retiring in the mid-1980s, and mostly played male roles; never married; employed in a creative and teaching capacity by the Company.

Informant DP (2001), interviewed in Takarazuka, 12 February. DP joined in the late 1950s, retiring in the late 1990s, and performed female roles for most of her career; never married; employed in a teaching capacity by the Company.

Informant EF (2001), interviewed in Takarazuka, 20 February. EF joined around 1960, retiring in the mid-1960s, and switched from playing male roles to female roles soon after her debut; married, with children.

Informant HO (2001), interviewed in Takarazuka, 20 February. HO joined in the early 1930s, retiring around 1980, and almost exclusively performed male roles; never married; employed as an instructor by the Company.

Informant IN (2001), interviewed in Takarazuka, 12 February. IN, a senior male administrator in the Takarazuka Revue Company, was asked selected questions which related to Takarazuka in general, not to his personal experience.

Informant KT (2001), interviewed in Takarazuka, 20 February. KT joined in the mid-1980s, and was still a member at the time of the interview; played only male roles.

Informant MH (2001), interviewed in Takarazuka, 18 February. MH joined in the mid-1930s, retiring in the late 1960s, and mainly performed female roles; widowed, with no children.

Informant NK (2001), interviewed in Tokyo, 27 February. NK joined around 1980, retiring in the mid-1990s, mostly playing male roles; married with children.

Informant PP (2001), interviewed in Takarazuka, 17 February. PP joined Takarazuka around 1930, retiring in the 1970s, and performed both stage genders, with a predominance of male roles; never married; employed as an instructor by the Company.

Informant PZ (2001), interviewed in Takarazuka, 17 February. PZ joined around 1960, retiring in the late 1990s, and almost exclusively performed male roles; never married.

Informant RX (2001), interviewed in Takarazuka, 12 February. RX joined in the mid-1980s, and was a member at the time of the interview; played only female roles.

Informant SS (2001), interviewed in Tokyo, 20 January (Q. 1–3) and 26 January (Q. 4–5). SS joined in the late 1950s, retiring in the mid-1970s, and performed only female roles; married, with children.

Informant TH (2001), interviewed in Takarazuka, 16 February. TH joined in the late 1930s, retiring in the mid-1940s, and only played female roles; widowed, with children.

Informant WF (2001), interviewed in Takarazuka, 19 February. WF joined in the mid-1980s, and was a member at the time of the interview; played only female roles.

Index